HANDBOOK

FOR MEMBERS AND VISITORS

MARCH 1997 TO MARCH 1998

CHASTLETON HOUSE

The National Trust

Contents

Properties open to the public

For enquiries please write to:
The National Trust, PO Box 39, Bromley, Kent BR1 3XL
or telephone 0181 315 1111
Registered Charity No. 205846
This handbook is also available in the internet at
http://www.ukindex.co.uk/nationaltrust

ISBN 0 7078 0218 0
© 1997 The National Trust
Editor: James Parry
Editorial Assistants: Charlotte Stewart and Penny Clarke
Production : Lorna Simmonds and Marjorie Norman
Managing Editor: Alex Youel
Designed by Pardoe Blacker Ltd, Lingfield, Surrey
Phototypeset in Monotype Photina Series 747
by Southern Positives and Negatives (SPAN), Lingfield, Surrey
Printed by Cox & Wyman Ltd, Reading, Berkshire

Illustrations by: Brian Delf, Brin Edwards, Peter Morter, Claude Page, David Peacock, Eric Thomas, Soun Vannithone

Front cover: Detail from *Belton House* by Paul Hogarth RA, 1996 (Foundation for Art/NTPL)

Back cover: Education Warden with young visitor at Ashridge Estate (NTPL/Ian Shaw)

About the National Trust

The National Trust

- is a registered charity

- is independent of government

- was founded in 1895 to preserve places of historic interest or natural beauty permanently for the nation to enjoy

- relies on the generosity of its supporters, through membership subscriptions, gifts, legacies and the contribution of many thousands of volunteers

- now protects and opens to the public over 200 historic houses, 230 gardens and 25 industrial monuments

- owns more than 240,000 hectares of the most beautiful countryside and 550 miles of outstanding coast for people to enjoy

- looks after forests, woods, fens, farmland, downs, moorland, islands, archaeological remains, nature reserves, villages – for ever, for everyone

- has the unique statutory power to declare land inalienable – such land cannot be sold, mortgaged or compulsorily purchased against the Trust's wishes without special parliamentary procedure. This special power means that protection by the Trust is for ever

- spends all its income on the care and maintenance of the land and buildings in its protection, but cannot meet the cost of all its obligations – four in every five of its historic houses run at a loss – and is always in need of financial support.

How you can support the National Trust

MAKING A DONATION

'Once surrendered, countryside is gone for ever; the National Trust is our best defence.'

HUGH MURLAND, *National Trust member*

Make a donation to the National Trust and help safeguard Britain's most loved places – for ever, for everyone.

To make a donation please telephone 0181 315 1111 or contact **The National Trust, PO Box 39, Bromley, Kent BR1 3XL.**

THE NATIONAL TRUST

Dear Members and Supporters,

It is a pleasure to introduce to you the 1997/8 edition of our Handbook, which is the essential guide to the National Trust's properties.

This year we have rearranged the way the Handbook is organised by grouping properties into geographical areas rather than in county-by-county order. For our members of long standing this may take a little time to get used to, but we are confident that it will make the Handbook easier to use while omitting none of the essential information. An explanation and map can be found on pages 24 and 25.

New properties opening in 1997 include Chastleton, near Oxford, which opens in September and for which all visitors, including National Trust members, will need to pre-book. At Nymans Garden, several rooms in the house will open for the first time in 1997. Please see the entries under 'South East' for visiting arrangements for Chastleton and Nymans.

Finally, I am pleased to say that in 1997 the Trust is making a special effort to offer an enjoyable visit to families with children, while continuing to extend the warmest of welcomes to all our visitors. The high point of the year for our younger visitors will occur in the school summer holidays with an extensive programme of events – many of them featuring Trusty the Hedgehog, the National Trust's own children's host.

May I take this opportunity to thank all our members for their support, and wish you many enjoyable visits during the course of this year.

Martin Drury
Director-General

How to use this Handbook

The Handbook gives details of how you can visit National Trust properties, including opening arrangements, admission charges and important information about visiting. In previous years property entries were listed alphabetically within their respective counties, but as a result of the local government re-organisation of April 1996 (and in anticipation of further changes in 1997 and beyond) the format has been changed in favour of a division into geographical areas. This arrangement should help avoid any confusion over new council names and the disappearance of some local authorities.

England, Northern Ireland and Wales are therefore divided into nine areas, listed alphabetically. The properties within each area are also arranged alphabetically. We have kept references to counties to a minimum to maintain clarity, but the current county location for each property is given in the index. If you are unsure of the area into which a particular county or property falls, please refer to the map and information given on pages 24 and 25.

Property features are indicated by symbols alongside the property name. More detailed information about specific facilities is represented by symbols down the left-hand side of each entry. The key to the symbols is on page 23. At the back of this year's Handbook is a tear-off bookmark which also shows the symbols.

The Trust's coast and countryside properties are described at the beginning of each area entry. A map of each area provides information on property location, major population centres and main access routes, but visitors are advised to consult the detailed access information given at the end of each property entry before setting out.

Please note the following points about this year's Handbook:

- it describes opening arrangements for the period from March 1997 to the end of March 1998

- in line with national guidelines for metrication, areas are shown in hectares (1ha = 2.47 acres) and heights and short distances in metres (1m = 3.28 feet); longer distances continue to be measured in miles (ml)

- although opening times and arrangements do vary considerably from place to place, and from year to year, most houses are open from the end of March to 2 November, usually on three or more afternoons per week between 1pm and 5pm (please note that last admission is usually 30 minutes before the stated closing time). However, always check the current Handbook for details and, if you are making a long or especially important journey, please telephone the property in advance for confirmation

- when telephoning, we can provide a better service if you call on a weekday morning, on days when the property is open to the public

- new properties, or properties featuring for the first time as separate entries in this year's Handbook: Chastleton House (South East), Croome Park (Midlands), Derrymore House (Northern Ireland), Hardy Monument (South West), Nymans House (South East), Selworthy Village (South West) and West Green House (South East)

- whilst every care has been taken in compiling the Handbook to ensure complete accuracy, members and visitors are asked to recognise that arrangements can change, as can telephone numbers and other details. The Trust reserves the right to amend opening arrangements during the period covered by this Handbook, should this prove necessary

- please note that some telephone information lines, usually those with an 0891 prefix, are charged at a rate higher than the normal tariff. At the time of publication, this amounts to 50p per minute at peak rate and 45p per minute at other times. Information provided on these lines will be kept as brief as possible, consistent with providing the necessary details.

How you can support the National Trust

JOIN AND ENJOY YOUR LOCAL MEMBERS' ASSOCIATIONS & CENTRES

Join your local Association and share your interest in the Trust with like-minded members from your area: more than 100,000 members already have.

A **National Trust Association or Centre** is a local club run by members, for members. There are 192 all over England, Wales and Northern Ireland and they offer coach outings, lectures, parties, rambles, tours and holidays in Britain and abroad – as well as **friendship**.

Last year they raised nearly £1 million for the National Trust, as well as providing practical help at Trust properties and offices.

To join please ask at any National Trust property for the free map leaflet 'Make the most of your membership'. This gives a contact name, address and telephone number for each Association. Alternatively, contact either the Membership Department at **PO Box 39, Bromley, Kent BR1 3XL, tel. 0181 315 1111** or Tom Burr, Associations Liaison Secretary at **Eastleigh Court, Bishopstrow, Warminster, Wiltshire BA12 9HW, tel. 01985 843586.**

Special Information for National Trust Members

- Membership of the National Trust allows you free entry to most properties open to the public during normal opening times and under normal opening arrangements, **providing you can present a valid membership card.**

- **Please check that you have your card with you before you set out on your journey. We very much regret that you cannot be admitted free of charge without it, nor can admission charges be refunded subsequently, due to the administrative costs of doing so.**

- Membership cards are **not transferable**.

- If your card is lost or stolen, please contact the Membership Department (address on p.21), tel. 0181 315 1111, Monday to Friday, 9am to 5.30pm.

- A replacement card can be sent to a temporary address if you are on holiday. Voluntary donations to cover the administrative costs of a replacement card are always welcome.

- Free entry is not guaranteed; additional charges may be made for the following:
    - When a special event is in progress at a property
    - When a property is opened specially for a National Gardens Scheme open day
    - Where the management of a property is not under the National Trust's direct control, eg Tatton Park, Cheshire
    - Where special attractions are not an integral part of the property, eg Steam Yacht *Gondola* in Cumbria

- The National Trust encourages educational use of its properties. Education Group Membership is open to all non-profit-making educational groups whose members are in full-time education. Subscription rates are banded according to the nature of the organisation and the number on roll.

- Life members of the National Trust who enrolled as such before 1968 have cards which admit one person only. Life members wishing to exchange these for 'admit two' cards, or those wishing to change from one category of Life membership to another, should contact the Membership Department in Bromley for the scale of charges.

- Entry to properties owned by the Trust but maintained and administered by English Heritage or Cadw (Welsh Historic Monuments) is free to members of the Trust, English Heritage and Cadw.

- Members of the National Trust are also admitted free to properties of the National Trust for Scotland. The National Trust for Scotland *Guide to over*

100 Properties can be obtained by sending a self-addressed adhesive label and £1.50 to the National Trust for Scotland (see address on p.22).

- Reciprocal visiting arrangements also exist with certain overseas Trusts, including Australia, New Zealand, Barbados, Bermuda, Canada, Jersey, Guernsey and the Manx Museum and National Trust on the Isle of Man. For a full list please send a s.a.e. to the National Trust Membership Department.

- National Trust members visiting properties owned by the National Trust for Scotland or overseas Trusts are only eligible for free entry on presentation of a valid membership card.

How you can support the National Trust

BECOME A MEMBER TODAY

You will be helping the Trust protect and care for much-loved countryside and coastline as well as the many important historic houses and gardens listed in this Handbook. Your subscription goes directly to support this work.

Benefits of membership:

- free admission to most of the properties listed in this Handbook
- three mailings a year which include a free copy of this Handbook, three editions of the full colour *National Trust Magazine*, a gift catalogue and two editions of your regional newsletter

There is a wide range of different membership categories for you to choose from (see form overleaf).

How to join:

For **immediate** membership, you can join at almost all National Trust properties or shops during your visit.

For **postal applications**, complete the form overleaf and return it to the address given.

Or just **telephone** the National Trust Membership Department on **0181 315 1111**. Enquiries and credit card applications are welcome. The lines are open Monday to Friday 9am to 5.30pm. Please allow 28 days for receipt of your membership card and new member's pack.

Application for membership

TO: THE NATIONAL TRUST, FREEPOST MB1438, BROMLEY, KENT BR1 3BR

Twelve-month membership

☐ **Individual:** £27 and, for each additional member living at the same address, £19. One card for each member.

☐ **Family group:** £51 for two adults and their children under 18, living at the same address. Please give names and dates of birth for all children. **One** card covers the family.

Under 26 membership

☐ **Child:** £13 Must be under 13 at time of joining. Please give date of birth.

☐ **Young person:** £13 Must be 13 to 25 at time of joining. Please give date of birth.

☐ **Education group membership:** See Special Information for National Trust Members, and tel. 0181 315 1111 for further details.

Life membership

☐ **Individual:** £650 (£430 if aged 60 or over and retired). One card admits the named member and a guest.

☐ **Joint:** £780 for lifetime partners (£510 if either partner is aged 60 or over and retired). Two cards, each admitting the named member.

☐ **Family joint:** £890 two cards, each admitting the named adult and their children under 18 living at the same address. Please give names and dates of birth for all children.

Rates valid until 31 March 1998.

SOURCE D73			DATE		
FULL ADDRESS					
			POSTCODE		
TITLE	INITIALS	SURNAME		DATE OF BIRTH	VALUE £

AMOUNT ATTACHED:
CHEQUE/POSTAL ORDER £
Delete as appropriate

Please allow 28 days for receipt of your membership card and pack

Credit/debit card payments can be made by telephoning 0181 315 1111 (office hours)

Immediate membership can be obtained by joining at a National Trust property, shop or countryside information point

We promise that any information you give will be used for National Trust purposes only. We will write to you about our work and will occasionally include details of products by third parties developed in association with the Trust. We would also like to send you separate details of such products but should you prefer not to receive these separate mailings, please tick this box.
The National Trust is an independent registered charity (no. 205846)

How you can support the National Trust

YOUR WILL CAN PROTECT THE PLACES YOU LOVE

Whatever their size, legacies are vital to the National Trust. They are used to fund major restoration projects or to acquire and endow new properties around the country. Legacies are not spent on administration costs.

Including a legacy to the National Trust in your Will could prevent your estate paying inheritance tax, and would certainly help maintain Britain's heritage for future generations.

We appreciate the concern you take in our work. We have now written a free booklet for our members, giving you all the information you need about making your Will, or adding a codicil to an existing one. Help us protect the places you love – send for our Will booklet today.

For more information contact: The Head of the Legacies Unit, 36 Queen Anne's Gate, London SW1H 9AS (tel: 0171 222 9251)

How you can support the National Trust in the USA

JOIN THE ROYAL OAK FOUNDATION

More than 30,000 Americans belong to the Royal Oak Foundation, the Trust's US membership affiliate. A not-for-profit organisation, the Royal Oak helps the National Trust through the generous tax-deductible support of members and friends by making grants towards its work. Member benefits include the National Trust Handbook, three editions of *The National Trust Magazine*, gift catalogue, the quarterly Royal Oak Newsletter, and free admission to properties of the National Trust and of the National Trust for Scotland.

Royal Oak also awards scholarships to US residents to study in Britain, and sponsors lectures, tours and events in both the US and the UK, designed to inform Americans of the Trust's work.

For further information please write, call or fax **The Royal Oak Foundation, 285 West Broadway, New York, NY 10013, USA. Tel. 00 1 212 966 6565, fax. 00 1 212 966 6619.**

Information and guidance for visitors

Please read these notes carefully as they apply to all National Trust properties. Visitors will recognise that the contents and fabric of many of the Trust's houses are fragile and valuable. After many years of thought and research into methods of improving preventive conservation and security, certain restrictive measures have been introduced. These constraints on visitors are essential to the safe-keeping of houses in the Trust's care – by respecting them you will be helping the Trust to ensure that its houses and contents are preserved for future generations to enjoy. Symbols indicating restrictions specific to that property are positioned to the right-hand side on the line following the property name. Restrictions on sharp-heeled shoes, bulky bags and photography apply at all Trust houses.

CHILDREN WELCOME

The National Trust's previous annual themes have always focused on what the Trust cares for – whether landscape, gardens, or historic buildings. In 1997, for the first time, the focus will be on a particular group of people – children and families. The Trust is reinforcing its commitment to provide a welcoming, worthwhile and enjoyable visit for families with children, by increasing and broadening what it offers – on both a practical and a fun level. The warmest of welcomes will of course continue to be extended to all our visitors! Family tickets are offered in every region, although not necessarily at every property. Many provide baby-feeding areas and baby-changing facilities (often combined in a purpose-designed parent and baby room). In restaurants there are high-chairs, together with children's menus, colouring sheets and, at some properties, play areas. There are children's guides, trails, or quiz sheets, and Trust shops stock a wide range of interesting and inexpensive items for children.

For 1997, we have selected a number of key 'Children Welcome' sites. These include both houses and countryside and all are particularly suitable for family outings. Each will be offering children's events during the school holidays, particularly in the summer. All other Trust properties will continue to welcome families, even if the properties themselves are less well equipped and may not be hosting special events.

There is also a new children's character for young visitors, Trusty the Hedgehog. Trusty appears in *Trust Tracks*, the newsletter for young members, sent to all Family Group members three times a year. As part of the Trust's aim to provide a more enjoyable visiting experience for children, 'Meet Trusty!' events will take place at many of our properties, at which Trusty stickers will be given out and children will get the chance to meet the cuddly hedgehog in person! There will also be children's concerts, family fun days and a whole range of exciting events on offer.

One note of caution on visiting historic houses: we ask parents to recognise the challenges which the Trust faces in preserving fragile interiors and delicate contents. Architecture, interior decoration and furnishings differ at every house, and therefore access arrangements for visitors vary too. Front slings for babies can be admitted but we regret that at the majority of historic houses (85), it is not possible to admit prams, pushchairs or baby back carriers, because of the considerable risk of accidents to babies and young children, damage to historic contents and inconvenience to other visitors on busy days. However, a few historic houses may admit back carriers on quiet days midweek, at the discretion of the staff on duty at the time.

The following houses are able to admit baby back carriers at all times: Aberconwy House; Ardress House; Canons Ashby; Castle Coole; Castle Drogo; Castle Ward; Charlecote Park; Clumber Chapel; Dunster Castle; Florence Court; Gibside Chapel; Hinton Ampner; Killerton; Knightshayes Court; Little Moreton Hall; Montacute House; Mount Stewart; Petworth House; Springhill; Tattershall Castle; Tatton Park; The Vyne.

For visitors with smaller babies, front slings are usually available on loan, and occasionally reins for toddlers. Prams can be stored at the entrance at the staff's discretion. We regret that the restriction on back carriers, prams and pushchairs can cause particular difficulties for parents with older and/or heavier babies. If you are unsure about restrictions, do please telephone a property in advance of your visit to check. Once at a property, please ask staff for help and advice, and do bear in mind that there is often plenty for children to see and do outdoors, whether on an estate with a garden and park, or at nearby countryside or coastal sites.

For a 'Children Welcome in '97' events list, send a s.a.e. to the **National Trust Membership Department, PO Box 39, Bromley, Kent BR1 3XL, or tel. 0181 315 1111.**

CONCESSIONS

As a registered charity, completely independent of government, the National Trust regrets it cannot afford to offer concessions on admission fees.

DOGS   🐕

Dogs (except guide dogs and hearing dogs for the deaf) are not allowed inside Trust houses and restaurants, and seldom in gardens. The symbol showing a dog on a lead indicates properties which welcome dogs on leads in their grounds (not gardens). In these cases dogs must be kept on the lead at all times to protect deer and grazing livestock.

Dogs are welcome at most countryside properties providing they are kept under control. However, the Trust has introduced restrictions on dogs at some family beaches during the summer to minimise conflict particularly between dogs and families with young children.

Conscious of the dangers associated with leaving dogs in cars, the Trust endeavours to provide a shady parking space in its car parks, water for drinking bowls, hitching posts where dogs may be safely left and advice on suitable areas where dogs may be exercised. These facilities will vary from property to property, and according to how busy it may be on a particular day. The primary responsibility for the welfare of dogs remains, of course, with the owner. Please ensure that wherever you park, your dog remains on a lead until clear of the car park and play/picnic areas, to minimise fouling.

FEEDBACK

We welcome feedback from our members and visitors on occasions when they have encountered especially good service, as well as when some element of a visit has proved less than satisfactory. Such feedback is most appropriately directed to the manager of the property concerned. Alternatively, please contact the relevant Regional Office or the Trust's London Head Office. Many properties provide their own suggestion forms and boxes which visitors are encouraged to use. All comments will be noted, and action taken where necessary, but it is not possible to answer every comment or suggestion individually.

The National Trust adheres to the English Tourist Board's Visitors' Charter for Visitor Attractions, and supports the 'Welcome Host' customer care training programme backed by the Wales, English and Northern Ireland Tourist Boards.

FREE ENTRY DAY

Each year the National Trust organises a day when all visitors are admitted free to many properties. It provides an opportunity to visit for those who would not normally be able to afford the admission charges. We are grateful to the many voluntary organisations who in 1996 provided transport and assistance to elderly and disadvantaged visitors on this day. Because Free Entry Day is generally very busy, National Trust members may prefer to plan their visits on other days. For the same reason we request groups planning to travel by coach to book their visits on Free Entry Day in advance with the property and to check beforehand for any restrictions.

The next Free Entry Day will be on **Wednesday, 17 September 1997**.

HEALTH AND SAFETY

We endeavour to provide a safe and healthy environment for visitors to our properties as far as is reasonably practicable, and to ensure that the activities of our staff, volunteers and contractors working on Trust properties do not in any way jeopardise the health and safety of visitors. You can help us by observing all notices and signs relating to this subject during your visit, by following any instructions given by Trust staff, by ensuring that children are properly supervised at all times and by wearing appropriate clothing and footwear at countryside properties.

HEAVILY VISITED PROPERTIES

Many properties are extremely popular at Bank Holidays and summer week-ends. At some houses and gardens timed tickets may be issued to smooth the flow of people entering the property (but not to limit the duration of a visit), and all visitors (including NT members) are required to use these tickets. This system is designed to create better viewing conditions for visitors and to min-imise wear-and-tear on the historic interiors or gardens. On rare occasions entry to the property may not be possible on that day. If you are planning a long journey, you are encouraged to telephone the property in advance of your trip. At a few properties special considerations apply and pre-booking is essential, eg Chastleton, Mr. Straw's House, Orford Ness.

HOW TO GET THERE →

At the end of each property entry is a brief description of location together with a grid reference. Car-parking is usually available within 100m of the property.

Travelling on foot, on horseback, by bike or on public transport is environ-mentally friendly and enjoyable. Details of access by public transport are given throughout the Handbook (correct as of October 1996). Regular updates are issued during the year; contact the Trust's London address (see p.21) and ask for 'Green Transport News'. Please note that no indication of frequency of transport services is given, so check the times of services before setting out. 'Passing ≋' indicates the bus service passes the station entrance or approach road and 'Passing close ≋' indicates that a walk is necessary. Unless otherwise stated, bus services pass the property (although there may be a walk from the bus-stop!), and the railway station name is followed by the distance from the property.

You can obtain train details from the national rail enquiry line 0345 484950 (at local rates) and Southern Vectis operates the train, bus and coach hotline on 0891 910910 (at premium rates – please mention this Handbook when calling). Many counties also provide a travel line for bus (and sometimes train) times.

Wheelchair users travelling by train should note that some stations are unstaffed. These are followed by a (U).

The National Trust is grateful to Barry Doe, a life member, for this travel information. If you experience difficulties following this information or have suggestions to make, he will be glad to reply to your comments. Please contact him at: Travadvice, 25 Newmorton Road, Moordown, Bournemouth, Dorset BH9 3NU (tel. 01202 528707).

LARGE OR BULKY BAGS

At some properties visitors will be asked to leave behind large items of hand luggage while they make their visit. This is to protect furniture and contents from accidental damage and to improve security. This restriction includes ruck-sacks, large handbags, carrier bags, bulky shoulder bags and camera/camcorder bags. These bags can be safely left at the entrance to any house where the restriction applies (principally historic houses with vulnerable contents, fragile decorative surfaces or narrow visitor routes). See Children Welcome section for additional information on back carriers and pushchairs.

LIGHT LEVELS

Light levels are regularly monitored and carefully controlled using blinds and sun-curtains to achieve the best balance between providing reasonable viewing conditions and preventing the deterioration of sensitive contents, especially tex-tiles and watercolours. Visitors are recommended to allow time for their eyes to adapt to darker conditions inside houses, particularly in rooms where light lev-els are reduced to preserve light-sensitive material.

THE NATIONAL GARDENS SCHEME

Each year many of the National Trust's gardens are opened on extra days in support of the National Gardens Scheme. Money raised on these days is donated by NGS to support nurses' and gardeners' charities, including National Trust gardens (for upkeep and for training of young gardeners). The National Trust acknowledges with gratitude the generous and continuing support of the National Gardens Scheme Charitable Trust.

OPENING ARRANGEMENTS AND ADMISSION FEES   O £

Members of the National Trust are admitted free to virtually all properties (see Special Information for National Trust Members, p.8). Each property entry shows the normal adult admission fee. This includes VAT and is liable to change if the VAT rate is altered.

Children: under 5s are free. Children aged 5–16 are half the adult price, unless stated. 17s and over pay the adult price. Children not accompanied by an adult are admitted at the Trust's discretion.

School parties: many properties offer educational facilities and programmes. Teachers are urged to make a free preliminary visit by prior arrangement with the property. Reductions are usually available for groups of 15 or more school-children aged under 19. Education Group Membership is recommended (see p.8 for more details).

Group visits: all groups are required to book in advance and confirm the book-ing in writing. Some properties have limited access for groups so early booking is recommended. A discount is usually available for groups of 15 or more at most properties. Full information on group visits to National Trust properties is available from the Travel Trade Office, tel. 0171 447 6700; fax. 0171 447 6701.

PHOTOGRAPHY

We welcome amateur photography out-of-doors at our properties. We regret, however, that such photography is not permitted indoors when houses are open to visitors.

However, special arrangements can be made for interested amateurs (as well as voluntary National Trust lecturers, research students and academics) to take interior photographs by appointment outside normal opening hours. **Applications must be made in writing to the property concerned, for a mutually convenient appointment. Please note that an admission charge will apply to everyone (including NT members) for this facility.**

All requests for commercial photography must be channelled through the Regional Public Affairs Manager at the appropriate regional office for permission.

PICNICS

Many properties welcome picnics; some make special provision, a few cannot accommodate them (this is usually indicated in the property entries). If you are planning a picnic at a Trust property for the first time, do please telephone in advance to check. Fires and barbecues are not allowed except where special provision is made.

SEATING

Seats for visitors' use are provided at various points in all the Trust's historic houses and gardens. Those visitors who wish to sit down – whether elderly, infirm, pregnant or simply tired – should feel free to use the seats available, or ask a room steward if seating is not immediately obvious.

SHOES

Any heel which covers an area smaller than a postage stamp can cause irreparable damage to all floors, carpets and rush matting. We regret, therefore, that sharp-heeled shoes are not permitted. When necessary, plastic slippers are provided for visitors with unsuitable or muddy footwear. Alternative slippers are available for purchase.

We would also like to remind visitors that ridged soles trap grit and gravel, which scratch fine floors. Boot-scrapers and brushes are provided for visitors' use. Overshoes may be provided at properties with vulnerable floors.

SMOKING

Smoking is not permitted inside Trust houses, restaurants or shops. Smokers are also invited to exercise reasonable restraint in gardens, since the scent of flowers is such an important part of visitors' enjoyment of a garden.

VISITORS WITH DISABILITIES

We warmly welcome to our properties visitors with physical, sensory and learning disabilities; also guide dogs for visually impaired and disabled people and hearing dogs for the deaf, so long as they are in harness. Most properties have a good degree of access, and provide manual wheelchairs. Self-drive and volunteer-driven powered buggies are available at some larger gardens and parks. (The Trust regrets that powered vehicles are rarely allowed in historic buildings; for exceptions please see individual entries.) The necessary companion of a disabled visitor is admitted free of charge on request, while the normal charge applies to the disabled visitor.

For properties with good access, the paragraph signed with the wheelchair symbol indicates the facilities available for visitors with disabilities. The Sympathetic Hearing Scheme operates at many properties, and Braille guides are available at most. General information and a free 56-page colour booklet on access (also available in large print and on tape), sponsored by Barclays Bank, are available from Mrs Valerie Wenham, Adviser, Facilities for Disabled Visitors (see p.21 for London Head Office address). Please enclose stamped self-addressed adhesive label (minimum postage).

The National Trust Magazine is available free on tape, as are several regional newsletters. Please contact Valerie Wenham if you wish to receive these regularly.

National Trust Enterprises

The Trust's shops, restaurants, tea-rooms and holiday cottages are all managed by National Trust Enterprises. The profit they generate goes to support the work of the National Trust, and in 1995/6 contributed £10.5 million to funds.

SHOPS

Many Trust properties have shops offering a wide range of related merchandise – much of which is exclusive to the National Trust. These shops and their opening times are indicated in relevant property entries by the shop symbol. Many are also open for Christmas shopping and dates are given in the appropriate entries. In addition the Trust now operates a number of shops in towns and cities throughout the country, which are open during normal trading hours (see p.20 for full list).

RESTAURANTS AND TEA-ROOMS

The National Trust operates over 130 tea-rooms and restaurants. They are usually located in very special old buildings including castles, lighthouses, stables, and even hot-houses! The Trust aims to offer traditional home cooking, warm hospitality and value for money. As well as providing services for visitors, the Trust caters for groups and private parties, and many properties offer festive meals in the run-up to Christmas. For more information on functions and private parties in National Trust properties, tel. 0181 315 1111.

HOLIDAYS WITH THE NATIONAL TRUST

The Trust owns and manages over 230 holiday cottages set in some of the most delightful localities in England, Wales and Northern Ireland. From a former lighthouse keeper's cottage in Northumberland to a mansion in Cornwall, all are described in the full-colour brochure available for £1 from the Holiday Booking Office, PO Box 536, Melksham, Wiltshire SN12 8SX. For bookings tel. 01225 791199

For a holiday overseas which also benefits the Trust, the National Trust Travel Collection features special-interest tours and cruises. The Collection also includes a selection of visits to Trust properties in this country. For a brochure tel. 0116 252 4400.

If you are interested in a self-catering holiday in Scotland please contact the National Trust for Scotland (see p.22).

Publications

The National Trust produces a wide range of books. Most of these are available in Trust shops and good bookshops, but you can also order them from the Mail Order Department, PO Box 101, Melksham, Wiltshire SN12 8EA. Copies of guidebooks to Trust properties can be obtained from 36 Queen Anne's Gate, London SW1H 9AS. If you would like a full list of publications, please write to this address (enclosing a stamped, self-addressed envelope).

Gardens of the National Trust, by Stephen Lacey, £29.99. An authoritative guide with superb photography showing the wide range of Trust gardens, from great landscape parks like Studley Royal and Stowe to small gems like the town gardens of Mompesson House in Salisbury and Peckover House in Wisbech. (This publication is sponsored by Land Rover.)

The National Trust Guide, by Lydia Greeves and Michael Trinick, £24.99. A revised edition of the Trust's illustrated 'bible' of information about all its properties.

The National Trust: The First Hundred Years, by Merlin Waterson, £17.99 hardback, £10.99 paperback. A history of the National Trust concentrating on the people behind the organisation – the donors, supporters and staff – brought to life with paintings and photographs. Revised edition published May 1997.

Behind the Scenes: Domestic Arrangements in Historic Houses, by Christina Hardyment, £24.99. A richly illustrated guide to how our ancestors kept themselves clean, warm and well-fed, using National Trust houses as examples. Published May 1997.

National Trust Town Shops

Barnstaple 5 High St
(tel. 01271 71551)

Bath Marshall Wade's House,
Abbey Churchyard
(tel. 01225 460249)

Cambridge 9 King's Parade
(tel. 01223 311894)

Canterbury 24 Burgate
(tel. 01227 457120)

Cardiff Castle
(tel. 01222 237997)

Chester 5 Northgate St
(tel. 01244 313465)

Cirencester Tourist Information Centre,
Cornhall, Market Place
(tel. 01285 654180)

Dartmouth 8 The Quay
(tel. 01803 833694)

Dorchester 65 High West St
(tel. 01305 267535)

Exeter 18 Cathedral Yard
(tel. 01392 274102)

Grasmere Information Centre & Shop
Church Stile, Grasmere
(tel. 01539 435621)

Hexham
25/26 Market Place
(tel. 01434 607654)

London
Brentford Syon Park
(tel. 0181 569 7497)

Regent St
British Travel Centre
(tel. 0181 846 9000)

Victoria Blewcoat School,
23 Caxton St
(tel. 0171 222 2877)

Melksham 5 Church St
(tel. 01225 706454)

Monmouth 5 Church St
(tel. 01600 713270)

Norwich – Shop & Tea-room 3/5 Dove St
(tel. 01603 610206)

St Alban's Tourist Information Centre,
Town Hall, Market Place
(tel. 01727 864511)

St David's
Captain's House, High St
(tel. 01437 720385)

Salisbury 41 High St
(tel. 01722 331884)

Shrewsbury 42 High St
(tel. 01743 350354)

Sidmouth Old Fore St
(tel. 01395 578107)

Solva 21 Main St
(tel. 01437 720661)

Stratford-upon-Avon
45 Wood St
(tel. 01789 262197)

Tewkesbury
39 Church St
(tel. 01684 292919)

Totnes Waterside,
The Plains
(tel. 01803 863475)

Truro 9 River St
(tel. 01872 41464)

Wells 16 Market Place
(tel. 01749 677735)

Windsor 14 High St
(tel. 01753 850433)

York – Shop & Tea-room
32 Goodramgate
(tel. 01904 659050)

Who to contact in the National Trust

We are very willing to answer questions and receive comments from our members and visitors. For queries about a particular place, please telephone the property (see property entry for address and tel. number). If your query relates to several properties in a region, or is about other regional matters, please telephone the appropriate regional office (see details below)

1. **National Trust Membership Department**, PO Box 39, Bromley, Kent BR1 3XL (tel. 0181 315 1111; fax. 0181 466 6824) for all straightforward queries, including membership and requests for literature

2. **London Head Office**, 36 Queen Anne's Gate, London SW1H 9AS (tel. 0171 222 9251; fax. 0171 222 5097) for queries of a national nature. National Trust guidebooks can be purchased from the reception desk

3. **Regional Offices**

Cornwall: Lanhydrock, Bodmin PL30 4DE
(tel. 01208 74281; fax. 01208 77887)

Devon: Killerton House, Broadclyst, Exeter EX5 3LE
(tel. 01392 881691; fax. 01392 881954)

East Anglia: Blickling, Norwich NR11 6NF
(tel. 01263 733471; fax. 01263 734924)

East Midlands: Clumber Park Stableyard, Worksop, Notts S80 3BE
(tel. 01909 486411; fax. 01909 486377)

Kent & East Sussex: The Estate Office, Scotney Castle, Lamberhurst, Tunbridge Wells, Kent TN3 8JN (tel. 01892 890651; fax. 01892 890110)

Mercia: Attingham Park, Shrewsbury, Shropshire SY4 4TP
(tel. 01743 709343; fax. 01743 709352)

North Wales: Trinity Square, Llandudno, Gwynedd LL30 2DE
(tel. 01492 860123; fax. 01492 860233)

North West: The Hollens, Grasmere, Ambleside, Cumbria LA22 9QZ
(tel. 015394 35599; fax. 015394 35353)

Northern Ireland: Rowallane House, Saintfield, Ballynahinch, Co. Down BT24 7LH (tel. 01238 510721; fax. 01238 511242)

Northumbria: Scots' Gap, Morpeth, Northumberland NE61 4EG
(tel. 01670 774691; fax. 01670 774317)

Severn: Mythe End House, Tewkesbury, Glos GL20 6EB
(tel. 01684 850051; fax. 01684 850090)

South Wales: The King's Head, Bridge Street, Llandeilo, Dyfed SA19 6BB
(tel. 01558 822800; fax. 01558 822872)

Southern: Polesden Lacey, Dorking, Surrey RH5 6BD
(tel. 01372 453401; fax. 01372 452023)

Thames & Chilterns: Hughenden Manor, High Wycombe, Bucks HP14 4LA
(tel. 01494 528051; fax. 01494 463310)

Wessex: Eastleigh Court, Bishopstrow, Warminster, Wiltshire BA12 9HW
(tel. 01985 843600; fax. 01985 843624)

Yorkshire: Goddards, 27 Tadcaster Road, Dringhouses, York YO2 2QG
(tel. 01904 702021; fax. 01904 707982)

4. **The National Trust London Information Centre**, Blewcoat School,
   23 Caxton Street, Westminster, SW1H OPY (tel. 0171 222 2877) for
   queries about visiting properties in Greater London

5. **Volunteers' Office**, 33 Sheep St, Cirencester, Glos GL7 1RQ
   (tel. 01285 651818), or contact the Regional Volunteers Coordinator in
   each region (see list of regional addresses, p.21) for offers of volunteer help

6. **National Trust Enterprises**, The Stable Block, Heywood House, Westbury,
   Wilts BA13 4NA (tel. 01373 858787) for matters relating to shops,
   restaurants, holidays and the catalogue. For **Mail Order**, write to
   PO Box 101, Melksham, Wiltshire SN12 8EA (tel. 01225 790800); for
   Holiday Cottage information, tel. 01225 791199

7. **National Trust for Scotland**, 5 Charlotte Square, Edinburgh EH2 4DU
   (tel. 0131 226 5922)

8. **Young National Trust Theatre (YNTT)**, The National Trust, Sutton House,
   2 & 4 Homerton High Street, Hackney, London E9 6JQ
   (tel. 0181 986 0242)

How you can support the National Trust

WORKING AS A VOLUNTEER

The National Trust invites the practical involvement of members through
its developing volunteer programme. Some 34,000 volunteers, members
and non-members of all ages and backgrounds, support the Trust's permanent staff as active partners. In over 140 different ways, they work on
tasks ranging from the highly skilled to those requiring only a gift of time
and enthusiasm.

To learn more about becoming an individual volunteer, joining one of
our 80 regional and property-based volunteer groups or taking part in
one of our 400 environmental working holidays for people of all ages,
please send a large s.a.e. to the **National Trust Membership Department,
PO Box 39, Bromley, Kent BR1 3XL.**

Key to Symbols

Castle

Historic house

Other buildings

Mill

Church, chapel etc

Garden

Park

Countryside

Coast

Prehistoric/Roman site

Industrial archaeology

Farm/farm animals

Nature reserve

Country walk*

Opening arrangements

Guided tours**

£ Admission details

Wheelchair access

For visually handicapped visitors

Parent & child facilities

Education

Information for dog-owners

Refreshments

How to find the property

Railway station

Shop

E Events

Map symbols:

▲ Buildings & gardens
■ Coast & countryside

*Waymarked routes or recommended walks. Leaflets describing many of these walks are available from Regional Offices.

**The symbol on the top line of an entry indicates that guided tours are the rule: in the left-hand margin the symbol indicates that guided tours are available at certain times or by arrangement.

List of Areas

The map opposite shows how England, Northern Ireland and Wales are divided into areas for the purposes of the Handbook. The areas are composed as follows:

1. **Eastern Counties:** the present counties of Cambridgeshire, Essex, Lincolnshire, Norfolk and Suffolk, plus the southern part of the former county of Humberside (replaced by the unitary authorities of North Lincolnshire and North East Lincolnshire).

2. **London:** the area covered by the present 32 London borough councils and the City of London.

3. **Midlands:** the present counties of Derbyshire, Gloucestershire, Hereford & Worcester, Leicestershire, Northamptonshire, Nottinghamshire, Shropshire, Staffordshire and the former county of West Midlands (replaced by the unitary authorities of Birmingham, Coventry, Dudley, Sandwell, Solihull, Walsall and Wolverhampton).

4. **North East:** the present counties/unitary authorities of Durham, East Riding of Yorkshire (the northern part of the former county of Humberside), Kingston-upon-Hull, North Yorkshire, Northumberland and York, as well as the former counties of Cleveland (replaced by the unitary authorities of Hartlepool, Middlesbrough, Redcar & Cleveland, Stockton-on-Tees and Sunderland), South Yorkshire (replaced by Barnsley, Doncaster, Rotherham and Sheffield), West Yorkshire (replaced by Bradford, Calderdale, Kirklees, Leeds and Wakefield) and Tyne & Wear (replaced by Gateshead, Newcastle upon Tyne, North Tyneside, South Tyneside and Sunderland).

5. **North West:** the present counties of Cheshire, Cumbria and Lancashire, plus the former counties of Greater Manchester (replaced by the unitary authorities of Bolton, Bury, Manchester, Oldham, Rochdale, Salford, Stockport, Tameside, Trafford and Wigan) and Merseyside (replaced by Knowsley, Liverpool, St Helens, Sefton and Wirral).

6. **Northern Ireland:** all present and former counties/authorities within the historical boundary.

7. **South East:** the present counties of Bedfordshire, Berkshire, Buckinghamshire, East Sussex, Hampshire, Hertfordshire, Kent, Oxfordshire, Surrey and West Sussex, plus the new unitary authority of the Isle of Wight.

8. **South West:** the present counties of Cornwall, Devon, Dorset, Somerset and Wiltshire, plus the former county of Avon (replaced by the unitary authorities of Bath & North East Somerset, Bristol, North West Somerset and South Gloucestershire).

9. **Wales:** all present and former counties/authorities within the historical boundary.

Note: The above information is correct as at October 1996. Further changes may take place in 1997.

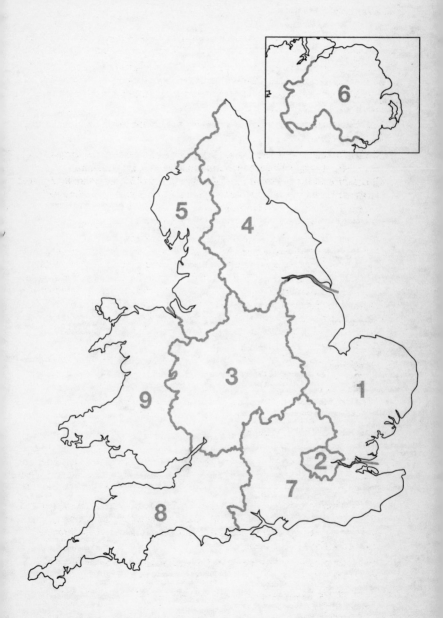

Eastern Counties

North Somercotes

Louth

Mablethorpe
Sutton on Sea

Gunby Hall
Whitegates Cottage
Skegness

Boston

Holbeach

Hunstanton

Brancaster
Stiffkey Marshes
A149
Blakeney Point
Blakeney
Sheringham Park
West Runton & Beeston Regis Heath
Morston Marshes
Cromer
Felbrigg Hall

Fakenham
North Walsham
Blickling Hall

Sandringham
A148

Horsey
Horsey Windpump

Wroxham
Wisbech
King's Lynn
St George's Guildhall
Peckover House
East Dereham
Norwich
Great Yarmouth
Elizabethan House Museum

Swaffham
March
Downham Market
Oxburgh Hall
Watton
Wymondham
A11
Darrow Wood
Beccles
Lowestoft

Chatteris
Brandon
Attleborough
Ramsey Abbey Gatehouse
Ely
Thetford
New Buckenham
Harleston
Southwold

St Ives
Soham
Mildenhall
Diss

Wicken Fen
Ixworth
Angel Corner
Dunwich Heath

Anglesey Abbey
Newmarket
Bury St. Edmunds
Theatre Royal
Saxmundham

Cambridge
Ickworth
Stowmarket

Wimpole Hall & Wimpole Home Farm
Lavenham Guildhall
Kyson Hill
Woodbridge
Orford Ness

Royston
Haverhill
Long Melford
Melford Hall
Ipswich
Pin Mill

Saffron Walden
Sudbury
Bridge Cottage, Flatford
Felixstowe
Harwich

Ware
Stansted
Halstead
Thorington Hall
Dedham
Paycockes & Coggeshall Grange Barn
Colchester
Bourne Mill
Walton-on-the-Naze
Frinton-on-Sea

Hertford
Bishop's Stortford
Braintree
Hatfield Forest
Witham
Copt Hall Marshes
West Mersea
Clacton-on-Sea

Harlow
Blake's Wood
Danbury & Lingwood Common
Maldon
Northey Island

Cheshunt
Waltham Abbey
Epping
Chipping Ongar
Billericay
Burnham-on-Crouch

Sutton House
Brentwood
Wickford
Rayleigh Mount
Southend-On-Sea

Eastbury Manor House
Basildon
Canvey Island
Shoeburyness

Rainham Hall
George Inn
Chislehurst Common, Hawkwood & Petts Wood
St John's Jerusalem Garden
Sheerness

COAST

There are entries on the following pages for the major coastal estates belonging to the Trust in **NORFOLK** and **SUFFOLK**: **Blakeney Point**, p.31, **Brancaster**, p.34, **Dunwich Heath**, p.35 and **Orford Ness**, p.44, which is one of the largest vegetated shingle spits in Europe.

In **ESSEX** the Trust owns the bird reserve of **Northey Island** in the Blackwater estuary. Permits to visit must be sought from the Warden, Northey Cottage, Northey Island, Maldon, Essex (tel. 01621 853 142) at least 24 hours in advance of a visit. It is a Grade 1 site for overwintering birds, and for saltmarsh plants. The island is cut off at high tide so access is limited. 8ml south of Colchester are the **Copt Hall Marshes**, near little Wigborough on the Blackwater estuary [168: TL981146]. The saltmarsh is extremely important for overwintering birds. 1½ml waymarked circular route. Footpath suitable for balloon-tyred wheelchairs. Small car park.

COUNTRYSIDE

In **NORFOLK** the Trust owns more than 810ha at **Horsey**, including **Horsey Windpump** (see p.40), marshland, marrams, farmland and the Mere. There is restricted access to the Mere, part of the Norfolk Broads, with brackish water because of seepage from the nearby sea, although it is separated from it by sand dunes. Car park and WCs.

At **West Runton** between Sheringham and Cromer the Trust owns about 28ha, known locally as the Roman Camp and including the highest point in the county [133: TG184414]. Adjoining **Beeston Regis Heath** is about 12ha of heathland and woodland giving fine views of the coastline. There is access to the long-distance coastal footpath. Car-parking for both properties at West Runton ('Roman Camp'). Also excellent coastal views from **Incleborough Hill**, above the Links Golf Course. (See also **Sheringham Park**, p.48.) **Darrow Wood** near Harleston is the site of a small motte-and-bailey castle [TM265894].

In **SUFFOLK**, at **Kyson Hill** just south of Woodbridge, there are lovely views of the winding River Deben from 1.5ha of parkland, with fine walks [169: TM269477]. Further south near Chelmondiston Village on the Orwell is **Pin Mill**, a well-known beauty spot for visitors from Ipswich. This natural woodland is accessible on foot in any weather, and there are fine views of the river and an extremely varied collection of fishing boats, Thames barges and pleasure craft of all types is drawn-up on the shore; waymarked walk [169: TM214380].

5ml east of Chelmsford in **ESSEX**, **Danbury & Lingwood Commons** [167: TL7805] are a survival of the medieval manors of St Clere and Herons, where commoners from the settlements roundabout grazed their animals on these heath and woodland areas. Danbury is more open with heather, bracken, broom and brambles, some oak and silver birch, and areas of hornbeam coppice and standard trees. A clearing on this common is one of the few known breeding grounds in this

WREN

country for the rosy marbled moth. Lingwood Common has more woodland, with open glades and a fine viewpoint. Near Little Baddow, 2ml to the north-west, the Trust owns **Blake's Wood** – more than 50ha of hornbeam and chestnut coppice and renowned for bluebells [167: TL773067]. All these areas are Sites of Special Scientific Interest. **Hatfield Forest**, near Bishop's Stortford on the Herts/Essex border, offers well over 480ha of undulating wooded country and open grassland for walkers and riders to explore (see p.39). **Rayleigh Mount** is an archaeological site in the centre of Rayleigh, the site of a motte-and-bailey castle recorded in the Domesday Book, now managed for plants and wildlife; circular walk, and footpath to the summit (see p.47). At Dedham the Essex Way passes through **Bridges Farm** and **Dalethorpe Park** [168: TM05333111].

ANGEL CORNER 🏠

8 Angel Hill, Bury St Edmunds IP33 1XB
Tel: (St Edmundsbury BC) 01284 763233

A Queen Anne house leased to the Borough of St Edmundsbury

🅾 Open by appointment only. Further details from The Mayor's Secretary, St Edmundsbury Borough Council

£ Free. No WC

➔ In Bury St Edmunds [155: TL855643] *Bus:* From surrounding areas (tel. 01473 583358) *Station:* Bury St Edmunds ½ml

---

ANGLESEY ABBEY AND GARDEN 🏠 ☒ ✝ ❀ Ⓔ

Lode, Cambridge CB5 9EJ Tel/fax: 01223 811200

The house, dating from 1600, is built on the site of an Augustinian abbey, and contains the famous Fairhaven collection of paintings and furniture. It is surrounded by an outstanding 40ha landscape garden and arboretum, with wonderful statues, a display of hyacinths in spring, and magnificent herbaceous borders and dahlia garden in summer. A watermill in the grounds is in full working order (flour on sale) and may be seen working on the first Saturday of each month

🅾 **House:** 22 March to 12 Oct: Wed to Sun & BH Mon 1–5. **Garden:** 22 March to 2 Nov: Wed to Sun & BH Mon 11–5.30; also open Mon & Tues 7 July to 7 Sept (but house closed Mon & Tues). **Lode Mill:** 22 March to 2 Nov: Wed to Sun & BH Mon 1–5. Last admission to house, garden and Lode Mill 4.30. Property closed Good Fri. *Note:* Timed tickets to the house are issued Sun & BH Mon to overcome problems of overcrowding. Visitors are advised that at BH periods the delay in gaining admission to the house may be considerable and very occasionally admission may not be possible. **Events:** please send s.a.e. for details of musical events, theatre and garden tours

£ House & garden £5.60; Sun & BH Mon £6.60; family discounts available. Parties £4.60 per person. Garden only £3.30 (parties £2.60). Lode Mill free on entry to garden. Parties please book with s.a.e. to Administrator (no reductions Sun & BH Mon)

🖆 Shop & plant centre open 22 March to 2 Nov: Wed to Sun & BH Mon (daily 7 July to 7 Sept) 11–5.30. 6 Nov to 21 Dec: Thur to Sun 11–4. Jan to March 1998: Sat & Sun 11–4

♿ Close car-parking arrangements: please contact Administrator at least 24hrs in advance. Self-drive vehicles available for access to garden, shop and restaurant; house difficult (only 3 rooms accessible to wheelchair users via 4 stone steps). Ground floor of Lode Mill accessible to wheelchair users. WC

◑ Braille guide to house only. Hyacinth garden in spring; other scented plants

🍴 Lunches and teas (full licence) in restaurant by car park, 22 March to 2 Nov: Wed to Sun & BH Mon 11–5.30; Christmas & New Year opening times as shop. Refreshments also open 7 July to 7 Sept: Mon & Tues. Picnic area. Seating:120 in restaurant, 60 in covered open-air area

👶 Children's guide to house; baby slings available. Restaurant: children's menu, baby food, highchairs, scribble sheets

🐕 In car park only, on leads. Guide dogs only in house and garden

➔ In village of Lode, 6ml NE of Cambridge on B1102 [154: TL533622]
Bus: Stagecoach Cambus 111/122 from Cambridge (frequent services link ≋ Cambridge and bus station) (tel. 01223 423554); also Neals 14 from Cambridge (Sun only) (tel. 01223 317740) *Station:* Cambridge 6ml

---

BELTON HOUSE 🏠 🏠 ✚ ✿ ♣ 👶 🎭 E

Grantham NG32 2LS Tel: 01476 566116 Fax: 01476 579071

The crowning achievement of Restoration country house architecture, built 1685–88 for Sir John Brownlow, and altered by James Wyatt in the 1770s. Plasterwork ceilings by Edward Goudge and fine wood carvings of the Grinling Gibbons school. The rooms contain portraits, furniture, tapestries, oriental porcelain, family silver gilt and Speaker Cust's silver. Formal gardens, an orangery and a magnificent landscaped park with a lakeside walk and the Bellmount Tower. Fine church (not NT) with family monuments

🔵 **House**: 29 March to 2 Nov: Wed to Sun & BH Mon (closed Good Fri) 1–5.30.
Garden & park: 11–5.30 (28 June 11–4.30; July & Aug 10–5.30). Last admissions to house, garden & park 5 (28 June 4). Please note that the visitor route is extensive so please allow at least one hour to take full advantage. Free access to park on foot only from Lion Lodge gates all year (this does not give admittance to house, garden or adventure playground). Access to Bellmount Woods and Tower from separate car park. Park may be closed occasionally for special events. **Events**: April, Belton Horse Trials; concerts in summer, including 28 June open-air 'Movie Classics' concert; 20 July, Family Fun Day; occasional events in the park; special exhibitions; children's craft workshops throughout the season; details from Property Manager (s.a.e. please)

💷 House & garden £4.80, children £2.40; family ticket £12 (£10 in July & Aug). Discount for parties

🎭 Guided tours for parties, outside normal hours only, may be arranged

🖆 Shop same days as house 12–5.30. Also Nov to 21 Dec: Sat & Sun 12–4

♿ House difficult; please arrange with Property Manager to visit Wed to Fri when less busy. Park, garden, restaurant, shop and refreshment kiosk accessible, but rough paths to playground, difficult in wet weather; close car parking by prior arrangement; WC; wheelchair available for use in house. Sympathetic Hearing Scheme. We recommend that people with disabilities contact property in advance

👁 Braille guide

☕ Licensed restaurant open as shop, serving wide variety of home-cooked hot and cold lunches 12–2, teas 2–5 (seats 96). Open for functions and pre-booked parties throughout year; details by written application (s.a.e. please) to Property Manager

🚸 Extensive adventure playground, incl. under-6 'corral'; miniature train rides in summer. Children's guide; parent and baby facilities; front baby slings available on loan; children's portions in restaurant

🏫 Educational visits from school parties welcomed (Education Liaison Officer, schoolrooms and teachers' pack available); also 'grounds only' arrangements available for school parties

🐕 In parkland only, on leads

➡ 3ml NE of Grantham on A607 Grantham–Lincoln road, easily reached, and signposted from A1 [130: SK929395] *Bus:* Road Car 601 Grantham–Lincoln; 609 Grantham–Sleaford (both pass close ✇ Grantham) (tel. 01522 553135) *Station:* Grantham 3ml

---

BLAKENEY POINT

Warden's address: 35 The Cornfield, Langham, Holt NR25 7DQ
April to Sept: Tel: 01263 740480; Oct to March: Tel: 01328 830401

A 3½ml long sand and shingle spit and national nature reserve, summer home for over eleven species of seabird, including common and sandwich tern, oystercatcher and ringed plover; winter visitors include large flocks of brent geese. Common seals breed off the point of the spit. Information centre at Morston Quay. Adjoining properties at Morston and Stiffkey comprise 405ha of saltmarsh and intertidal mudflats. In July the marshes are coloured purple with sea lavender

O All year

£ No landing fee. Access on foot from Cley Beach (3½ml) or by ferry from Morston and Blakeney (tidal). Restricted access to certain areas of the Point during the main bird breeding season (May to July). Car park at Blakeney Quay and Morston Quay £1, NT members free

i For pre-booked school parties and special interest groups (small charge)

♿ A 133m long wheelchair walkway provided on the Point; local boatmen will help disabled visitors with wheelchairs; please give advance notice of a visit to Warden (address above). WC at Lifeboat House

◄ Sea and bird sounds; atmosphere

▶ Light refreshments and exhibition in the Old Lifeboat House (April to Sept); open subject to tide times

▤ Resource book available from Warden; price £1.50 plus postage

🐕 Must be on leads. No dogs west of Old Lifeboat House on Blakeney Point, April to Sept

→ Morston Quay, Blakeney [133: TG0046] and Cley are all off A149 Cromer–Hunstanton road *Bus:* Sanders Coaches, Eastern Counties Coastliner, from ➤ Sheringham (tel. 0500 626116) *Station:* Sheringham (U) 8ml

---

BLICKLING HALL, GARDEN AND PARK 🏠 🏨 ❋ ♦ ♿ i E

Blickling, Norwich NR11 6NF Tel: 01263 733084 Fax: 01263 734924

One of the greatest houses in East Anglia, Blickling dates from the early 17th century. Its collections include fine furniture, pictures and tapestries. A spectacular Jacobean plaster ceiling in the 40m long gallery is particularly impressive. The gardens are renowned for massive yew hedges and magnificent herbaceous borders and contain a late 18th-century orangery; the parkland has a lake and good walks

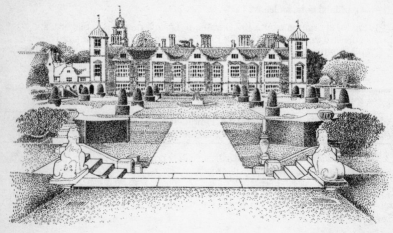

⭕ **House:** 28 to 31 March: daily 1–4.30; April to end June: Thurs to Sun & BH Mons 1–4.30; 1 July to 14 Sept: Tues to Sun & BH Mon 1–4.30; 15 Sept to 2 Nov: Thurs to Sun 1–4.30. Last admission 4.30. 'Taster' guided tours frequently available. **Garden:** same days as house 10.30–5.30 (gates close at 6), and open daily 1 July to 14 Sept. **Park and woods:** daily all year dawn to dusk. **Events:** wide-ranging programme; details from Property Manager

💷 House & garden £5.50 (Sun & BH Mon £6.50). Family and group discounts available. Groups please book with s.a.e. to Property Manager. Garden only £3.20 (Sun & BH Mon £3.50). Coarse fishing in lake; permits available from Warden at 1 Park Gate (tel. 01263 734181). Free access to South Front, shop, restaurant and plant centre on open days

🧍 Private and school party guided tours of hall, garden and estate available outside normal opening hours. Evening tour with supper in hall possible. Partner programmes compiled; details from Property Manager

🛍 Shop and plant centre open as garden; 28 March to 2 Nov 10.30–5.30. Also 3 Nov to 21 Dec: Thur to Sun 10.30–5.30; Jan to end March 1998: Sat & Sun only 11–4

♿ Designated parking area near house for elderly visitors and visitors with disabilities. Steep ramp at East Gate; entrance to house ramped; ground floor on one level; lift to upper floor. Garden routes available avoiding steps; two battery-operated vehicles available. Steep ramp to shop and restaurant. Plant centre accessible. WCs at reception and in buildings to east of Hall. Sympathetic Hearing Scheme. *Note*: British Gas ADAPT Commendation, 1993

👁 Braille guide

☕ Lunches & teas in restaurant (capacity 110): 28 Mar to 2 Nov when house and garden open 10.30–5.30; 3 Nov to 21 Dec; Thur to Sun 10.30–5.30; Jan to end March 1998: Sat & Sun only 11–4; table licence (parties by arrangement). Picnic area in orchard. Private lunch, supper & dinner parties in Hall

👶 Children's guide. Baby slings available. Baby-changing facilities. Restaurant: children's menu, baby food, highchairs, scribble sheets

🏫 School visits welcome, details from Property Manager

🐕 In park and picnic area only, on leads. Guide dogs only in Hall and garden

➡️ On N side of B1354, 1½ml NW of Aylsham on A140, 15ml N of Norwich, 10ml S of Cromer [133: TG178286] *Bus:* Eastern Counties 53/8, X58 Norwich–Sheringham; Sanders Coaches 40/1 (passing close ≆ Norwich), alight Aylsham, 1½ml (tel. 0500 626116) *Station:* Aylsham (Bure Valley Railway from ≆ Hoveton & Wroxham) 1¾ml, North Walsham (U) 8ml

---

BOURNE MILL ✖

Bourne Road, Colchester CO2 8RT Tel: 01206 572422

Originally a fishing lodge built in 1591, it was later converted into a mill, with a 2ha mill pond. Much of the machinery, including the waterwheel, is intact

⭕ BH Sun & BH Mon only, plus Sun & Tues in July & Aug: 2–5.30

[£] £1.50. Children must be accompanied by an adult. No reduction for parties. No WC

[→] 1ml S of centre of Colchester, in Bourne Road, off the Mersea Road (B1025) [168: TM006238] *Bus:* Colchester Transport 8/A, Eastern National 67 from Colchester (passing ⇌ Colchester) (tel. 0345 000333) *Station:* Colchester Town ¾ml; Colchester 2ml

---

BRANCASTER [icons]

Dial House, Brancaster Staithe, King's Lynn PE31 8BW Tel: 01485 210719

810ha of beach with 4ml of tidal foreshore, sand dunes, and saltmarsh, including the site of the Roman Fort of Branodunum

Note: A boat can be hired at Brancaster Staithe (weather permitting) to take visitors to the National Nature Reserve on Scolt Head Island. It is managed by English Nature (EN Warden: tel. 01485 518050). The Island is an important breeding site for four species of tern, oystercatcher and ringed plover. Nature trail. It is inadvisable to walk at low tide over the saltmarshes and sand flats

[O] All year. Information centre and cycle hire at Brancaster Staithe harbour: April to mid Sept; Sat & Sun 10–5. Daily 10–5 during summer school holidays. **Events:** guided walks programme; leaflet from Warden

[£] Golf club car park at Brancaster Beach, parking charge (incl. NT members)

[♿] Access to Brancaster Staithe and information centre

[🍴] Near the harbour (not NT)

[🐕] Under control at all times on the beach and not on Scolt Head Island from mid April to mid Aug. Dog-free area on Brancaster Beach, W of golf clubhouse May to Sept

[→] Brancaster Staithe is halfway between Wells and Hunstanton on A149 coast road [132: TF800450] *Bus:* Sanders/Dunthorne/Eastern Counties Coastliner Hunstanton–Wells, with connections from King's Lynn (passing close ⇌ King's Lynn) (tel. 0500 626116)

COGGESHALL GRANGE BARN [icon]

Grange Hill, Coggeshall, Colchester CO6 1RE Tel: 01376 562226

The oldest surviving timber-framed barn in Europe, dating from c.1140, and originally part of the Cistercian monastery of Coggeshall. It was restored in the 1980s by the Coggeshall Grange Barn Trust, Braintree District Council and Essex County Council. Features a small collection of farm carts and wagons

[O] 30 March to 12 Oct: Tues, Thur, Sun and BH Mon 1–5

[£] £1.50. Parties £1. Joint ticket with Paycocke's £3. Car park at Grange Barn

[♿] Barn accessible, parking nearby. WC next to Barn

34

🍴 Refreshments available at the Clockhouse Tea-rooms (not NT) in the centre of Coggeshall (tel. 01376 563242)

➡️ Signposted off A120 Coggeshall bypass; ½ml from centre of Coggeshall, on Grange Hill (signposted) [168: TQ848223] *Bus:* Eastern National/ Hedingham 70 Braintree–Colchester (passing close ⇌ Marks Tey) (tel. 0345 000333) *Station:* Kelvedon 2½ml

---

DUNWICH HEATH & MINSMERE BEACH 🏖️ 🏨 ♿ 👤 E

Dunwich, Saxmundham IP17 3DJ Tel: 01728 648505/648501 Fax: 01728 648384

86ha of Sandlings heathland with sandy cliffs and 1ml of beach. One of Suffolk's most important conservation areas with good walks from the property and access to a public hide at the adjacent Minsmere Reserve. Information and observation room in the converted Coastguard Cottages which also have a restaurant, shop and three holiday flats and a holiday cottage for rent

🕐 All year: dawn to dusk. Introductory talks available for group visits.
Events: family events programme; send s.a.e. to Property Enterprises Manager for list. Private function and events catered for

💷 Parking charge: season tickets £15; cars (pay-and-display) £1.50; coaches £6 (but free with 2 weeks' written notice). Members should display membership card on dashboard or obtain pass from Coastguard Cottages

👤 On request for groups

🛍️ Shop open as restaurant in Coastguard Cottages

♿ Car park viewing point and some footpaths accessible. Please contact the Warden for further information. Adapted WC at Coastguard Cottages (RADAR lock); stairlift to viewing room. Chauffeur-driven/self-drive powered vehicle available (booking preferred). Shop and tea-room accessible. Holiday flat for disabled guests at the Coastguard Cottages

👁️ Guided walks for visually impaired people; Braille guide

🍴 Restaurant (located in Coastguard Cottages) open for morning coffee, lunch & tea: Jan to Feb & Nov to Dec: Thur to Sun; March & April: Tues to Sun; May to Oct: daily

👶 Restaurant: children's menu, baby food, highchairs, scribble sheets. Baby-changing facilities and children's outdoor play area

🏛️ Education Officer and Field Study Centre. Groups must book in advance

🐕 Must be under tight control

➡️ 1ml S of Dunwich, signposted from A12 [156: TM475683] *Bus:* Eastern National 167 Colchester–Lowestoft, Sun only (tel. 01473 583358) *Station:* Darsham (U) 6ml

COMMON TERN

ELIZABETHAN HOUSE MUSEUM 🏠

4 South Quay, Great Yarmouth NR30 2QH Tel: 01493 855746

A 16th-century building with panelled rooms and 19th-century frontage, leased to the Norfolk Museums Service as a museum of domestic life

🅾 24 March to 6 April: Mon to Fri 10–5, Sun 2–5 (closed Good Fri); 25 May to 26 Sept: Sun to Fri 10–5. Please telephone in advance to confirm opening arrangements (possible major renovation work during 1997)

💷 Joint ticket lasting two days also gives entry to Maritime Museum for East Anglia and Tollhouse Museum and Brass Rubbing Centre. Adult £1.10, concessions 60p, children 50p; family ticket (2 adults, 4 children) £2.70. NT members admitted free to Elizabethan House Museum only. Prices subject to change

➔ In Great Yarmouth [134: TG523073] *Bus:* Local services from surrounding areas (tel. 0500 626116) *Station:* Great Yarmouth ½ml

FELBRIGG HALL, GARDEN AND PARK 🏠 🏠 ✝ ❀ ♠ 🐾 ℹ E

Felbrigg, Norwich NR11 8PR Tel: 01263 837444 Fax: 01263 837032

One of the finest 17th-century houses in Norfolk, with its original 18th-century furniture and Grand Tour paintings; there is also an outstanding library and interesting domestic wing. The Walled Garden has been restored, complete with dovecote, greenhouses and the traditional layout of herbaceous plants and fruit trees, including the national collection of colchicums. There are extensive walks in the 200ha Great Wood and through the historic parkland with its church and lake

🅾 House: 29 March to 2 Nov: Sat to Wed 1–5 (but open Good Fri); BH Mon & Sun preceding BH Mon 11–5; last admission 4.30. **Garden:** same days 11–5.30. **Woodland, lakeside walks and parkland:** daily all year, dawn to dusk (closed Christmas Day). **Events:** for details of full programme please send s.a.e. to Property Manager or contact Events Box Office (tel. 01263 838297)

💷 House & garden £5.20; family discounts available. Parties £4.20; please book with s.a.e. to Property Manager. Garden only £2; family ticket £4. A car-parking charge for non-members will be introduced during 1997

𝐊 Guided tours of Hall outside normal opening times available; details from Property Manager

🛍 Open same days as house 11–5.30. Also 6 Nov to 21 Dec: Thur to Sun 11–4; Jan to end March 1998: Sat & Sun 11–4 (tel. 01263 837040)

♿ Parking area in main car park by information board. Wheelchairs available from visitor reception building 100m. One self-drive single-seater vehicle. Access to ground floor only, shop, restaurant, tea-room & garden; photograph album of upper floor rooms for visitors unable to climb stairs. WC. Sympathetic Hearing Scheme

◉ Braille guides to house and walks

☕ Park restaurant (waited service) and Turret tea-room (counter service) both licensed. 29 March to 2 Nov: same days as house 11–5.15 (occasionally only one of these facilities available). Booking advisable for park restaurant and Sun lunches. Private functions catered for (tel. 01263 838237). Also 6 Nov to end March 1998: same days as shop 11–3.30

👶 Baby slings available. Parent & baby room. Highchairs in restaurant. Children's menu. Scribble sheets. Free Family Woodland Trail

📖 Details of Education Programme from Education Officer. Teachers' resource book Key Stage 2 & 3 and teachers' pack available. 32-bed base camp available with all facilities; s.a.e to Property Manager for details

🐕 In woods under close control; in park and on farmland on leads only

➔ Nr Felbrigg village, 2ml SW of Cromer; entrance off B1436, signposted from A148 and A140 [133: TG193394] *Bus:* Coastliner from Wells-next-the-Sea and 🚆 Sheringham, Sun, Tues, Wed, Thur & Fri, June–Sept only (tel. 0500 626116) *Station:* Cromer (U) or Roughton Road (U), both 2¼ml

---

FLATFORD: BRIDGE COTTAGE 🏠 🚆 E

Flatford, East Bergholt, Colchester CO7 6OL
Tel: 01206 298260 Fax: 01206 299193

Just upstream from Flatford Mill, the restored thatched cottage houses a display about John Constable, several of whose paintings depict this property. Facilities include a tea-garden, shop, boat hire and an information centre. Access by foot to Trust land in Dedham Vale

Note: Flatford Mill, Valley Farm & Willy Lott's House are leased to the Field Studies Council which runs arts-based courses for all age groups. For further information on courses tel. 01206 298283. There is no general public access to the buildings, but the Field Studies Council will arrange tours for groups

🅾 1 March to end April: Wed to Sun 11–5.30 (closed Good Fri); May to Sept: daily 10–5.30; Oct: Wed to Sun 11–5.30; Nov: Wed to Sun 11–3.30. Limited opening in Dec (telephone for details). **Events:** special evening events in tea-room (also available for private functions); details from Property Manager

£ Guided walks £1.50, accompanied children free (subject to availability). Also available for school parties and coach parties; pre-booking essential. Parking 200m; private car park, charge (NT members incl.). Free admission to Bridge Cottage

🏃 Guided walks of the area: 29, 30 & 31 March and every afternoon June to end Sept, subject to availability

🛍 Shop open as cottage

♿ Close car-parking; 25m from cottage, or main car park, 200m. Access to tea-garden and shop. Wheelchair, powered self-drive buggy and walking aid available at Bridge Cottage

👁 Braille guide

🍽 Open as cottage for morning coffee, lunches and teas (table licence)

🧒 Tea-room; children's menu, baby food, highchairs, scribble sheets. Children's play table. Flatford trail on sale in cottage

🐕 Guide dogs only in Bridge Cottage complex

➡ On N bank of Stour, 1ml S of East Bergholt (B1070) [168: TM077332]. Accessible on foot from East Bergholt, Dedham and Manningtree *Bus:* Eastern Counties/Eastern National 92/3, 166–8 Ipswich–Colchester (passing ≋ Ipswich and close ≋ Colchester Town), alight E Bergholt, ¾ml (tel. 01473 583358) *Station:* Manningtree 1¾ml by footpath, 3½ml by road

---

GRANTHAM HOUSE 🏠 ❖ ♠

Castlegate, Grantham NG31 6SS
Tel: (Regional Office) 01909 486411 Fax: 01909 486377

The house dates from 1380, but has been extensively altered and added to throughout the centuries, resulting in a pleasant mixture of architectural styles. The walled gardens run down to the river, and on the opposite bank Sedgwick Meadows, also NT, form an open space in the centre of the town

Ⓞ **Ground floor only**: 29 March to end Sept: Wed 2–5 by written appointment only with the tenant, Major-General Sir Brian Wyldbore-Smith

£ £1.50. Limited space; numbers in parties should not exceed seven. No WC

➡ Immediately E of Grantham Church [130: SK916362] *Bus:* Road Car 601 Grantham–Lincoln, to within ¼ml (tel. 01522 553135) *Station:* Grantham 1ml

---

GUNBY HALL 🏠 🏃 £

Gunby, nr Spilsby PE23 5SS
Tel: (Regional Office) 01909 486411 Fax: 01909 486377

A red-brick house with stone dressings, built in 1700 and extended in 1870s. Within the house, there is good early 18th-century wainscoting and a fine oak staircase, also English furniture and portraits by Reynolds. Contemporary stable block, a walled garden, sweeping lawns and borders. Gunby was reputedly Tennyson's 'haunt of ancient peace'

O **Ground floor & basement of house & garden**: 29 March to end Sept: Wed 2–6. Last admission 5.30. Closed BHols. Garden also open Thur 2–6. House & garden also open Tues, Thur and Fri by written appointment only with J. D. Wrisdale at above address. **Events**: occasional concerts

£ House & garden £3.50. Garden only £2.50. No reduction for parties. Access roads unsuitable for coaches which must park in layby at gates ½ml from house

& Access to garden only; cobbled stableyard. Wheelchair available

♣ Rose & herb garden

♦ No refreshments available

♦ In garden only, on leads

➔ 2½ml NW of Burgh le Marsh, 7ml W of Skegness on S side of A158 (access off roundabout) [122: TF467668] *Bus:* Road Car 6 Skegness–Lincoln (passing close ≋ Skegness) (tel. 01522 553135) *Station:* Skegness 7m

---

GUNBY HALL ESTATE: WHITEGATES COTTAGE 🏠

Mill Lane, Bratoft, nr Spilsby Tel: 01754 890533

A small cottage on the Gunby Hall Estate, built c.1770 to provide accommodation for workers next to land which lay some distance from the main body of the farm. Constructed in the once common, now extremely rare, Lincolnshire vernacular tradition of mud and stud walling under a long-straw thatch roof, the cottage is currently being restored using traditional methods and materials

Note: Further restoration work will be carried out in 1997, but visitors are welcome to view work in progress

O 29 March to end Sept: Wed 2–6 by written appointment only with the tenant, Mr J. Zaremba

£ £1.50. Numbers in parties visiting the property should not exceed six at any one time, due to the small size of rooms. WCs at Gunby Hall (above)

➔ 2ml W of Burgh le Marsh, 8ml W of Skegness. Approached by Gunby Lane off A158 just W of the roundabout N of Gunby Hall. Public transport: as for Gunby Hall (see above)

HATFIELD FOREST 🖼 🏠 🚻 E

Takeley, nr Bishop's Stortford CM22 6NE Tel: 01279 870678 Fax: 01279 871938

Over 480ha of ancient woodland and rare surviving example of a medieval royal hunting forest. This historic landscape has been designated a National Nature Reserve. The chases and rides afford excellent walks and there is good coarse fishing on the two lakes. Waymarked nature trail

O All year. Vehicle access restricted to entrance car park Nov to Easter. **Events:** 2 Aug, Children's Fun Day; 30 & 31 Aug, Wood Fair

£ Car park £2.60; mini-buses £5; coaches £20; school coaches £10. Parties must book in advance with Property Manager. Riding for members of Hatfield Forest Riding Association only; contact Property Manager

♿ Reserved car-parking; accessible paths and grassland; self-drive powered vehicle available, please book in advance. WC

☕ Refreshments available near the lake

🚼 Baby-changing facilities

▣ Full education programme; details from Education Officer

🐕 Must be kept on leads where cattle and sheep are grazing and around lake. There is a dog-free area near the lake

➔ Signposted off A120 at Takeley, E of Bishop's Stortford [167: TL547208/546199] *Bus:* Biss 317 � Bishop's Stortford–� Elsenham, or Townlink 133 Bishop's Stortford–Braintree, on both alight Takeley Street (Green Man), thence ¾ml; otherwise Eastern National 33/X � Bishop's Stortford–Southend or 133 Bishop's Stortford–Braintree, alight Takeley (Four Ashes), thence 1½ml (tel. 0345 000333) *Station:* Stansted Airport 3ml

HORSEY WINDPUMP ▣

Horsey, Great Yarmouth NR29 4EF
Tel: (Regional Office) 01263 733471 Fax: 01263 734924

A drainage windmill which was working until 1943, when lightning severely damaged it. Acquired by the Trust in 1948 and restored

🅾 29 March to 30 Sept: daily 11–5

£ £1.20. No reduction for parties. Car-parking charge for non-members, 30p per hour

🛍 Small shop

☕ Light refreshments

🐕 On leads only

➔ 2½ml NE of Potter Heigham, 11ml N of Yarmouth near B1159 [134: TG457223] *Bus:* Eastern Counties 623/6, 723/6 Great Yarmouth–Martham (passing close � Yarmouth), alight W Somerton School, 1¾ml (tel. 0500 626116) *Station:* Acle (U) 10ml

HOUGHTON MILL ▣ 🛗

Houghton, nr Huntingdon PE17 2AZ Tel: 01480 301494

A large timber-built watermill on an island on the River Great Ouse, 2ml downstream from Huntingdon. Much of the 19th-century machinery is intact and is operational on milling days, every Sun from April to end Aug, when corn is ground and the flour sold. An art gallery displays local artists' work

[O] **Mill**: 29 March to 12 Oct: Sat, Sun & BH Mon 2–5.30; also 23 June to 3 Sept: Mon to Wed 2–5.30. Last admission 5.15. Parties and school groups at other times by arrangement with Custodian. **Art gallery**: June to end Sept: Sat & Sun 2.30–5.30

[£] £2.50 (£3 on milling days); family discounts available. Car park on adjacent private land (no street parking); charge £1 (NT members 40p on days when the mill is open). Coaches must park 300m away in village

[X] By prior arrangement

[&] Access to ground floor only; steep wooden stairs

[◉] Braille guide. Many items can be enjoyed by touch

[†] Children's guide

[▥] Guided tours for pre-booked school parties

[→] In village of Houghton, signposted off A1123 to Huntingdon, to St Ives [153: TL282720] *Bus*: Stagecoach United Counties 74, Whippet 1A, 4 from Huntingdon (passing close ≠ Huntingdon) (tel. 01223 317740) *Station*: Huntingdon 3½ml

---

ICKWORTH HOUSE, PARK & GARDEN [▦] [▥] [✿] [♣] [†] [E]

Ickworth, The Rotunda, Horringer, Bury St Edmunds IP29 5QE
Tel: 01284 735151/735270 Fax: 01284 735270

The eccentric Earl of Bristol (also Bishop of Derry) created this equally eccentric house, started in 1795 to display his collections. The paintings include works by Titian, Gainsborough and Velasquez and the magnificent Georgian silver collection is displayed in the oval Rotunda which is linked by curved corridors to flanking wings. The house is surrounded by an Italianate garden and set in a 'Capability' Brown park with several waymarked woodland walks, a deer enclosure with hide and an adventure playground. The house has been extensively redecorated and the recently purchased paintings hung in their original places in the state rooms

[O] **House**: 22 March to 2 Nov: Tues, Wed, Fri, Sat, Sun & BH Mon 1–5. **Park**: all year: daily 7–7. **Garden**: 22 March to 2 Nov: daily 10–5; 4 Nov to end March 1998: daily 10–4. Garden & park closed 25 Dec. **Events**: most weekends throughout the season. Regular programme of music in the house during normal opening hours. Contact the Property Manager's office for details

[£] House, garden & park £5, children £2; family discounts available. Pre-booked parties £4 (no party rate Sun & BH Mon). Admission to park & garden £2, children 50p (access to shop & restaurant with park ticket)

[X] Guided tours and pre-booked special openings for groups with particular interests

[▣] Shop open same days as house 12–5. Also 1 Nov to 21 Dec: Sat & Sun 11–4

[&] Disabled visitors may be driven to the house; disabled drivers are given a temporary parking permit to park outside the house. Ramp available for access to house; then all ground-floor rooms are level. Wheelchairs and powered self-drive vehicle available. Much of garden accessible, but gravel drive and paths. 1½ml woodland walk accessible to wheelchair users. Adapted WC on ground floor.

Stairlift to shop and restaurant. Batricars available free of charge for use in park and garden

Braille guides; scented woodland walk with tapping rail. Special guided tours if booked in advance

Lunches & teas; table licence, open as shop. Last orders 5. (Nov & Dec: Sat & Sun 11–4) Capacity: 60 plus overflow 50. Picnic area

Children's playground next to car park. Children's guide. Children's quiz trails during spring and summer holidays. Baby slings available. Restaurant: children's menu, baby foods, highchairs, scribble books. Baby-changing table

School groups welcome

In park only, on leads. Guide dogs allowed in house

In Horringer, 3ml SW of Bury St Edmunds on W side of A143 [155: TL8161]
Bus: Eastern Counties 141-4 Bury St Edmunds–Haverhill; Suffolk Bus 757 from ☰ Colchester (Sun only); both pass close ☰ Bury St Edmunds (tel. 01473 583358) *Station:* Bury St Edmunds 3ml

---

LAVENHAM: THE GUILDHALL OF CORPUS CHRISTI

Market Place, Lavenham, Sudbury CO10 9QZ Tel: 01787 247646

This late 15th-century timber-framed Tudor building, originally the hall of the Guild of Corpus Christi, overlooks and dominates the market place. Within the nine rooms of the Guildhall are displays of 500 years of local history, farming, industry and the development of the railway, and a unique exhibition of 700 years of the medieval woollen cloth trade. There is a delightful walled garden including dye plants, and a 19th-century lock-up and mortuary

29 March to 2 Nov: daily 11–5. The building, or parts of it, may be closed occasionally for community purposes

£ £2.70. Accompanied children free. Parties £2.30. School parties by prior arrangement, 60p per child

⌷ Shop open as Guildhall. Also 6 Nov to 21 Dec: Thur to Sun 11–4

♿ Access to shop & tea-room only

✋ Studwork and carved wood may be touched

☕ Tea-room for coffee, light lunches & teas, open as Guildhall, 11–5 (but reduced opening in April & Oct). Seats 43

👶 Children's guidebook. Tea-room: children's menu, highchairs, scribble sheets

➔ A1141 and B1071 [155: TL917494] *Bus:* Chambers Bury St Edmunds–Colchester (passing close ⇌ Bury St Edmunds); Suffolk Bus 757 ⇌ Colchester–Lavenham, Sun only. All pass close ⇌ Sudbury (tel. 01473 583358) *Station:* Sudbury (U) 7ml

---

MELFORD HALL 🏛 ✤

Long Melford, Sudbury CO10 9AH Tel: 01787 880286

A turreted brick Tudor mansion, little changed since 1578 with the original panelled banqueting hall, an 18th-century drawing room, a Regency library and a Victorian bedroom, showing fine furniture and Chinese porcelain. There is also a special Beatrix Potter display and a garden. New walk open in the park

🅾 April: Sat, Sun & BH Mon 2–5.30; May to end Sept: Wed, Thur, Sat, Sun & BH Mon 2–5.30; Oct: Sat & Sun 2–5.30. Last admission 5

£ House, garden & park £4. Pre-arranged parties £3 per person Wed & Thur only; please book with s.a.e. to Administrator

♿ Disabled visitors may be driven to the Hall. Ground-floor rooms easily accessible; stairlift available to first floor. Some steps in garden. WC (by car park)

✋ Braille guide

☕ In Long Melford (not NT)

👶 Children's guide

→ In Long Melford off A134, 14ml S of Bury St Edmunds, 3ml N of Sudbury [155: TL867462] *Bus:* Beestons/Chambers various services (but frequent) from Sudbury; Suffolk Bus 601 Colchester–Saffron Walden & 757 ⇌ Colchester–Lavenham (Sun). All pass close ⇌ Sudbury (tel. 01473 583358) *Station:* Sudbury (U) 4ml

---

ORFORD NESS

Quay Office, Orford Quay, Orford, Woodbridge IP12 2NU
Warden Tel/fax: 01394 450900

Orford Ness is the largest vegetated shingle spit in Europe; the site contains a variety of habitats, including shingle, saltmarsh, mud-flat, brackish lagoons and grazing marsh. The shingle flora has a significant number of nationally rare species and rare plant communities; it is also an important location for breeding and passage birds. The Ness was a secret military site from 1915 and was successively a Royal Flying Corps and RAF experimental station. Early experiments in radar were carried out on the Ness and from the 1950s to the 1970s it was a testing centre for the Atomic Weapons Research Establishment. Visitors go on a $4\frac{1}{2}$ml route which includes grazing and saltmarshes, the shingle, and some of the areas of historic and defence interest; the route is available to walk in total or in parts. The full route involves walking on shingle

Note: It is advisable to book a ferry trip in advance through Orford Ness Ferry, Walnut Tree Cottage, Orford, Woodbridge, IP12 2NF (tel. 01394 450057). The maximum number of visitors is limited to 96 per day for both conservation and safety reasons. Pedestrian access on site only

🄾 April to Oct: Thur, Fri & Sat. Access to the Ness is by ferry only from Orford Quay. Outward journeys are at 20min intervals 10–12.40. The maximum stay on the Ness is $3\frac{1}{2}$ hours. Nov to March: contact Orford Ness Warden for access details

£ Admission includes the ferry crossing; for details tel. 01394 450057. Pay-and-display car-parking in Orford town

🕭 A number of guided walks will be available in 1997; contact Warden for details

🍴 In Orford town

🏛 Education Warden (tel. 01394 450900). Some of the buildings are open to the public and include displays on natural history and history of the site

🐕 Strictly no dogs allowed

→ Access from Orford Quay, Orford town 10ml E of A12 (B1084), 12ml NE of Woodbridge

AVOCET

OXBURGH HALL, GARDEN AND ESTATE 🏰 ✝ ❀ 👤 E

Oxborough, King's Lynn PE33 9PS Tel: 01366 328258 Fax: 01366 328066

This moated house was built in 1482 by the Bedingfeld family, who still live here. The rooms show the development from medieval austerity to Victorian comfort, with embroidery worked by Mary Queen of Scots during her captivity on display. The magnificent Tudor gatehouse rises 25m above the moat, and the garden includes lawns, fine trees, colourful borders and a French parterre. There are also delightful woodland walks, including a new 2ml walk through Home Covert

🅾 **House**: 29 March to 2 Nov: Sat to Wed 1–5; BH Mon 11–5. **Garden**: same days as house 11–5.30. **Events**: programme of brass band concerts and garden open days; s.a.e. to Administrator for details

£ House, garden & estate £4.60; family discounts available. Pre-arranged parties £3.60 per person; please book with s.a.e. to Administrator. Garden & estate only £2.20

📷 Open same days as house 11–5

♿ Parking adjoining ticket office. Access to house 200m; shallow ramp to 4 ground-floor rooms; difficult stairs to upper floors. WC in west wing of house. Easy access to tea-room and shop. Garden largely accessible, gravel paths; route map available; care necessary near moat. 2 shallow steps to Chapel, 100m from Hall. Wheelchairs available at ticket office

👁 Braille guide

🍴 Light lunches and teas in Old Kitchen 11–5 on open days. Table licence. Seats 100. Private functions catered for. Pantry with open air seating area in car park, serving light refreshments, home-made fudge and ice-cream; opening times vary according to season

👶 Baby slings available. Children's guide. Restaurant: children's menu, baby foods, highchairs, scribble sheets

🐕 No dogs

➡ At Oxborough, 7ml SW of Swaffham on S side of Stoke Ferry road [143: TF742012] *Station*: Downham Market 10ml

PAYCOCKE'S 🏠 ❊

West Street, Coggeshall, Colchester CO6 1NS Tel: 01376 561305

*A merchant's house, dating from c.1500, with unusually rich panelling and wood carving.
A display of lace for which Coggeshall was famous is on show, and there is a pleasant garden*

O 30 March to 12 Oct: Tues, Thur, Sun & BH Mon 2–5.30. Last admission 5

£ £2. Parties of 6 or more must book in advance with the tenant. No reduction for
parties. Children must be accompanied by an adult. Joint ticket with Coggeshall
Grange Barn £3. Parking at Grange Barn (10min walk) until 5

& Access to garden and ground floor; but one awkward step at front door.
The house is small

◉ Braille guide

➔ Signposted off A120, on S side of West Street, about 300m from centre of
Coggeshall, on road to Braintree next to the Fleece Inn, 5½ml E of Braintree
[168: TL848225] *Bus:* Eastern National/Hedingham 70 Colchester–Braintree
(passing ⇌ Marks Tey) (tel. 0345 000333) *Station:* Kelvedon 2½ml

PECKOVER HOUSE & GARDEN 🏠 🐘 ❊

North Brink, Wisbech PE13 1JR Tel/fax: 01945 583463

*A town house, built c.1722, with fine plaster and wood rococo decoration. The notable 0.8ha
Victorian garden includes an orangery, summerhouses, roses, herbaceous borders, a fernery,
a croquet lawn and the recently restored Reed Barn with its flat maze. The newly-restored
Octavia Hill Birthplace Museum (not NT) is virtually opposite Peckover House. The museum
charts Octavia Hill's career and includes a section on her as a founder of the National Trust.
The museum is open the same hours as the House and by appointment through the year; for
further details contact the Octavia Hill Birthplace Museum Trust, 1 South Brink Place,
Wisbech, PE13 1JE (tel. 01945 476358)*

O **House & garden**: 29 March to 2 Nov: Sat, Sun, Wed & BH Mon 2–5.30. Last
admission 5. **Garden only**: Mon & Tues 2–5.30. Last admission 5. Parties on
house open days by appointment.

£ £3 (£2 on garden only days); family discounts available. Parties £2.50.
Note: Members may, by written appointment with the tenants, view Nos. 14
and 19 North Brink

◊ Out of hours tours of house and/or garden available; please contact the Property
Manager for details

& Access to garden and Reed Barn only. Adapted WC at Reed Barn. Parking in
courtyard by prior arrangement

◉ Scented flowers and plants

◉ In Servants' Hall when house open. Reed Barn available for private functions

🐾 No dogs

➡️ On N bank of River Nene, in Wisbech (B1441) [143: TF458097] *Bus:* Eastern Counties X94, Stagecoach Viscount 336 from Peterborough (passing close ⊠ Peterborough); Eastern Counties 46, X94 from King's Lynn (passing close ⊠ King's Lynn) (tel. 01223 317740) *Station:* March 9½ml

RAMSEY ABBEY GATEHOUSE 🏠

Abbey School, Ramsey, Huntingdon PE17 1DH
Tel: (Regional Office) 01263 733471 Fax: 01263 734924

Remains of a 15th-century gatehouse of the Benedictine abbey

🅾️ 1 April to end Oct: daily 10–5. Other times by written application to Curator

£ Free (but collection box for contributions). No WC

➡️ At SE edge of Ramsey, at point where Chatteris road leaves B1096, 10ml SE of Peterborough [142: TL291851] *Bus:* Enterprise 330/1 Huntingdon–Peterborough (passing close ⊠ Huntingdon & Peterborough) (tel. 01354 692504) *Station:* Huntingdon 10ml

RAYLEIGH MOUNT

Rayleigh Tel: (Regional Office) 01263 733471 Fax: 01263 734924

A 2ha site in the middle of Rayleigh town, on which once stood the Domesday castle erected by Sweyn of Essex

🅾️ All year. Summer 7am–7.30pm; winter 7am–5pm

£ Free

➡️ 6ml NW of Southend, path from Rayleigh station (A129) [178: TQ805909] *Bus:* From surrounding areas (tel. 0345 000333) *Station:* Rayleigh 200m

ST GEORGE'S GUILDHALL 🏠 E

27 King Street, King's Lynn PE30 1HA Tel: 01553 773578

The largest surviving English medieval guildhall, with adjoining medieval warehouse, now in use as an Arts Centre

🅾️ All year Mon to Fri (closed Good Fri & Aug BH Mon) 10–4; Sat 10–1 & 2–3.30 (opening times may vary during July & Aug). Closed 25, 26 Dec & 1 Jan. The Guildhall is not usually open on the days when performances are taking place in the theatre (please refer to current King's Lynn Arts Centre brochure for details). **Events:** July, King's Lynn Festival. Performances, workshops and art exhibitions throughout the year; for details write to address above or tel. 01553 773578

£ 50p adult, 25p child

📷 Crafts. Christmas shop (open from mid-Nov)

♿ Access to galleries; please telephone for advice before a visit

🍽 Light lunches & teas from Crofters Coffee Bar. Also, restaurant open for lunch and dinner Mon to Sat

➡ On W side of King Street close to the Tuesday Market Place [132: TF616202] *Bus:* From surrounding areas (tel. 0500 626116) *Station:* King's Lynn ¾ml

---

SHERINGHAM PARK 🔲🏞🚂👤

Warden: Gardener's Cottage, Sheringham Park, Upper Sheringham NR26 8TB Tel: 01263 823778

This 311ha property includes the outstanding landscaped park by Humphry Repton, with fine, mature, mixed woodland, plus large area of rhododendrons and azaleas, which flower in May/June. Spectacular views of coast and countryside from viewing towers. Wonderful walks all year round. Includes route through Weybourne Heath to North Norfolk railway station at Weybourne (private full gauge steam railway open to the public)

🅾 **Park**: all year, dawn to dusk. Numerous waymarked walks through woodland, parkland and to the coast; guide on sale in car park. Sheringham Hall is privately occupied. Limited access is available to selected rooms only, April to Sept, by written appointment with the leaseholder

💷 £2.50 per car, incl. all passengers. Coaches £7.50; please book in advance for May/June visits with Warden. Pay-and-display car park. Coaches display 3 valid tickets. Members display membership card or pass (available when staff on duty)

👤 Morning/afternoon tours during rhododendron season (subject to guide availability)

♿ Raised walkway from car park to park viewpoints. Self-drive powered vehicle & wheelchair on request when car park staff present, Easter to end Sept. WC

🍽 Light refreshments available Easter to end Sept

🐕 On leads in park

➡ 2ml SW of Sheringham, access for cars off A148 Cromer–Holt road; 5ml W of Cromer; 6ml E of Holt [133: TG135420] *Bus:* Sanders Coaches Norwich–Holt (passes ⇌ Sheringham) (tel. 0500 626116) *Station:* Sheringham (U) 2ml

---

TATTERSHALL CASTLE 🏰🏠Ⓔ

Tattershall, Lincoln LN4 4LR Tel: 01526 342543

A vast fortified tower built c.1440 for Ralph Cromwell, Lord Treasurer of England. The castle is an important example of an early brick building, with a tower containing state apartments, rescued from dereliction and restored by Lord Curzon 1911–14. Four great chambers, with ancillary rooms, contain late Gothic fireplaces and brick vaulting. There are tapestries; information displays in turret rooms. Lincoln Cathedral and Boston Stump are visible from the 33m high battlements on clear days

[O] 29 March to 2 Nov: Sat to Wed & BH Mon (closed Good Fri) 10.30–5.30. Nov to 21 Dec: Sat & Sun only 10.30–4. Last admissions 30min before closing. Ground floor of castle may occasionally be closed for functions or events. Please contact the Custodian for dates. **Events:** details from Custodian

[£] £2.50, children £1.20; family ticket £6.20. Discount for parties; contact Custodian. Advance booking essential for coach parties

[🛍] Shop open same times as castle

[♿] Access via three steps to ground floor of castle, museum not accessible; easy access to shop and grounds (gravel paths). WC. Special parking area nearer the castle – please contact Custodian for details

[🍴] Limited service of drinks and ice creams available from shop. Picnicking welcome in grounds

[👶] WC with baby-changing facility; child back-packs allowed; family guidebook

[🎓] Castle is particularly suitable for school groups

[🐕] In car park only, on leads. No shade in car park; hooks are provided in shade by entrance to grounds, where dogs may be left

[→] On S side of A153, 15ml NE of Sleaford; 10ml SW of Horncastle [122: TF209575] *Bus:* Bryline Boston–Woodhall Spa (passing close ⇌ Boston) (tel. 01205 364087) *Station:* Ruskington (U) 10ml

THEATRE ROYAL [🏠][E]

Westgate Street, Bury St Edmunds IP33 1QR
Tel: 01284 755127 Fax: 01284 706035

Built in 1819 by William Wilkins, a rare example of a late Georgian playhouse with fine pit, boxes and gallery. Theatre Royal is a working theatre and presents a year-round programme of professional drama, comedy, dance music, mime, pantomime and amateur work. It boasts a national reputation and attracts the best touring companies in the country

[O] All year: daily, except Sun, 10–8 (closed every BH except for performances). No access to auditorium if theatrical activity is in progress. Please check in advance that theatre is open (tel. 01284 755469). **Events:** For 1997 events programme please send large s.a.e. (tel. 01284 769505)

[£] Free. Ticket prices for performances in brochures. Limited parking in Westgate Street. No parking in front of the theatre

[🚶] Organised guided tours and talks are available by prior arrangement: £1 per head; £25 minimum fee. To book tel. 01284 755127

[🛍] Wide selection of souvenirs available in box office

[♿] Induction loop system available. Signed performances. Limited wheelchair access. For full details tel. 01284 769505

[👁] Guide dogs admitted

[🍴] Meals; licensed bar in theatre for all performances. For reservations tel. 01284 766755

▥ For details of education initiatives and teachers' magazine tel. 01284 755127

▨ Guide dogs only

➔ On Westgate Street on S side of A134 from Sudbury (one-way system)
[155: TL855637] *Bus:* From surrounding areas (tel. 01473 583358)
Station: Bury St Edmunds ¾ml

THORINGTON HALL **▦**

Stoke by Nayland, Colchester CO6 4SS

Oak-framed, plastered, gabled house built in c.1600 and extended c.1700

O By written appointment with the tenant

➔ 2ml SE of Stoke by Nayland [155: TM013355] *Bus:* Hedingham 84, Carters 755
Colchester–East Bergholt (passing **⇌** Colchester), thence 1¼ml (tel. 01473
583358) *Station:* Colchester 7ml

WICKEN FEN NATIONAL NATURE RESERVE **▨ ▨ ▨ E**

Lode Lane, Wicken, Ely CB7 5XP Tel: 01353 720274 Fax: 01353 720274

*Britain's oldest nature reserve is a delight for the naturalist and rambler alike. Wide droves
and lush green paths take visitors into the heart of this special place; a unique fragment of
the wilderness that once covered much of East Anglia. The William Thorpe Visitor Centre,
refurbished in 1996, now offers a viewing gallery, children's activities, new exhibitions and
gift shop. Four new observation hides will open in 1997. The boardwalk offers easy access
to the fen throughout the year, although stout footwear is recommended for those following
the longer nature trail. The traditional Fen Cottage, with its charming cottage garden, was
restored using fen materials. From the glorious winter skies and frosts to the living tapestry
of the fen in summer, Wicken offers you a visit to remember at any time of the year*

O Fen: all year: daily except Christmas Day, dawn to dusk. Some paths will be
closed in very wet weather. **Visitor centre:** daily 9–5 (but occasionally closed
in winter). **Fen Cottage:** April to Oct: Sun & BH Mon 2–5 (plus some other days
in summer). **Fen Cottage Garden:** open as Fen. **Windpump:** in operation
occasionally in summer. **Events:** expert-led guided walks, family events, dawn
chorus, swallowtail watch, ghost walk and many other activities throughout
the year; please tel. for details

£ Fen & Cottage £3.50 (family discounts available). Cottage only £1.50.
Pre-booked parties £2.80, special rates for school/educational groups; contact
the Education Officer or write enclosing s.a.e

▨ Guided tours by special arrangement

▢ New bookshop and giftshop in visitor centre

▨ Raised boardwalk; adapted bird hides; close parking by arrangement. Visitor
centre fully accessible. WC in car park. Access to Fen Cottage by prior arrangement

▨ Hot and cold drinks, sweets and snacks from visitor centre

👶 Children's activities in visitor centre. Family events throughout the year

📰 Full-time Education Officer, pond-dipping, minibeast hunts and many other activities for school or educational groups at all levels. Simple self-catering accommodation for groups of up to 28 people available

🐕 Welcome if kept on lead at all times; there are other walks nearby where dogs can be exercised freely. No dogs allowed in Fen Cottage

➡️ S of A1123, 3ml W of Soham (A142), 9ml S of Ely, 17ml NE of Cambridge via A10 [154: TL563705] *Bus:* Stagecoach Cambus 19 Cambridge–Ely (Sun only); Greys 117 from Ely (Thur, Sat only); Stagecoach Cambus 122 Cambridge–Ely (Wed, Fri, Sat only); otherwise Stagecoach Cambus 116, 122 from Cambridge, Ely & Newmarket, alight Soham Downfields 3ml, or 109 Cambridge–Ely, alight Stretham 3½ml (tel. 01223 317740). All pass ➡️ Ely *Station:* Ely 9ml

---

WIMPOLE HALL 🏠 🐴 ✝ ✿ 🌳 👤 E

Arrington, Royston SG8 0BW Tel: 01223 207257 Fax: 01223 207838

This magnificent 18th-century house has a fine interior which is both intimate and formal, with work by Gibbs, Flitcroft and Soane. Servants' quarters include the housekeeper's room, butler's pantry, steward's room and a servant's bedroom. A 142ha park, landscaped by Bridgeman, Brown and Repton, includes a grand folly, Chinese bridge, lakes and extensive walks (leaflet). Heavy horses operate from the Victorian stable block to the farm

🔘 **Hall:** Sat & Sun 15/16 March 1–5, then 22 March to 2 Nov: Tues, Wed, Thur, Sat & Sun 1–5 (BH Sun & BH Mon 11–5). Additional opening Good Fri 1–5, BH Sun & BH Mon 11–5, Fri in July & Aug 1–5. **Garden:** open as Hall, 10.30–5 and daily in Aug. **Park:** open daily sunrise to sunset, but will close at 5 during open air concerts 18–20 July. **Events:** 27–29 June, East Anglia Flower & Garden Show; 18–20 July, open-air concerts with fireworks ; for bookings tel. 01223 207001. For details of musical and countryside events please send s.a.e. to Property Manager

💷 Hall & garden £5.20. Family discounts available for Hall. Parties £4.20; please send s.a.e. to Property Manager. Joint ticket with Home Farm £7. Car park 200m

51

🎁 By special arrangement outside normal opening hours

🛍 Shop open same days as Hall 11–5.30. Also 4 Nov to 23 Dec & Jan to end March 1998: Tues, Wed, Thur, Sat & Sun 11–4

♿ Parking near stable block. Disabled visitors may be set down near Hall. Stairlift usually available to ground floor rooms, which are fully accessible. WC open 10.30–5.30 at stable block; 12–5.30 at Hall. 1 self-drive vehicle available; please book in advance. New restaurant fully accessible

👁 Braille guide

🍴 Full lunches and teas in new restaurant, open same days as Hall 11–5 (lunches 12–2). Also 4 Nov to 23 Dec Tues to Thur & Sat & Sun 11–4; Jan to mid March 1998 11–4. Table licence. Stable block: light refreshments same days as Hall 10.30–5, also Tues to Thur & Sat & Sun Jan to 9 March 1998 11–4. Picnic area.

👶 Children's guide. Parent & baby room in stable block; baby slings available. Restaurant: children's menu, baby food, highchairs, scribble sheets

🏫 Full education programme; details from Education Officer (tel. 01223 207801)

🐕 In park only, on leads

➔ 8ml SW of Cambridge (A603), 6ml N of Royston (A1198) [154: TL336510] *Bus:* Whippet 175, Neals 14 Cambridge–Biggleswade (passing close ⊒ Biggleswade & Cambridge) *Station:* Shepreth 5ml

---

WIMPOLE HOME FARM 🏠 👁 🌳 ♿ E

As Wimpole Hall

Built in 1794 as a model farm. The Great Barn, designed by Sir John Soane, houses a collection of farm machinery of the kind used here over 200 years. Rare breeds of animals, including sheep, goats, cattle, pigs and horses, can be viewed in paddocks and the thatched buildings. There is an adventure woodland and horse and cart rides are usually available

🅾 8 March to 2 Nov: Tues, Wed, Thur, Sat & Sun, plus Good Fri & BH Mons 10.30–5. Open daily in July and Aug 10.30–5. 3 Nov to 7 March 1998: Wed, Sat & Sun 11–4 (closed 24 Dec). Also open Feb half-term week. **Events:** full programme; please tel. for details

💷 NT members £2, children £1. Non-members £4. Children (over 3) £2.50. Parties £3, children £1.50, please book with s.a.e. to Property Manager, Wimpole Hall. Joint ticket for hall & farm £7. School parties especially welcome (£1.50 per child, Education Group members £1 per child). Part of a building is reserved for their use. Parking 400m, at Hall

🎁 By special arrangement

🛍 Shop open same times as farm

♿ Ask for directions and parking at stable block. Level access throughout farm and ramps to most farm buildings. Light refreshments in stableyard. Shop next to Great Barn accessible. WC at farm. Wheelchairs available. Battery-operated vehicle available at stable block; please book in advance

BLEWCOAT SCHOOL

23 Caxton Street, Westminster SW1H 0PY Tel: 0171 222 2877

Built in 1709 at the expense of William Green, a local brewer, to provide an education for poor children. The building was in use as a school until 1926, bought by the Trust in 1954 and restored in 1975. It is now the NT London Information Centre and Shop

O All year: Mon to Fri 10–5.30; also Sat 29 Nov and Sat 6 & 13 Dec 11–4.30. Closed BH Mon, Good Fri, 25 Dec to 1 Jan 1998 (inclusive)

£ Free

⌖ Several steps to shop, difficult for wheelchair users; then level access

→ Near the junction with Buckingham Gate. *Bus:* Frequent local services (tel. 0171 222 1234) *Station:* Victoria ¼ml *Underground:* St James's Park, 100m

CARLYLE'S HOUSE

24 Cheyne Row, Chelsea SW3 5HL Tel: 0171 352 7087

This Queen Anne town house was the home of the Victorian writer and historian Thomas Carlyle and his wife Jane from 1834 until their deaths. The life and times of the Carlyles can be seen through the original furniture and decoration of the house, together with the many books, portraits and personal relics acquired during Carlyle's 47 years here. Dickens, Chopin, Tennyson, George Eliot and Emerson were among the many illustrious Victorians who visited Thomas and Jane at home. The house is part of a terrace in a quiet backwater of old Chelsea. A restored Victorian walled garden also reflects the Carlyles' life here.

O 29 March to 2 Nov: Wed to Sun & BH Mon 11–5. Last admission 4.30. Closed Good Fri. **Events:** NT/Chelsea Society guided themed walks around Chelsea. Annual Carlyle Memorial Lecture. Evening performances of works by Chelsea writers and readings from the letters of Thomas and Jane Carlyle; for details please send s.a.e. to Custodian

£ £3; child £1.50

Ì Groups welcome; introductory talk and tour can be booked in advance with Custodian

→ Off Cheyne Walk, between Battersea and Albert Bridges on Chelsea Embankment, or off the King's Road and Oakley Street [176: TQ272777] *Bus:* Frequent local services (tel. 0171 222 1234) *Station:* Victoria 1½ml *Underground:* Sloane Sq 1¼ml

EASTBURY MANOR HOUSE 🏛 E

Barking IG11 9SN Tel: 0181 507 0119 Fax: 0181 507 0118

Set in 0.6ha of land, Eastbury Manor is a rare example of a medium-sized Elizabethan manor house, now surrounded by 20th-century housing. The interior contains notable wallpaintings, depicting fishing scenes. It is leased to the London Borough of Barking & Dagenham and the house and grounds are used for a wide range of arts and heritage activities

🕐 1 Feb to 30 Nov: Mon to Fri 10–5 by appointment with Administrator. Also open one Sat ('Visitor Day') every month 10–4. Tel. for details. **Events:** exhibitions, Tudor evenings and concerts; please tel. for details

£ £1.50. Group visits by prior arrangement. Rates on application

🚶 Guided tours available

♿ Wheelchair access to ground floor only

☕ Tea-room open on 'Visitor Day'

🏫 Teachers' resource book available. School visits by prior arrangement

🐕 In garden only

➔ In Eastbury Square, 10min walk S from Upney station [177: TQ457838]
Bus: LT 287, 368 ⇌ Barking–Rainham/Chadwell Heath (tel. 0171 222 1234)
Station: Barking, then one stop on Underground District line to Upney ¼ml

FENTON HOUSE 🏛 ❀ E

Windmill Hill, Hampstead NW3 6RT Tel/fax: 0171 435 3471

A late 17th-century house with an outstanding collection of porcelain and early keyboard instruments. Large walled garden

Note: For permission to use the early keyboard instruments, please apply in writing one month in advance to the Keeper of Instruments, c/o Fenton House

🕐 1 to 23 March: Sat & Sun only 2–5. 29 March to 2 Nov: Sat, Sun & BH Mon 11–5.30; Wed, Thurs & Fri 2–5.30; last admission 30min before closing. Parties received at other times by appointment. **Events:** for details of events please send s.a.e. to Custodian

£ £3.60; family ticket £9. No reduction for pre-booked parties. No parking facilities. No picnics in garden

♿ Access to ground floor only

🐕 No dogs

→ Visitors' entrance on W side of Hampstead Grove *Bus:* Frequent local services (tel. 0171 222 1234) *Station:* Hampstead Heath 1ml; *Underground:* Hampstead 300m

---

GEORGE INN 🏠

The George Inn Yard, 77 Borough High St, Southwark SE1 1NH Tel: 0171 407 2056

The only remaining galleried inn in London, famous as a coaching inn in the 17th century, and mentioned by Dickens in Little Dorrit. *The George Inn is leased to and run by Whitbread plc as a public house*

○ During licensing hours

🍽 Bar food daily; à la carte restaurant Mon to Fri & Sat evening; please telephone for reservations

🚹 Children admitted subject to normal licensing regulations

🐕 In courtyard only

→ On E side of Borough High Street, near London Bridge Stn *Bus:* Frequent local services (tel. 0171 222 1234) *Station:* London Bridge ⦰ & Underground, few mins walk

---

HAM HOUSE 🏠 ✸ E

Ham, Richmond TW10 7RS Tel: 0181 940 1950 Fax: 0181 332 6903

Outstanding Stuart house built on the banks of the River Thames in 1610 and enlarged in the 1670s. Contains rare and unique survivals of the 17th century, including exquisite closets, fine furniture, textiles and pictures. The centre of Restoration court life and intrigue in the 1670s when the Duke of Lauderdale, one of Charles II's most powerful ministers, married Elizabeth, Countess of Dysart. Her descendants, the Tollemaches, lived in the house until 1948. 17th-century formal gardens surround the house and there is a continuing programme to restore their decorative glory

○ **House:** 29 March to 2 Nov: Sat & Sun 12–5, Mon to Wed 1–5; last admission 4.30. **Garden:** open daily except Fri 10.30–6 (or dusk if earlier). Closed 25/26 Dec & 1 Jan. **Events:** 7 June, 5 July, 2 Aug & 6 Sept, family picnic evenings (house open till 7); for details contact Regional Box Office, tel. 01372 451596; garden tours throughout the season, and dairy demonstrations (butter-making etc) during school hols; Great Hall licensed for civil weddings & Orangery available for private functions (tel. 0181 332 6644 for details)

£ House: £4.50, family ticket £12. Pre-booked groups 15+ during opening hours £3.50, children £2. Garden free. Free parking 400m (not NT)

💺 Guided tours for groups of 15+, Wed mornings only between 10–12; essential to book in advance (rates on application)

🛍 Shop open 1 to 23 March: Sat & Sun 11–4.30; 29 March to 2 Nov: Sat to Wed 11–5.30; 8 Nov to 14 Dec: Sat & Sun 12–4.30

♿ Parking near house for disabled visitors. Access to house by steep ramps only suitable for assisted wheelchair users. Lift access to all showrooms on request. Grounds include mostly firm, but some deep gravel, paths. Orangery restaurant accessible via ramps. Shop accessible. Sympathetic Hearing Scheme. WC. 2 wheelchairs available

👁 Braille guide; scented plants

☕ Orangery tea-room and tea garden licensed for lunches; dates and times as shop. Last orders 30min before closing. Special rates for weekday group bookings; tel. 0181 940 0735. Picnics in orangery garden

👶 Baby-changing facility. House unsuitable for back-packs or pushchairs, but reins and baby-slings available. Highchairs in tea-room; children's portions available. Children's quiz (from front desk)

🎒 School pack available; tel. 0181 940 1950

🐕 No dogs except guide dogs

➜ On S bank of Thames, W of A307, at Petersham [176: TQ172732] *Bus:* LT 65 Ealing Broadway–Kingston; 371 Richmond–Kingston; London & Country 415 Victoria–Guildford; (all passing ⇌ Richmond & Kingston) (tel. 0171 222 1234) *Station:* Richmond ⇌ & Underground 1½ml via Thames towpath, 2ml by road; Kingston 2ml. Also foot ferry from Marble Hill House, tel. 0181 940 1950 for details

LINDSEY HOUSE 🏠

99/100 Cheyne Walk SW10 0DQ Tel: (Regional Office) 01494 528051

Part of Lindsey House. Built in 1674 on the site of Sir Thomas More's garden, overlooking the River Thames. It has one of the finest 17th-century exteriors in London

O This is a tenanted property. At the time of going to press the lease is being re-negotiated. Please contact Regional Office for details of opening arrangements, which are limited to the ground floor entrance hall and garden room, main staircase to first floor, and the front and rear gardens

£ Free. No parking (nearest car park Battersea Park)

♿ Inaccessible

🐕 No dogs

➔ On Cheyne Walk, W of Battersea Bridge near junction with Milman's Street on Chelsea Embankment [176: TQ268775] *Bus:* Frequent local service (tel. 0171 222 1234) *Station:* Victoria 1¾ml; *Underground:* South Kensington 1¼ml

MORDEN HALL PARK ♠ E

Morden Hall Road, Morden SM4 5JD Tel: 0181 648 1845 Fax: 0181 687 0094

A green oasis in the heart of SW London, this former deer park has an extensive network of waterways, a tree-lined avenue, ancient hay meadows and an interesting collection of vernacular buildings. Old estate workshops house a selection of local craftspeople whose work is on view. Riverside walk. Independently managed City Farm on Bunce's Meadow in the park. Garden centre (not NT). Modern Hall is independently managed as a restaurant by Whitbread plc

O Park only open all year during daylight hours. *Note:* Car park by the café/shop and garden centre closes at 6 daily. **Events:** 3–5 May, Craft Fair; details from Four Seasons Events (tel. 01344 874787). There will be a charge for all visitors to the fair, incl. NT members

£ Free

🏃 Guided tours by arrangement; contact Warden's office

🏠 Daily throughout the year 10–5. Closed 25 & 26 Dec and 1 Jan 1998 (tel. 0181 687 0881). Shop closed 21 & 22 Jan 1998. Garden centre independently run by Capital Gardens plc as National Trust tenants (tel. 0181 646 3002)

♿ Restaurant, shop & garden centre fully accessible. (Some thick gravel in garden centre.) WC in restaurant. Access available from car park through garden centre to riverside walkways. Wheelchair path through rose garden and beside river. 2 wheelchairs available on request

👂 Flowing water sounds by mill

🍽 Licensed riverside café serving coffee, lunches (12–2) and teas daily throughout the year 10–5. Closed 25 & 26 Dec and 1 Jan (tel. 0181 687 0881)

[👶] Baby-changing facilities and highchairs

[🏭] Snuff Mill Environmental Centre for school education groups. Contact Education Officer (tel. 0181 542 4232)

[🐕] Please keep dogs under control at all times and on leads around buildings, paths & picnic area

[→] Off A24, and A297 S of Wimbledon, N of Sutton [176: TQ259687] *Bus:* Frequent from surrounding areas (tel. 0171 222 1234) *Station:* Morden Road, not Sun, ½ml. *Underground:* Morden 500m

---

OSTERLEY PARK [🏠][♿][E]

Isleworth, Middlesex TW7 4RB Tel: 0181 560 3918 Fax: 0181 758 2116

Completed in 1575, Osterley was transformed by Robert Adam into an elegant 18th-century villa for the founders of Child's Bank. The superb interiors contain one of the country's most complete examples of Adam's work and include plasterwork, carpets and furniture. Interesting kitchen. Set in 140ha of landscape park and farmland. There are ornamental lakes and pleasure grounds with classical garden buildings. Osterley's Tudor origins can be seen in the magnificent stable block which still has working stables

[🅾] **House:** 26 March to 2 Nov: Wed to Sun 1–5; BH Mon 11–5. Closed Good Fri. Last admission 4.30. **Grand Stable:** Sun afternoons in summer. **Park and pleasure grounds:** all year 9–7.30 or sunset if earlier. Park will close early during major events. Car park closed 25 & 26 Dec. **Events:** 12–20 July, Osterley Community Week; July, Shakespeare in the stable yard; Aug, annual summer 'Big Band' concert. For details send s.a.e. to Box Office, P O Box 180, High Wycombe, Bucks HP14 4XT

[£] £3.80; family ticket £9.50. Parties Wed to Sat £3, advance booking required. Park and pleasure grounds free. £1 off adult ticket for holders of valid LT travelcard. Car park £2, refundable on purchase of ticket to house, but free 3 Nov to March 1998

[🎫] Pre-booked out-of-hours guided 'Private View' Wed to Fri mornings £6 per person (incl. NT members). Minimum charge £120

[🛍] Shop in stable yard open 26 March to 2 Nov 1–5.30, Nov to 21 Dec 12–4: Wed to Sun and BH Mon (incl. Good Fri)

[♿] Car park is 250m from house, tea-room and shop. Courtesy vehicle runs between car park, house, tea-room & shop during house opening hours. Tea-room, walled tea-garden and shop are accessible. WC in park. Park is level and accessible to wheelchairs. Indoor & outdoor wheelchairs available. Stairclimber gives wheelchair access to principal floor of house (20 steps) but must be pre-booked. Self-drive battery-powered vehicles are available free of charge on Wed, Thur & Sun afternoons during the summer months

[👁] Braille guide

[☕] Coffee, light lunches & teas in Stables tea-room, 26 March to 2 Nov: Wed to Sun & BH Mon (incl. Good Fri) 11.30–5; open 8 Nov to 21 Dec: Sat & Sun 12–4. Groups of 20 or more must book in advance (tel. 0181 569 7624)

![] Baby-changing facilities in WC. House unsuitable for pushchairs or back-packs. Highchairs in tea-room

![] Pre-booked school groups welcome. Study base in stable block available for pre-booked parties. Children's guide and quiz, teachers' resource book.

![] In park only (guide dogs and hearing dogs excepted). Must be on leads unless indicated

![] Access via Thornbury Road on N side of A4 between Gillette Corner and Osterley underground station; M4, Jn 3 [176: TQ146780] *Bus:* LT H91 Hounslow–Hammersmith, not Sun, to within ½ml (tel. 0171 222 1234) *Station:* Syon Lane 1½ml *Underground:* Osterley ¾ml

RAINHAM HALL ![]

The Broadway, Rainham RM13 9YN Tel: (Regional Office) 01494 528051

An attractive red-brick house with stone dressing, built in 1729 on a symmetrical plan. There are fine contemporary wrought-iron gates in front of the house and original panelling inside

![] April to end Oct: Wed & BH Mon 2–6; also Sat by written application to tenant

![] £2. No reduction for parties. Parking limited. No WC

![] Guide dogs by arrangement with tenant

![] Just S of the church, 5ml E of Barking [177: TQ521821] *Bus:* Frequent local services (tel. 0171 222 1234) *Station:* Rainham, few metres

ROMAN BATH

5 Strand Lane WC2 Tel: 0171 798 2064 (answerphone)

The remains of a bath, restored in the 17th century, believed by some to be Roman

Note: The Roman Bath is administered and maintained by Westminster City Council

O Bath visible through window from pathway all year. Otherwise May to end Sept: every Wed 1–5 by appointment only (24hrs' notice) during office hours

£ 50p. Children under 16 and OAPs 25p. No WC

→ Just W of Aldwych station (Piccadilly Line now closed), approach via Surrey Street [176: TQ309809] *Bus:* Frequent local services (tel. 0171 222 1234) *Station:* Blackfriars or Charing Cross, both ½ml *Underground:* Temple, not Sun, few metres; Embankment ½ml

SUTTON HOUSE

2 & 4 Homerton High Street, Hackney E9 6JQ Tel: 0181 986 2264

In London's East End: a rare example of a Tudor red-brick house, built in 1535 by Sir Rafe Sadleir, Principal Secretary of State for Henry VIII, with 18th-century alterations and later additions. The recent restoration has revealed many 16th-century details which are displayed even in rooms of later periods. Notable features include original linenfold panelling and 17th-century wallpaintings. The Edwardian chapel contains an audiovisual presentation. There is also a permanent exhibition on the history of the house and its occupants and a multi-media presentation of local archive material. Changing shows of contemporary art and sculpture

O 5 Feb to 26 Nov & 4 Feb 1998 onwards: Wed, Sun & BH Mon 11.30–5.30 (closed Good Fri). Last admission 5. Contemporary exhibitions open as café bar. **Events:** for full programme of concerts, exhibitions, fairs, lectures, craft workshops and other events, please contact Property Manager on above number. Rooms available for private functions, rates on application. Licensed for civil marriages

£ £1.80, family ticket £4.50. Group visits by prior arrangement, also on Thur & Sat. Rates on application. Public car park in Morning Lane and St John's Churchyard, ¼ml. Pay-and-display parking in immediate vicinity

Ⓚ Guided tours and walks available. Rates on application

⌂ Open as house

♿ Ground floor only accessible to wheelchairs. No lift. WC. Induction loop in concert hall and lecture room

👁 Braille guide

☕ Café bar open all year except 22 Dec to 14 Jan 1998; Wed, Sun & BHs 11–5

🚼 Baby-changing facilities in WC. Family trails

📖 Teachers' resource book. School visits by prior arrangement. Rates on application

➔ At the corner of Isabella Road and Homerton High Street [176: TQ352851]
Bus: Frequent local services (tel. 0171 222 1234) *Station:* Hackney Central ¼ml; Hackney Downs ½ml

---

2 WILLOW ROAD 🏠 🛈

2 Willow Road, Hampstead NW3 1TH Tel: 0171 435 6166

Erno Goldfinger's house designed and built by him in 1939. The central part of a block of three, it was his family's home until his death in 1987, and that of his widow Ursula until 1991. Filled with furniture designed by Goldfinger and works of art he and his wife collected from such artists as Henry Moore and Max Ernst. Cinema showing introductory film

Note: Entry by timed ticket only. Difficult access for the elderly

🅾 3 April to 1 Nov: Thur, Fri & Sat 12–5 (closed BH Mon). Last admission 4. Guided tours every 45min (of 1hr duration; max 12 people). Organised groups to be booked in advance with Custodian

💷 £3.60. No parking at house. Limited on-street parking. East Heath Road municipal car park (100m), open intermittently

♿ Wheelchair access provided for on ground floor only. Filmed tour of whole house available. Cinema equipped with induction loop

👁 Braille guide

➔ *Bus:* Frequent local services (tel. 0171 222 1234) *Station:* Hampstead Heath ¼ml *Underground:* Hampstead or Belsize Park ½ml

Midlands

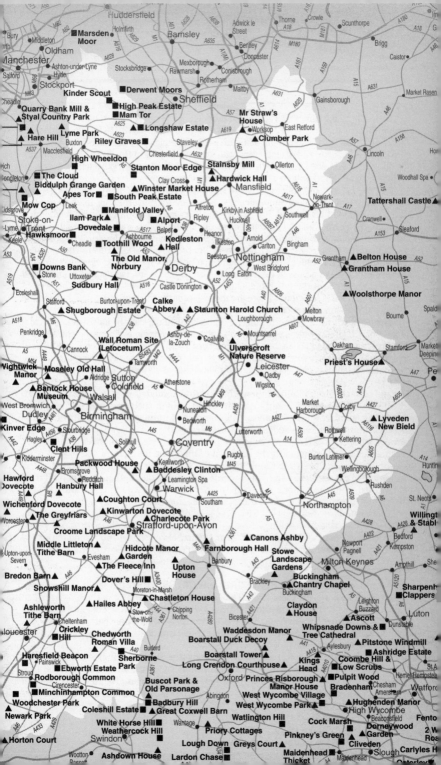

COUNTRYSIDE

Dover's Hill, 1ml north of Chipping Campden, [151: SP135395] forms a natural amphitheatre on a spur of the Cotswolds in **GLOUCESTERSHIRE**, giving glorious views over the Vale of Evesham. The Cotswold 'Olympick Games' have been held here since 1612, and are re-enacted every year on the evening of the first Friday following Spring Bank Holiday. There is a waymarked woodland walk. Wheelchair access to viewpoint and topograph.

6ml to the east of Gloucester is **Crickley Hill** [163: SO930163], on the Cotswold escarpment, commanding magnificent views over the Severn Vale to the Forest of Dean and Welsh hills beyond. It is run as a country park in conjunction with adjoining land owned by the County Council; leaflets of various guided walks are available at the information point. The promontory is the site of an Iron Age and Neolithic hillfort.

3ml north-west of Stroud is **Haresfield Beacon** [162: SO820089]. The site of a hillfort, and over 100ha of nearby woodland, it provides spectacular views towards the Severn estuary and across to the Forest of Dean. A topograph (signposted from a small car park) is sited on the adjoining spur known as Shortwood; it displays the area in relief and indicates the views. There are many footpaths through the woodland and the Cotswold Way long distance footpath traverses the property.

The Ebworth Estate close to Sheepscombe, 2ml north-east of **Painswick**, provides excellent woodland walking through magnificent beechwoods rich in wildlife. Access to Workmans Wood [163: SO897107] and Lord's and Lady's Woods [163: SO888110] is by public rights of way only and there are no parking facilities. Blackstable Wood [163: SO894097] is also accessible by public rights of way with car-parking available nearby.

2ml south of Stroud, **Minchinhampton** and **Rodborough Commons** [162:SO855010 & SO850038] together amount to nearly 480ha of high open grassland and woods for walking and other quiet recreation. The commons form a steep-sided plateau, rich in wild flowers and other wildlife, with views across the Stroud valleys which contain former wool and cloth mills, to distant hills beyond. There are a number of interesting archaeological sites, including the impressive Minchinhampton Bulwarks.

3ml south-west of Newent and 9ml west of Gloucester are **May Hill** and **May Hill Common** [162: SO694218]. Walks to the pine trees on the summit (not NT) are signposted from the minor road below the hill. This is a wild and romantic area of heath and grassland, from which there are spectacular views in every direction.

Sherborne Park Estate [163: SP157144] is off the A40, 3ml east of Northleach. Attractive waymarked walks through woods and parkland, with fine views. **Woodchester Park** [162: SO796014], near Nympsfield off the B4066 Stroud to Dursley road, is a wooded valley of approximately 200ha with five lakes running through it. Waymarked walks, some steep in places, provide spectacular views.

Just south of Stourbridge in **HEREFORD & WORCESTER**, at the south-western edge of Birmingham, are the **Clent Hills**. The Trust owns over 161ha of these hills, which are covered with heathy grassland. This is ideal country for walkers and riders with superb views in every direction. There is an excellent wheelchair path to a toposcope which explains all the views, with perching points and seats from which to enjoy the surrounding countryside [139: SO9379].

At **Croft Castle** (see p.82), the Trust owns nearly 566ha, including the high open grassland of **Bircher Common**, where local people still graze their animals. The Iron Age hillfort of Croft Ambrey, on a 300m limestone ridge, can give views over several counties. The estate is home to hares, squirrels, fallow deer, stoats, weasels and even polecats which have ventured here from across the Welsh border. Britain's largest finch, the hawfinch, is sometimes seen feeding on hornbeam seeds on Croft Ambrey. There are walks through the park to the hillfort; butterflies and wild flowers abound on the estate.

At **Bradnor Hill** near Kington [148: SO282584] is 138ha of commonland rising to 385m with the highest golf course in Britain on the summit.

At the **Brockhampton Estate** near Bromyard, the Trust owns nearly 688ha, including wonderful woodlands and parkland which is open to the public. There are a number of waymarked footpaths to follow, with magnificent views. Within the woodlands are a sculpture trail and an easy access trail. Visitors may also like to visit **Lower Brockhampton** (see p.93) [149: 693548].

Perhaps one of the most famous landmarks in **SHROPSHIRE** is the **Long Mynd** [137: SO430940], a heather-covered upland of which the Trust owns some 2368ha. A good starting point is the **Carding Mill Valley** (see p.77), from which paths lead to the high moorland and its prehistoric remains. These include burial mounds, hillforts and the ancient Port Way track which traverses the hill. Vehicle access is by a steep road which is liable to congestion in summer. On fine days there are views from the summit to Snowdonia, the **Brecon Beacons** (see p.298), the **Clent Hills** and the **Cotswolds**. Wheelchair users may reach some viewpoints on the Long Mynd, and visit the shop and restaurant at Carding Mill Valley.

The patchwork of heather provides a home for red grouse and for a variety of other upland birds, including raven, buzzard and dipper, which are often joined by wheatear and ring ouzel in the summer months.

Since 1981 the Trust has acquired about 223ha of **Wenlock Edge**, including **Easthope Wood** [138: SO570965], **Harley Bank** [127: SO605002], **Blakeway Coppice** [138: SO595988] and **Longville Coppice** [137: SO54899400]. This wooded limestone escarpment runs from Craven Arms to Ironbridge and is internationally famous for its geology, in particular its coral-reef exposures. A rich limestone flora includes the wild service tree and nine species of orchid. Public and permitted paths traverse the Edge; the road along the escarpment gives extensive views and passes close by the Elizabethan **Wilderhope Manor** (see p.107). Exhibition in Much Wenlock Museum.

On the **STAFFORDSHIRE/DERBYSHIRE** border is **Apes Tor**, a rock face in the gorge of the River Manifold below Hulme End [119: SK100586]. It is of particular geological interest since it shows clearly the folding and faulting processes which have formed the landscape of this part of the southern Peak District.

The Trust owns over 404ha of farmland and rock hills in the **Manifold** and **Hamps Valleys** and **Dovedale**; (see also p.69). The Manifold and Hamps are beautiful, but lesser-known perhaps than their sister river, the Dove. In dry weather both the Manifold and the Hamps vanish underground down 'swallet' holes in the limestone, leaving a dry watercourse for some miles until they reappear at Ilam. These river valleys support a wide range of limestone-loving plants. At Wetton Mill on the Manifold is a car park and refreshments (not NT). A well-surfaced, disused railway with adjacent car parks gives good access to the Manifold and Hamps Valleys. The Manifold joins the Dove between Ilam and Thorpe, near **Ilam Park** (see p.90).

A fourth river, the Churnet, flows through **Hawksmoor** [128: SK035445], an area of some 122ha of woodland and farmland. There are several walks through Hawksmoor, including a nature trail.

Further south near Alton Towers (not NT), is 4ha of **Toothill Wood** [128: SK066425]. The property includes part of the Staffordshire Way long-distance footpath, and the viewpoint of Toothill Rock.

To the south-west and not far from the industrial landscape of Stoke-on-Trent is **Downs Banks** [127: SJ902370], just north of Stone – undulating moorland with a stream, given to the Trust as a war memorial in 1946.

DERBYSHIRE is a county of contrasts – gentle river valleys, pastures, woodland and the high peat moorlands and towering limestone crags of the Peaks. The Trust's holdings amount to some 12 per cent of the **PEAK DISTRICT NATIONAL PARK**, the first of ten to be designated in England and Wales by Government in the 1950s and '60s. While the Trust and the National Park Authorities work closely together, they are entirely separate bodies; the National Parks are statutory authorities, and the Trust is an independent charity. The Trust's extensive ownership in the Peak District is managed in three estates.

High Peak Estate (tel. 01433 670368): An important part of the Trust's High Peak Estate is over the county border in Yorkshire; the Derwent Moors extend to some 2024ha, with an extra 567ha which spill over into Derbyshire [110: SK1944]. This vast stretch of moorland on the east bank of the River Derwent rises to 533m and overlooks the three main reservoirs in the Peak District, created at the turn of the century by flooding the dales – the Ladybower, the Derwent and the Howden.
By far the largest single holding of the Trust's 14,772ha in Derbyshire is the **Hope Woodlands**, 6680ha, 12ml west of Sheffield [110: SK135935]. This has less woodland than its name suggests; it is largely wild and dramatic Pennine moorland adjoining Kinder Scout and giving superb views over the Peak District. The moors are open except on a few grouse-shooting days. The property is crossed by the Pennine Way.
Kinder Scout [110: SK0888] came to the Trust in 1982. Probably the most famous landmark in the Peak District at 600m high, known not only for its magnificence, but because of the mass trespass here in 1932 when ramblers campaigned, eventually with some success, for the right of access to uplands in England.
The Kinder estate marches with the Trust's holdings in Edale, where several hill farms are owned with viewpoints such as **Lord's Seat** and **Lose Hill Pike** [110: SK153853]. But perhaps the most fascinating landmark here is **Mam Tor** – the 'shivering mountain' of which Celia Fiennes said in 1697 '... a high hill that looks exactly round but on the side next Castleton ... it's all broken that it looks just in resemblance as a great Hayricke thats cut down one halfe ... and on that broken side the sand keeps trickling down all walyes ...' This description fits today, and there are views from its 510m summit towards Kinder and the High Peak [110: SK1383].
Next to Mam Tor is the spectacular limestone gorge of **Winnats Pass** close to the Blue John mines of Treak Cliff (not NT) which yield an amethyst-coloured stone from which ornaments have been made since the 18th century.

Longshaw Estate (tel. 01433 670368); see also entry on p.93.
At **Longshaw** near Hathersage the Trust owns nearly 729ha of moor, pasture and woodland by the Burbage Brook which varies from a raging torrent in wet weather to a babbling brook in summer. In a disused quarry are half-finished millstones – a reminder of the end of the millstone-making industry centred here about a hundred years ago.
In 1665 the Plague came to Eyam near Tideswell, carried there from London in some clothing. When it was discovered the villagers – led by their rector – took a terrible decision: they isolated the village and no one was allowed in or out until the infection had burnt itself out. Three-quarters of the inhabitants died and seven members of one family, the Hancocks, are buried in the **Riley Graves** in a meadow

called the **Righ Lea**. The Trust owns the graves and protects the meadow [110: SK229766].

South Peak Estate (tel. Estate Office: 01335 350503).
This area of outstanding natural beauty in the southern limestone region of the Peak District extends to 1600ha and straddles the Derbyshire/Staffordshire border. It consists of **Dovedale**, internationally famous for its ashwoods and geological features, with limited access for wheelchairs; the former **Manifold and Hamps Light Railway**, now a well-surfaced tarmac track providing easy access (including wheelchairs) into dramatic limestone scenery; and the grounds of **Ilam Park** (see p.90), at the heart of which is **Ilam Hall** (now a youth hostel). Ilam Park has an information centre, shop and tearoom and there is also a school visit room available for groups (further details from the Education Coordinator, South Peak Estate Office, tel. above). There is also an information shelter at Milldale.

ASHLEWORTH TITHE BARN 🏠

Ashleworth Tel: (Regional Office) 01684 850051

A 15th-century tithe barn with two projecting porch bays and fine roof timbers with queenposts

O April to end Oct: daily 9–6 or sunset if earlier. Closed Good Fri. Other times by prior appointment only (please tel. 01684 850051)

£ 60p

→ 6ml N of Gloucester, 1¼ml E of Hartpury (A417), on W bank of Severn, SE of Ashleworth [162: SO818252] *Bus:* Swanbrook Transport Gloucester–Tewkesbury (passing close ≋ Gloucester), alight Ashleworth ¼ml (tel. 01242 574444) *Station:* Gloucester 7ml

---

ATTINGHAM PARK 🏠 🌳 👤 E

Shrewsbury SY4 4TP Tel: 01743 709203 Fax: 01743 709352

An elegant neo-classical mansion of the late 18th century with magnificent state rooms, built for 1st Lord Berwick. His eldest son added a top-lit picture gallery by Nash to display his Grand Tour collection. The 3rd Lord Berwick contributed splendid Regency silver, Italian neo-classical furniture and more pictures, making this one of the richest displays of Regency taste to survive. The park was landscaped by Humphry Repton; there are attractive walks along the river and through the deer park

O **House:** 22 March to 2 Nov: Sat to Wed (and Good Fri)1.30–5; BH Mon 11–5. Last admission to house 4.30. **Deer park & grounds:** March to Oct: daily 8–8; Nov to Feb daily 8–5 (closed Christmas Day). **Events:** please send s.a.e. to Property Manager

£ House & park £3.80; family ticket £10. Park & grounds only £1.50. Pre-booked parties £3

👤 Tours for pre-booked parties at 11 and 4.30; £5 per head (NT members £3). Evening visits by special arrangement with the Property Manager

🛍 Shop same days as house 12.30–5; BH Mon 11–5; also Nov to 21 Dec: Sat & Sun 12.30–4

♿ Prior notice of visit appreciated as access to house is by rear lift with staff help; then rooms easily accessible; disabled visitors may be driven to side of tea-room or outer courtyard. Self-drive powered vehicle available for use in grounds; park easily accessible. Tea-room access difficult; some outside tables accessible. WC at brewhouse. Sympathetic Hearing Scheme

📖 Braille and large-print guides at house

🍴 Light lunches and refreshments in tea-room same days as house 12.30–5, lunches 12.30–2.30, BH Mon 11–5. Also Nov to 21 Dec: Sat & Sun 12.30–4; March 1998: Sat & Sun 2–4. Licensed. Lunches & suppers at other times for pre-booked parties. Separate tea-room available. Picnic sites along Mile Walk

🚼 Baby-changing facilities. Highchairs available in tea-room

📷 Environmental education resource pack; park exhibition in Bothy. Education room available for pre-booked parties (max. 30 children)

🐕 No dogs in deer park, on leads in immediate vicinity of house

➔ 4ml SE of Shrewsbury, on N side of B4380 in Atcham village [126: SJ550099] *Bus:* Williamsons 96, X96, Midland Red 81/2/4, 481 Shrewsbury–Telford/ Wellington (all passing close ⇌ Shrewsbury & Telford Central (tel. 0345 056785) *Station:* Shrewsbury 5ml

---

BADDESLEY CLINTON 📷 ✝ ❖ ♣ E

Rising Lane, Baddesley Clinton Village, Knowle, Solihull B93 0DQ
Tel: 01564 783294 Fax: 01564 782706

A romantically sited medieval moated manor house, dating from the 14th century, and little changed since 1634. Contents include family portraits and priest holes. Also a chapel, garden, ponds and lake walk

🅾 5 March to 2 Nov: Wed to Sun & BH Mon (closed Good Fri) March, April & Oct 1.30–5; May to end Sept 1.30–5.30 (grounds open from 12). March 1998: Wed to Sun 1.30–5. Last admission to house 30min before closing. **Events:** autumn lecture programme and other events; please contact the Administrator for details

£ £4.60; family ticket £11.50. Grounds, restaurant & shop only, £2.30. Parties of 15 or more and coaches (not Sun) by prior written arrangement. Free parking. No prams, back-carriers or pushchairs in house. Timed tickets issued to control numbers in house

✗ Wed/Thur evenings by appointment. Supper can be included

△ Shop open same days as house, March, April & Oct: 12–5; May to end Sept: 12–5.30; 5 Nov to 14 Dec: Wed to Sun 12–4.30

♿ Access to ground floor and most of garden, moat and grounds, lakeside walk, restaurant & shop; some thick gravel. Parking by visitor reception area. Wheelchairs available. WC near shop. Sympathetic Hearing Scheme

👁 Braille guide; please enquire about items to touch

♨ Licensed restaurant same days as house; lunches 12–2; teas 2.30–5.30 (March, April & Oct closes 5). Also Nov & Dec as shop. Party lunches and dinners arranged. No picnicking in garden

⚥ Baby-changing and feeding room

▮ School parties by appointment: Wed, Thur & Fri mornings. Schools base and resource book available

⚲ In car park only. Reasonable walks available outside property

➜ ¾ml W of A4141 Warwick–Birmingham road, at Chadwick End, 7½ml NW of Warwick, 6ml S of M42 exit 5; 15ml SE of central Birmingham [139: SP199715] *Station:* Lapworth (U), not Sun (except June to Sept), 2ml; Birmingham International 9ml

---

THE BALSTON COLLECTION, BANTOCK HOUSE MUSEUM **E**

Bantock Park, Bradmore Road, Wolverhampton WV3 9LQ Tel: 01902 312132

Thomas Balston's collection of Victorian Staffordshire portrait figures, which he presented to the Trust in 1960, is on permanent view at Bantock House Museum (not NT); also on view are the town's important collections of 18th-century English enamels, Georgian and Victorian japanned tin and papier mâché, good collections of Worcester porcelain, dolls and toys, and some local history. Located in public park with free access

◯ All year: Mon to Sat 10–5; Sun 2–5. Closed Good Fri, Easter Sun, other Suns before a BHol, 25 & 26 Dec and other days at Christmas. 1 Jan, BHols subject to arrangement. **Events:** contact Museum for details

£ Free. Car & coach parking 300m, access via Finchfield Road

✗ Guided tours by arrangement with the Curator

♿ Access for wheelchair users. Ground floor only, includes Balston Collection; cars may draw up to the front door, access via Bradmore Road

👁 Interpretation of the collections is currently being improved for visually impaired visitors

♨ Morning coffee and afternoon teas available; also for group parties by prior arrangement

⬛ Education pack and children's worksheet available. Schools workshops linked to the National Curriculum; INSET workshops are available by prior appointment with the Education Officer

🐕 In park only, on leads

➡ SW of Wolverhampton town centre on B4161; access via Bradmore Road
Bus: West Midlands Buses 513/4, 585–7 from 🚆 Wolverhampton (tel. 0121 200 2700) *Station:* Wolverhampton 2ml

---

BENTHALL HALL 🏠 ✝ ❀ E

Broseley TF12 5RX Tel: 01952 882159

A 16th-century stone house with mullioned windows and moulded brick chimneys. The interior includes an intricately carved oak staircase, decorated plaster ceilings and oak panelling; also family collections of furniture, ceramics and paintings. Carefully restored plantsman's garden. Restoration church

⭕ 26 March to 28 Sept: Wed, Sun & BH Mon 1.30–5.30. Last admission 5. House and/or garden for parties at other times by arrangement: Tues & Wed am. **Events:** church services most Suns 3.15; visitors welcome

💷 £3, children £1. Reduced rates for booked parties. Garden only £2. Parking 150m. Coaches by appointment

♿ Access to ground floor and parts of garden. WC. No wheelchairs available

👁 Braille and large-print guides

🍴 Catering for groups (Wed only) by arrangement at Dudmaston. No picnics

➡ 1ml NW of Broseley (B4375), 4ml NE of Much Wenlock, 1ml SW of Ironbridge [127: SJ658025] *Bus:* Midland Red 9 & 99 Telford/Wellington–Bridgnorth, alight Broseley, 1ml (pass close 🚆 Telford Central) (tel. 0345 056785) *Station:* Telford Central 7½ml

---

BERRINGTON HALL 🏠 ❀ E

nr Leominster HR6 0DW Tel: 01568 615721 Fax: 01568 613263

An elegant neo-classical house of the late 18th century, designed by Henry Holland and set in a park landscaped by 'Capability' Brown. The formal exterior belies the delicate interior with beautifully decorated ceilings and fine furniture, including the Digby collection and a recently restored bedroom suite. Also, a nursery, Victorian laundry and pretty tiled Georgian dairy. There is an attractive garden with interesting plants and an historic apple orchard in walled garden

⭕ 26, 27 & 29 March to end April & Oct: Fri, Sat & Sun (open BH Mon but closed Good Fri) 1.30–5.30 (closes 4.30 in Oct). May to end June & Sept: Wed to Sun & BH Mon 1.30–5.30. July & Aug open 7 days a week 1.30–5.30. Also 24 to 31 Oct: Wed to Sun 1.30–4.30. Last admission 30min before closing. Garden from 12.30–6 (Oct 5.30). Park walk open July, Aug, Sept & Oct same days and times as house. **Events:** August horse trials; for details of this and other events please contact the Property Manager

£ £3.80; family ticket £9.50. Grounds only £1.70. Parties of 15 or more by prior written arrangement only. Free car and coach park

⚐ By prior arrangement with Property Manager

⬚ Shop open same days as house 1–5.30. Also 1 Nov to 14 Dec: Sat & Sun 1–4.30. Tel. 01568 610134

♿ Access to house via 12 steps; thereafter ground floor level; advisable to avoid peak visiting times. Two wheelchairs and powered self-drive buggy (please book in advance). WC. Access to garden; firm gravel paths. No wheelchair access to restaurant (5 steps) but a table can be set up in the courtyard in good weather on request. Parking: please enquire at ticket office

♨ Braille guide

▣ Licensed restaurant in Servants' Hall open same days as house: home-made lunches 12.30–2, teas 2.30–5.30. Edwardian tea-room open BH weekends and for pre-booked groups. Last orders 30min before closing. Oct: 12.30–4.30. Also open as shop Nov & Dec 12.30–4.30. Picnic tables near car park. Tel. 01568 610134

⚼ Children's outdoor and indoor quizzes. Baby-changing facilities. Play area in walled garden

⌂ No dogs in house, garden or on parkland

→ 3ml N of Leominster, 7ml S of Ludlow on W side of A49 [137: SO510637] *Bus:* Midland Red West/Go Whittle 192, 292 Birmingham–Hereford (passing close ⇌ Ludlow & Leominster), alight Luston, 2ml (tel. 0345 125436) *Station:* Leominster (U) 4ml

---

BIDDULPH GRANGE GARDEN ❁ **E**

Biddulph Grange, Biddulph, Stoke-on-Trent ST8 7SD Tel: 01782 517999

An exciting and rare survival of a High Victorian garden, acquired by the Trust in 1988 and focus of an extensive restoration project. Conceived by James Bateman, the 6ha are divided into a number of smaller gardens designed to house specimens from his extensive and wide-ranging plant collection. An Egyptian Court, Chinese Pagoda, Joss House, Bridge and Pinetum, together with many other settings, all combine to make the garden a miniature tour of the world

O 29 March to 2 Nov: Wed to Fri 12–6, Sat, Sun & BH Mon 11–6. Last admission 5.30 or dusk if earlier. Also open 8 Nov to 21 Dec: Sat & Sun 12–4 or dusk if earlier **Events:** for details please send s.a.e. to Property Manager

£ 29 March to 2 Nov: £4; family ticket £10. Pre-booked parties £3 per person. Joint ticket with Little Moreton Hall £6; family ticket £15. 8 Nov to 21 Dec: Sat & Sun, £2; family £5. Free car park 50m. Coach party organisers must book in advance

⚐ Pre-booked guided tours in groups of 10 or more, at 10 on Wed, Thur & Fri; £5 per person (NT members incl.)

⬚ Shop open as garden

Access for visitors with impaired mobility extremely difficult; unsuitable for wheelchairs but access possible to tea-room & terrace with views over garden. Please contact Garden Office for details. WC

Suitable for accompanied visually impaired visitors, with care. Braille & large-print guides

Tea-room serving coffee, teas and light refreshments open as garden. Light lunches 12–2 (waited service). Seating for 50. Last admission 5.30. Picnics in car park only

2 highchairs in tea-room

School visits by arrangement

No dogs in garden, car park only

½ml N of Biddulph, 3½ml SE of Congleton, 7ml N of Stoke-on-Trent. Access from A527 (Tunstall–Congleton road). Entrance on Grange Road [118:SJ895591]. *Bus:* PMT 6 from Hanley; Bakers/Stevensons 86–8 from Congleton (passing ⭆ Congleton) (tel. 01785 223344) *Station:* Congleton 2½ml

BREDON BARN

Bredon, nr Tewkesbury Tel: (Regional Office) 01684 850051

A 14th-century barn, approx. 44m long, with fine porches, one of which has unusual stone chimney cowling. The barn was restored with traditional materials after a fire in 1980

April to end Nov: Wed, Thur, Sat & Sun 10–6 or sunset if earlier. Dec to Feb: by prior appointment only (tel. 01684 850051)

60p

3ml NE of Tewkesbury, just N of B4080 [150: SO919369] *Bus:* Boomerang/Spring & Son Evesham–Cheltenham (passing ⭆ Evesham) (tel. 0345 125436) *Station:* Pershore (U) 8½ml

CALKE ABBEY 🏛 🏚 ✝ ❀ ♣ ♿ 🎣 E

Ticknall, Derby DE73 1LE Tel: 01332 863822 Fax: 01332 865272

The house that time forgot; a baroque mansion built 1701–3 for Sir John Harpur and set in a landscaped park. Little restored, Calke is preserved by a programme of conservation as a graphic illustration of the English country house in decline; it contains the family's collection of natural history, a magnificent 18th-century state bed and interiors that are virtually unchanged since the 1880s. Walled garden, pleasure grounds and newly restored orangery. Early 19th-century church. Historic parkland with Portland sheep and deer. Staunton Harold Church is nearby.

Note: One-way system operates in the Park; access only via Ticknall entrance. Entry to the house is by timed ticket (incl. NT members). Waiting time may be spent in the park, garden, church, stables, restaurant or shop; visitors are advised that at BH periods the delay in gaining admission to the house may be considerable, and very occasionally admission may not be possible

🅾 **House, garden & church**: 29 March to 2 Nov: Sat to Wed incl. BH Mon (closed Good Fri). **House & church**: 1–5.30. **Garden**: 11–5.30. **Ticket office**: 11–5. Last admission 5. Admission to house for all visitors (incl. NT members) is by timed ticket, obtained on arrival. This gives the time of entry to the house, but does not restrict the time visitors may spend on their tour. **Park**: open during daylight hours all year; April to Oct closed 9pm (or dusk if earlier); Nov to March closes at dusk. **Events**: August, outdoor classical concert; details of this and other events from Property Manager (s.a.e. please)

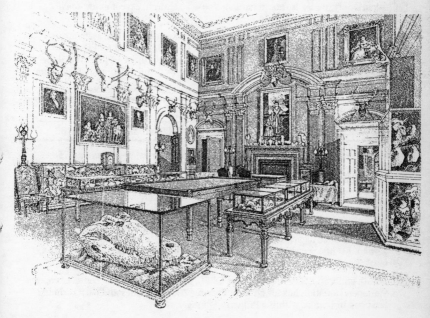

£ All sites: £4.85, children £2.40; family ticket £12.10. Garden only: £2.20. Discount for parties. Vehicle charge £2 (refundable on entry to the house when open)

🏃 Guided tours for parties outside normal open hours may be arranged; Sat, Mon, Tues, Wed mornings (not BH weekends). Tours last approx 1hr 20min (extra charge incl. NT members); evening meals are also available with house tours. Parties must book through Calke office (tel. 01332 863822)

🛍 Shop and information room open same days as house 11–5.30. Also Nov to 21 Dec: Sat & Sun 12–4

♿ Access above ground floor difficult; advisable to avoid peak visiting times. Moderate access to garden, park and church (some steps), good access to stables and all visitor facilities. WC at stable block. 4-seater volunteer-driven buggy (ask at ticket office). Sympathetic Hearing Scheme

👁 Braille guide

🍽 Licensed restaurant open 11–5 serving wide variety of home-cooked hot and cold lunches 12–2 and teas 2–5 (Nov to 21 Dec: Sat & Sun 12–4). Seats 126. Booked meals available for large groups. Kiosk serving snacks and ice creams on busy afternoons

👶 Parent & baby facilities; highchairs available; children's portions of selected dishes

🏫 Curriculum-related tours and other activities for school groups. Teachers must book (tel. 01332 863822)

🐕 In park only, on leads (not in garden, house or church, except guide dogs). No shaded areas in car parks

➔ 10ml S of Derby, on A514 at Ticknall between Swadlincote and Melbourne [128: SK356239] *Bus:* City Rider C68A/69, Derby Integrated 69B Derby–Swadlincote (passing close ⮕ Derby), alight Ticknall, thence 1¼ml walk along drive to house (tel. 01332 292200) *Station:* Derby 10ml; Burton-on-Trent 10ml

---

CANONS ASHBY HOUSE 🏠 ✝ ✿ ♠ E

Canons Ashby, Daventry NN11 3SD Tel: 01327 860044 Fax: 01327 860168

Home of the Dryden family since the 16th century, this manor house was built c.1550, added to in the 1590s, and altered in the 1630s and c.1710; largely unaltered since. Within the house, Elizabethan wallpaintings and outstanding Jacobean plasterwork are of particular interest. A formal garden includes terraces, walls and gate piers of 1710. There is also a medieval priory church and a 28ha park

O **House & Garden:** 29 March to 2 Nov: Sat to Wed incl. BH Mon (closed Good Fri) 1–5.30 or dusk if earlier. Last admission 5. **Park:** open as house, access through garden. **Events:** occasional outdoor events; details from Property Manager (s.a.e. please)

£ £3.50; children £1.70; family ticket £8.70. Discount for parties; contact Property Manager. Donation box for church. Parking 200m; coaches and parties should pre-book in writing with the Property Manager.

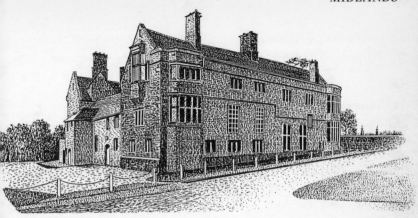

 Shop open 12.30–5

Disabled visitors may be set down at front door; car park 200m. Access to garden and ground floor via 3 steps. House access via 7 steps. WC. Guidebook for hearing-impaired visitors. Sympathetic Hearing Scheme

Braille and taped guides

Light lunches 12–2 and afternoon teas 2–5 in Brewhouse; same days as house. Party bookings by prior arrangement. 36 seats

Teachers' pack available; contact Property Manager

On leads, in Home Paddock only

Easy access from either M40, exit 11 or M1, exit 16. From M1, signposted from A5 2ml S of Weedon crossroads, along unclassified road (3ml) to Banbury. From M40 at Banbury take A422 exit, then left along B4525 and after 3ml turn left up unclassified road (signposted) [152: SP577506] *Bus:* Occasional Sun services from Northampton (tel. 01604 236712) *Station:* Banbury 10ml

CARDING MILL VALLEY & LONG MYND

Chalet Pavilion, Carding Mill Valley, Church Stretton SY6 6JG
Tel: 01694 722631 Fax: 01694 723068

2368ha of historic upland heath, part of the Long Mynd, extending for 4ml, and including the Carding Mill Valley where the Trust has a tea-room, shop and information centre in the Chalet Pavilion. The land rises to some 560m, providing magnificent views of the Shropshire and Cheshire plains and the Black Mountains

Heathland: all year. **Chalet Pavilion (tea-room, shop & information centre):** 24 March to 28 Sept: daily 11–5; 4 Oct to 21 Dec & Jan to March 1998: weekends only 11–4 (or dusk if earlier)

Car park charge: £1.70, motorcycle 50p, minibus £2.50, minicoach £3.50, coach £5. Education coaches £5 if pre-booked, £10 if unbooked

Guided walks in summer

⬛ See above for opening times

♿ Viewpoints on Long Mynd accessible by car. Tea-room, shop & information centre accessible. Parking immediately outside building. WC

⬛ Light lunches & teas at the Chalet Pavilion. Seating capacity 80

⬛ Highchairs available; baby-changing facilities

⬛ School parties must pre-book visits (tel: 01694 724536). Environmental education programme available

⬛ Must be kept under control on moorland; not admitted to the Chalet Pavilion

➔ 15ml S of Shrewsbury, W of Church Stretton valley and A49; approached from Church Stretton and, on W side, from Ratlinghope or Asterton [137: SO443945] *Bus:* Midland Red West 435 Shrewsbury–Ludlow, alight Church Stretton, ½ml (tel. 0345 056785) *Station:* Church Stretton (U) 1m

---

CHARLECOTE PARK 🏠 ✿ ♣ 🔊 🚹 E

Warwick CV35 9ER Tel: 01789 470277 Fax: 01789 470544

Home of the Lucy family since 1247. The present house was built in 1550s and later visited by Queen Elizabeth I. Rich Victorian 'romantic' interiors were created from the 1820s onwards, and contain important objects from William Beckford's Fonthill Abbey. The River Avon flows through the park, landscaped by 'Capability' Brown, which supports herds of red and fallow deer, reputedly poached by Shakespeare, and a flock of Jacob sheep, first introduced in 1756

⭕ 29 March to end Oct: Fri to Tues 11–6. House open 11–1 & 2–5.15.
Events: 29 May, Family Day; 19 to 25 June, Midsummer Music Festival; 1 to 3 Aug, Medieval Craft Fayre; 7, 14, 21 & 28 Oct, deer park tours. NT members are charged for events. Details from Administrator

💷 £4.60; family ticket £11.50. Parties (max. 60) by prior arrangement. Group rate and introductory talk available, weekdays only. Car and coach park 300m. Video film of life at Charlecote Park in the Victorian period

🕺 Evening guided tours for pre-booked parties May to Sept: Tues 7.30–9.30 (£4.60, incl. NT members; minimum charge £115 for party)

⬛ Shop & Victorian kitchens open as property 11–5.30. Also 1 Nov to 14 Dec: Sat & Sun 1.30–4.30 for Christmas shopping

♿ Access to all open rooms, except the gatehouse museum. Wheelchairs available. Restaurant accessible. Shop & Victorian kitchens have alternative access avoiding steps. WCs behind orangery and near gatehouse. Arrangements can be made at the kiosk to drop off disabled visitors or park near house. Video can be viewed in the gatehouse. Sympathetic Hearing Scheme

👁 Braille guide available at gatehouse; arrangements can be made to enhance a visit

⬛ Morning coffee, lunches, afternoon teas in the orangery restaurant (licensed); open as property 11–5.30. Picnicking in deer park only

⬛ Changing and feeding room

School parties by arrangement: schools base and resource book available

In car park only. Reasonable walks available outside park

1ml W of Wellesbourne, 5ml E of Stratford-upon-Avon, 6ml S of Warwick on N side of B4086 [151: SP263564] *Bus:* Stagecoach Midland Red 18, X18 Leamington Spa (Coventry Sun)–Stratford-upon-Avon (passing ⇌ Leamington Spa) (tel. 01788 535555) *Station:* Stratford-upon-Avon, not Sun, except June to Sept, 5½ml; Warwick 6ml; Leamington Spa 8ml

CHEDWORTH ROMAN VILLA 🏛 Ⓔ

Yanworth, nr Cheltenham GL54 3LJ Tel: 01242 890256 Fax: 01242 890544

The remains of a Romano-British villa, excavated 1864. Set in beautiful wooded combe. Includes fine 4th-century mosaics, two bath houses, spring with temple. A museum houses the smaller finds. There is a 9min introductory film

4 Feb to 28 Feb: Tues to Fri 10–4 site open for pre-booked parties; 1 March to 30 Nov: Tues to Sun & BH Mon 10–5 (closes 4 from 4 Nov onwards). Open Good Fri. Also 6 & 7 Dec: 10–4. **Events:** 25/26 May, Archaeology Activity Weekend; 2 Aug, outdoor jazz concert; mid-Sept, National Archaeology Days

£3; family ticket £7.50. School and other parties are given an introduction to the site, but must be booked in advance. No reduction for parties. Free coach and car park

For pre-booked parties only

Shop open as villa

Ramps to reception building and onto site which is partly accessible but some steps & slopes so strong companions necessary. WC (RADAR lock) in reception building

Braille guide

➔ 3ml NW of Fossebridge on Cirencester–Northleach road (A429), approach from A429 via Yanworth or from Withington (coaches must avoid Withington) [163: SP053135] *Station:* Cheltenham Spa 9ml

---

CLUMBER PARK 🏠 ✝ ❀ ♠ 🏃 Ⓔ

The Estate Office, Clumber Park, Worksop S80 3AZ
Tel: 01909 476592 Fax: 01909 500721

1538ha of parkland, farmland, lake and woodlands. The mansion was demolished in 1938, but the fine Gothic Revival chapel, built 1886–89 for the 7th Duke of Newcastle, survives. Park includes the longest double lime avenue in Europe and a superb 32ha lake. Also, classical bridge, temples, lawned Lincoln Terrace, pleasure grounds and the stable block with restaurant, shop and information room. Walled garden including working Victorian apiary, vineries and tools exhibition. Clumber Conservation Centre near cricket ground

Note: Enquiries to Estate Office (tel. 01909 476592). Guided walks may be booked for parties throughout the summer. Information room open April to Oct, afternoons (tel. 01909 484977). 166-berth caravan site run by Caravan Club; open to non-members. NT & Caravan Club members have priority (tel. 01909 484758). Camp site run by Camping & Caravanning Club of Great Britain (booking advisable due to limited spaces): April to end Sept (tel. 01909 482303). Clumber Conservation Centre for school and other groups (book with Head Warden): open weekends April to end Sept and other times by arrangement

🅾 **Park:** open all year during daylight hours. **Walled garden, Victorian apiary, fig house, vineries, orchard & garden tools exhibition:** 6 April to end Sept: Sat, Sun & BH Mon 10–5. Last admission 4.30. **Conservation Centre:** 6 April to 21 Sept: Sat, Sun & BH Mon 1–5. **Chapel:** please tel. Estate Office for opening times. **Events:** full programme; please ring 01909 476592 for events leaflet. Credit card line for outdoor events (tel. 01909 530424/531171)

💷 Pedestrians free. Cars, motorbikes & caravanettes £3 (exemption for NT members only); cars with caravans & mini coaches £4.30; coaches midweek £7, weekends and BH £14. Parking 100m from visitor facilities. Bicycle hire (identification essential) including cycles with child carriers £3.50 for 2hrs; (midweek party bookings for min. 20 cycles) book through Estate Office. Orienteering by arrangement (orienteering packs £1.50). Horse riding by permit. Coarse fishing: 16 June to 14 March; 7am to dusk; day ticket £3; season ticket £50. Day tickets available on the bank from fishing bailiff. Walled garden, Victorian apiary, vineries & garden tools exhibition 70p

🏃 Guided walks may be booked for parties throughout the summer. Details from Estate Office

🏪 Clocktower shop (tel. 01909 474468) open daily: Jan to 29 March 10.30–5; 30 March to 25 Oct 10.30–6; 26 Oct to 24 Dec 10.30–4; 27 Dec to end March 1998 10.30–4. Plant sales centre: open daily 30 March to 25 Oct 10.30–6

♿ 13ml of tarmac roads, most areas accessible; Walled garden, Victorian apiary, fig house, kitchen garden, vineries & garden tools exhibition fully accessible. Restaurant & shop accessible. Wheelchairs (incl. child size) available (identification required) from cycle hire. Access across grass for special events (see below). WCs.

WC at cricket ground (RADAR lock). Visitors with special needs please contact Visitor Liaison Officer. Powered self-drive vehicle available free of charge weekdays – booking essential from Estate Office (identification required)

Nature trails recommended to accompanied visually impaired visitors; map and guide available

Self-service cafeteria: daily Jan to 29 March: 10.30–5; 30 March to 25 Oct: 10.30–6; 26 Oct to 24 Dec: 10.30–4; 27 Dec to end March 1998: 10.30–4. Restaurant open daily 12–2. Open for functions and booked parties throughout the year. Bookings and enquiries tel. 01909 484122. Seats 150

Parent & baby facilities; highchairs and children's portions in restaurant; cycles with child carriers or buggies; open parkland ideal for family activities

Conservation Centre available for school parties; educational exhibitions; please contact Warden, Estate Office

4½ml SE of Worksop, 6½ml SW of Retford, 1ml from A1/A57, 11ml from M1 exit 30 [120: SK645774 or 120: SK626746] *Bus:* Unity 30 from Worksop; otherwise Stagecoach E Midland 33 Worksop–Nottingham (passing close ⇌ Worksop), alight Carburton, 1¼ml (tel. 0115 9240000) *Station:* Worksop 4½ml; Retford 6½ml

---

COUGHTON COURT 🏠 ✝ ✽ E

nr Alcester B49 5JA
Office Tel: 01789 400777 Visitor Information: 01789 762435 Fax: 01789 765544

An impressive central gatehouse dating from 1530 with Elizabethan half-timbered courtyard. During the Civil War this mainly Elizabethan house was attacked by both Parliamentary and Royalist forces. It has important connections with the Gunpowder Plot and contains priests' hiding places. The contents of the gatehouse and south wing include some notable furniture, porcelain, portraits and memorabilia of the Throckmorton family who have lived here since 1409. There are two churches, a tranquil lake, riverside walk and new formal walled garden. Also Gunpowder Plot and children's clothes exhibitions

Note: Coughton Court is lived in and managed by the Throckmorton family

81

O 15 March to end April: Sat & Sun 12–5. Easter Mon to Wed 11.30–5 (closed Good Fri). May to end Sept: Sat to Wed 11.30–5; also every Fri from 25 July to 29 Aug 11.30–5. 4 to 19 Oct: Sat & Sun 11.30–5. Grounds open 11–5.30 (Oct closes 5). Last admission to house and grounds 30min before closing. The house may occasionally close on Sat afternoons; the gardens and grounds will remain open (tel. visitor information line to check). On busy days entry to the house is by timed ticket. **Events**: concerts & other events; please tel for details

£ £5.75; family ticket £18.50. Parties of 15 or more by prior arrangement (not BH). Grounds only £3.50. New walled garden (financed by the family) £2 (incl. NT members)

Ẋ Evening guided tours for pre-booked parties Mon to Wed. Garden tours by appointment. No party rate or membership concessions for out of hours visits

⌷ Shop & plant sales centre open as grounds (managed by family)

⌷ Access to three rooms on ground floor, restaurant and shop. Wheelchairs available. WC. Grounds, garden & riverside path suitable for wheelchairs. Disabled drivers please contact Admissions for advice on parking

⌷ Braille guides

⌷ Restaurant managed by family, open for morning coffee, lunches & teas same days as house 11–5.30. Picnics in car park picnic area

⌷ School visits by arrangement

⌷ Dogs on leads in car park only

→ 2ml N of Alcester on A435 [150: SP080604] *Bus:* Midland Red West 146, Birmingham–Evesham; Stagecoach Midland Red 228 Redditch–Stratford-upon-Avon (passing ⇌ Redditch & close ⇌ Evesham) (tel. 0345 125436) *Station:* Redditch 6ml

CROFT CASTLE ⛫ ✝ ❀ ♣ 🏛 Ẋ

nr Leominster HR6 9PW Tel: 01568 780246

Home of the Croft family since Domesday (with a break of 170 years from 1750). The walls and corner towers date from the 14th and 15th centuries, while the interior is mainly 18th century, when the fine Georgian-Gothic staircase and plasterwork ceilings were added. A splendid avenue of 350-year-old Spanish chestnuts runs through the park, and an Iron Age fort (Croft Ambrey) may be reached by footpath (an uphill walk of approx. 40min)

O Easter Sat, Sun & Mon (29 to 31 March) 1.30–4.30 (closed Good Fri). April & Oct: Sat & Sun 1.30–4.30. May to end Sept: Wed to Sun & BH Mon 1.30–5.30. Last admission to house 30min before closing. Car park, parkland and Croft Ambrey open all year

£ **House & grounds:** £3.20; family ticket £8. **Grounds only:** car park charge £1.50 per car; £10 per coach. Parties of 15 or more by prior written arrangement. Picnics in the car park only

⌷ Access to all rooms (one ramped step), garden (gravelled terrace difficult) and part of grounds; parking near castle

⊙ Braille guide; some carved furniture may be touched on request

🧍 Children's quiz

🐕 In parkland only, on leads

➔ 5ml NW of Leominster, 9ml SW of Ludlow; approach from B4362, turning N at Cock Gate between Bircher and Mortimer's Cross; signposted from Ludlow–Leominster road (A49) and from A4110 at Mortimer's Cross [137: SO455655] *Bus:* Midland Red West/Go Whittle 192, 292 Birmingham–Hereford (passing close ⇌ Ludlow & Leominster), alight Gorbett Bank, 2¼ml (tel. 0345 125436) *Station:* Leominster (U) 7ml

---

CROOME LANDSCAPE PARK ✿ ♠

The National Trust Estate, Office Builder's Yard, High Green Severn Stoke WR8 9JS

Croome Park was 'Capability' Brown's first significant landscape; it made his reputation and was highly influential. The exquisite park buildings and other structures (seven in total) are mostly by Robert Adam and James Wyatt. The Trust acquired 270ha in 1996 with grant aid from the Heritage Lottery Fund.

The Trust is embarking on a 10 year restoration plan, including dredging the water features, extensive tree planting in the park and woodland and the provision of facilities for visitors. The Royal & Sun Alliance Group is making a major financial contribution towards the cost of this restoration.

🅾 The estate is crossed by public and other footpaths, which are open throughout the year. Major restoration work will start in 1997 on the Lake Garden and Temple Greenhouse Walk, which will be open only to pre-booked guided tours; booking is by written application only to: The National Trust, Mythe End House, Tewkesbury, Glos. GL20 6EB. There is car-parking at Punch Bowl Gates, but no other facilities

£ By pre-booked guided tour only, £2 (incl. NT members)

♿ Wheelchair access to Lake Garden and Temple Greenhouse Walk

🐕 Dogs are welcome, but must be kept on leads

➔ 8ml S of Worcester and E of A38 and M5 [150: SO878448] *Bus:* Midland Red West 372–4 Worcester–Gloucester, alight Severn Stoke, thence 2ml (tel. 0345 125436) *Station:* Pershore 7ml

---

CWMMAU FARMHOUSE 🏠 🔧

Brilley, Whitney-on-Wye HR3 6JP Tel: 01497 831251

Early 17th-century timber-framed and stone-tiled farmhouse

🅾 May to Aug inclusive: Wed only, 2–5.30

£ £2. Not suitable for coaches

⚔ Viewing by guided tours only

🍽 Tea-room (managed by tenant)

➜ 4ml SW of Kington between A4111 & A438; approach by a narrow lane leading S from Kington–Brilley road at Brilley Mountain [148: SO267514]

DUDMASTON 🏠 ❀ 🖼 E

Quatt, nr Bridgnorth WV15 6QN Tel: 01746 780866 Fax: 01746 780744

Late 17th-century house with fine furniture; Dutch flower paintings, modern pictures, watercolours and botanical art, modern sculpture, family and natural history; lakeside garden and walk through the Dingle. Estate walks starting from Hampton Loade

🅾 23 March to 28 Sept: Wed & Sun only 2–5.30. Last admission 5. Special opening for pre-booked parties only, Thur 2–5.30. **Events:** please send s.a.e. to Administrator

£ House & garden £3.50, children £2; family ticket £8. Garden only £2.50. Parking 100m

⚔ For pre-booked parties

🛍 Shop open as house

♿ Ramp to entrance; access to main and inner halls, Library, Oak Room, No 1 & Darby galleries and Old Kitchen. Tea-room accessible. Shop accessible via ramp. For access arrangements apply to Administrator; wheelchairs and self-drive powered vehicle available; signed route in garden (some steep slopes) and through Gerard's Wood. WC by car park. Sympathetic Hearing Scheme

👁 Braille & large-print guides for house and woodland; taped guide for house with cassette players. Scented plants in garden

🍽 Home-made teas 2–5.30. Light lunches Wed and Sun 1–2.15. Light lunches for booked parties by arrangement on Wed and Thur. (Please note that the tea-room is open to the general public and not restricted to those visiting the house or garden)

🚼 Highchair in tea-room. Baby slings available. Baby-changing facilities

🐕 In Dingle and on estate only, on leads

➜ 4ml SE of Bridgnorth on A442 [138: SO746887] *Bus:* Midland Red West 297 Kidderminster–Bridgnorth (passing close ⇌ Kidderminster) (tel. 0345 056785) *Station:* Hampton Loade (Severn Valley Rly) 1½ml; Kidderminster 10ml

---

FARNBOROUGH HALL 🏠 ❀ ♣

Banbury OX17 1DU Tel: 01295 690002

A classical mid 18th-century stone house, home of the Holbech family for 300 years. The entrance hall, staircase and two principal rooms are shown; the plasterwork is particularly notable. The grounds contain charming 18th-century temples, a ¾ml terrace walk and an obelisk

Note: Farnborough Hall is occupied and administered by Mr & Mrs Holbech

O **House, grounds & terrace walk:** April to end Sept: Wed & Sat 2–6: also 4 & 5 May 2–6. **Terrace walk only:** Thur & Fri 2–6. Last admission 5.30

£ House, grounds & terrace walk £2.80. Garden & terrace walk £1.50. Terrace walk only Thur & Fri £1. Parties by written arrangement only, no reduction. Coach and car park. Strong shoes advisable for terrace

& Ground floor of house and garden accessible (terrace walk is very steep)

↑ Welcome, on leads in grounds only

➔ 6ml N of Banbury, ½ml W of A423 [151: SP430490]

THE FLEECE INN 🏠

Bretforton, nr Evesham WR11 5JE Tel: 01386 831173

A medieval farmhouse in the centre of the village, containing family collection of furniture. It became a licensed house in 1848, and remains largely unaltered

O During normal public house licensing hours

£ Car-parking in village square. Coaches by written appointment only

◖ Lunchtime snacks

➔ 4ml E of Evesham, on B4035 [150: SP093437] *Bus:* Barry's/Cresswell/Spring & Son/Midland Red West 554 from Evesham (tel. 0345 125436) *Station:* Evesham 3ml

---

THE GREYFRIARS 🏠 ❉ **E**

Friar Street, Worcester WR1 2LZ Tel: 01905 23571

Built in 1480, with early 17th- and late 18th-century additions, this timber-framed house was rescued from demolition at the time of the Second World War and has been carefully restored and refurbished; interesting textiles and furnishings add character to the panelled rooms. An archway leads through to a delightful garden

Note: The house will be closed during the early part of the season because of repair works

O 5 May to end Oct: Wed, Thur & BH Mon 2–5. **Events:** 4,5 & 6 Dec, Street Fayre

£ £2.20; family ticket £5.50. Parties of 15 or more by written appointment. No reductions. Not suitable for large parties of children. Public car park in Friar Street. No WC

➔ In centre of Worcester [150: SO852546] *Bus:* From surrounding areas (tel. 0345 125436) *Station:* Worcester Foregate Street ½ml

HAILES ABBEY ✝

nr Winchcombe, Cheltenham GL54 5PB Tel: 01242 602398

Seventeen cloister arches and extensive excavated remains in lovely surroundings of an abbey founded by Richard, Earl of Cornwall, in 1246. There is a small museum and covered display area. Free audio tour

Note: Hailes Abbey is in the guardianship of English Heritage. For further information contact Regional Office (tel. 01179 750700)

O **Site & Museum:** 22 March to end Oct: daily 10–1 & 2–6 (or dusk if earlier); Nov to end March 1998: Wed to Sun 10–1 & 2–4 (closed 24 to 26 Dec)

£ £2.40. OAP/student/UB40 holder £1.80; children £1.20 (incl. of tape guide)

⌂ Small English Heritage shop in museum

⟐ Access to most of site and museum. WC. Loop system for hearing-impaired visitors

⦿ Braille guide. Some touch prints available; taped guides, including basic tape for people with learning disabilities

⫯ Baby-changing facilities available

▮ Teachers' handbook available. Free admission for pre-booked school parties; for information contact the property

⛨ On leads only in abbey grounds, but not in museum

→ 2ml NE of Winchcombe, 1ml E of Broadway road (B4632) [150: SP050300]
Bus: Castleways from Cheltenham (passing close ⭙ Cheltenham) alight Didbrook, 1½ml, or more frequent to Greet, 1¾ml by footpath (tel. 01242 602949)
Station: Cheltenham 10ml

HANBURY HALL ⌂ ⌂ ✿ ♣ E

Droitwich WR9 7EA Tel: 01527 821214 Fax: 01527 821251

William & Mary-style red-brick house, completed in 1701. Hanbury is a typical example of an English country house built by a prosperous local family, with outstanding painted ceilings and staircase by Thornhill. The Watney Collection of porcelain is also on display in the house. There is an 18th-century orangery in the garden and an ice house. Reinstatement of the formal 18th-century garden commenced in autumn 1993

O 30 March to 29 Oct: Sun to Wed 2–6. Last admission 5.30 (dusk if earlier).
Events: varied programme through the year: for details and inclusion on mailing list please send s.a.e. to the property

£ House & garden £4.10; family ticket £10. Garden only £2.50. House is available for private and commercial functions and civil wedding ceremonies; please contact Property Manager. Free car- and coach-parking

⫯ Evening guided tours for pre-booked parties, May to Sept, £4.10 (incl. NT members), minimum charge £82

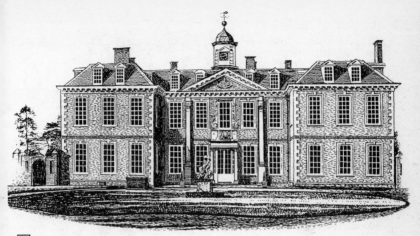

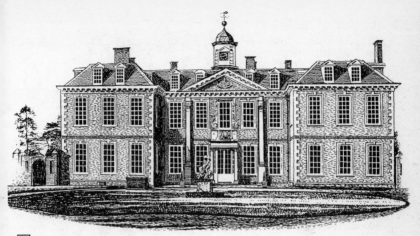 Shop open as house

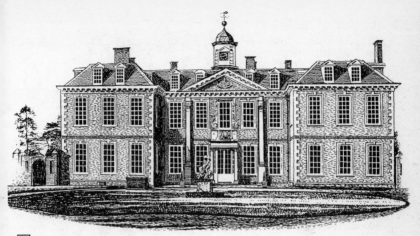 Wheelchair access to ground floor, tea-room; easy access to garden; disabled visitors may be driven to front door. Self-drive powered vehicle. WC

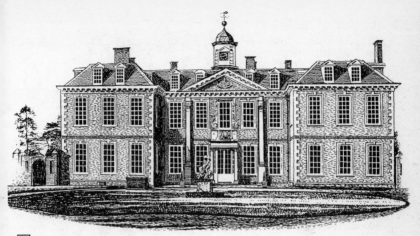 Braille guide

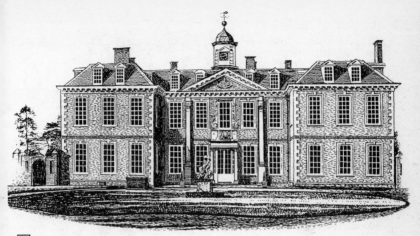 Cream teas in tea-room in house, open as house. Picnic area in car park

 No dogs in garden, but allowed on leads in park on footpaths only

 4½ml E of Droitwich, 1ml N of B4090, 6ml S of Bromsgrove, 1½ml W of B4091 [150: SO943637] *Bus:* Midland Red West 142/4 Worcester–Birmingham (passing close ⮂ Droitwich Spa), alight Wychbold, 2½ml (tel. 0345 125436) *Station:* Droitwich Spa 4ml

HARDWICK HALL ⌂ ❀ ♠ ♿ ♟ E

Doe Lea, Chesterfield S44 5QJ Tel: 01246 850430 Fax: 01246 854200

A late 16th-century 'prodigy house' designed by Robert Smythson for Bess of Hardwick. The house contains outstanding contemporary furniture, tapestries and needlework, many pieces identified in an inventory of 1601; a needlework exhibition is on permanent display. Walled courtyards enclose fine gardens, orchards and a herb garden. The country park contains Whiteface Woodland sheep and Longhorn cattle. Information point in country park. Fishing permits available from Bailiff. 400 years ago, Bess of Hardwick moved into her magnificent new home, Hardwick Hall, and this important occasion will be celebrated in 1997

Note: Due to limited light in the Hall's ancient rooms, visitors wishing to make a close study of tapestries and textiles should avoid dull days early and late in the season. To avoid congestion, access to the house may be limited at peak periods. The remains of Hardwick Old Hall in the grounds are in the guardianship of English Heritage.

 Hall: 26 March to 2 Nov: Wed, Thur, Sat, Sun & BH Mon 12.30–5 (closed Good Fri). Last admission to hall 4.30. **Garden:** 26 March to 2 Nov: daily 12–5.30. No picnics in garden; only in car park & country park. Car park gates close 6.

Country park open daily throughout the year, dawn to dusk. **Old Hall** (EH): 26 March to 2 Nov: Wed to Sun & BH Mon (but closed Good Fri) 10–6. **Events**: a series of special events to mark the 400th anniversary is planned; details from the Property Manager (s.a.e. please); 11 May, Airborne Forces Memorial Service

£ Hall & garden £5.80, child £2.90; family ticket £14.50. Garden only £2.50, child £1; family £6. No reduction for parties; parties of 10+ only by written arrangement with Property Manager; please send s.a.e. Vehicle charge £2 (refundable on purchase of house and garden ticket; NT members free). Car park charge for country park to non-members 50p. Joint ticket available for Hall (NT) and Old Hall (EH): adult £7, child £3.60. Children under 15 must be accompanied by an adult

By special written arrangement with Property Manager

Shop open as restaurant (shop/restaurant tel. 01246 854088)

Access to garden and some parts of park and ponds. Great Kitchen and shop accessible by ramp. Access to house limited to ground floor via ramp to main entrance. WC. Wheelchair available; please pre-book. Sympathetic Hearing Scheme

Herb & flower garden particularly recommended to visually impaired visitors (pre-booking advised); herbs may be touched. Braille guide to hall, park, garden, children's guide

Lunches 12–2 & teas 2–4.45 (closes 5.15) in licensed restaurant in the Great Kitchen, on days hall is open. Party bookings by written application only (s.a.e. please). Limited seating of 60 in Great Kitchen and 30 in Still Room

Parent & baby facilities, accessible from car park; highchair and children's portions available

School parties Wed and Thur only; pre-booking essential (s.a.e. please). Schools resource pack and environmental education facility available

In Country Park only, on leads; not in garden

Note: All visitors please note that a one-way traffic system operates in the Park; access only via Stainsby Mill entrance (leave M1, exit 29, follow brown signs), exit only via Hardwick Inn. Park gates closed at night (7 in summer, 5.30 in winter) 6½ml W of Mansfield, 9½ml SE of Chesterfield; approach from M1 (exit 29) via A6175 [120: SK463638] *Bus:* Cosy Coaches C1 from Workshop to Hall (Sun,

July–Aug only); otherwise Stagecoach E Midland X2, 63
Sheffield/Chesterfield–Nottingham, 48 Chesterfield-Bolsover (local buses link
with Chesterfield ⬛ station), alight Glapwell 'Young Vanish', 1½ml (tel. 01332
292200) *Station:* Chesterfield 8ml

HAWFORD DOVECOTE 🏠

Hawford Tel: (Regional Office) 01684 850051

A 16th-century half-timbered dovecote. Access (on foot only) via the entrance drive to
adjoining house

🅾 April to end Oct: daily 9–6 or sunset if earlier. Closed Good Fri. Other times by
prior appointment only with Severn Regional Office

£ 60p

➔ 3ml N of Worcester, ½ml E of A449 [150: SO846607] *Bus:* Midland Red West 303
Worcester–Kidderminster (passing ⬛ Worcester Foregate Street & Kidderminster),
alight Hawford Lodge, ¼ml (tel. 0345 125436) *Station:* Worcester Foregate Street
3ml; Worcester Shrub Hill 3½ml

HIDCOTE MANOR GARDEN ✽

Hidcote Bartrim, nr Chipping Campden GL55 6LR
Tel: 01386 438333 Fax: 01386 438817

One of the most delightful gardens in England, created by the great horticulturist Major
Lawrence Johnston. A series of small gardens separated by walls and hedges, Hidcote is
famous for rare shrubs, trees, herbaceous borders, 'old' roses and interesting plant species

🅾 26 March to end Sept: daily except Tues & Fri 11–7 (closed Good Fri). Also open
Tues in June & July only 11–7. Oct: daily except Tues & Fri 11–6. Last admission
1 hr before closing

£ £5.30; family ticket £13.20. Coaches & parties by appointment only (tel. 01386
438333); no party concessions. No picnicking and no games in garden. Free car
park 100m. Liable to overcrowding on BH Mon and fine Suns. Number of parties
limited per day; party leaders should therefore check with the property before
booking transport

🛍 Shop open as garden; also open 1 Nov to 14 Dec: Sat & Sun 12–4. Plant sales
centre open same days as garden to end Sept: 10.30–5.45

♿ Gravelled car park; disabled visitors may be set down at garden entrance. Access
limited for wheelchair users due to the nature of some informal stone paved paths
and some steps. Wheelchair users requiring refreshments contact Restaurant
Manager; level access can be arranged. Tea Bar accessible. WC in plant sales
centre adjacent to car park

❁ Scented plants; Braille guide

ILAM PARK ✛ ⏣ 🐾 🤾

Ilam, Ashbourne DE6 2AZ Tel: 01335 350245

34ha of attractive park and woodland on both banks of the River Manifold, in the South Peak Estate, with magnificent views towards Thorpe Cloud and the entrance to Dovedale

O **Grounds and Park**: all year, daily. Hall is let to YHA and is not open. *Note*: small caravan site run by NT (basic facilities) open to Caravan Club/NT members; Easter to Oct (tel. 01335 350310)

£ Free. Pay-and-display car park (NT members free); minibuses & coaches £1.50; no coaches Sun or BH Mon

🤾 Guided walks around the estate may be booked by groups; contact Property Manager (tel. 01335 350503)

🛍 Shop and information centre with an exhibition on Ilam and the South Peak Estate: 4 Jan to 29 March: Sat & Sun 11–4; 30 March to 25 Oct: daily 11–5; 26 Oct to 21 Dec: Sat & Sun 11–4; Jan to end March 1998: Sat & Sun 11–4

♿ Access to information centre and shop only; limited access in grounds near Hall. WC. No wheelchair available

🍽 Manifold tea-room open for selection of light refreshments & teas: 4 Jan to 29 March: Sat & Sun 11–4; 30 March to 18 May: Sat & Sun 11–5; 19 May to end Sept: Fri to Tues 11–5; Oct to 21 Dec: Sat & Sun 11–4; Jan to end March 1998: Sat & Sun 11–4. Seats 58

👶 Children's portions available in tea-room

🏫 School visit room, resource material, teachers' resource book for Dovedale, illustrated talks and guided walks available for educational groups. Further details from the Education Coordinator, South Peak Estate Office, Home Farm (tel. 01335 350503)

🐕 On leads only

➜ 4½ml NW of Ashbourne [119:SK132507] *Bus:* Warrington 443 from Ashbourne, Thur & Sat only, with connections from Derby; also various services from ⊒ Buxton and Derby, summer Sun only; otherwise GMS 201 Derby–Manchester (passing close ⊒ Derby & Macclesfield), alight Ilam Cross Roads, 2ml (tel. 01332 292200)

KEDLESTON HALL 🏛 ✛ ❊ ⏣ Ⓔ

Derby DE22 5JH Tel: 01332 842191 Fax: 01332 841972

Palladian mansion set in a classical park landscape, built 1759–65 for Nathaniel Curzon, 1st Baron Scarsdale, whose family has lived at Kedleston since the 12th century. The house has the most complete and least-altered sequence of Robert Adam interiors in England, and the rooms still contain their great collection of family portraits, Old Masters, and their original furniture and other contents. The Indian Museum houses objects collected by Lord Curzon during his travels and when he was Viceroy of India (1899–1905). There is an exhibition of Robert Adam architectural drawings for the house and grounds, an Adam bridge

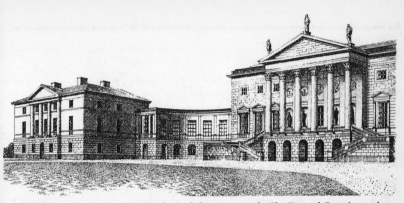

and fishing pavilion in the park, a garden and pleasure grounds. The 'Peacock Dress' worn by Lady Curzon at the Delhi Coronation Durbar 1903 is on display. Late 13th-century parish church (not NT) with important family monuments

House: 29 March to 2 Nov (closed Good Fri): Sat to Wed 1–5.30 (11–5.30 on BH Sun & Mon only). Last admissions to house 5. **Garden & church**: same days as house 11–6. **Park**: 29 March to 2 Nov: daily 11–6; Nov to 21 Dec: Sat & Sun only 12–4. **Events**: for an events leaflet contact Property Manager (s.a.e. please)

£4.50, children £2.20; family ticket £11.20. Reduced rate for booked parties on application. Park & garden only: £2 per adult, £1 per child (refundable on purchase of tickets for house); Thur & Fri vehicle charge of £2 for park only (other facilities closed).

Guided walks around the park and/or gardens may be booked (tel. 01332 842393/842191)

Shop open as house. Also Nov to 21 Dec: Sat & Sun only 12–4

Hall access via difficult steps for wheelchairs; please telephone Property Manager in advance. Wheelchairs and self-drive vehicle available for garden and limited use in park. Tarmac paths throughout park. Garden accessible. WC. Access to restaurant and shop. Sympathetic Hearing Scheme

Braille guide

Licensed restaurant same days as house serving drinks 11–12, home-cooked hot and cold lunches 12–2, teas 2–5. Light lunches and teas only, Nov to 21 Dec, Sat & Sun 12–4. Party bookings by written application (s.a.e. please). Seats 50

WC with baby-changing facility; children's guide and quiz; children's portions available in restaurant

Teachers' leaflets available, please contact Education Coordinator

In park only, on leads. No dogs on Long Walk or in gardens

5ml NW of Derby, signposted from roundabout where A38 crosses A52 close to Markeaton Park [SK312403] *Bus*: Derby Integrated 69B from ≋ Derby to Hall (Sun only); otherwise Dunn Line 109 Derby–Ashbourne, alight the Smithy (1ml); Trent R51/2 from Derby to Askerfield Avenue, thence 2ml. All pass close ≋ Derby (tel. 01332 292200) *Station*: Duffield (U) 3½ml; Derby 5½ml

KINVER EDGE 🈂️🚹

The Warden's Lodge, The Compa, Kinver, nr Stourbridge DY7 6HU
Tel: 01384 872418

*128ha of wood and heath-covered sandstone ridge from which are views across Shropshire
and the West Midlands. Rock houses, inhabited until 1950s: one rebuilt in 1993 for resident
tenants (not open to public)*

O Kinver Edge open all year. Rock house grounds open: April to Sept: daily 9–7;
Oct to March: daily 9–4. Access to upper terrace usually available: prior
confirmation with Custodian advisable (tel. 01384 872553)

£ Free

♿ Route to lower caves at Holy Austin Rock is suitable for wheelchair users; limited
access onto escarpment from east side. Roadside parking

🐕 On leads within grounds of rock houses

➔ 5ml W of Stourbridge, 6ml N of Kidderminster. 2½ml off A458 [138:SO836836]
Bus: West Midlands/Midland Red West 242 ⇥ Stourbridge–Kinver (tel. 01785
223344) *Station:* Stourbridge Town 5ml

KINWARTON DOVECOTE 🏠

Kinwarton, nr Alcester Tel: (Regional Office) 01684 850051

A circular 14th-century dovecote, with ogee doorway. It retains its potence, a rare feature

O April to end Oct: daily 9–6 or sunset if earlier. Closed Good Fri. Other times by
prior appointment only with Regional Office. Key obtainable from Glebe Farm
next door

£ 60p

➔ 1½ml NE of Alcester, just S of B4089 [150: SP106585] *Bus:* As Coughton
Court, but alight Alcester, 1½ml except on the 228 which passes the Dovecote
Station: Wilmcote (U), not Sun except May to Sept, 5ml; Wootton Wawen (U),
not Sun, 5ml

LITTLE FLEECE BOOKSHOP 🏠

Bisley Street, Painswick GL6 6QQ Tel: 01452 812103

*17th-century building in the heart of Painswick, originally part of Great Fleece Inn. An
exemplary restoration carried out in 1935 with the advice of Sir George Oakley, enhancing
the existing 17th-century features and character. Ground-floor room only, open as a bookshop*

O 4 April to 31 Oct: Tues to Sat 10–1 & 2–5. Closed Good Fri. Nov & Dec: Sat only
10–1 & 2–5

➔ 3ml N of Stroud A46, 6ml SE of Gloucester B4073. Off main High Street,

Painswick [162: SO868098] *Bus:* Stagecoach Stroud Valleys 46 Stroud–
Cheltenham Spa (passes close ≉ Stroud) (tel. 01453 763421) *Station:* Stroud 4ml

LONGSHAW ESTATE ❀ ⬛ ⬛ ⬛ ⬛ ⬛ E

Sheffield S11 7TZ
Visitor Centre Tel: 01433 631708 Wardens' Office Tel/fax: 01433 631757

*688ha of open moorland, woodland and farms in the Peak District National Park, with
dramatic views and varied walking. Stone for the Derwent and Howden Dams was quarried
from Bolehill, and millstones may be seen in quarries on the estate. There is a quarry winding
house above Grindleford station*

🅾 **Estate**: open at all times. Lodge is converted into flats and is not open. **Visitor
centre** (café, shop and information centre): 4 Jan to Easter: weekends only; Easter
to end Oct: Wed to Sun & BH Mon; 1 Nov to 21 Dec: weekends only: 11–5 or
sunset if earlier. Reopens 3 Jan 1998. Booked parties at other times by
arrangement. **Events**: 4–6 Sep, Longshaw Sheepdog Trials

£ Car park 200m from visitor centre [SK266800]; access difficult for coaches;
no coaches at weekends or BH. Car parks for estate at Haywood [110/119:
SK256778] and Wooden Pole [110/119: SK267790]. Riding permits available.
Longshaw Walks & Family leaflets from visitor centre

🏃 Guided walks around the estate may be booked by groups: contact Wardens'
office (tel. 01433 631757)

📷 Shop open as visitor centre

♿ WC. Limited access to the estate. One car-parking space available at visitor centre
– please book in advance with Visitor Centre Manager

🍽 Selection of home-made light lunches and teas at visitor centre. Seats 40

🚼 Baby-changing facilities. Highchairs in café

🐕 On leads only; no dogs in visitor centre

➡ 7½ml from Sheffield, next to A625 Sheffield–Hathersage road; Woodcroft car park
is off B6055, 200m S of junction with A625 [110/119: SK266802] *Bus:* Mainline
240 Sheffield–Bakewell (passing ≉ Grindleford); Mainline/Hulley's 272 Sheffield–
Castleton (passing ≉ Hathersage). All pass close ≉ Sheffield (tel. 01332 292200)
Station: Grindleford (U) 2ml

LOWER BROCKHAMPTON 🏠 🏃

Bringsty WR6 5UH Tel: 01885 488099

*A late 14th-century moated manor house, with an attractive detached half-timbered 15th-
century gatehouse, a rare example of this type of structure. Also, the ruins of a 12th-century
chapel*

🅾 **Medieval hall & parlour, gatehouse & chapel:** 29 March to end Sept: Wed to Sun
& BH Mon 10–5 (closed Good Fri). Oct: Wed to Sun 10–4

💷 £1.60; family ticket £4

♿ Access to most parts. Gatehouse & upper floor not accessible

🐾 Braille guide; timber-framing and oak furniture may be touched

➡ 2ml E of Bromyard on Worcester road (A44); reached by a narrow road through 1½ml of woods and farmland [149: SO682546] *Bus:* Midland Red West 419/20 Worcester–Hereford (passing ⇌ Worcester Foregate Street & close ⇌ Hereford) (tel. 0345 125436)

LYVEDEN NEW BIELD 🏚 ✝

nr Oundle, Peterborough PE8 5AT Tel: 01832 205358 Fax: 01832 205358

The shell of an uncompleted 'lodge' or garden house, begun c.1595 by Sir Thomas Tresham, and designed in the shape of a cross. The exterior incorporates friezes inscribed with religious quotations and signs of the Passion. Sir Thomas died before the building was completed, and his son, Francis Tresham, was then imprisoned in connection with the Gunpowder Plot. Viewing platform at the east window

🅾 All year: daily. Parties by arrangement with the Custodian, Lyveden New Bield Cottage, Oundle, Peterborough PE8 5AT. Elizabethan water gardens open selected Sun during July & Aug

💷 £1.70. Limited roadside parking; access on foot ½ml along farm track; no parking for coaches which may drop and return to pick up passengers. No WC

🚹 Tours of the remains of the late Elizabethan water gardens by prior arrangement with the Custodian

🐕 On leads only

➡ 4ml SW of Oundle via A427, 3ml E of Brigstock, off Harley Way [141: SP983853] *Bus:* Stagecoach United Counties X65 Northampton–Peterborough (passing close ⇌ Peterborough); alight Lower Benefield, 2ml by bridlepath; Stagecoach United Counties/Blands 8 Kettering Corby, alight Brigstock, 2½ml. Both pass close ⇌ Kettering (tel. 01604 20077) *Station:* Kettering 10ml

MIDDLE LITTLETON TITHE BARN 🏚 🔑

Middle Littleton, Evesham

Magnificent 13th-century tithe barn, built of blue lias stone, and still in use as a farmbuilding

🅾 April to end Oct: daily 2–5. Access is by key only; a notice at the property gives details of how to obtain the key

💷 60p

➡ 3ml NE of Evesham, E of B4085 [150: SP080471] *Bus:* Midland Red West 146, Evesham–Birmingham (passing close ⇌ Evesham), alight Middle Littleton School Lane, ½ml (tel. 0345 125436) *Station:* Honeybourne (U) 3½ml; Evesham 4½ml

MORVILLE HALL 🏠 ❖ ♨

nr Bridgnorth WV16 5BN

An Elizabethan house of mellow stone, converted in the 18th century. The Hall is in a fine setting, with three attractive gardens

O By written appointment only with the tenant, Mrs J. K. Norbury

🏃 For pre-booked parties

♿ Ground floor and most of garden accessible

➔ [138: SO668940] *Bus:* Midland Red West 436/7 Shrewsbury–Bridgnorth (passing close ➤ Shrewsbury & Severn Valley Rly Bridgnorth) (tel. 0345 056785) *Station:* Bridgnorth (Severn Valley Rly) 3½ml

MOSELEY OLD HALL 🏠 ❖ Ⓔ

Moseley Old Hall Lane, Fordhouses, Wolverhampton WV10 7HY
Tel: 01902 782808 Fax: 01902 782808

An Elizabethan house with later alterations. Charles II hid here after the Battle of Worcester, and the bed in which he slept is on view, as well as the hiding place he used. A new special exhibition in the barn tells the story of the King's escape using contemporary accounts. The small garden has been reconstructed in 17th-century style with formal box parterre; 17th-century plants only are grown. The property holds three Sandford Heritage Education Awards

O 15 March to 21 Dec; March & April: Sat & Sun, BH Mon, and following Tues 1.30–5.30 (BH Mon 11–5); May to Oct: Sat, Sun, Mon and Tues after BH Mon; also Tues in July & Aug 1.30–5.30 (BH Mon 11–5); Nov & Dec: Sun 1.30–4.30 (guided tours only, last tour at 4). Pre-booked parties at other times incl. evening tours. Special arrangements for NT Members' Centres and Associations on Weds. **Events:** for programme please send s.a.e. to Property Manager

£ £3.30; family ticket £8.25

🏃 Optional free guided tours

🛍 Shop open as house. Christmas shop

♿ Access to ground floor (3 rooms) and garden only. Two tables for wheelchair users on ground floor of tea-room. WC in garden. Wheelchair available

👁 Braille and large-print guides; some items, including fabric samples, may be touched

🍽 Tea-room in 18th-century barn. Teas, as house, 1.30–5.30. Light lunches BH Mon, also Sun July & Aug, from 1. Christmas shop & tea-room open 2 Nov to 21 Dec: Sun 1.30–4.30. Other times for parties by prior arrangement. Licensed. Seating for 54

👶 Highchair available in tea-room

🏛 Education programme includes living history

→ 4ml N of Wolverhampton; S of M54 between A449 and A460; traffic from N on M6 leave motorway at exit 11, then A460; traffic from S on M6 & M54 take exit 1; coaches must approach via A460 to avoid low bridge [127: SJ932044] *Bus:* Midland Red 870–2 Wolverhampton–Cannock, alight Bognop Road, ¾ml; West Midlands Buses 613 from Wolverhampton, thence ¾ml (all pass close ⇌ Wolverhampton) (tel. 0121 200 2700) *Station:* Wolverhampton 4ml

NEWARK PARK 🏠 👤

Ozleworth, Wotton-under-Edge GL12 7PZ Tel: (Regional Office) 01684 850051

Tudor 'standing' or hunting lodge built on the edge of a cliff by the Poyntz family, made into a four-square castellated country house by James Wyatt, 1790. Restoration work on the garden and house is in progress. The house is of specialist architectural interest

🅾 By prior appointment only; please tel. 01684 850051

💷 £2. No reduction for parties. Car park. Not suitable for coaches. No WC

→ 1½ml E of Wotton-under-Edge, 1¾ml S of junction of A4135 & B4058 [172: ST786934] *Bus:* Badgerline 309 Bristol–Dursley, alight Wotton-under-Edge, 1¾ml. Frequent services link ⇌ Bristol Temple Meads with the bus station (tel. 0117 955 3231) *Station:* Stroud 10m

THE OLD MANOR 🏠 🏠 ✚ ❈

Norbury, Ashbourne DE6 2ED

A stone-built 13th- to 15th-century hall with a rare kingpost roof, undercroft and cellars; the hall is of specialist architectural interest only. (Also, a late 17th-century red-brick manor house, incorporating fragments of an earlier Tudor house, tenanted and not open). The church (not NT) is well worth a visit

🅾 Medieval hall by written appointment only with the tenant, Mr C. Wright. 29 March to end Sept: Tues, Wed & Sat

💷 £1.50 *Bus:* Stevensons 409 Uttoxeter–Belper (passing close ⇌ Uttoxeter), alight Ellastone, ¾ml (tel. 01332 292200) *Station:* Uttoxeter (U) 7½ml

PACKWOOD HOUSE 🏠 ❈ 👤 🄴

Lapworth, Solihull B94 6AT Tel: 01564 782024

The house, originally 16th-century, is a 20th-century evocation of domestic Tudor architecture. Created by Graham Baron Ash, its interiors reflect the period between the World Wars and contain a fine collection of 16th-century textiles and furniture. Important gardens with renowned herbaceous borders and a famous yew garden based on the Sermon on the Mount

🅾 26 March to end Sept: Wed to Sun & BH Mon 2–6, garden 1.30–6. Closed Good

Fri. Oct: Wed to Sun 12.30–4.30. Last admission to house 30min before closing. **Events**: 11/12 July, 1920s Follies event; tel. bookings from 1 April. For full summer events leaflet please send s.a.e. to Administrator

£4; family ticket £10. Garden only £2. Car park £2, refunded on entry to house & garden. Walks available through parkland and woodland. Picnic site in avenue opposite main gates

Shop open as house

Access to ground floor (except great hall which can be seen from door) and part of garden.Wheelchairs available. WC (in car park) with handrails, otherwise unadapted. Shop inaccessible to wheelchair users

Braille guide; enquire in house about items to touch. Yew trees and hedges may be touched

School parties by appointment Wed, Thur & Fri mornings

2ml E of Hockley Heath (on A3400), 11ml SE of central Birmingham [139: SP174722] *Bus*: Stagecoach Midland Red X20 Birmingham–Stratford-upon-Avon, alight Hockley Heath, 1½ml (tel. 0121 200 2700) *Station*: Lapworth (U), not Sun (except June to Sept), 1½ml; Birmingham International 8ml

PRIEST'S HOUSE

Easton on the Hill, nr Stamford

Pre-Reformation priest's lodge, of specialist architectural interest. There is a small museum of village bygones upstairs

By appointment only. Please tel. Regional Office 01909 486411

Free. Unsuitable for coaches

Ground-floor room only

→ Approx. 2ml SW of Stamford off A43 [141: TF011045] *Bus:* Road Car 180, Blands from Stamford (passing close ⭢ Stamford), alight Easton, ½ml (tel. 01522 553135) *Station:* Stamford 2ml

---

SHUGBOROUGH ESTATE 🏠 🏠 ✕ ✿ ♣ 🔲 E

Milford, nr Stafford ST17 0XB Tel: 01889 881388 Fax: 01889 881323

The 364ha Shugborough Estate is being restored as a 19th-century working estate. Shugborough Hall is the magnificent seat of the Earls of Lichfield. The house was enlarged c.1750, and altered by Samuel Wyatt 1790–1806, with collections of French and English china, silver, paintings and furniture, and rococo plasterwork by Vassalli. The County Museum in the stable block houses the original kitchens and butler's pantry, laundry and restored working brew-house. In the parkland the Georgian farmstead built in 1805 for Thomas, Viscount Anson, as home farm for the estate, is now a working farm museum with rare breeds, restored working corn mill and demonstrations of traditional farming methods. There are Victorian terraces, an Edwardian rose garden and extensive parkland, with neo-classical monuments

Note: Shugborough is financed and administered by Staffordshire County Council. NT members are entitled to free entry to the Mansion, reduced rate to County Museum & Farm but must pay site admission charge per vehicle and any special event charge which may be in operation. Admission charges and opening arrangements may vary when special events are held. Tel. property for details of 1997 events programme

O **House, County Museum, Farm & Gardens:** 29 March to 26 Oct: daily 11–5 until 28 Sept; Suns only in Oct. Open daily all year from 10.30 for booked parties. (County Museum, Farm, Gardens and tours of house: tel. property for details). **Events:** a wide range of events, incl. open-air concerts, theatre and themed activities, Christmas evenings and craft festivals take place through the year; please tel. for details

£ Parkland £1.50 per vehicle (NT members incl.), coaches free, giving access to parkland, gardens, picnic area and walks and trails. Free car park at Farm for Farm visitors. House £3.50 (NT members free), concessions £2.50; Farm £3.50 (NT members and concessions £2.50); County Museum £3.50 (NT members and concessions £2.50); all sites £8 (concessions £6). *Note:* concessions apply to children, OAPs, registered unemployed and parties. Guided walks and trails for booked parties throughout the year £3 per head. Evening visits for booked parties (min. 30): prices on request. Guided tours available for school parties at £2 per head per site (2 sites for £3); working demonstrations available from Oct to Easter £2.50–£5; schools must book in advance

🕴 Available throughout year; evening guided tours and garden tours also available. Range of connoisseur talks and tours designed for special-interest groups

🛍 NT shop at main site (tel. 01889 882122). Open 29 March to 28 Sept: daily 11–5. NT shop also open 29 Sept to 21 Dec: daily (except Sat) 11–4

♿ County Museum and Farm accessible (reduced admission charge); access can be arranged to ground floor of house for wheelchairs using step-climber. WC. Some staff have been trained in basic sign language. Tours and demonstrations can be adapted to your special needs. Self-drive powered vehicles and wheelchairs available for park and garden; accessible picnic tables

Braille, taped and large-print guides; rose garden

Lunches, high teas and snacks in Lady Walk Restaurant on main site; dinners available to pre-booked parties (min. 15). Tea-room at farm for light refreshments open as house. Picnic sites by main and farm car parks. Main site car park picnic area features special picnic tables for wheelchair users

Farm gives children chance to see and touch domestic and rare breeds of animal and poultry. Games gallery in corn mill. Children's play area. Extensive puppet collection in County Museum. Highchairs; baby-changing facilities

Extensive schools and adult demonstration programme. Education rooms can be booked at each of the three sites

On leads in parkland only. Guide dogs admitted to house and County Museum

Signposted from M6 exit 13; 6ml E of Stafford on A513; entrance at Milford. Pedestrian access from E, from the canal/Little Haywood side of the Estate [127: SJ992225] *Bus:* Midland Red 825 ⇌ Stafford–Tamworth (passing close ⇌ Lichfield City) (tel. 01785 223344) *Station:* Stafford 6ml

---

SNOWSHILL MANOR ⊞ ❖ E

Snowshill, nr Broadway WR12 7JU Tel: 01386 852410

A Cotswold Tudor manor house, best known for Charles Paget Wade's collections of craftsmanship and design, including musical instruments, clocks, toys, bicycles, weavers' and spinners' tools, Japanese armour. His cottage and charming cottage garden are also on view

Note: The manor is a 10min walk (500m) along an undulating country path

24 March to end Oct: daily except Tues 1–5 (closed Good Fri); Also open Tues in July & Aug. **Grounds & visitor facilities** open at 12. **Grounds & shop** open till 5.30 May to Sept. Last admission to house and restaurant 45min before closing. Timed tickets will be issued for the house. Due to re-roofing work there will be scaffolding on part of the manor for most of the season. **Events:** please tel. for details

£5.40; family ticket £13.50. Grounds, restaurant & shop £2. Coach and school parties by prior written appointment only. No pushchairs or back-packs allowed in house. Photography only by prior written arrangement with Curator

Shop open same days as house 12–5 (to 5.30 May to Sept). Also 1 Nov to 7 Dec: Sat & Sun 12.30–4.30

Access to visitor facilities but house and grounds unsuitable

Braille guide for house and description of garden

Restaurant open for coffees, lunches & teas on same days as house 12–5. Also Nov & Dec as shop. No picnicking. Tel. 01386 858685

Parent & baby room

3ml SW of Broadway, approach only from turning off the A44 by Broadway Green [150: SP096339] *Bus:* Thames Trains buslink ⇌ Moreton-in-Marsh– ⇌ Evesham (June–Sept) (tel. 01865 722333); otherwise Castleways ⇌ Evesham– Broadway, thence 2½ml (tel. 01242 602949) *Station:* Moreton-in-Marsh 7ml

STAINSBY MILL: HARDWICK ESTATE ▣ E

Doe Lea, Chesterfield S44 5QJ Tel: 01246 850430 Fax: 01246 854200

There has been a water-powered flour mill at Stainsby since the 13th century. It passed to Bess of Hardwick with the purchase of the Manor of Stainsby in 1593. It is remarkably complete, with newly reconstructed 1849–50 machinery. Includes a kiln, drying floor, three pairs of millstones and an iron water wheel. In working order

O 26 March to 2 Nov: Wed, Thurs, Sat, Sun & BH Mon 11.30–4.30; July, Aug & Sept also open Fri 11.30–4.30. Last admission 4. **Events**: 11 May, National Mills Day; 23 Aug, Son et lumière; for events leaflet contact Property Manager (s.a.e. please)

£ £1.50, children 70p; family £3.70. Children under 15 must be accompanied by an adult. Parties by prior arrangement only (no reduction) with Property Manager, Hardwick Hall. *Note*: No WC at mill, but available at Hardwick Hall car park

🚹 On request at the mill

📷 Available at Hardwick Hall

♿ Limited access to ground floor only; no wheelchairs available

👁 Panelling and mill stones on display may be touched

☕ Refreshments available at Hardwick Hall

👥 School parties Wed & Thurs only. Please send s.a.e. to Property Manager at Hardwick Hall for further information

🐕 In country park only on leads. Not in Mill

➔ From M1 exit 29 take A6175 signposted to Clay Cross then first left and left again to Stainsby Mill *Bus*: As for Hardwick Hall, but, except for the C1, alight Heath, thence 1ml (1½ml on X2) *Station*: Chesterfield 7ml

STAUNTON HAROLD CHURCH ✚ ♣

Staunton Harold, Ashby-de-la-Zouch Tel: 01332 863822 Fax: 01332 865272

One of the very few churches to be built during the Commonwealth, erected by Sir Robert Shirley, an ardent Royalist. The interior retains its original 17th-century cushions and hangings, and includes fine panelling and painted ceilings. The wrought-iron screen was designed by Robert Bakewell. The church is in an attractive parkland setting and stands next to Staunton Harold Hall (not NT). Calke Abbey is nearby

Note: A voluntary vehicle charge may be requested on busy summer Sundays and Bank Holidays at which time a one-way system will be in operation on the estate

O 29 March to end Sept: Sat to Wed & BH Mon (closed Good Fri) 1–5 or sunset if earlier; Oct: Sat & Sun only 1–5

£ Donations of £1 requested, collection box. WCs (not NT) 300m

♿ Church and park largely accessible; no wheelchair available

🕒 Light refreshments available at Hall (Sue Ryder Foundation)

→ 5ml NE of Ashby-de-la-Zouch, W of B587 [128: SK379208] *Bus:* City Rider C68/A, 69; Derby Integrated 69B Derby–Swadlincote (passing close ⇄ Derby), alight Melbourne, 3ml or Ticknall via Calke Park, 3ml (tel. 01332 292200)

MR STRAW'S HOUSE 🏠

7 Blyth Grove, Worksop S81 0JG Tel: 01909 482380

A semi-detached house built at the turn of the century, belonging to William Straw and his brother, Walter. The interior has been preserved since the death of their parents in the 1930s with 1920s wallpaper, furnishings and local furniture. Museum room contains displays of family memorabilia, and there is a suburban garden

Note: Blyth Grove is a private road; there is no access without booking in advance. There is a car park with picnic area opposite the house for visitors with timed tickets

🅾 29 March to 2 Nov: Tues to Sat (closed Good Fri) 11–4.30. Last admission 4. Admission for all visitors (incl. NT members) by pre-booked timed ticket only. All bookings by telephone or letter (s.a.e. please) to Custodian

£ £3, children £1.50, family ticket £7.50. *Note*: Guided tours for groups (max. 16) may be arranged on Wed & Fri mornings only (£10 extra per group, incl. NT members)

♿ Wheelchair access not possible

👁 Access advisable outside peak viewing times; house is small and quickly becomes congested; please telephone in advance. Braille guide; audio cassette

→ In Worksop, follow signs to Bassetlaw General Hospital. House signposted from Blyth Road (B6045) [120: SK590802] *Bus:* From surrounding areas (tel. 0115 9240000) *Station:* Worksop ½ml

SUDBURY HALL 🏠 ✳ E

Sudbury, Ashbourne DE6 5HT Tel: 01283 585305 Fax: 01283 585139

One of the most individual of late 17th-century houses, begun by George Vernon c.1661. The rich decoration includes wood carvings by Gibbons and Pierce, superb plasterwork, and mythological decorative paintings by Laguerre. The Great Staircase is one of the finest of its kind in an English house

Note: Owing to low light levels, visitors wishing to study the Hall's plasterwork or paintings in detail should avoid dull days and late afternoons towards end of season

🅾 29 March to 2 Nov: Wed to Sun & BH Mon (closed Good Fri) 1–5.30 or sunset if earlier. Last admission 5. Grounds open 12.30–6. *Note:* New visitor car park 400m from Hall. No WC in car park. **Events:** details of concerts & special events from the Administrator (s.a.e. please)

£ Hall £3.50, children £1.50; family ticket £8.50; joint individual ticket for Hall & Museum recommended £5; joint family ticket £12.50. All party bookings by prior arrangement with the Bookings Secretary

🕅 Guided and specialist tours available; contact Administrator

🗋 Shop open as Hall. Also Nov to 21 Dec: Sat & Sun only 12–4

♿ Parking in visitor car park. Multi-seater volunteer-driven buggy. Hall and garden difficult. Lake, tea-room and shop accessible; one wheelchair available for inside use only; for entrance arrangements, please contact Administrator. WC in museum (see following entry); Sympathetic Hearing Scheme

◉ Braille guide

▣ Coach House tea-room open same days as house 12.30–5.30 (last orders 5); also Nov to 21 Dec: Sat & Sun 12–4. Coaches by appointment only, booking form by written application (s.a.e. please). Seats 68

🚼 Changing facilities in Museum of Childhood; children's portions available in tea-room

▣ Special facilities linked to National Curriculum for pre-booked school parties, by arrangement with Education Officer (tel. 01283 585022)

🐾 In visitor car park only

→ 6ml E of Uttoxeter at the crossing point of A50 Derby–Stoke and A515 Lichfield–Ashbourne roads [128: SK160323] *Bus:* Stevensons 401 Burton-on-Trent–Uttoxeter (passing ⇌ Tutbury & Hatton and close ⇌ Burton-on-Trent (tel. 01332 292200) *Station:* Tutbury & Hatton (U) 5ml

SUDBURY HALL – THE NATIONAL TRUST MUSEUM OF CHILDHOOD ▣ 🕅 E

As Sudbury Hall

Situated in the 19th-century service wing of Sudbury Hall, the Museum of Childhood contains fascinating and innovative displays about children from the 18th century onwards, but with particular emphasis on life in Victorian and Edwardian periods. There are chimney climbs for the adventurous 'sweep-sized' youngster. Betty Cadbury's fine collection of toys and dolls is displayed in the specially designed 'Playthings Past' gallery

🅞 29 March to 2 Nov: Wed to Sun & BH Mon (closed Good Fri) 1–5.30. Last admission 5. **Events:** special events and activities for children; details from Education Officer (s.a.e. please)

£ Museum & Garden £3, children £1.50; family ticket £7.50. Joint individual ticket for Hall & Museum £5; joint family ticket £12.50. Party bookings by arrangement with the Bookings Secretary

🕅 Guided tours available; contact Administrator

🗋 Shop open as Hall; also Nov to 21 Dec, Sat & Sun 12–4

♿ Most of Museum accessible. WC. Wheelchair available for inside use only

⬛ Coach House tea-room open same days as Museum 12.30–5.30 (last orders 5); also Nov to 21 Dec, Sat & Sun 12–4. Coaches by appointment only, by written application (s.a.e. please). Seats 68

🧍 Baby-changing facilities; back-pack baby carriers accepted; pushchairs difficult

📖 Educational materials available. Special facilities for schools as for Sudbury Hall

🐕 In car park only

➔ 6ml E of Uttoxeter at the crossing point of A50 Derby–Stoke and A515 Lichfield–Ashbourne roads [128:SK160323] *Bus:* Stevensons 401 Burton-on-Trent–Uttoxeter (passing ⇌ Tutbury & Hatton and close ⇌ Burton-on-Trent) (tel. 01332 292200) *Station:* Tutbury & Hatton (U) 5ml

TOWN WALLS TOWER 🏠

Shrewsbury SY1 1TN Tel: (Regional Office) 01743 709343

The last remaining watchtower, built in the 14th century and overlooking the River Severn

🅾 By written appointment only with the tenant, Mr A. A. Hector, Tower House, 26a Town Walls, Shrewsbury SY1 1TN

➔ A few mins walk from town centre, on S of Town Walls *Bus:* From surrounding areas (tel. 0345 056785) *Station:* Shrewsbury ½ml

ULVERSCROFT NATURE RESERVE 🐦

nr Loughborough Tel: (Regional Office) 01909 486411 Fax: 01909 486377

Part of the ancient Charnwood forest, the area is especially fine in spring during bluebell time

🅾 Access by permit only, from The Secretary, Leicestershire & Rutland Trust for Nature Conservation, Leicester LE1 6UU

➔ *Bus:* Midland Fox 109, 117–9, 217/8 Leicester–Swadlincote (passing close ⇌ Leicester) (tel. 0116 251 1411) *Station:* Barrow upon Soar 7ml, Loughborough 7½ml

UPTON HOUSE 🏠 ❀ 🅴

Banbury OX15 6HT Tel: 01295 670266

The house, built of a mellow local stone, dates from 1695, but the outstanding collections it contains are the chief attraction. Assembled this century by the 2nd Lord Bearsted, they include paintings by English and Continental Old Masters, Brussels tapestries, Sèvres porcelain, Chelsea figures and 18th-century furniture. The garden is also of great interest, with terraces descending into a deep valley from the main lawn; herbaceous borders, the national collection of asters, over 0.4ha of kitchen garden, a water garden laid out in the 1930s and pools stocked with ornamental fish

Note: Entry to house by timed tickets at peak times on Sun & BHols, when delays are possible

🅾 29 March to 2 Nov: Sat to Wed (incl. BH Mon) 2–6. Closed Thur & Fri (incl. Good Fri). Last admission 5.30 (5 after 26 Oct). **Events:** fine arts study tours, jazz concert and other events; please send s.a.e. or tel. for details

£ £4.80; family ticket £12. Garden only £2.40. Parties of 15 or more by written arrangement. Free parking

🕴 Evening guided tours by written arrangement

🏠 Shop open as house. Plant and garden produce on sale (when available) by admission kiosk

♿ Access to ground-floor rooms via ramped side door, tea-room and part of garden. Access to lower floor (avoiding stairs) can be provided by prior arrangement. Wheelchair available for use in house. WC. Parking near house for disabled drivers. Motorised buggy with driver available for access to/from lower garden

♦ Braille guide

☕ Tea-room in house. Last teas 5.30; 5 on weekdays in April & Oct

🚼 Parent & baby room

➡ On A422, 7ml NW of Banbury, 12ml SE of Stratford-upon-Avon [151: SP371461]
Bus: Stagecoach Midland Red X70, 270 from Banbury (tel. 01788 535555)
Station: Banbury 7ml

WALL ROMAN SITE (LETOCETUM BATHS & MUSEUM)

Watling Street, Wall, nr Lichfield WS14 0AW Tel: 01543 480768

The excavated bath-house of a Roman posting station on Watling Street; the most complete example of its kind in Britain. Interesting museum

Note: Letocetum is in the guardianship of English Heritage

🅾 1 April to 30 Sept: daily 10–6; Oct: daily 10–4 or dusk if earlier (closed for lunch 1–2). Closed in winter. **Events:** send s.a.e. to property for details

£ Museum & site £1.50, children 80p. OAPs and UB40 holders £1.10 (all prices provisional). Parties of 11 or more 15% discount. School bookings (tel. 01604 730332)

[🏃] Informal talk given in museum for small parties only, on prior request

[📷] Open same times as property

[♿] Access to museum only. Site on uneven ground

[🔊] Audio tape available at small extra charge

[▓] Free entry for education groups who book in advance

[🐕] On leads only

[➜] 2ml SW of Lichfield, on N side of A5 [139: SK099066] *Station:* Shenstone 1½ml

---

THE WEIR [❀]

Swainshill, nr Hereford HR4 8BS

Delightful riverside garden particularly spectacular in early spring, with fine views over the River Wye and Black Mountains

[O] 14 Feb to end Oct: Wed to Sun (incl. Good Fri) & BH Mon 11–6

[£] £1.50; free car park (unsuitable for coaches). No WC

[♿] Not advisable for wheelchair users

[🐕] In car park only (no shade or water)

[➜] 5ml W of Hereford on A438 [149: SO435421] *Bus:* Yeoman's Canyon 446 from Hereford; otherwise Midland Red West 101 Hereford–Credenhill (both passing close ≈ Hereford), thence 1½ml (tel. 0345 125436) *Station:* Hereford 5ml

---

WESTBURY COURT GARDEN [❀][E]

Westbury-on-Severn GL14 1PD Tel: 01452 760461

A formal water garden with canals and yew hedges, laid out between 1696 and 1705. It is the earliest of its kind remaining in England, restored in 1971 and planted with species dating from pre-1700, including apple, pear and plum trees

[O] 29 March to end Oct: Wed to Sun & BH Mon 11–6 (closed Good Fri). Other months by appointment only. **Events:** Pillowell Silver Band concert; please contact property for details

[£] £2.50. Free car park. Parties of 15 or more by written arrangement. Picnic area

[♿] All parts of garden accessible; wheelchair available. WC

[🔊] Scented plants; Braille guide

[🐕] Strictly no dogs except guide dogs

[➜] 9ml SW of Gloucester on A48 [162: SO718138] *Bus:* Stagecoach Red & White 73 ≈ Gloucester–Newport (passing close ≈ Newport); 31 ≈ Gloucester–Coleford (tel. 01633 266336) *Station:* Gloucester 9ml

WICHENFORD DOVECOTE 🏠

Wichenford

A 17th-century half-timbered dovecote

O April to end Oct: daily 9–6 or sunset if earlier. Closed Good Fri. Other times by prior appointment only with Regional Office (tel. 01684 850051)

£ 60p

→ 5½ml NW of Worcester, N of B4204 [150: SO788598] *Bus:* Midland Red West 310/2/3 from Worcester (passing close ⇌ Worcester Foregate Street), alight Wichenford, ½ml (tel. 0345 125436) *Station:* Worcester Foregate Street 7ml; Worcester Shrub Hill 7½ml

WIGHTWICK MANOR 🏠 ❀ 🚶 E

Wightwick Bank, Wolverhampton WV6 8EE
Tel: 01902 761108 Fax: 01902 764663

Begun in 1887, the house is a notable example of the influence of William Morris, with many original Morris wallpapers and fabrics. Also of interest are Pre-Raphaelite pictures, Kempe glass and de Morgan ware. The Victorian/Edwardian garden has yew hedges and topiary, terraces and two pools

O **House:** 1 March to 31 Dec and March 1998: Thur & Sat 2.30–5.30. Also open BH Sat, Sun & Mon 2.30–5.30 (ground floor only, no guided tours). Open for pre-booked parties Wed & Thur and special evening tours. Admission to house by timed ticket, issued from 2 at front door. Owing to the fragile nature of contents and the requirements of conservation, some rooms cannot always be shown; tours will therefore vary during the year. School visits on Wed & Thur, contact Property Manager for details. **Garden:** Wed & Thur 11–6; Sat, BH Sun & BH Mon 1–6. Other days by appointment. **Events:** details from Property Manager; please send s.a.e.

£ £5. Students £2.50. Garden only £2.25. Parking: only room for one coach in lay-by outside main gate; car park (120m) at bottom of Wightwick Bank (no parking in Elmsdale opposite the property)

🚶 Except BHols

📷 William Morris Arts & Craft shop open Wed and Thur 11–5.30; Sat, BH Sun & BH Mon 1–5.30. Pottery (not NT) open as shop. *Note:* the William Morris shop, tea-room and pottery are open to the general public, independent of visiting the house and garden

♿ Access (via steps to ground floor) to 5 rooms & garden (but site slopes; strong companions necessary). No wheelchairs available. Ring for parking advice

👁 Braille guides to house and Pre-Raphaelite collection

☕ Tea-room open as shop

🏫 Pre-booked school visits; details from Property Manager

⊟ In garden only, on leads

➔ 3ml W of Wolverhampton, up Wightwick Bank (off A454 beside the Mermaid Inn) [139: SO869985] *Bus:* Midland Red 890 Wolverhampton–Bridgnorth; 516 Wolverhampton–Pattingham (both pass close ⇌ Wolverhampton) (tel. 0121 200 2700) *Station:* Wolverhampton 3ml

---

WILDERHOPE MANOR ⊞ ⊞ ⊞

Longville, Much Wenlock TF13 6EG Tel: 01694 771363

This limestone house stands on the southern slope of Wenlock Edge in remote country with views down to Corvedale. Dating from 1586, it is unaltered but unfurnished; features include remarkable wooden spiral stairs, unique bow rack and fine plaster ceilings. Let to the Youth Hostels Association. Circular walk through farmland and woods

O April to end Sept: Wed & Sat 2–4.30. Oct to end March 1998: Sat only 2–4.30

£ £1. No reduction for parties

⊡ YHA shop

⊡ Access to house via steep section of path (strong companion needed) then ground floor accessible. Shop (not NT) accessible

⊡ Tea and coffee available

⊡ Field Study Centre run by YHA

⊟ On leads in area around Manor

➔ 7ml SW of Much Wenlock, 7ml E of Church Stretton, ½ml S of B4371 [138: SO545929] *Station:* Church Stretton (U) 8ml

---

WINSTER MARKET HOUSE ⊞

nr Matlock Tel: 01335 350245

A market house of the late 17th or early 18th century. The ground floor is of stone with the original five open arches filled in, while the upper storey is of brick with stone dressings. The building was bought in 1906, the first Peak District acquisition, and restored; it is now an NT information room (no attendant)

O 29 March to end Oct: open daily

£ Free. Public WC in side street near house

➔ 4ml W of Matlock on S side of B5057 in main street of Winster [119: SK241606] *Bus:* Hulley's 170/2 Matlock–Bakewell (passing close ⇌ Matlock) (tel. 01332 292200) *Station:* Matlock (U) 4ml

North East

COAST

The Trust's many holdings on the **YORKSHIRE** coast are best viewed from the Cleveland Way long distance footpath. **Newbiggin Cliffs**, 10ha, 2ml north-east of Filey [93: TA827105], provide nesting places for guillemot and razorbill. At **Cayton Bay**, south of Scarborough [101: TA0635850], there is a wide variety of habitats contained within its 36ha. The woodland is being selectively felled to encourage the abundance of wild flowers. 6ml north of Scarborough at **Hayburn Wyke**, there are 26ha of wooded valley and cliffs, with a stream running through to a waterfall by the rocky beach.

Ravenscar, at the south of Robin Hood's Bay, has the **Coastal Centre** (open 10.30–5.30 daily, 29 March to 28 September), including rock pool aquarium, shop and local information. Refreshments and WC available in village [94: NZ980025]. The remains of the **Peak Alum Works** [94: NZ973024], just north of Ravenscar, are permanently accessible with information panels which explain the Alum industry and the Trust's consolidation of this early industrial site. Moving north, **Boggle Hole**, the headland at **Bayness**, and **Bottom House Farm** provide spectacular clifftop views. **Saltwick Nab**, just south of Whitby, is home to a variety of wild flowers and insects. North of Whitby, the Trust owns 11ha just north of **Runswick** village, and a further acquisition at **Port Mulgrave** has increased the holding of cliff and farmland there to almost 26ha.

The first acquisition on the Cleveland Heritage Coast was 61ha of cliff and farmland, capped by Warsett Hill – a popular local viewpoint. The Trust has also acquired 23ha of coastal land at **Hummersea**, to the north-east of Loftus, and 62ha at Loftus Alum Quarra, to the north-east of Loftus, and 62ha at **Loftus Alum Quarries**, near Boulby.

Further north, near Horden in **COUNTY DURHAM**, are two denes, **Warren House Gill** and **Foxholes Dene** (the Trust owns the southern half of this dene), connected by a narrow coastal strip; access from B1283 via footpaths [88: NZ444427]. This piece of coast marks the 500th mile acquired through the Trust's coastal appeal, Enterprise Neptune. South of Horden, the Trust owns around 53ha of clifftop, including **Blackhills Gill**: access via A1086. Just north of Easington, the Trust owns part of Hawthorne Dene and adjoining coastal strip, together with **Beacon Hill**, the highest point on the Durham coast. It provides spectacular views; access on foot through Hawthorne Dene [88: NZ425460].

At South Shields, the Trust owns 2½ml of spectacular coastline, from Trow Point to Lizard Point [88: NZ400650]. The property consists of **The Leas**, a large open area of grassland, bordered on the east by limestone cliffs, and **Marsden Rock**, with its famous bird colony of kittiwakes, cormorants and fulmars. Guided walks with the Warden take place on a regular basis during the season. At the southern end of this area is **Souter Lighthouse** (see p.130) with its complex of buildings [88: NZ641408].

The coast of **NORTHUMBERLAND** is one of the most beautiful stretches of English coastline, with its castles – some ruined, some in splendid repair – where you can enjoy miles of sandy beaches, links and sand dunes, nature reserves and rocky offshore islands.

If you are visiting Northumbria or Scotland by car, the A189 from the A1 north of Newcastle will take you within easy reach of **Druridge Bay** [81: NZ2896]; here the Trust owns a mile of coastline with 40ha of golden sand dunes and grassland, and further north there are dunes at **Alnmouth**. The A189 road rejoins the A1 at Alnwick, but B-roads lead to the starkly dramatic ruin of **Dunstanburgh Castle** (see p.118). From Craster the Trust owns a 5ml stretch of coastline, including **Embleton Links** [75:

NU243235] and **Low Newton-by-the-Sea** [75: NU241246]. Almost the whole of the square at Low Newton is owned by the Trust as well as **Newton Pool** [75: NU243240], a freshwater lake behind the dunes. This nature reserve is home to breeding birds such as blackheaded gull, teal, mute swan, dabchick, sedge warbler and reed bunting, and in winter goldeneye and pochard. Two hides are provided for birdwatchers, one adapted for disabled visitors with a wheelchair pathway. There are parking bays for disabled visitors at Low Newton. From Craster to Low Newton there is a beautiful 2½ml walk along the rocky coastline and the dunes. Information boards have been placed at the access points to help introduce this coastline to visitors.

The road leads on to **Beadnell Harbour** where the Trust owns the 18th-century sandstone **Lime Kilns** and just to the north, a ½ml of sand dunes [75: NU237286]. From Beadnell the B1340 hugs the coast for about 6ml to Bamburgh, passing **St Aidan's Dunes** [75: NU211327] with spectacular views of the **Farne Islands** (see p.120) on clear days. On the way, at Seahouses, is a Trust information centre and shop – and access to the Farnes. The Trust's coastal holdings in Northumberland culminate at **Lindisfarne Castle** on Holy Island (see p.124), from where there are views not only seawards, but inland to the Cheviot Hills. On all properties dogs must be kept under control at all times. Please keep to rights of way and permitted paths.

COUNTRYSIDE

Situated at the heart of the **SOUTH PENNINES**, **Hardcastle Crags** lies 1½ml north of Hebden Bridge. The estate, a wooded oasis surrounded by large tracts of moorland, comprises two steep-sided valleys covered by mixed woodland with craggy outcrops and tumbling streams. Rich in flowers, ferns, fungi and woodland fauna, the site is home to the rare northern hairy wood ant. Three waymarked trails run the length of the main Hebden valley. Self-guiding trail leaflets (small charge) are available from the information caravan, (open Sun all year; weekends in April, May, June & Oct; daily from last week June to first week Sept, incl. BHols). Wheelchair users can enjoy the main track, but most of the property is not accessible.

The riverside path passes the now disused **Gibson Mill**, built during the early 19th century, originally as a cotton mill. In later years the site was used by the Victorians as an entertainments centre. The mill is currently undergoing renovation work. Causeys, ancient paved packhorse trails, cross the estate. One leads up past **Slurring Rock**, a large boulder formerly used by children, who used to slide down it in their iron-shod clogs. Information on the programme of organised walks is available from the information caravan or the Warden (tel. 01422 844518). Parking at the entrance; cars £2 weekends and BHols, midweek £1.50; motorcycles 60p; minibuses £5; coaches £15 and by arrangement only. WC (not NT) located outside entrance to property [103: SD988291].

Nearly 2429ha of unenclosed SSSI moorland, almost surrounding the town of Marsden, form the **Marsden Moor Estate**. Stretching from Buckstones Moor north of the A640 to Wessenden Moor, north of the A635 [109: SE0210/0611]. This is wild, open country, forming the northern tip of the Peak District National Park, yet it has a surprising diversity of interest; valleys, reservoirs, peaks and crags and archaeological remains dating from pre-Roman settlements to the great engineering structures of the canal and railway age. Guided walks and events are held throughout the year and details, together with a new leaflet detailing five walks, can be obtained from the Marsden Moor Estate Office, The Old Goods Yard, Station Road, Marsden, Huddersfield HD7 6DH (please send s.a.e.). An information caravan is out and about on the estate most weekends between April and Sept, for details tel. 01484 847016. Whilst at

Marsden, also visit the Tunnel End Canal and Countryside Centre (not NT) to find out more about this fascinating area.

The two upland properties of **Malham Tarn Estate** and **Upper Wharfedale** protect some of the finest landscapes of the **YORKSHIRE DALES**, having impressive scenery with waterfalls and limestone pavements, hay meadows rich in wild flowers, and an internationally important wetland nature reserve. Tel/fax 01729 830416.

The 2860ha **Malham Tarn Estate** [98: SD8966] includes several large hill farms. In 1996 the 26ha New House Farm was acquired for nature conservation reasons. It has flower-rich hay meadows and the footpath from Lee Gate to Bordley runs through it. The Tarn and its wetlands are a National Nature Reserve and a wetland of international importance under the Ramsar Convention. The reserve is jointly managed by the National Trust and the Field Studies Council. Tarn House, overlooking the Tarn, was built in 1780 and is leased to the Field Studies Council and run as a Field Centre. The area has a rich flora, and characteristic upland breeding birds such as wheatear, curlew, lapwing and redshank. Great crested grebe, coot and tufted duck breed on the Tarn and can be seen from a bird hide situated at the north-west corner. The Pennine Way runs through the estate. Access to the Tarn on foot only; vehicular access for disabled visitors from Streetgate to the south-east of the Tarn along the estate road for about 1½ml, passing the Tarn shore. Near Malham village, the Trust owns the waterfall at **Janet's Foss**, and 38ha of the area forming the impressive amphitheatre of Malham Cove were acquired in 1992.

Upper Wharfedale, between Kettlewell and Beckermonds, amounts to some 2470ha, with grazing rights over a further 810ha. This area has some of the finest features of Dales landscape, including flower-rich hay meadows containing over a hundred field barns, mostly near the River Wharfe. On the hillsides, limestone pasture and acid moorland stretch to over 600m at the summit of Buckden Pike. The estate is criss-crossed with stone walls, dividing eight farms, and also includes 162ha of magnificent woodlands, waterfalls and a former deer park. The Dales Way runs through the property.

At **Stainforth**, the Trust owns a 17th-century single-span packhorse bridge across the River Ribble; once part of the route from Ripon to Lancaster [98: SD818672].

Hudswell: 54ha of semi-natural ancient woodland known as Calf Hall, Round Howe and Billy Bank Woods on the south bank of the River Swale, between Richmond and Hudswell village [92: NZ158005]. The woodlands are rich in flora and fauna and there are fine views across the River Swale. Part of the property is within the Lower Swaledale Woods and Grasslands SSSI. Access from Richmondshire DC car park off A6108, ¾ml west of Richmond town centre. 16ha of land at Hag Wood situated ½ml north-west of Hudswell. Access from the A6108.

Near the Cleveland Hills to the north, **Scarthwood Moor** gives fine views of the Pennines [94/100: SE465995] from its moorland heights. It provides a popular picnic site beside the stream at its valley floor. Further east, the Trust owns 13ha of mixed woodland known as **Farndale Woodlands** [94: SE654994]; Sonley, Sikehill & Hall Woods in Upper Farndale lie 8ml north of Kirkbymoorside, a valley famed for its wild daffodils. Access by foot from minor public highways running north from Church Houses.

Bridestones Moor [94: SE8791] lies within the **NORTH YORK MOORS NATIONAL PARK** on the edge of Dalby Forest, 12ml south of Whitby, 7ml north-east of Pickering and 1ml east of the A169. Part of the property is a nature reserve which can be reached by taking the Forestry Commission's Dalby Forest Drive, for which a charge is made. A car park with WCs [94: SE879904] is situated 3ml north-east of Low Dalby.

The reserve contains a variety of plants and animals typical of the North York Moors, in addition to the Bridestones, which are impressive and oddly-shaped sandstone outcrops. The Trust is currently carrying out important conservation work on this area of considerable natural history interest. Nature walk leaflet available.

Crosscliff and Blakey Topping. Crosscliff is an area of heather moorland ½ml north of Bridestones Moor, situated approximately 1½ml east of the Pickering-Whitby road, A169, 11ml south of Whitby. At the northern end of the property lies **Blakey Topping**, a curiously shaped conical hill, rising to a height of 263m above sea level. There are impressive all-round views from this point. The nearest car-parking is either at the National Park car park at the Hole of Horcum on the A169 [101: SE852938], or the Forestry Commission's Crosscliff viewpoint car park, just off the Dalby Forest Drive [101: SE896915].

The strange and fantastic rock formations of **Brimham Rocks** [99: SE2165], 8ml south-west of Ripon, off B6265, and 10ml north-west of Harrogate off the B6165, are set in open moorland overlooking Nidderdale. Information centre, shop & refreshment kiosk open daily June–Sept; April, May, Oct weekends; BHols and local school holidays; some winter weekends: 11–5. Parking: cars £1.80; motorcycles 70p; minibuses £3; coaches £7. An adapted WC for wheelchair users, special car-parking by arrangement, and a wheelchair are available. Dogs must be on leads in April, May & June, and thereafter under strict control; grazing animals. Tel. 01423 780688; fax 01423 781020.

To the north-east, and with panoramic views over the **CLEVELAND HILLS** and across Teeside to the North Sea. the bent pinnacle of **Roseberry Topping** [93: NZ575126) has been described as a miniature Matterhorn. The summit rises to 317m and the area has a long and romantic history. Prehistoric herdsmen and hunters occupied the site and to the Vikings it was a sacred hill. The Topping was used as a beacon station at the time of the Spanish Armada and during the Napoleonic Wars. Captain James Cook, one of the world's great navigators, worked with his father at Aireyholme Farm on the Topping's southern slopes. The Topping lies on the northern edge of the North York Moors National Park, south-west of Guisborough, and about 8ml south-east of Middlesbrough. Access is from the car park on the A173, 1ml north-east of Great Ayton [93: NZ571128]. The Trust's purchase of **Roseberry Common** and part of **Roseberry Topping** in 1985 included the northern and eastern slopes of the hill, as well as a stretch of heather moorland and an oakwood on its western flank; a total of some 122ha. Some 5ml to the north-west is **Ormesby Hall** (see p.128).

Just to the north of the city of **DURHAM** the Trust-owned **Moorhouse Woods** [88: NZ305460] offer peaceful woodland walks along the banks of the River Wear. Access to Moorhouse Woods can be gained from Leamside across a footbridge over the A1(M). At the village of **Ebchester** [88: NZ100551], in north-west County Durham, is a short woodland walk along the banks of the River Derwent.

Further east near the village of Penshaw, just off the A183 Sunderland road, can be found the well-known landmark of **Penshaw Monument** [88: NZ334544]. A Doric temple built in 1844 to commemorate the first Earl of Durham, it can be seen from miles around; car-parking in disused road at foot of monument. At **Gibside** (see p.123) new walks have been opened around the 18th-century landscaped park.

In **NORTHUMBERLAND**, the Allen and Tyne rivers meet 3ml west of Haydon Bridge off the A69, where nearby the Trust owns **Allen Banks** [86/87: NY799630] and leases **Staward Gorge**, together totalling over 202ha of hillside, woodland and riverside walks along the steep banks of the Allen; there is a picnic site in the car park, which is accessible to wheelchair users. **Bellister Pele Tower** [86: NY699631], sits in 445ha of Trust land, crossed by footpaths. Across the Tyne valley, 4ml north on the B6318, is access to the Trust's **Hadrian's Wall Estate** (see p.123). More than 1093ha of farmland, about 5ml of the course of the Hadrian's Wall, Vallum etc, including stretches of the stone wall and ditch, **Housesteads Fort**, several milecastles and, at Shield on the Wall, one of the best preserved sections of the Vallum, form one of the Trust's most fascinating and breathtaking antiquities. There is an adapted WC for wheelchair users at **Housesteads** car park; dogs on leads only.

7ml west of Rothbury at Holystone on the edge of the Cheviots is **The Lady Well**, which has probable associations with St Ninian [81: NT953029]. Views of the Cheviots, Lindisfarne, and surrounding countryside can be seen from the hilltop of **Ros Castle** [75: NU081253] near Wooler between the A1 and the A697. North-east of Wooler near Holburn Grange is a natural stone cave in the Kyloe Hills – **St Cuthbert's Cave**, where the saint's body is said to have rested on its journey from Lindisfarne to Durham [75: NU059352].

At Wallington (see p.131), the Trust owns 5263ha of beautiful countryside. The land is farmed, but with the agreement of the farmers, circular walks are open during the summer months for visitors to the estate. Walks leaflets are available at Wallington and they introduce the walker to the geology, history, flora and fauna of the area. The 405ha **Cragside House, Garden and Grounds** (see p.116) is a must for walkers: 40ml of footpaths and carriage drives are available. The Power Circuit, a 1½ml circular walk, highlights the industrial archaeology of Cragside. It includes the restored hydraulic and hydro-electric machinery at the Ram and Power Houses and the Iron Bridge, one of the first steel bridges in the world. Walks leaflets are available at the visitor centre. During June, the grounds come alive with a superb display of rhododendrons and azaleas and in the autumn the colours are quite breathtaking. There is also the Armstrong Energy Centre, an exhibition of energy technology, and the formal garden originally part of Lord Armstrong's estate.

BENINGBROUGH HALL AND GARDENS 🏠 🏠 ❖ 🏃 E

Shipton-by-Beningbrough, York YO6 1DD Tel: 01904 470666 Fax: 01904 470002

John Bourchier built this imposing Georgian hall in 1716. The beautiful house, set in 148ha, contains over 100 pictures on loan from the National Portrait Gallery, an impressive cantilevered staircase, furniture and porcelain. There is a Victorian laundry, a potting shed and a 3ha garden. Exciting new walled garden (picnic and events area remain open). Garden gallery exhibition describes plans, progress reports and news. Also Pike Ponds walk, monthly exhibition and croquet available for hire

Note: Most rooms have no electric lights. Visitors wishing to make a close study of the interior and portraits should avoid dull days early and late in the season. The house may be closed for up to 1hr on Fri for wedding ceremonies to take place. Contact the property for more information

🅾 29 March to 2 Nov: Sat to Wed, Good Fri & Fri in July and Aug. **House:** 11–5. Last admission 4.30. **Grounds:** 11–5.30. Last admission 5. **Events:** 7 Sept, Great Autumn Plant Fair; Christmas concerts; wedding ceremonies and receptions; contact Assistant Property Manager for details

£ House, garden & exhibition: £4.50, children £2.30; family ticket (2 adults & 3 children) £9. Discount ticket for cyclists. Party rates available; for full details tel. 01765 601005 and ask for group visits information or contact the Assistant Property Manager (tel. 01904 470666). Garden & exhibition only: £3, children £1.50; family ticket £6. School groups and parties by prior arrangement. For conservation reasons pushchairs are not allowed in the house

K Guided garden walks most weekends, 1.30 and 3

⬚ Open as grounds

♿ Access to ground floor only, by ramp; level garden paths (embedded gravel); parking spaces by stable block. Restaurant, shop, garden exhibition and laundry accessible; WC in stable block. Wheelchairs available

👁 Braille guides for house and garden; guided tours by arrangement

🍽 Home-made hot & cold lunches, coffee & teas in licensed restaurant, open as grounds. Kiosk open busy days. Special functions and pre-booked parties by arrangement

👶 Baby-changing and feeding room. Baby slings available. Children's menu & highchairs in restaurant. Children's guidebook. Wilderness playground. Full programme of events for families

▦ Victorian 'Below-stairs'; artwork with portraits; archive of materials

🐕 Strictly no dogs allowed in house or garden

➔ 8ml NW of York, 2ml W of Shipton, 2ml SE of Linton-on-Ouse (A19) [105: SE516586] *Bus:* Rider York 31/B, 32 from ⭍ York–Newton-on-Ouse, thence 1ml (tel. 01904 624161) *Station:* York 8ml; also, on Route 65 of National Cycle Network

---

BRAITHWAITE HALL 🏠

East Witton, Leyburn DL8 4SY Tel: 01969 640287

This 17th-century hall is now a working farmhouse with 303ha of moor and farmland. It is a family home, furnished by the tenants, and contains oak panelling, staircase and fireplaces

⬚ By arrangement with the tenant, Mrs David Duffus

£ £1 incl. leaflet. No reduction for children. No access for coaches. No WC

➔ 1½ml SW of Middleham, 2ml W of East Witton (A6108) [99: SE117857]

CHERRYBURN 🏠🏠❈🚜🔸 E

Station Bank, Mickley, Nr Stocksfield NE43 7DB Tel: 01661 843276

The birthplace of Thomas Bewick, Northumbria's greatest artist, wood-engraver and naturalist (b.1753). The 19th-century farmhouse, latter home of the Bewick family, houses a small exhibition on Bewick's life and works. Printing house in adjoining barn. Also birthplace cottage, farmyard animals and garden for picnics. Beautiful views of Tyne Valley and short walk from the south bank of the River Tyne, where Bewick spent much of his childhood

🅾️ 28 March to end Oct: daily except Tues and Wed 1–5.30. Last admission 5. **Events**: wood-engraving, book-binding and printing; free demonstrations most days. Please tel. for details. Maypole, country and clog dancing on May Day. 9 August, Grand Ceilidh to celebrate Bewick's birthday (tickets £5 each, cheques payable NT, s.a.e. to Administrator)

💷 £2.70. Pre-booked coach parties welcome; exclusive use of property Mon, Thur & Fri mornings only (s.a.e. to Administrator for booking form)

🅰️ Shop selling prints from Bewick's original engravings, books & mementoes, located in the farmhouse at Cherryburn

♿ Some gravel paths; few steps; cobbled farmyard, companion necessary; ramped pathway from car park, level entry to front of property (usual visitor entrance), then two steps inside property. WC. Car park 100m from house entrance

👁️ Braille booklet 'Discover Thomas Bewick at Cherryburn'; smooth and engraved woodblocks may be touched

☕ Morning coffee available for pre-booked parties

🧒 Farmyard animals usually include donkeys, pigs, poultry, lambs. Picnicking in grounds. Play lawn. Annual art competition

🏫 Pre-booked school parties welcome Mon, Thur & Fri mornings only. Wood-engraving and printing demonstrations. Art, artists. Local history and life in 17th- and 18th-centuries. Farmyard animals. Maypole and country dance with instruction. Exclusive use of property for each school visit. 'School Visits' leaflet available (s.a.e. to Administrator)

🐕 No dogs

➡️ 11ml W of Newcastle, 11ml E of Hexham; ¼ml N of Mickley Square (leave A695 at Mickley Square and follow signposts). Cherryburn situated close to S bank of River Tyne [88: NZ075627]. Free car park at property *Bus:* Northumbria 602 Newcastle–Hexham (passes ⮂ Newcastle) (tel: 0191 212 3000) *Station:* Stocksfield (U) 1½ml; Prudhoe (U) 1½ml

CRAGSIDE HOUSE, GARDEN AND GROUNDS
🏠 🅰️ ✽ 🌳 ⬆️ 🧍 🅴

Rothbury, Morpeth NE65 7PX Tel: 01669 620333/620266

A Victorian mansion, mainly designed by R. Norman Shaw, in 405ha of grounds created by the 1st Lord Armstrong. It was the first house in the world to be lit by hydroelectricity; the system was developed by Armstrong with manmade lakes and underground piping. He also planted millions of trees and shrubs and built 40ml of drives and footpaths. 'The Power Circuit', a 1½ml circular walk, includes the restored Ram and Power Houses with their hydraulic and hydroelectric machinery, and, in the visitor centre, the Armstrong Energy Centre. The remarkable Orchard House, ferneries, rose loggia and Italian garden are within walking distance of the house; car-parking on site. The restored 19th-century clocktower can be seen by visitors to the garden

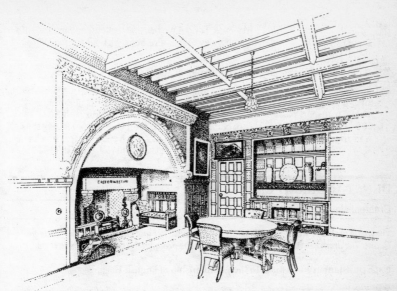

House: 28 March to end Oct: daily except Mon but open BH Mon, 1–5.30. Last admission 4.45. **Grounds:** same days as house 10.30–7. Last admission 5. Also 1 Nov to 14 Dec: Tues, Sat & Sun 10.30–4. **Garden:** 28 March to end Oct; same days as grounds 10.30–6.30 and 1 Nov to 14 Dec 10.30–4. **Events:** for details please send s.a.e. to Property Manager

House, garden, grounds & visitor centre £5.80; family ticket (2 adults, 2 children) £15; pre-booked parties £5.50. Garden, grounds & visitor centre only £3.80; pre-booked parties £3.50. Accompanied children 12 and under free during school holidays. Car park 100m from house (9 car parks in grounds). New car park to rear of gardens: access from main entrance. Coach park 350m (advance booking essential). Please note coaches cannot tour grounds as drive is too narrow in places. Mini-bus for tour of grounds available to groups visiting by coach, must be booked in advance

Visitor centre (including shop), Vickers Rooms restaurant, information centre, Armstrong Energy Centre and natural history exhibition: same days as house: 10.30–5.30; 1 Nov to 14 Dec: Tues, Sat & Sun 12–4 (tel. 01669 620448)

Parking for disabled drivers in designated areas of car parks; disabled passengers may be set down at house. Access to house (lift to first floor) & shop and restaurant in visitor centre. WC at visitor centre & by house and Crozier Drive car park; wheelchair path, adapted picnic tables & parking at Nelly's Moss Upper Lake

Braille guides

Morning coffee, lunches and teas in Vickers Rooms restaurant in visitor centre (tel. 01669 620134). Picnicking in all car parks and around Nelly's Moss Lakes

Front sling baby carriers available; facilities for parents and babies, including use of private room for nursing mothers. Adventure playground at Dunkirk car park. Children's guide

⬛ Education Room/School party base. School parties may visit all attractions with a guide. Resource book for teachers available. Pre-book with Education Officer (tel. 01669 621445)

🐾 In grounds only (not in formal garden)

➡ 13ml SW of Alnwick (B6341) and 15ml NW of Morpeth on Wooler road (A697), turn left on to B6341 at Moorhouse Crossroads, entrance ¾ml N of Rothbury; public transport passengers enter by Reivers Well Gate from Morpeth Road (B6344) [81: NU073022] *Bus:* Northumbria 516 Morpeth–Thropton, Postbus 817 (both passing ⇌ Morpeth) with connections from Newcastle (passing Tyne & Wear Metro Haymarket), alight Reivers Well Gate, ¾ml (tel. 01670 533128)

DUNSTANBURGH CASTLE 🏚 🖼 🧍

Craster, Alnwick Tel: 01665 576231

The castle was built in 1316 by Thomas Earl of Lancaster and enlarged later by John of Gaunt. The dramatic ruin encloses 4.5ha of dolerite promontory with sea cliffs to the north

Note: Dunstanburgh Castle is in the guardianship of English Heritage

🅾 27 March to 31 Oct: daily 10–6 (closes 4 in Oct); 1 Nov to 31 March 1998: Wed to Sun 10–4 (closed 24 to 26 Dec & 1 Jan)

£ Adults £1.60; concessions £1.20; children 80p. Car parks at Craster & Embleton, 1½ml (no coaches at Embleton)

🛍 Shop

♿ Castle unsuitable for wheelchairs. WC at Craster car park

🍽 In Craster (not NT)

⬛ Free school visits. Book through EH (tel. 0191 261 1585)

🐾 Must be kept on leads

➡ 9ml NE of Alnwick, approached from Craster on S and Embleton on N (pedestrians only) [75: NU258220] *Bus:* Northumbria 501 Alnwick–Berwick-upon-Tweed (passing close ⇌ Berwick-upon-Tweed) with connections from Newcastle (passing Tyne & Wear Metro Haymarket), alight Craster, 1½ml (tel. 0191 212 3000) *Station:* Chathill (U), not Sun, 5ml from Embleton, 7ml from Castle; Alnmouth, 7ml from Craster, 8¼ml from Castle

---

EAST RIDDLESDEN HALL 🏠 🏠 ✳ E

Bradford Road, Keighley BD20 5EL Tel: 01535 607075 Fax: 01535 691462

A charming 17th-century West Yorkshire manor house with panelled rooms, fine plasterwork and mullioned windows, providing an ideal setting for embroideries, pewter and Yorkshire oak furniture. Attractive garden with herbaceous borders, monastic fish pond and grass maze in the picnic field. Also an impressive timber-framed Great Barn with a collection of traditional agricultural implements

29 March to 2 Nov: Sat 1–5, Sun 11–5, Mon to Wed 12–5; closed Thur & Fri, except for Good Fri & Thur in July & Aug, when open 12–5. Last admission 4.30. **Events:** July & Aug, costumed interpretation; for details of this and of full events programme send s.a.e. marked 'Events' to the Property Manager

£3, child £1.50; family ticket (2 adults & 3 children) £7.50. Party rates available; for full details tel. 01765 601005 and ask for group visits information or contact the Property Manager. Parking 100m; coaches must book as space limited. School groups and parties by arrangement. Open for pre-booked parties outside normal opening hours, private functions and wedding ceremonies and receptions

Shop and information area in Bothy, open as house (but opens at 12 on Sat). Also some Christmas opening

Access to ground floor and garden; some uneven surfaces; loose gravel paths. Spaces reserved for disabled drivers in car park. Shop accessible via some steps. Tea-room on first floor of Bothy. Unadapted WC with access via some steps. Access to Great Barn (uneven floor) and Airedale Barn for events only. Sympathetic Hearing Scheme

Braille guide, large-print guide and tactile book; panelling and carving may be touched. Guided tours for groups of visually impaired visitors, Mon only

Tea-room serving lunches and afternoon teas, open as property (but opens at 12 on Sat); also some Christmas openings. Open for pre-booked parties during and outside normal opening hours. Tea-room and Airedale Barn available for private functions. Picnic area in field

Changing facilities; highchairs and children's menu in tea-room. Children's guidebook. Children's activity days & workshops

Living History for schools (details from Assistant Property Manager)

In grounds only, on leads. Not permitted in garden

1ml NE of Keighley on S side of the Bradford Road in Riddlesden, close to Leeds & Liverpool Canal [104: SE079421] *Bus:* Frequent services from ⇌ Bradford Interchange, Bingley & Keighley (tel. 0113 245 7676) *Station:* Keighley 1ml

FARNE ISLANDS ✝ 🏞 ▶ 🚶

Information Centre Tel: 01665 721099 Warden Tel: 01665 720651

The islands provide a summer home for over 17 different species of seabird, including puffin, kittiwake, eider duck, guillemot, fulmar and terns. Large colony of grey seals. St Cuthbert died on Inner Farne in 687 and there is a chapel built in his memory in the 14th century and restored 1845

O Inner Farne and Staple Islands only are open to visitors. 28 March to 30 April & 1 Aug to 30 Sept: daily 10.30–6. During breeding season (1 May to 31 July) access is limited to Staple 10.30–1.30, Inner Farne 1.30–5. Visitors to Inner Farne are advised to wear hats!

£ May to end July £3.80; pre-booked school parties £1.80 (per island). At other times £2.90; pre-booked school parties £1.50 (per island). Public car park in Seahouses opposite harbour. Admission fees do not include boatmen's charges. Tickets may be bought from Warden on landing and boat tickets from boatmen in Seahouses Harbour. No landing in bad weather. Enquiries about landing answered by Property Manager: The Sheiling, 8 St Aidan's, Seahouses, Northumberland NE68 7SR (tel. 01665 720651). WC on Inner Farne

🛒 NT Information Centre and shop at 16 Main Street, Seahouses (tel. 01665 721099); open 24 March to 30 Sept: 10–5 (till 6 during July & Aug); Oct: daily 11–4.30 (except half-term, when 10–5); Nov to 24 Dec: Wed to Sun 11–4

♿ Nature walks on Inner Farne & Staple Island. Islands are difficult for disabled or visually impaired visitors and largely unsuitable for wheelchairs; some wheelchair access to Inner Farne. Please tel. Property Manager before attempting this. WC on Inner Farne

🍴 Refreshments (not NT) in Seahouses (none on islands)

📕 Teachers' resource book. Guided walks available

➡ 2–5ml off the Northumberland coast, opposite Bamburgh: trips every day from Seahouses Harbour, weather permitting [75: NU2337] *Bus:* As for Dunstanburgh Castle, but alight Seahouses *Station:* Chathill (U), not Sun, 4ml

---

FOUNTAINS ABBEY & STUDLEY ROYAL WATER GARDEN
🏠 🏡 ✝ ♣ ♠ 🚶 E

Fountains, Ripon HG4 3DY Estate Office Tel: 01765 608888; fax: 01765 608889
Visitor Centre Tel: 01765 601005; fax: 01765 601002

One of the most remarkable sites in Europe, sheltered in a secluded valley, Fountains Abbey and Studley Royal, a World Heritage Site, encompasses the spectacular ruin of a 12th-century Cistercian abbey, an Elizabethan mansion, and one of the best surviving examples of a Georgian green water garden. Elegant ornamental lakes, avenues, temples and cascades provide a succession of unforgettable eye-catching vistas in an atmosphere of peace and tranquillity. St Mary's Church, built by William Burges in the 19th century, provides a dramatic focal point to the medieval deer park with over 600 deer

Note: Audiovisual programme and exhibition at visitor centre; small museum near to Abbey; exhibitions in Fountains Hall and Swanley Grange. Abbey maintained by English Heritage: St Mary's Church owned by English Heritage, managed by the NT

◐ Abbey and water garden: open all year daily except Fri in Nov, Dec, Jan and 24/25 Dec. April to Sept: 10–7 (closes at 4 on 11/12 July & 9 Aug); Oct to March 1998: 10–5 (dusk if earlier). Last admission 1hr before closing. **Deer park:** open all year daily during daylight hours. **Floodlighting:** Abbey is floodlit on Fri and Sat evenings until 10pm, 22 Aug to 11 Oct. **Fountains Hall & St Mary's Church:** restoration in progress, apply to Estate Office for opening times. Charge may be reduced on and around event days (11/12 July) due to restricted access to parts of estate. **Events:** extensive programme of concerts, plays, walks & talks available all year, incl. 19 to 21 June, Shakespeare theatre; 11/12 July, Music by Moonlight; 24 to 26 July, theatre; 9 Aug, outdoor promenade entertainment. Details from Box Office (tel. 01765 609999). All outside events wheelchair-accessible. Join free events mailing list

£ Fountains Abbey and Studley Royal Water Garden: £4.20, children £2; family ticket (2 adults & 3 children) £10. Parties over 15 £3.70, children £1.90; parties over 40 (pre-booked only) £3.20, children £1.70. Visitor centre, deer park, St Mary's Church: free. Parking: visitor centre free; deer park £2

⚑ Free guided tours of the Abbey and water garden plus extended tours of the complete estate. Floodlit tours of the Abbey 22 Aug to 10 Oct, Fri 7.45pm & 8.15pm. Specialist guides for pre-booked parties (50p per person) (tel. 01765 601005)

⌂ Visitor centre shop: open all year except 24/25 Dec & Fri in Jan, April to Aug 10–6, Sept to March 10–5 (or dusk if earlier) (tel. 01765 601004). Lakeside shop open as estate

♿ Minibus available from visitor centre; wheelchairs and self-drive powered vehicle available by prior booking only (tel. 01765 601005); Sympathetic Hearing Scheme. WCs at visitor centre, lakeside tea-room and near Fountains Hall. Wheelchair access: most of the estate accessible, enquire for best route. Paths from visitor centre unsuitable for any self-drive vehicle due to gradient; it is also strongly advised that three-wheeled powered vehicles are not used elsewhere on the estate because of the terrain. Four-wheel battery cars restricted to certain areas. For level access to Abbey use West Gate entrance (see information boards in disabled car park)

◉ Large-print and Braille guides available from visitor centre. Tactile wall frieze and model of Abbey at visitor centre

⬛ Visitor centre restaurant: licensed, serving coffee, teas and a wide variety of home-made lunches; party bookings and functions welcome (tel. 01765 601003). Open daily, same times as visitor centre shop. Lakeside tea-room: light lunches, teas & refreshments; open daily April to end Sept 10–5.30 or dusk if earlier (tel. 01765 604246). *Note:* tea-room may close for major building work Oct to March 1998

👶 Parent & baby rooms available at visitor centre and near Fountains Hall. Highchairs & children's menu in restaurant. Children's guide, programme of family and children's activities

📕 Special facilities linked to National Curriculum for pre-booked parties; for details contact Education Officer (tel. 01765 608888); also new study centre at Swanley Grange

🐕 On short leads

➔ 4ml W of Ripon off B6265 to Pateley Bridge, signposted from the A1, 10ml N of Harrogate (A61) [99: SE271683] *Bus:* Angloblue 802 Bradford–Ripon (with connections from 🚉 Harrogate), Sun, June to Aug only (tel. 01609 780780); otherwise United 145 from Ripon (with connections from 🚉 Harrogate), Thur & Sat only (tel. 01325 468771)

GEORGE STEPHENSON'S BIRTHPLACE 🏠 👶 🎓

Wylam NE41 8BP Tel: 01661 853457

A small stone tenement built c.1760 to accommodate four pitmen's families. The furnishings reflect the age of George Stephenson's birth here in 1781; the room in which he was born and in which the whole family lived, is open to visitors

🅾 28 March to 2 Nov: Thur, Sat & Sun, BH Mon & Good Fri 1–5.30. Last admission 5. The property may be closed for building works for part of the season. Please contact the Regional Office before visiting (tel. 01670 774691)

💷 80p. Accompanied children aged 12 and under free during school summer holidays. Access by foot and bicycle through Country Park. No parties. No WC. Parking by War Memorial in Wylam village, ½ml

➔ 8ml W of Newcastle, 1½ml S of A69 at Wylam. Access on foot and bicycle through Country Park, ½ml E of Wylam [88: NZ126650] *Bus:* OK Travel 684 Newcastle–Ovington, alight Wylam, 1ml (tel. 01388 450000) *Station:* Wylam (U) ½ml

GIBSIDE ✝ 👤 ♿ 🚻 🚶 Ⓔ

nr Rowlands Gill, Burnopfield, Newcastle-upon-Tyne NE16 6BG
Tel: 01207 542255

Gibside's 18th-century landscape, one of the finest in the north, was created by George Bowes and his successors, the Bowes-Lyon Earls of Strathmore. The landscape of this great 'Forest Garden' is being gradually restored. 143ha of grounds embrace many miles of walks in woodland, along grand vistas and beside the River Derwent, and provide a setting for outstanding buildings: Paine's Palladian chapel, the Column of Liberty, Garrett's banqueting house (a Landmark Trust property) and others, including the orangery and hall, now picturesque ruins awaiting consolidation

🅾 28 March to 2 Nov: Grounds & chapel, daily except Mon (open BH Mon) 11–5. Last admission 4.30. *Note:* the property will be closed 3 to 8 November incl. Winter opening (grounds only): 9 Nov to 29 March 1998, Sun only: 10–4. **Events:** service in Chapel first Sun each month at 3. 18 & 19 July, open-air concerts; for details of these and other events, including guided walks, please send s.a.e. to Administrator

£ £3. Pre-booked parties £2.60. Winter opening (grounds only) £2

🛍 Shop (tel. 01207 545801)

♿ Please contact Administrator for access arrangements. Stairclimber available for Chapel steps; essential to book in advance. 1 wheelchair available. WC

👁 Braille guide

🍴 Tea-room (tel. 01207 545801). Picnic area in car park

🐕 In the grounds, on leads only

➔ 6ml SW of Gateshead, 20ml W of Durham; entrance on B6314 between Burnopfield and Rowlands Gill [88: NZ172583] *Bus:* Go-Ahead Gateshead 611, M21; Northern 745 from Newcastle (passing close ⭫ Newcastle). On all, alight Rowlands Gill, ½ml (tel. 0191 232 5325) *Station:* Blaydon (U) 5ml

HADRIAN'S WALL & HOUSESTEADS FORT ♿ 🏛

Bardon Mill, Hexham NE47 6NN Tel: (EH Custodian) 01434 344363

The Trust owns approx. 5ml of the Wall running west from Housesteads Fort (including the Fort itself) and over 1000ha of farmland. Access to the Wall and the public rights of way is from car parks at Housesteads, Steel Rigg and Cawfields Quarry. Housesteads Fort is owned by the National Trust, and maintained and managed by English Heritage

🅾 **Housesteads Fort & Museum:** 27 March to 30 Sept: daily, 10–6. 1 Oct to 31 March 1998: daily 10–4 (closed 24 to 26 Dec & 1 Jan)

£ Hadrian's Wall, NT information centre and shop free. Housesteads Museum & Fort: Adults £2.50. OAP/UB40/students £1.90, children £1.30. Free admission to English Heritage members. Car & coach parks at Housesteads (free to NT members), ½ml walk to the Fort, and at the western end at Steel Rigg and Cawfields Quarry, managed by the Northumberland National Park

▦ For details of guided walks send s.a.e. to information centre and shop

▣ Shop & information centre at Housesteads car park (times subject to revision):
March: Sat & Sun 11–5; April & Oct: daily 11–5; May to end Sept: daily 10–5;
Nov: Sat & Sun 11–dusk (tel. 01434 344525)

♿ Access to information centre and shop only; parking available near Housesteads
Fort; ask at information centre for details. WC at information centre and shop.
Fort not suitable for wheelchair users

▣ Braille guides

▣ Hot and cold drinks, sandwiches and ice cream at shop. Picnicking

▣ Children's guide

▣ Must be kept on leads

➔ 6ml NE of Haltwhistle, 3ml N of Bardon Mill Rly station; ½ml N of B6318; best
access from car parks at Housesteads and Cawfields [87: NY790688]
Bus: Waugh's 890 Hadrian's Wall service, Apr–Oct only, ⇌ Hexham–
⇌ Haltwhistle (tel. 01670 533128) *Station:* Bardon Mill (U) 4ml

---

LINDISFARNE CASTLE ▦ ❀ ▥ ⬚

Holy Island, Berwick-upon-Tweed TD15 2SH Tel: 01289 389244

*Built in 1550 to protect Holy Island harbour from attack, the castle was restored and
converted into a private house by Sir Edwin Lutyens in 1903. Small walled garden was
designed by Gertrude Jekyll. 19th-century lime kilns in field by the castle*

Note: It is impossible to cross to the island between the 2hrs before high tide and the
3½hrs following. Tide tables are printed in local newspapers, and displayed at the
causeway. *Special note*: To avoid disappointment please check safe crossing times
coincide with castle opening times before making a long/special journey

◎ 28 March to 30 Oct: daily except Fri (but open Good Fri) 1–5.30. Last admission
5. Admission to garden only when gardener is in attendance (usually Fri but
please check with Administrator before making a special journey). Tide and
staffing levels permitting, open 11–5 in July & Aug (certain days only; tel. for
details)

£ £3.80; family ticket (2 adults, 2 children under 17) £10. No party rate. Parties
of 15 or more must pre-book. No WC. Main public car park approx. 1ml away;
parking off approach road to castle for disabled orange badge holders only, car-
parking charges (incl. NT members). No large camera cases, boxes or rucksacks

▣ NT shop in Main Street, Holy Island Village (tel. 01289 389253)

♿ Difficult for ambulant disabled people and not recommended to wheelchair users;
steep, cobbled access ramp, many steps and stairs within castle

▣ Braille guide

▣ In Holy Island Village (not NT)

▣ No back-packs in castle (including framed baby carriers); front sling baby carriers
available

⊞ On leads as far as Lower Battery only

→ On Holy Island, 6ml E of A1 across causeway [75: NU136417] *Bus:* Northumbria 477 from Berwick-upon-Tweed (passing close ≈ Berwick-upon-Tweed). Times vary with tides (tel. 01670 533128 – bus times only) *Station:* Berwick-upon-Tweed 10ml from causeway

---

MAISTER HOUSE ⊞

160 High Street, Hull HU1 1NL Tel: 01482 324114

Rebuilt in 1744, the house contains a superb staircase hall designed in the Palladian manner and ironwork by Robert Bakewell; let as offices

◯ Staircase and entrance hall only: all year: Mon to Fri 10–4; closed BH Mon, Good Fri & 1 Jan

£ 80p, incl. guidebook. Unsuitable for parties. No parking at property. No WC

→ Hull city centre *Bus:* Local services to within 100m (tel. 01482 222222); services from surrounding areas (tel. 01482 327146) *Station:* Hull ¾ml

---

MOULTON HALL ⊞ 🏛

Moulton, Richmond DL10 6QH Tel: 01325 377227

Compact manor house of 1650, with fine carved-wood staircase

◯ By arrangement with tenant, the Hon. J. D. Eccles

£ 50p. Unsuitable for coaches

♿ Please enquire about access when arranging a visit

→ 5ml E of Richmond; turn off A1, ½ml S of Scotch Corner [99: NZ235035] *Bus:* United 35/A Darlington–Richmond (passing close ≈ Darlington), alight Moulton village, ½ml (tel. 01325 468771) *Station:* Darlington 9½ml

---

MOUNT GRACE PRIORY ✚ 🛈 ℇ

Osmotherley, Northallerton DL6 3JG Tel: 01609 883494

The greater part of the remains of a 14th-century priory, this is the most important Carthusian ruin in England. There is a reconstructed and furnished cell on show, an exhibition on the Carthusians and NT/EH information room. Nature trail at front of priory. Leaflet available in shop. Herb garden

Note: The priory is financed, administered and maintained by English Heritage

◯ 27 March to 31 October: daily 10–6 (closes 4 in Oct). 1 Nov to 31 March: Wed to Sun 10–4; closed 1–2. **Events:** diary of events available in shop free of charge, or tel. 0191 261 1585

£ £2.50; OAPs, students and UB40 holders £1.90; children (under 16) £1.30. Parties of 11 or more 15% discount. NT members free, except on certain special event days, when full admission price will be charged. School visits Mon to Fri, free, but must be booked with EH (tel. 0191 261 1585). Bulky bags and pushchairs may be left in reception

🛍 Shop; herbs for sale May to Aug

♿ Disabled visitors may bring car up to entrance. Access to grounds, shop and ground floor of reconstructed cell and the herb garden

❋ Wild flowers and herbs; bird song and animal sounds

🍴 Light refreshments i.e. canned drinks, biscuits, available in shop. Picnics welcome

🏫 School visits free Mon to Fri. Must be booked in advance through EH (tel. 0191 261 1585)

🐕 No dogs, except guide dogs

➜ 6ml NE of Northallerton, ½ml E of A19 and ½ml S of its junction with A172 [99: SE449985] *Bus:* Tees 90, 190 ⇌ Northallerton–Middlesbrough, alight Priory Road End, ½ml (tel. 01642 210131) *Station:* Northallerton 6ml

---

NOSTELL PRIORY 🏛 ❀ 👤 E

Doncaster Road, Nostell, nr Wakefield WF4 1QE
Tel: 01924 863892 Fax: 01924 865282

A fine Palladian house, built for the Winn family in the 18th century. An additional wing and many of the state rooms were designed by Adam. Fine collection of Chippendale furniture, specially made for the house. Delightful lakeside walks through the grounds

Note: Nostell Priory is managed by Lord St Oswald

🅾 29 March to 26 Oct: April, May, June, Sept & Oct: Sat 12–5, Sun 11–5; July, Aug to 4 Sept: daily except Fri 12–5, Sun & BH Mon 11–5 & following Tues 12–5. Closed Good Fri & May Day Tues. Last admission 4.30. **Events:** 20 July, Country Fair

£ House & grounds: £3.80, children £2; family ticket (2 adults & 3 children) £9.50. Party rates available; for full details tel. 01765 601005 and ask for group visits information or contact the Administrator. Grounds only: £2.50, children £1.30; family ticket £6.30. Pre-booked parties welcome outside published opening times (no reduction and charge made for NT members). Min. charge for parties of fewer than 30. Parking 350m. NT members may be expected to pay additional charge for access to grounds during special events. For conservation reasons pushchairs must be left in reception

👤 Guided tours only on weekdays (last tour 4); free-flow visiting at weekends

🛍 2 gift shops (not NT)

♿ Disabled visitors may usually be driven to front door. Level access to ground floor. Lift to first floor; grounds accessible; wheelchairs and powered self-drive venicle available. Restaurant accessible. WC. Tape guide; loop system; rollators

⊙ Braille guide and audio tour; tactile books

☕ Light lunches and teas in stable block (not NT). Meals available to parties, by arrangement (tel. 01924 862205 or 375910). Picnic site

⚲ Baby-changing facilities and feeding area; baby carriers

⚮ In grounds only, on leads

➔ On the A638 out of Wakefield towards Doncaster [111: SE407172] *Bus:* W Riding/Yorkshire Traction/Yorkshire Rider 485, 497/8 Wakefield–Doncaster; W Riding 123 from Wakefield; Yorkshire Traction 245 from Pontefract (tel. 0113 245 7676) *Station:* Fitzwilliam 1½ml

---

NUNNINGTON HALL 🏛 ✳ E

Nunnington, York YO6 5UY Tel: 01439 748283 Fax: 01439 748284

The sheltered walled garden on the bank of the River Rye with its peacocks, ducks, orchard and clematis collection, complements this mellow 17th-century manor house. From the magnificent oak-panelled hall, follow three staircases to discover family rooms, the nursery, the haunted room and the attics, with their fascinating Carlisle collection of miniature rooms fully furnished to reflect different periods

◉ 26 March to 2 Nov: daily except Mon & Tues (but open BH Mon & every Tues during June, July & Aug) 1.30–6 (1.30–5.30 April & Oct); last admission 1hr before house closes. **Events:** varied programme of exhibitions and events through the year; contact Visitor Manager for details

£ House & garden £3.80, children £1.90; family ticket £9. Party rates available, for full details tel. 01765 601005 and ask for Group Visits Information or contact the Visitor Manager (tel. 01439 748283). Garden only £1; children free. For conservation reasons pushchairs, prams and back-packs are not allowed in the house. Car parking 50m; unsuitable for trailer caravans

▣ Open as house

♿ Access to ground floor and tea-room only. Garden tables by river. Ramp to main garden; loose gravel paths. For close parking please apply at Reception; adapted WC. Wheelchairs available

👁 Braille guide; river, peacock and duck sounds; garden scents

🔒 Tea-room and tea-garden serving home-made teas, sandwiches, scones, cakes and pastries. Open as house, closes 30min after last admission

💀 Baby-changing facilities. Children's menu and highchairs in tea-room. Collection of miniature rooms. Children's guide. Quiz

💀 Contact the Visitor Manager for details

💀 In car park only; shaded woodland

➡ In Ryedale, 4½ml SE of Helmsley (A170) Helmsley–Pickering road; 1½ml N of B1257 Malton–Helmsley road [100: SE670795]; 21ml N of York, B1363. Nunnington Hall is 7½ml SE of the NT Rievaulx Terrace and Temples
Bus: Yorkshire Coastliner 94 ⋙ Malton–Helmsley (tel. 01653 692556); otherwise Scarborough & District/Stephensons 128 Scarborough–Helmsley (passing close ⋙ Scarborough & Seamer), alight Wombleton, 3ml (tel. 01609 780780)

ORMESBY HALL ■ ■ ■ ■ E

Ormesby, Middlesbrough TS7 9AS Tel: 01642 324188 Fax: 01642 300937

A mid 18th-century house, home of the Pennyman family, with fine plasterwork and carved woodwork; Victorian laundry and kitchen with scullery and game larders. A large model railway exhibition housed in the 17th-century wing, where the family crest survives over the door from the earlier house. An attractive 2ha garden with holly walk. The stable block, attributed to Carr of York, is a particularly fine mid 18th-century building which is leased to Cleveland Constabulary Mounted Police

🔷 29 March to 2 Nov: Wed, Thur, Sat, Sun, BH Mon & Good Fri 2–5.30; June, July & Aug: Wed to Sun 1.30–5.30. Last admission 5. *Note:* Fri access is by guided tour only, last tour starts 3.30. **Events:** for a detailed programme and inclusion on the mailing list, send s.a.e. to the House Manager

£ House, garden, railway & exhibitions: £3, children £1.50; family ticket (2 adults & 3 children) £7.50. Party rates available; for full details tel. 01765 601005 and ask for group visits information or contact the House Manager. Garden, railway & exhibitions: £2, children £1. Parking 100m

🕴 Special evening tours for pre-booked parties

💰 Shop as house. Also certain dates in Nov & Dec. Tel. for details

♿ Access via one shallow step to ground floor of house, shop, tea-room & garden; cars may bring disabled visitors to front door; disabled drivers may park near house; please notify House Manager in advance of visit; WC

👁 Braille guide. Specialist tours for groups by arrangement

💀 Tea-room serving home-made teas open as house and certain dates in Nov & Dec

[📋] Baby-changing facilities; children's menu, highchairs in tea-room; children's play area

[🖼] School groups on Mon, Tues & Wed mornings during season. Laundry and kitchen visits

[🐕] In park only, on leads

[→] 3ml SE of Middlesbrough, W of A171 [93: NZ530167]. From the A19 take the A174 to the A172. Follow signs for Ormesby Hall. Car entrance on Ladgate Lane (B1380) *Bus:* From Middlesbrough (passing close ≋ Middlesbrough) (tel. 01642 210131) *Station:* Marton (U), not Sun, except May to Sept, 1½ml; Middlesbrough 3ml

---

RIEVAULX TERRACE & TEMPLES [🏠][♿][👶][E]

Rievaulx, Helmsley, York YO6 5LJ Tel: 01439 798340 Fax: 01439 748284

A ½ml long grass-covered terrace and adjoining woodlands with vistas over Rievaulx Abbey (English Heritage) and Rye valley to Ryedale and the Hambleton Hills. Abundance of wild spring flowers. There are two mid 18th-century temples: the Ionic Temple has elaborate ceiling paintings and fine 18th-century furniture

Note: No access to Rievaulx Abbey from Terrace. No access to property Nov to end March

[🅾] 26 March to 2 Nov: daily 10.30–6 (or dusk if earlier). Last admission 5. Ionic Temple closed 1–2. **Events:** contact the Visitor Manager at Nunnington Hall for information (tel. 01439 748283)

[£] £2.80, children £1.40; family ticket £7. Party rates available; for full details tel. 01765 601005 and ask for group visits information or contact the Visitor Manager at Nunnington Hall. Parking at reception, but coach park 200m; unsuitable for trailer caravans

[🛍] Shop and information centre open as property

[♿] Terrace recommended; access to Ionic Temple not possible because of steps. Unadapted WCs. Powered self-drive vehicle available; level gravel path through woods. Ramped access to shop and reception. Manual wheelchair available

[👆] Braille guide

[🍦] Ice cream only. Teas at Nunnington Hall, 7ml (see entry, above)

[👶] Baby-changing facilities

[🖼] Contact the Visitor Manager at Nunnington Hall for information

[🐕] On leads only

[→] 2½ml NW of Helmsley on B1257 [100: SE579848] *Bus:* Moorsbus from Helmsley (connections from ≋ Scarborough), Sun, June to Sept, plus Tues & Wed in Aug; otherwise Scarborough & District/Stephensons 128 from Scarborough or Stephensons 57 from ≋ York, alighting Helmsley, thence 2½ml (tel. 01609 780780)

SOUTER LIGHTHOUSE

Coast Road, Whitburn, Sunderland SR6 7NR Tel: 0191 529 3161

This shore-based lighthouse was the first to be powered by alternating electric current. It was opened in 1871. Visitors can view the engine room, light tower, fog signal station and lighthouse keeper's cottage. Video, model and information displays

O 28 March to 2 Nov: daily except Fri (but open Good Fri) 11–5. Last admission 4.30. **Events:** 20 July, Family Fun Day; story-telling sessions for schools, Christmas lunches and talks; for full details please send s.a.e. to Property Manager

£ £2.50. Pre-booked parties £2. Accompanied children aged 12 and under free during school summer holidays. Car and coach park 100m

K For pre-booked parties

□ Access to shop is free. Open as lighthouse

& Good access to ground floor of lighthouse, including engine room, shop and interpretation area with video. WC (limited wheelchair access). Restaurant, limited access. Light tower not accessible for wheelchairs

◉ Braille guide. Morse code signaller and engines are among items to touch

◘ Tea-room serving morning coffee, lunch and teas, open as lighthouse. Access is free. Children's pirate parties, meetings and other functions by arrangement; details from Property Manager. Picnicking in grounds

▦ Education room; school base. School visits bookable when property is closed to public. Full details from Education Officer or Property Manager

⌖ Dogs in grounds only

→ 2½ml S of South Shields on A183, 5ml N of Sunderland on A183 [88: NZ641408] *Bus:* Stagecoach Economic E1 ⇌ Sunderland–South Shields (passes ⇌ Sunderland & Tyne & Wear Metro South Shields) (tel. 0191 232 5325) *Station:* East Boldon (U) 3ml

TREASURER'S HOUSE 🏠✹🚶E

Chapter House Street, York YO1 2JD Tel: 01904 624247

York's 'hidden treasure', this elegant house stands within the tranquil surroundings of the Minster Close. A series of period rooms are the setting for a wonderful collection of furniture and artefacts given to the National Trust by the Yorkshire industrialist Frank Green, who lived here from 1897 to 1930. An introductory video and exhibition show the development of the house from Roman times

- **O** 29 March to 2 Nov: daily except Fri 10.30–5. Last admission 4.30. **Events:** contact Property Manager for details of function hire and full calendar of special events

- **£** House & garden: £3.30, children £1.50; family ticket (2 adults & 3 children) £8. Party rates available; for full details tel. 01765 601005 and ask for group visits information or contact the Property Manager (tel. 01904 624247). No parking facilities, but car park nearby in Lord Mayor's Walk

- **🚶** Guided tours by arrangement. Evening opening for pre-booked parties £4.50 per person (min. charge £90) incl. guided tour; contact Property Manager

- **🛍** NT shop at 32 Goodramgate open all year, Mon to Sat 9–5.30

- **♿** Cars may set down passengers with disabilities at the door. Ground floor accessible with helper and introductory video available on ground floor. Access to tea-room difficult, but possible to have refreshments brought up. Induction loop in video room. Garden level

- **👁** Braille guide. Tactile pictures in exhibition and short 'scented' pathway in garden

- **🍴** Licensed tea-room for coffee, lunches & teas. Open for pre-booked parties during and outside normal opening hours and for private functions (tel. 01904 646757)

- **👶** Facilities for babies & nursing mothers; children's guidebook, activity sheets, children's menu and highchair. Recipient of York City Council Child Friendly Award, 1995. For conservation reasons pushchairs are not allowed in the house

- **🏫** Pre-booked school parties welcome

- **🐕** In garden only, on leads

- **➔** In Minster Yard, on N side of Minster [105: SE604523] *Bus:* From surrounding areas (tel. 01904 624161). Park and Ride scheme from outskirts of city *Station:* York ½ml

WALLINGTON 🏠🏡✹🌳🍴🚶E

Cambo, Morpeth NE61 4AR Tel: 01670 774283

The family home of the Trevelyans, built of warm Northumberland stone. Rooms range from elegant mid-Georgian to the Victorian nursery, and the 19th-century Central Hall contains paintings by William Bell Scott. Doll's house collection and Children's Room. Enchanting terraced walled garden with themed mixed borders and splendid conservatory. Estate room with exhibition

House: 28 March to 29 Sept: daily except Tues 1–5.30. Last admission 5. 1 Oct to 2 Nov: daily except Tues 1–4.30. Last admission 4. **Walled garden**: 28 March to end Oct: daily 10–7 or dusk if earlier; Nov to March 1998 10–4 (or dusk if earlier). **Grounds**: all year during daylight hours. **Events**: open air concerts, family fun day, Shakespeare on the lawn; for details send s.a.e. to Visitor Manager. Wallington is available for weddings, corporate bookings and special events

House, walled garden & grounds £4.80; family ticket (2 adults & their children) £12. Accompanied children aged 12 and under free during school summer holidays. Parties £4.30. Walled garden & grounds £2.80; parties £2.30. Parties must book in advance

Guided tours available outside normal opening hours; contact House Manager for details (tel. 01670 774283)

Shop open 28 March to 29 Sept: daily except Tues 10.30–5.30; 1 Oct to 2 Nov: daily except Tues 10.30–5; 5 Nov to 14 Dec: Wed to Sun 12–4 (tel. 01670 774249). Plant centre (access through shop) 28 March to 29 Sept (except Tues) 10.30–5.30

Access via ramp to ground floor of house only; wheelchairs available. Apply to parking attendant for reserved bays in main car park and walled garden; most of grounds, conservatory and walled garden accessible, self-drive powered vehicle. WC in courtyard and restaurant. Restaurant upstairs, but refreshments available in Harness Room on ground floor on request

Braille guides; scented roses in garden

Coffee, lunches & teas in tea-room and Harness Room (tel. 01670 774274) same times as shop, see above. Picnics in grounds. Access to shop and restaurant is free from 5 Nov to 14 Dec, Wed to Sun

⊕ Front sling baby carriers to be used in house, provided at front desk; please enquire about other facilities for parents & babies. Doll's houses and toy soldier collections. Children's guide. 'Spot the odd thing out' competition during summer holidays

▦ School visits on Wed & Thur mornings, must be booked in advance

🐾 In grounds and in walled garden on leads

➔ 12ml W of Morpeth (B6343), 6ml NW of Belsay (A696), take B6342 to Cambo [81: NZ030843] *Bus:* Northumbria 419, from Morpeth (Wed, Fri, Sat only) (passing close ⇌ Morpeth); Northumbria 508 from ⇌ Newcastle, Sun, May to Aug only; otherwise National Express from Newcastle (passing close ⇌ Newcastle), alight Capheaton Road End, 2ml (tel. 01670 533128)

WASHINGTON OLD HALL ▦ ❀ E

The Avenue, Washington Village NE38 7LE Tel: 0191 416 6879

The home of George Washington's direct ancestors from 1183–1288, remaining in the family until 1613. Substantially rebuilt in the 17th century

🅞 28 March, then 30 March to 2 Nov: closed Thur, Fri & Sat when the property is used for parties, weddings and meetings (but open Good Fri) 11–5. Last admission 4.30. **Events:** 30 March, free refreshments; 6 July, Independence Day celebrations; 8 to 19 Sept, Young NT Theatre; 18 Sept, wedding exhibition. In addition, the Old Hall and garden are available for various functions; full details from the Property Manager

£ £2.50. Accompanied children aged 12 and under free during school summer holidays. Parties £2 on application to Property Manager. Coaches must park on the Avenue

🏃 Introductory talks for group visits

🛍 Small shop in entrance hall, open as house

♿ Access to ground floor only. Access to part of garden. Please contact Property Manager for access arrangements

👁 Please ask about tactile opportunities. Braille guide. Garden has scented plants

🍵 Tea, coffee and cake available during opening hours

▦ Teachers' notes available; please contact the Property Manager

🐾 No dogs allowed

➔ 5ml W of Sunderland, 2ml E of A1, S of Tyne tunnel, follow signs, Washington New Town, District 4, then Washington village; situated on E side of Avenue [88: NZ312566] *Bus:* Wear Buses X85, 194, 293/4/7, Calvary 293/4/7 from Tyne & Wear Metro Heworth; also other services from surrounding areas (tel. 0191 232 5325) *Station:* Heworth (Tyne & Wear Metro) 4ml; E Boldon (U) 6ml; Newcastle 7ml

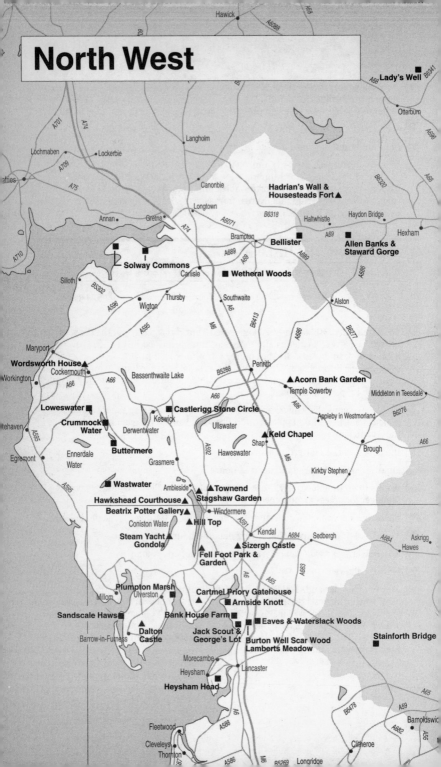

North West

Hawick

Lady's Well

Otterburn

Lochmaben
Lockerbie

Langholm

Canonbie

Hadrian's Wall &
Housesteads Fort ▲

Annan
Gretna
Longtown

Haltwhistle
Haydon Bridge
Hexham

Brampton
Bellister ■

Allen Banks &
Staward Gorge ■

Silloth

Solway Commons ■
Carlisle

Wetheral Woods ■

Thursby

Southwaite

Wigton

Alston

Maryport

Wordsworth House ▲
Cockermouth

Bassenthwaite Lake

Penrith

Acorn Bank Garden ▲
Temple Sowerby

Workington

Middleton in Teesdale

Loweswater ■

Keswick
Castlerigg Stone Circle ■

Appleby in Westmorland

Crummock
Water ■

Derwentwater

Ullswater

Keld Chapel ▲

Whitehaven

Shap

Buttermere ■

Brough

Ennerdale
Water

Grasmere

Haweswater

Kirkby Stephen

Egremont

Wastwater ■

Ambleside

Townend ▲

Hawkshead Courthouse ▲

Stagshaw Garden ▲

Beatrix Potter Gallery ▲
Windermere

Coniston Water

Hill Top ▲

Kendal

Sedbergh

Askrigg
Hawes

Steam Yacht
Gondola ▲

Sizergh Castle ▲

Fell Foot Park &
Garden ▲

Plumpton Marsh ■
Millom
Ulverston

Cartmel Priory Gatehouse ▲

Sandscale Haws ■

Arnside Knott ▲

Bank House Farm ■

Eaves & Waterslack Woods ■

Barrow-in-Furness

Dalton
Castle ■

Jack Scout &
George's Lot

Burton Well Scar Wood
Lamberts Meadow

Stainforth Bridge ■

Morecambe

Heysham
Lancaster

Heysham Head ■

Fleetwood

Cleveleys
Thornton

Clitheroe

Bamoldswic

Longridge

LAKE DISTRICT LANDSCAPE

The Trust's most important work in **CUMBRIA** is the conservation of about one quarter of the **LAKE DISTRICT NATIONAL PARK**. Almost all the central fell area and the major valley heads are owned or held on lease by the Trust, and six of the main lakes and much of their shoreline are also fully protected. These 50,000ha are about a quarter of the Trust's entire holding throughout the country and by far the largest portion of any National Park protected by the Trust.

The Trust bought its first property in the Lake District, **Brandelhow Woods** [89: NY250200], in 1902 to guarantee public access to the shore of Derwentwater. Some of the most important of the Trust's 2834ha of woodland in the National Park are in the Borrowdale Valley: **Great Wood** [89: NY2721], with a well-screened car park (charge for non-members) and lake access, **Manesty Wood** [89: NY251191], with its caravan site run by the Caravan Club, and **Johnny Wood** [89: NY252142], a Site of Special Scientific Interest. Ruskin called the view from **Friar's Crag** [89: NY264223], on the north shore of Derwentwater, one of the finest in Europe: his memorial stands upon the crag which itself is a memorial to Canon Hardwicke Rawnsley, whose inspiration and energy began the great work of the Trust. Further along the valley the Trust owns the tiny hamlet of **Watendlath**, which includes a car park [89: NY274163]. At the Keswick boatlandings is an NT information centre and shop. To the east of Keswick on a magnificent site is **Castlerigg Stone Circle** [89: NY293236], a free-standing megalithic circle of 40 stones.

Loweswater [89: NY1221], **Crummock Water** [89: NY1518] and **Buttermere** [89: NY1815] (car park charge for non-members) are all under Trust protection; a boat can be hired on all three lakes for fishing. There are further car parks at **Lanthwaite Wood** [89: NY153209] and **Honister** [89: NY225135], beside the slate quarry. The Trust owns the Honister pass road and its verges. Around the lakes the Trust is increasing native hardwoods, mostly by natural regeneration. **Scale Force** [89: NY150171], south-west of Crummock Water, is the highest waterfall in a district renowned for its falls.

Much of the northern and all of the southern shore of **Ennerdale Water** [89: NY1015] is protected by the Trust, as are all the high fells to the west and south.

Further south still is dramatic **Wasdale**, arguably the wildest of all the valleys [89: NY1606], almost entirely protected by the Trust: from **Scafell Pike** [89: NY215071] England's highest mountain, and **Great Gable** [89: NY215106] at its head, to the awesome screes sliding down into **Wastwater**, England's deepest lake. Even the bed of the lake is in the Trust's care. There is a Trust campsite here, and a car park at the lake head (charge for non-members).

There are dramatic views of the lakeless Eskdale from the top of **Hardknott Pass** [89: NY230015]. In this valley alone the Trust protects 1518ha of land, including the summit of **Bowfell** [89: NY247064] and all the surrounding fells. One of the Trust's isolated holiday cottages, Bird How, is situated in this quiet and beautiful valley.

Dunnerdale [96: SD2093], beloved of the poet Wordsworth (whose birthplace in Cockermouth is under Trust care and open to the public, see p.159), with the tumbling River Duddon, scattered woods and steep side-valleys, leads up to **Wrynose Bottom** [89: NY260020], where much work has been done in repairing dilapidated dry stone walls.

Wrynose Pass leads down to the Langdale Valleys. **Great Langdale** [89: NY3006] is climbing country: here there is a Trust campsite. For those less hardy the Old Dungeon Ghyll Hotel [89: NY286060] provides much more comfortable accommodation. Evidence of some of the huge amount of footpath repair undertaken in recent years can be seen just a short walk up the fell from the well-screened and landscaped car park beneath **Stickle Ghyll** (car park charge for non-members) [89: NY295064]. 6819ha of land in this area are held on lease from the 7th Earl of Lonsdale. This large area includes the famous **Langdale Pikes**, together with all the high land from **Seat Sandal** on the slopes of Helvellyn to the head of Great Langdale, the bed of **Grasmere Lake**, and part of **Rydal Water**, **White Moss** and **Elterwater Commons**.

Moving to the softer hills of the south, Trust ownership around Coniston is centred on the vast Monk Coniston Estate which includes **Tarn Hows** [89: NY3300]; (car park charge for non-members). Here the Trust has created a new section of the path round the tarns to enable those with walking difficulties to enjoy this beautiful place to the full. But there are unavoidably some steep inclines: two strong helpers and great care are needed by those attempting a circumnavigation in wheelchairs. Tarn Hows was bought by Beatrix Potter, better known locally as Mrs William Heelis. She sold half at cost to the Trust (the purchase of Tarn Hows being funded by Sir Samuel Scott), and then bequeathed to it the other half. The beauty of Tarn Hows is described in a 'talking postcard' on cassette, available from the information vehicle. Restored and relaunched by the National Trust in 1980, the Victorian steam yacht **Gondola**, first launched in 1859, gently plies the length of Coniston Water (see p.155). In **Hawkshead village** there is a National Trust shop [96: SD352982] and the **Beatrix Potter Gallery**, with a selection of her original watercolours on display (see p.141). **Hill Top** [89: SD370956], Beatrix Potter's first acquisition in the Lake District, in Near Sawrey, is best visited at off-peak times (see p.147).

It was through money raised by Beatrix Potter that the Trust was able to purchase **Cockshott Point** [96: SD396965] on the shore of Windermere. On this lake, the most popular of all, the Trust protects some 90% of the land from which the public has free access to the shore. On the west side is **Low Wray Campsite** [89: NY372011] and **Claife Woods**, along some 3ml of shore stretching from near Ferry Nab to Wray Castle [96: SD3898]. At the southern tip of the lake, near Newby Bridge, is **Fell Foot Park & Garden** [96: SD382870], with picnic areas, boats for hire, tea-room and shop (see p.144). Here the Trust is restoring a Victorian garden to its former glory.

Bridge House, perched over Stock Ghyll in Ambleside, once home to a family of six, is now the Trust's oldest information centre and smallest shop [89: NY375045]. Between Ambleside and Grasmere lies **White Moss Common** (car park charge for non-members) [89: NY348065], where the Trust has provided a wheelchair path leading from the car park to the river. **Church Stile** houses a Trust shop and information centre [89: NY336074] in Grasmere village, while at the head of the valley the Trust has pitched a totally new footpath up Helm Crag to overcome the massive erosion problems and provide a more attractive route to the summit of this family favourite.

Aira Force [89: NY399205] (car park charge for non-members) provides a glimpse of a landscaped Victorian park with dramatic waterfalls, arboretum and rock scenery. An audio trail on cassette is available from the information vehicle for those with impaired vision, together with a 'talking postcard' on cassette. Wheelchair and pram access to Aira Beck is now possible. There is also a tea-room. After a walk along this shore of Ullswater, Wordsworth wrote 'I wander lonely as a cloud'. Trust purchase in 1913 ensured that this area would not be developed into a housing estate.

In the small area of the Lake District are tranquil lakes, quiet valleys, gently rolling vales and awesome mountains, each individual and with its own special character. Today it is still a working community of farmers and sheep where the Trust's protection of so much of this glorious landscape is aimed at maintaining the delicate balance between man and nature. Tree coverage is a balanced mixture of broadleaves and conifers, developed by natural regeneration and planting programmes, which helps preserve the special mosaic of woodlands and trees which clothes the fellsides. In the past twelve years 40 major footpath rebuilding projects have been completed, as well as many smaller projects right across the Lake District. Since 1985 major works, including repairs and improvements, have been completed on nearly all of the Trust's 91 Lake District farms. Many miles of walls have also been repaired by Trust gangs, although with an estimated 2,000ml of wall on Trust land alone, there remains much to do.

COAST AND COUNTRYSIDE ELSEWHERE IN THE REGION

While most of the countryside under the Trust's protection in **CUMBRIA** lies within the National Park, there are some outstanding areas in other parts of the county. Near Carlisle, **Wetheral Woods** [86: NY470533] provide riverside walks by the River Eden, while at the other end of the county the limestone escarpment of **Arnside Knott** [89: SD456774] and **Heathwaite** offers wonderful views over Morecambe Bay. Only 2ml north of Barrow is **Sandscale Haws** (car-parking) [96: SD200756], signed Roanhead along the Dalton-in-Furness bypass (A590), an internationally renowned nature reserve with beach, flora-rich dunes and marshes, the breeding site of the rare natterjack toad and with a strong population of the coral root orchid; Braille guide available. Nearby stands **Dalton Castle**, a 14th-century pele tower in the main street of Dalton-in-Furness (see p.142). 3ml from Kendal is the **Sizergh Castle Estate** [89: SD498878] with not only the castle and its extensive garden (see p.153), but also long walks through surrounding woods and hills. On a smaller scale is **Keld Chapel** [90: NY554145] (see p.147), a charming pre-Reformation building near Shap. **Cartmel Priory Gatehouse** (see p.142) also dates from before the Reformation and is the only building, other than the church, which remains of the Augustinian Priory. **Plumpton Marsh** [96/97:XX3198] is a small but intriguing coastal saltmarsh 1ml east of Ulverston with views of the Leven estuary and adjacent to the mouth of the Ulverston Canal (not NT). At the opposite end of the county is **Acorn Bank Garden** [91: NY612281] (see p.141), a fascinating contrast of well-established herb garden and newly opened-up woodland. The most northwesterly of the Trust's properties are the **Solway Commons** [85: NY3156], 69ha of commonland and 1½ml of coastline with a solitary beauty and magnificent views.

Holiday Cottages. The National Trust's holiday cottages in the Lake District do not attempt to be anything but homely and reasonably comfortable bases from which to explore. The cottages can be conveniently categorised as either fell or waterside. The waterside cottages stand within yards of lakeshores and river banks. They tend to be of easier access and slightly more modern in their facilities. As their name implies the fell cottages are at a higher level, often at the end of rough tracks; some are quite isolated.

Restharrow Cottage, on the quiet western shore of Windermere, has been adapted for disabled visitors, who will be given booking preference. For a leaflet or bookings for all cottages, contact the NT Holiday Booking Office on 01225 791133.

Boating and Fishing. A leaflet detailing the boating and fishing available on National Trust waters in the Lake District is available from NT information centres or from The Public Affairs Department, The Hollens, Grasmere, Ambleside LA22 9QZ (please send s.a.e.). NT rowing boats are available for hire on Buttermere, Crummock Water, Loweswater and Windermere.

Tarn Hows, White Moss Common, Fell Foot Park & Garden, Castlerigg Stone Circle, Aira Force, Friar's Crag, Buttermere, Blea Tarn, the Bowder Stone and Sizergh Castle have special provision for disabled visitors: details are given in a special leaflet.

Campsites. A leaflet detailing the campsites run by the Trust is also available.

In **LANCASHIRE** the Trust owns nearly 81ha of land at **Silverdale**, overlooking the saltmarshes of the Kent estuary just over the Cumbrian border. Silverdale village was once on the River Kent, but the river changed its course in the 1920s and now flows some 4ml away. In 1994, through public subscription, the Trust acquired **High and Low Town Fields**, in order to protect the middle of the village from development. 23ha of Bank House Farm [97: SD460752] on the northern fringe of the village are owned by the Trust, where neat limestone walls enclose a patchwork of small fields and spinneys. The shoreline is marked with low limestone cliffs. A coastal footpath crosses this property. **Jack Scout**, 6.5ha of clifftop land on the fringe of Morecambe Bay, was the first coastal property north of the River Ribble to be owned by the Trust [97: SD459737]. It was acquired in 1983, and has much to interest historians, scientists, botanists, bird-watchers and country-lovers. There are extensive views to the Lake District hills across the Kent estuary.

More recently still the Trust acquired **George's Lot**, a 3.5ha cliff field, to extend the length of foreshore open to the public [97: SD459750]. All this coastal limestone pasture and scrub is crossed by public footpaths, and a little further inland 43ha of **Eaves and Waterslack Woods** present a fine variety of trees and other flora, with many woodland birds and animals and a 2ml self-guided walk [97: SD465758]. **Burton Well Scar Wood** [97: SO470754] is 4ha of attractive woodland over limestone pavement. A public footpath passes right through the wood to **Lambert's Meadow** [97: SD471754], 1.5ha of wet meadowland, with a great variety of trees, shrubs and wild flowers, making it an excellent site for invertebrates. In 1996 the Trust increased its protection of Lancashire's coastline by acquiring 4.5ha of **Heysham Head** [97: SD419618] with funds given by all six of the Region's centres and associations. The **Barrows Field** includes the remains of a Saxon chapel and rock-cut graves. Stunning views of the Lakeland fells can be seen across Morecambe Bay.

North of Bury, astride the B6214, is the **Stubbins Estate**, 177ha of agricultural land with numerous public footpaths through fields and woodland full of interesting wildlife and flowers. The Estate, given to the Trust in 1943, provides access from the industrial Rossendale Valley to **Holcombe Moor**, a bleak area of rough grassland and heath, notable especially for its numerous bird species [109: SD785177]. In 1994 the Trust acquired 371ha of this moorland, which is the Trust's largest acquisition in Lancashire to date.

To the south west, the Trust owns over 200ha of ecologically interesting foreshore and woodland at **Formby**: see entry on p.145.

On the north bank of the Mersey at **Speke Hall** (see p.154) the Trust now owns much of the historic landscape surrounding the Hall, consisting of farmland and **Stocktons Wood** [108: SJ4223826]. Research indicates that this wood has never been cultivated, which accounts for its rich variety of insects.

The Wirral Peninsula has a 12ml long country park, several parts of which are owned by the Trust. **Caldy Hill** [108: SJ224855] gives views across the mouth of the River Dee where birdwatchers will find many varieties of duck and waders in large numbers. It has been estimated that 20,000 oystercatchers roost here. At **Heswall** [108: SJ246825] are 16ha of meadow and farmland on the Dee Estuary with fine views to Wales. The acid heathland of **Thurstaston Common** [108: SJ244853] is rich in insect life.

Several of the Trust's beauty spots in **CHESHIRE** are very near the great industrial conurbations which fringe its northern and eastern boundaries. **Styal Country Park** (see p.156) is the closest to Manchester. **Alderley Edge** [118: SS860775] is also within easy reach of Manchester and Macclesfield and gives splendid views over the Cheshire Plain. Its wooded sandstone escarpment (180m) once harboured a large Neolithic settlement; Bronze Age pottery and tools have been found here. A footpath has been created which is linked to the Trust's nearby **Hare Hill Garden** (see p.146); walkers are asked to return by the same route, rather than along the highway. A path is signposted from the car park along the Edge, giving fine views: although the path is suitable for wheelchairs, a strong pusher may be necessary. WC. 1ml away is **Nether Alderley Mill** (see p.150). In the north-east corner of Cheshire is **Lyme Park**, just outside Stockport (see p.149).

On the south-east boundary, and hence close to the Potteries, are two Trust properties with extensive views: Mow Cop and the Cloud. On the Staffordshire border, **Mow Cop** [118: SJ857573] is topped by a Gothic folly in the shape of a ruined castle. Just over 300m above sea level, it marks the beginning of the Staffordshire Way footpath and gives views towards Alderley Edge and beyond to Manchester to the north, north-east to the Peak District, south to Cannock Chase and Shropshire, and west to Wales and the Berwyn Mountains. From Mow Cop you can walk 3ml to the timber-framed **Little Moreton Hall**, Congleton (see p.148). There is a car park at Mow Cop but the summit of the Cloud can only be reached on foot. **The Cloud**, [118:SJ903636] 3ml east of Congleton, is a hill rising to 337m. Mainly heath with some wooded areas and farmland on the lower slopes; the summit gives very fine views over three counties: Cheshire, Staffordshire and Derbyshire.

In the west of the county, close to Chester, is **Helsby Hill** [117: SJ492754], a sandstone outcrop overlooking the Mersey, and giving views of the mountains of North Wales. The climb to the summit takes about fifteen minutes and you will pass an Iron Age hillfort near the top. On the Wirral lies **Burton Mill Wood**, 8ha of woodland adjacent to the village of Burton, 8ml north-west of Chester. Easy walking with views across the Dee estuary to the Welsh hills beyond [117:SJ315745].

Bickerton Hill [117: SJ504529] lies at the southern tip of the Peckforton Hills, close to the Welsh border – over 113ha of mixed woodland, heathland and fields accessible by public footpath. The Peckforton Hills are a wooded red sandstone ridge running from Maiden Castle, an Iron Age fort in the south, to the 13th-century Beeston Castle in the north. The Sandstone Trail, a long-distance footpath (30ml), traverses the length of the hills from Grindley Brook to Frodsham, passing a variety of dwellings from black-and-white cottages to prehistoric hillforts.

ACORN BANK GARDEN AND WATERMILL ✿

Temple Sowerby, nr Penrith CA10 1SP Tel: 017683 61893

A 1ha garden protected by fine oaks under which grow a vast display of daffodils. Inside the walls there are orchards containing a variety of fruit trees, surrounded by mixed borders with shrubs, herbaceous plants and roses, while the impressive herb garden has the largest collection of culinary and medicinal plants in the north. A circular woodland walk runs beside the Crowdundle Beck to Acorn Bank watermill. Although work to restore the mill continues, it will be open to visitors at the same times as the garden. The house is not open to the public.

- 🅞 28 March to 2 Nov: daily 10–5.30. Last admission 5

- 💷 £2.10, children £1; family ticket £5.50. Pre-arranged parties £1.50 per person. Car-parking

- 🗍 Small shop and plants for sale, open 1 April to 5 Oct, same times as garden. From 6 Oct to 2 Nov: weekends only

- ♿ Access to herb garden, herbaceous borders, greenhouse & shop. WC

- 👁 Herbs, sounds of water from beck

- 👶 Baby-changing facilities, children's guide and quiz sheet

- 🐕 Admitted on leads to woodland walk, but not to walled garden

- ➔ Just N of Temple Sowerby, 6ml E of Penrith on A66 [91: NY612281]
  Bus: Stagecoach Cumberland 100 Penrith–Appleby (passes close ⇌ Penrith & ⇌ Appleby) (tel. 01946 63222) *Station:* Langwathby (U) 5ml; Penrith 6ml

BEATRIX POTTER GALLERY 🏠

Main Street, Hawkshead LA22 0NS Tel: 015394 36355

An annually changing exhibition of original illustrations from the children's stories. One of many historic buildings in this picturesque village, this was once the office of the author's husband, the solicitor William Heelis, and the interior remains largely unaltered since his day

- 🅞 28 March to 2 Nov: Sun to Thur (closed Fri and Sat except Good Fri) 10.30–4.30. Last admission 4. Admission is by timed ticket (incl. NT members)

- 💷 £2.70, children £1.30. No reduction for parties. Car- and coach-parking in town car park, 200m

- 🗍 Shop (30m) open daily 9.30–5.30, 28 March to 24 Dec. Closed Thur & Fri. Out of season tel. 015394 36471

♿ We regret Gallery unsuitable for wheelchairs

♿ Braille guide

♿ Available in Hawkshead

♿ Children's guide to Beatrix Potter. We regret the Gallery is not suitable for baby back-packs or pushchairs

⏩ In The Square [96: SD352982] *Bus:* Stagecoach Cumberland 505/6 Ambleside–Coniston (connections from ⊜ Windermere) (tel. 01946 63222) *Station:* Windermere 6½ml via ferry

CARTMEL PRIORY GATEHOUSE 🏠✝

Cavendish Street, Cartmel, Grange-over-Sands LA11 6QA
Tel: (Regional Office) 015394 35599 Fax: 015394 35353

All that is left, apart from the church, of the Augustinian priory, dating from about 1330. A picturesque building which served as a grammar school from 1624–1790

○ Opening times under review; please tel. 015394 35599 for latest information

£ Free. Parking in the village

⏩ [96: SD378788] *Bus:* Stagecoach Cumberland 530/1 Kendal–Cartmel (passing ⊜ Grange-over-Sands) (tel. 01946 63222) *Station:* Cark (U) 2ml

DALTON CASTLE 🏠

Market Place, Dalton-in-Furness LA15 8AX
Tel: (Regional Office) 015394 35599 Fax: 015394 35353

A 14th-century tower in the main street of Dalton-in-Furness. Local exhibition by Friends of Dalton Castle

○ Easter to end Sept: Sat 2–5

£ Free but donations welcome

⏩ In main street of Dalton [96: SD226739] *Bus:* From surrounding areas (tel. 01946 63222) *Station:* Dalton ¼ml

DUNHAM MASSEY 🏛🏠🍽♣🌳🚹🇪

Altrincham WA14 4SJ Tel: 0161 941 1025 Fax: 0161 929 7508

Georgian house with Edwardian additions set in a 101ha wooded deer park, a rare survivor of 18th-century formal design. Until 1976 this was the home of the 10th and last Earl of Stamford. Over 30 rooms are open, with fine furniture, paintings and outstanding Huguenot silver collected by the 2nd Earl of Warrington; also a fine library, kitchen and laundry. The moat provides power for a working sawmill. The richly planted garden contains an 18th-century orangery, a Victorian bark house and well house; all set amongst mixed shrubs,

herbaceous borders, mature trees and waterside plantings. There is also a collection of unique late-flowering azaleas

House: 22 March to 2 Nov: Sat to Wed 12–5. Last admission 4.30 (last audio tour 4). **Garden**: 22 March to 2 Nov: daily 11–5.30. Last admission 5. The Mill machinery will normally operate on Wed & Sun 2–4. **Park**: daily throughout the year. **Events**: concerts, theatre and walks. Plantsman's Day in May. Please send s.a.e. for details

House & garden: £4.50, children £2; family ticket £11. House only: £3, children £1.50. Garden only £2.50, children £1. Audio tour of house 50p. Reduced rate for booked parties Sat & Mon to Wed (but not BH Mon). Park only: £2.50 per car, £1 per motorbike, £5 per coach/minibus. NT members and coaches bringing booked parties park free. Car park and adjacent picnic area 250m from house. Visitors to house must leave large bags, video cameras, pushchairs etc. at reception

Outside normal hours, guided tours for booked parties min. charge £200

Daily throughout the year, Mon to Fri 11–5.15, Sat & Sun 11–6 (or dusk if earlier), closed 25 to 31 Dec 1997 (tel. 0161 941 2815)

Regret house difficult, steps to ground floor and throughout house. The less accessible rooms are illustrated in an album of photographs. Access to garden and park, on smooth, level paths; shop, refreshments and WCs in main lavatory block and next to restaurant accessible over cobbled yard (restaurant accessible by lift). Car-parking by prior arrangement. Wheelchairs and self-drive powered vehicles available, advance notice requested. Sympathetic Hearing Scheme

Induction loops for audio tour of house. Braille guide; large-print guide

Licensed self-service Stables Restaurant on first floor with variety of lunches and teas, vegetarian choice; open daily throughout the year, 11–5.15 or dusk if earlier (closed 25 to 31 Dec 1997). Seating for 150. Functions and parties welcome by arrangement. The Piers Davenport Room available for booked parties (tel. 0161 941 2815). Picnics welcome in North Park adjacent to car park, but not in deer park or garden

📖 Baby slings available; baby-changing unit in WC; children's menu, highchairs and activity table in restaurant; children's guidebook, seek & find quiz, garden trail, park trail. Please send s.a.e. for details of children's activities

▣ Victorian living history in house and environmental studies in deer park based on National Curriculum Key Stages 1 & 2; by arrangement with Education Coordinator (tel. 0161 941 4986). Teachers' resource pack. Schoolrooms for booked parties

🐕 Good walks in park for dogs on leads. No dogs in house or garden

→ 3ml SW of Altrincham off A56; exit 19 off M6; exit 7 off M56 [109: SJ735874] *Bus:* North Western/Warrington Transport 38 ⇥ Altrincham Interchange–Warrington (tel. 01244 602666) *Station:* Altrincham (⇥ & Metro) 3ml; Hale 3ml

---

DUNHAM MASSEY: WHITE COTTAGE 🏠 👤

Little Bollington, Altrincham WA14 4TJ

An important timber-framed cottage built as a cruck trussed open hall c.1500 and altered in the 17th century. Recently restored by the NT using traditional methods and materials. Private residence open by kind permission of our lessees

🅾 April to end Oct: last Sun of month 2–5. All visits to be pre-booked through the Stamford Estate Office (tel. 0161 928 0075) open Mon to Fri 9–1 and 2–5

💷 Voluntary contributions to be made at the White Cottage

→ As Dunham Massey above

FELL FOOT PARK AND GARDEN 🌳 ⛵

Newby Bridge, Ulverston LA12 8NN Tel: 015395 31273 Fax: 015395 30049

7ha park and garden in the process of being restored and landscaped to its former Victorian glory; with lakeshore access and magnificent views of the Lakeland fells. Good shows of daffodils and rhododendrons. Boat launching, rowing boats for hire, adventure play area, picnics; ideal for a day's outing

Note: No launching or landing of speedboats or jet skis

🅾 All year 9–7 or dusk if sooner. Facilities (such as rowing boat hire) 1 April to 31 Oct: daily incl. Good Fri 11–4 (buoyancy aids available)

💷 Car park £3 (over 4hrs), £1.80 (up to 4hrs), £1.20 (up to 2hrs). Coaches £10 by arrangement. Please note car park has pay and display meters so NT membership or season ticket must be displayed in car. Season tickets available from most NT outlets in Cumbria

🛍 April to Oct: daily 11–5; Nov and Dec: weekends only 12–4

♿ Accessible but please be careful; slopes and unfenced water. Access to tea-room and shop; WC beside tea-room. A 2-seater buggy is available

🔊 Braille guide planned

⬛ Coffee, light lunches, teas and ice creams in tea-room, 29 March to 2 Nov: 11–5; Nov & Dec: weekends only 12–4

🧒 Highchairs in tea-room, children's menu, scribble sheets

🐕 On leads only

➡️ At the extreme S end of Lake Windermere on E shore, entrance from A592 [96/97: SD381869] *Bus:* Stagecoach Cumberland 518 Ulverston–Ambleside (passing ≋ Windermere) (tel. 01946 63222) *Station:* Grange-over-Sands 6ml

FORMBY 🦑 🏔 🧒 E

Victoria Road, Freshfield, Formby L37 1LJ Tel: 01704 878591 Fax: 01704 874949

202ha of dune, foreshore and pinewood between the sea and the town of Formby, 2ml inland. Red squirrels can frequently be seen in the pine trees and the shoreline attracts waders such as oystercatchers and sanderlings

🅾️ All year during daylight hours. Country walks around the property and the Sefton coast. **Events:** details from Property Manager (s.a.e. please)

💷 Entrance per car: April to end Oct: weekdays £2; Sat, Sun & BH Mon £2.50. Nov to end March 1998: £2. Coaches £10 all year. Motorcycles £1 all year. Coaches must pre-book; details from Property Office

♿ Hard surface paths to red squirrel viewing area and Cornerstone Walk. Large car park in sand dunes gives access to beach via boardwalks. Picnic sites. WC (radar key)

🧒 Red squirrel booklet for children £1. Baby-changing facilities in WC

🎒 School groups must book in advance. Environmental education programme; for information tel/fax 01704 874949

🐕 On leads around the squirrel walk

➡️ 15ml N of Liverpool, 2ml W of Formby, 2ml off A565 [108: SD275080] *Bus:* ABC 161/4/5, ≋ Formby–≋ Freshfield, to within ½ml (tel. 0151 236 7676) *Station:* Freshfield 1ml

GAWTHORPE HALL 🏛 ❀ E

Padiham, nr Burnley BB12 8UA Tel: 01282 771004 Fax: 01282 770178

The house was built in 1600–5, and restored by Sir Charles Barry in the 1850s; Barry's designs have been re-created in the principal rooms. Gawthorpe was the home of the Shuttleworth family, and the Rachel Kay-Shuttleworth textile collections are on display in the house; private study by arrangement. Collection of portraits on loan from the National Portrait Gallery

Note: Gawthorpe Hall is financed and administered by Lancashire County Council

🅾️ **Hall:** 28 Mar to 30 Oct: daily except Mon & Fri, but open Good Fri & BH Mon,

1–5. Last admission 4.15. **Garden**: all year: daily 10–6. **Events**: exhibitions during high season

£ Hall: £2.90, children £1.30; family ticket £8. Garden: free. Parties by prior arrangement. Free parking 150m. We regret that the Hall is not suitable for baby back-packs or pushchairs

Access limited to grounds only

Rose garden

Tea-room open same days as Hall, 12.30–4.30

→ On E outskirts of Padiham; ¾ml drive to house on N of A671 [103: SD806340] *Bus*: Frequent services from Burnley. All pass close Burnley Barracks & Burnley Manchester Road (tel. 01282 423125) *Station*: Rose Grove (U) 2ml

HARE HILL

Over Alderley, Macclesfield SK10 4QB

A woodland garden surrounding a walled garden with pergola, rhododendrons and azaleas; parkland; link path to Alderley Edge (2ml)

O 28 March to 30 Oct: Wed, Thur, Sat, Sun & BH Mon 10–5.30. Special opening to see rhododendrons and azaleas: 12 May to 1 June: daily 10–5.30. Closed Nov to March

£ £2.50. Entrance per car £1.50 refundable on entry to garden. Parties either by written appointment c/o Garden Lodge, Oak Road, Over Alderley, Macclesfield SK10 4QB, or by tel. Gardener-in-charge on 01625 828981. Not suitable for school parties

Ample car-parking, but on slope; gravel paths, strong companion advisable. Wheelchair available

Braille guide. Scents & sounds of wooded parkland; scented plants in walled garden

No dogs in garden, elsewhere on leads

→ Between Alderley Edge and Prestbury, turn off north at B5087 at Greyhound Road [118: SJ875765] *Bus*: Stevensons 287 Manchester Airport–Macclesfield (passing Prestbury), to within ¾ml (tel. 01244 602666) *Station*: Alderley Edge 2½ml; Prestbury 2½ml

HAWKSHEAD COURTHOUSE

Hawkshead, nr Ambleside Tel: (Regional Office) 015394 35599 Fax: 015394 35353

Dating from the 15th century, the Courthouse is all that is left of the manorial buildings of Hawkshead, once held by Furness Abbey

O 1 April to 31 Oct: daily 10–5, by key from NT shop, The Square, Hawkshead. May occasionally be in use by the local community

£ Free. No WC. No parking facilities

→ At junction of Ambleside and Coniston roads, ½ml N of Hawkshead on B5286 [96/97: SD349987] *Bus:* Stagecoach Cumberland 505/6 Ambleside–Coniston (connections from ⇌ Windermere) (tel. 01946 63222) *Station:* Windermere 6½ml via vehicle ferry

HILL TOP 🏠 ❊

Near Sawrey, Ambleside LA22 0LF Tel: 015394 36269

Beatrix Potter wrote many of her famous children's stories in this little 17th-century house, and traditional cottage garden; the house still contains her furniture and china. A selection of her original illustrations is displayed at the Beatrix Potter Gallery, Hawkshead (see p.141)

Note: Hill Top is a very small house and a timed entry system is operated, with a daily limit of 800 visitors. During the busiest periods this may give rise to long delays and some visitors may not gain admission at all. Please help to preserve Hill Top by avoiding peak times if you can, particularly mornings in school holidays (closed Thur & Fri except Good Fri)

O 28 March to 2 Nov: Sat to Wed & Good Fri 11–5. Last admission 4.30

£ £3.60, children £1.70. No reduction for parties. Parking 200m; no parking for coaches

📷 Shop daily 10–5 during season

♿ Ground floor access for wheelchairs by prior arrangement

👁 Accompanied visually impaired people welcome, but are advised to visit outside peak times as house is so small and often crowded. Some items in house may be touched; Braille guide

🍴 Bar lunches and evening meals at the Tower Bank Arms (NT owned, and let to tenant) next door, during licensing hours (tel. 015394 36334)

🚶 Unsuitable for back-packs or pushchairs. Children's guide to Beatrix Potter

→ 2ml S of Hawkshead, in hamlet of Near Sawrey, behind the Tower Bank Arms [96/97: SD370955] *Bus:* Stagecoach Cumberland 505/6 Ambleside–Coniston service (connections from ⇌ Windermere); also frequent service from ⇌ Windermere to Bowness Pier, thence ferry and 2ml walk (tel. 01946 63222) *Station:* Windermere 4½ml via vehicle ferry

KELD CHAPEL ✠

Shap, nr Kendal Tel: (Regional Office) 015394 35599 Fax: 015394 35353

Small pre-Reformation building, still used occasionally for services

O At all reasonable hours; key available in village; notice on chapel door

£ Free. Unsuitable for coaches. No WC

Tea-shop (not NT) between car park and chapel, open Easter to Nov

1ml SW of Shap village, close to River Lowther [90: NY554145] *Bus:* Stagecoach Cumberland 107 Penrith–Shap (passing close ⇌ Penrith), thence 1ml (tel. 01946 63222) *Station:* Penrith 10ml

LITTLE MORETON HALL 🏠 ✝ ✿ E

Congleton CW12 4SD Tel: 01260 272018

Begun in 1450 and completed in 1580 Little Moreton is regarded as the finest example of a timber-framed moated manor house in the country. The drunkenly reeling South Front opens onto a cobbled courtyard and the main body of the Hall. The Chapel, Elizabethan Long Gallery, Great Hall, wall paintings and Knot Garden are of particular interest. Location for Granada TV's recent (1996) adaptation of Daniel Defoe's novel Moll Flanders

22 March to 2 Nov: Wed to Sun 12–5.30 or dusk if earlier (opens at 11 Wed to Sun 26 July to 31 Aug). BH Mon 11–5.30. Last admission 5. 8 Nov to 21 Dec: Sat & Sun 12–4, access to Great Hall, Parlour, garden, shop and restaurant only. Special openings at other times, for pre-booked parties, including evening tours with buffet supper. **Events**: 23 March to 2 Nov: Chapel Service every Sun 3.45. Open-air theatre in July

£3.80; family ticket £9.50. Pre-booked parties £3. Joint ticket with Biddulph Grange Garden available £6; family ticket £15. 2 Nov to 22 Dec: free admission. Extra charge for special openings. Parking 150m £2, refundable on entry to Hall (NT members free); car park open from 11

Optional free guided tours most afternoons, 22 March to 2 Nov

Shop as house

🚹 Access to ground floor; includes Great Hall, Parlour, chapel, tea-room, shop, exhibition room. Cars may be driven to entrance, but then must park in car park. Garden accessible. Self-drive vehicle and wheelchairs available by arrangement. WC. Sympathetic Hearing Scheme

👁 Braille guide; large-print guide; opportunities to touch

🍴 Light lunches and home-made teas (waited service); licensed; limited seating – no reservations. Last admission 5. Picnic area adjacent to car park

🚼 Baby-changing unit; highchair and children's portions available; children's guidebook

🏫 School parties April to end Oct: Thur & Fri, mornings only, by prior arrangement with Property Manager. Schoolroom available; teachers' resource pack

🐕 In car park only

➔ 4ml SW of Congleton, on E side of A34 [118: SJ832589] *Bus:* PMT 77 Congleton–Hanley (passing close ⇌ Kidsgrove & Congleton), alight Brownlow Heath, 1½ml (tel. 01244 602666); PMT Flexibus from ⇌ Stoke-on-Trent, July to Sept only (tel. 01782 747000) *Station:* Kidsgrove 3ml; Congleton 4½ml

---

LYME PARK 🏠 ❀ ♠ 🚹 E

Disley, Stockport SK12 2NX Tel: 01663 762023/766492 Fax: 01663 765035

Home of the Legh family for 600 years and one of the largest houses in Cheshire. Part of the original Elizabethan house survives with 18th- and 19th-century additions by Giacomo Leoni and Lewis Wyatt. The collection includes Mortlake tapestries, Grinling Gibbons carvings and a renowned collection of English clocks. Set in an extensive garden with conservatory by Wyatt, lake and formal 'Dutch' garden. 567ha park, home to red and fallow deer. Magnificent views of Pennine Hills and Cheshire Plain from recently restored buildings within the park. Setting for exterior filming of BBC's recent adaptation of Jane Austen's novel Pride and Prejudice

Note: Lyme Park is owned and managed by the NT and partly financed by Stockport Metropolitan Borough Council

🅾 **House:** 29 March to 29 Oct: Sat to Wed 1.30–5 (BH Mon 11–5). Last admission 4.30. **Garden:** 29 March to 29 Oct: daily 11–5; for garden winter opening please tel. for details. **Park:** April to Oct: daily 8am–8.30pm; Nov to March: 8–6 daily. **Events:** details from estate office (please send s.a.e.)

£ House & garden £4; family £9. House only £3; garden only £2. Park only £3.30 per car (NT members free)

🏃 House: outside normal opening hours, by arrangement. Park or garden, by arrangement

📷 Park shop open as park coffee shop (see below); hall shop open as hall tea-room (see below)

♿ Limited parking at house. Refreshment facilities in park and hall courtyard accessible. First floor of house accessible, wheelchair users please telephone in advance. Garden (including rose garden) and park; prior arrangement advisable. Wheelchairs available. Steep terrain throughout park

⬛ Park shop and coffee shop open 29 March to 29 Oct: daily 11–5. Nov to March: please tel. for details. Hall tea-room and gift shop open 29 March to 29 Oct: Sat to Wed 11–5; Nov to March: please tel. for details

⬛ Play area with multi-play apparatus. Highchairs available in hall tea-room and park coffee shop

⬛ Extensive education programme in house and park

⬛ No dogs in garden; under close control in park

⬛ Entrance on A6, 6½ml SE of Stockport, 9ml NW of Buxton (house and car park 1ml from entrance) *Bus:* Glossopdale 361 from Stockport to car park (Sun, May to Sept only); for other services from surrounding areas to park entrance (tel. 0161 228 7811) *Station:* Disley, ½ml from park entrance

---

NETHER ALDERLEY MILL ⊠ 🚻

Congleton Road, Nether Alderley, Macclesfield SK10 4TW Tel: 01625 523012

Correspondence and bookings: 7 Oak Cottages, Styal, Wilmslow SK9 4JQ (tel. 01625 523012). A fascinating overshot tandem-wheel watermill, dating from the 15th century, with a stone-tiled low-pitched roof. The machinery was derelict for 30 years, but has now been restored to full working order, and grinds flour occasionally for demonstrations

⬛ 30 March to end May & Oct: Wed, Sun & BH Mon 1–4.30. June to Sept: Tues to Sun & BH Mon 1–5

⬛ £1.80. Parties (max. 20) by prior arrangement (tel. 01625 523012). Parking space for one coach at a time; must book. No WC

⬛ As required

⬛ Ladder stairs. No access for wheelchairs

⬛ Working machinery provides fascinating range of sounds

⬛ Visits by arrangement. Teachers' resource book available

⬛ No dogs

⬛ 1½ml S of Alderley Edge, on E side of A34 [118: SJ844763] *Bus:* Stevensons/Timeline 127, 130 Manchester–Macclesfield (passing ⇌ Alderley Edge) (tel. 01244 602666) *Station:* Alderley Edge 2ml

---

QUARRY BANK MILL & STYAL COUNTRY PARK 🏠⊠♨🚻 Ⓔ

Wilmslow SK9 4LA Tel: 01625 527468 Fax: 01625 539267

A Georgian cotton mill, built in 1784 by Samuel Greg, an early pioneer of the factory system. Still in working order, it gives a fascinating insight into the evolution of the cotton textile industry and the early industrial revolution. The restored Apprentice House provides a glimpse into the life of the pauper apprentice children who did menial tasks at the mill. The mill is powered by a magnificent 50-ton waterwheel. During 1997 a project to restore steam power using an 1840s beam engine will take place. The engine and new displays will be installed in the original engine house, not previously opened to the public

Note: The Mill is managed for the National Trust by the tenant, Quarry Bank Mill Trust Ltd. NT members pay charges for special events. Entry to the Apprentice House is not included in special offers due to restricted visitor numbers

April to Sept: **Mill:** daily 11–6. Last admission 4.30. Also pre-booked specified evenings in May, June & Sept. **Apprentice House & garden:** (closed Mon except BH Mon) Tues to Fri 2–4.30. Weekends & during Aug: as Mill. Timed entry tickets: to avoid disappointment please reserve timed ticket at reception on arrival. Oct to March: **Mill:** daily 11–5 except Mon. Last admission 3.30. Pre-booked groups from 9.30 except weekends & BH Mon. **Apprentice House and garden:** Tues to Fri 2–4.30; weekends: as Mill. **Events:** details of programme available from property

Mill & Apprentice House £4.70, children/concessionaries £3.20; family ticket £12. Mill only £3.70, children/concessionaries £2.50. Apprentice House & garden only £3.20, children/concessionaries £2.30. Advance booking essential for groups of 10 or more (please apply for booking form at least 3 weeks in advance; guides may be booked at same time). Groups of 20 or more admitted at concessionary rate

Available for pre-booked parties

Mill shop sells goods made from cloth woven in the mill and wide range of gifts & souvenirs. Mail order catalogue for Styal Calico, send A4 s.a.e. (60p)

Exterior, and route through part of interior, accessible using ramps and step lift. Access to waterwheel and waterforce gallery by arrangement. Also to three rooms on ground floor of Apprentice House. Wheelchair available on request; cars may set down passengers in Mill Yard. Disabled drivers may park in Tilt Yard. Please tel. for special access leaflet. WC. Sympathetic Hearing Scheme; audio tapes with induction loop. 1995 Holiday Care Award

Braille and large-print guides. Audio tape tour of mill. Mill unsuitable for guide dogs. Talking map, varied scents, smells and noises from machinery, etc; cotton samples and other items to handle

📖 The Mill Kitchen: licensed. Mill Pantry for snacks, drinks and ice cream. Conference and banqueting facilities

🚼 Parent & baby room; back-packs admitted; baby sling and back-packs available

🏭 Education programme (for pre-booked parties) linked to national curriculum; living history, hands-on activities and textile workshops. Information available from Education Dept

➡ 1½ml N of Wilmslow off B5166, 2½ml from M56, exit 5, 10ml S of Manchester [109: SJ835835] *Bus:* Stevensons 287 Manchester Airport–Macclesfield, passing ⊠ Wilmslow (tel. 01244 602666) *Station:* Styal, ½ml (not Sun)

RUFFORD OLD HALL 🏠 ❄ E

Rufford, nr Ormskirk L40 1SG Tel: 01704 821254 Fax: 01704 821254

There is a legend that William Shakespeare performed here for the owner, Sir Thomas Hesketh, in the Great Hall of this, one of the finest 16th-century buildings in Lancashire. The playwright would have delighted in the magnificent Hall, with its intricately carved movable wooden screen. Built in 1530, it established the Hesketh family's seat for the next 250 years. In the Carolean Wing, altered in 1821, there are fine collections of 16th- and 17th-century oak furniture, arms, armour and tapestries

O **House:** 29 March to 2 Nov: Sat to Wed 1–5. Last admission 4.30. **Garden:** same days 12–5.30. **Events:** please send s.a.e. for details

£ House and garden £3.30, children £1.60; family ticket £9. Garden only £1.70. (Children free during school holidays.) Reduction for pre-booked parties (£2.60, but no parties Sun & BH Mon)

🏪 Shop open as garden. Also 4 Nov to 20 Dec: daily except Mon & Fri 12–4, Sun 2–5

♿ Access to entrance hall, Great Hall, tea-room, shop & garden only, otherwise many steps & narrow passages; two wheelchairs available. Photograph albums of rooms available to those unable to reach them. Parking on firm gravel; level paths to hall and garden

🐾 Braille guide and large-print house guide; great screen and carved oak doors may be touched

☕ Light lunches 12–2 (licensed for cider & wine) and teas 12–5 (last serving 4.30); 4 Nov to 20 Dec, as shop, see above. Picnic site adjacent to car park

👶 House not suitable for baby back-packs or pushchairs, but following available: highchairs in tea-room, baby slings, children's menu, children's quiz sheet, scribble sheets, baby-changing facility in women's WC, bottle-warming service. Early learning toys

🏫 Accompanied visits and teachers' pack

🐕 In grounds only, on leads. Fresh water and bowl available. Tether rings in yard

➡ 7ml N of Ormskirk, in village of Rufford on E side of A59 [108: SD463160]
Bus: N Western X11 Liverpool–Preston; Blackpool Transport X54, 754/8 Liverpool–Blackpool (tel. 01695 579062) *Station:* Rufford (U), not Sun, ½ml; Burscough Bridge 2½ml

---

SIZERGH CASTLE 🏛 ❀ 🧍

Sizergh, nr Kendal LA8 8AE Tel: 015395 60070

The Strickland family have lived here for more than 750 years. This impressive 14th-century pele tower was extended in Tudor times, with some of the finest Elizabethan carved overmantels in the country. Contents include good English and French furniture and family portraits. The castle is surrounded by gardens (including the Trust's largest limestone rock garden) of beauty and interest; good autumn colour. Large estate; walks leaflet available in shop

🅾 **Castle:** 30 March to 30 Oct: Sun to Thur 1.30–5.30. **Garden:** as Castle from 12.30. Last admission 5

💷 £3.80, children £1.90; family ticket £10. Garden only £1.90. Parties of 15+ £3 by arrangement (not BH). Car park 100m

🏬 Shop open as garden. Also on various days in Nov and Dec; tel. 015395 60070

♿ Access to most of garden mainly via gravel paths; battery-powered and manual wheelchairs available. Lower Hall & tea-room accessible. Picnic tables with wheelchair access. WC

🐾 Garden & first floor suitable for accompanied visually impaired visitors. Some wooden articles may be touched; Braille guide

☕ Tea-room in basement of pele tower opens 1.30. Picnic tables in car park

👶 Young Explorers quiz sheet, garden treasure hunt. Unsuitable for baby back-packs and pushchairs

🐕 Not allowed in garden

➡ 3½ml S of Kendal NW of interchange A590/A591 [97: SD498878] *Bus:* Stagecoach Cumberland 555 Keswick–Lancaster (passing close 🚋 Lancaster and Kendal) (tel. 01946 63222) *Station:* Oxenholme 3ml; Kendal (U) 3½ml

SPEKE HALL 🏠 ❀ ♨ E

The Walk, Liverpool L24 1XD
Tel: 0151 427 7231 Infoline (local rate): 0345 585702 Fax: 0151 427 9860

One of the most famous half-timbered houses in the country. The Great Hall, Oak Parlour and priest holes evoke Tudor times while the small rooms, some with William Morris wallpapers, show the Victorian desire for privacy and comfort. Fine plasterwork and tapestries, plus a fully-equipped Victorian kitchen and servants' hall. The restored garden has spring bulbs, rose garden, rhododendrons, summer border and stream garden; bluebell walks in the ancient Clough Woodland; spectacular views of grounds and the Mersey basin from a high embankment 'the Bund'; peaceful walks in wildlife oasis of Stocktons Wood

Note: Speke Hall is administered and financed by the National Trust with the help of a grant from the National Museums & Galleries on Merseyside

🅾 **House**: 29 March to 26 Oct: daily except Mon (but open BH Mon) 1–5.30. 1 Nov to 14 Dec: Sat & Sun 1–4.30. **Garden**: 29 March to 26 Oct: open as house from 12; Nov to March 1998: daily except Mon 12–4 (closed 24, 25, 26, 31 Dec & 1 Jan). *Note*: on BH Mon and summer weekends the house can become very crowded. **Events**: for details please send s.a.e. to Events Manager

£ House, garden & grounds £3.80; family ticket £9.50. Garden only £1.20. Grounds only £1.20. Reduction for pre-booked groups. Car park 200m

🏃 Programme of guided tours of roof, gardens, estate & house (latter by arrangement)

🛍 Shop open as house

♿ Close parking by arrangement; self-drive powered vehicle available for use in grounds. Wheelchairs available by arrangement on arrival or at house; access to ground floor (includes most principal rooms) and tea-room. WC ramp and 5cm step to tea-room; cobbled courtyard. Easy access to much of garden and woodlands; wheelchair path around Stocktons Wood. Sympathetic Hearing Scheme

♨ Braille and large-print guides; some objects may be touched; guided tours bookable

☕ Refreshments and teas; tea-room open same days as house from 12; light lunches 12–2; parties should book. Also open Sun in March 1–4.30 for drinks; seating capacity 40. Picnics in orchard

🧒 Children's guide. Highchairs in tea-room; baby-changing facilities

🎒 School visits welcome, but must be pre-booked; details from Education Assistant

🐕 On leads in Stocktons Wood only. No dogs in garden

➡️ On N bank of the Mersey, 1ml off A561 on W side of Liverpool airport. Follow airport signs from M62 exit 6, A5300; M56 exit 12 [108: SJ419825] *Bus:* North Western H25 ⊒ Garston–Runcorn, Sun, May to Oct only; otherwise Merseybus 80, 180 ⊒ Liverpool Lime Street–Liverpool Airport (passing ⊒ Garston) or 81/2 Bootle–Speke (passing ⊒ Hunt's Cross or Cressington), both to within ½ml (tel. 0151 236 7676) *Station:* Garston 2ml; Hunt's Cross 2ml

STAGSHAW GARDEN ❖

Ambleside LA22 0HE Tel: (Regional Office) 015394 35599 Fax: 015394 35353

This woodland garden was created by the late Cubby Acland, Regional Agent for the National Trust. It contains a fine collection of azaleas and rhododendrons, planted under the thinned oaks on the hillside; also magnolias, camellias and embothriums

⭕ 1 April to end June: daily 10–6.30. July to end Oct: by appointment with Regional Office. Please send s.a.e.

💷 £1.30. No reduction for parties. Parking very limited; access dangerous; visitors may park at Waterhead car park and walk to Stagshaw. No access for coaches: park in Waterhead car park, Ambleside. No WC

🧒 Difficult for pushchairs

➡️ ½ml S of Ambleside on A591 [90: NY380030] *Bus:* Stagecoach Cumberland 518, 555/9 from ⊒ Windermere (tel. 01946 63222) *Station:* Windermere 4ml

STEAM YACHT GONDOLA

National Trust (Enterprises) Ltd, Gondola Bookings, Pier Cottage, Coniston LA21 8AJ Tel: 015394 41288

The steam yacht Gondola, *first launched in 1859, and now completely renovated by the Trust, provides a steam-powered passenger service, carrying 86 passengers in opulently upholstered saloons. Travel aboard* Gondola *is an experience in its own right, and a superb way to see Coniston's scenery*

⭕ **Sailings:** Steam Yacht *Gondola* sails to a scheduled daily timetable 26 March to 2 Nov, weather permitting, starting at 11, except Sat, when sailings start at 12.05. The Trust reserves the right to cancel sailings in the event of high winds or lack of demand. Piers at Coniston, Park-a-Moor at SE end of the lake and Brantwood (not NT). Parties from Coniston Pier only. Free parking & WC at Coniston Pier

£ Ticket prices and timetable on application and published locally. Family ticket available. No reduction for NT members as *Gondola* is an enterprise and not held solely for preservation. Parties & private charters by prior arrangement. Contact may be made direct between 9 and 10.30; answerphone in operation at other times

⌂ Guidebook and *Gondola* souvenirs available on board

♿ Not suitable for wheelchairs

👁 Access for visually impaired visitors; guide dogs admitted

🚼 Children's quiz sheet

→ Coniston (½ml to Coniston Pier) *Bus:* Stagecoach Cumberland 505/6 from Ambleside (connections from ≋ Windermere) (tel. 01946 63222) *Station:* Foxfield (U), not Sun, 10ml; Windermere 10ml via vehicle ferry

STYAL COUNTRY PARK 🏠❌✝🦆♿

Estate Office, 7 Oak Cottages, Styal, Wilmslow SK9 4JQ Tel: 01625 523012

Part of the valley of the River Bollin, combining natural beauty with historic interest. There are pleasant riverside walks in fine woodlands; the Country Park includes Quarry Bank Cotton Mill, the factory colony village of Styal and associated farmland

◯ All year during daylight hours

£ Admission charge per car to country park, £1.50

🏃 Guided tours of woodlands and village from main car park on second Sun in each month at 2.30

⌂ Shop at mill

♿ A recently extended circular woodland route is available from the Twinnies Bridge car park (not NT) at the end of the country park. (No access from main car park)

👁 Braille and large-print guides

[symbol] Available from Mill

[symbol] Baby-changing facilities at Mill

[symbol] Environmental education; booking as for Quarry Bank Mill, see above

[symbol] Dogs welcome

[symbol] As for Quarry Bank Mill *Bus:* As for Quarry Bank Mill *Station:* Styal ½ml (not Sun)

TATTON PARK [symbols] [E]

Knutsford WA16 6QN
Tel: 01565 654822 Infoline: 01565 750250 Fax: 01565 650179

One of the most complete historic estates in England open to visitors. The 19th-century Wyatt house, set in more than 400ha of deer park, contains the Egerton family collection of pictures, books, china, glass, silver and specially commissioned Gillow furniture; servants' rooms and cellars depict life downstairs. The 20ha garden contains an authentic Japanese garden, Italian garden, orangery, fernery, rose garden and pinetum. Also, a medieval old hall, an 18th-century farm working as in 1930s and many varieties of wildfowl. There is a new outdoor and sailing centre for pre-booked groups, and a walk round the Landscape History Trail begins the interpretive theme, A Story for Every Age

Note: Members please note: Tatton Park is financed, administered and maintained by Cheshire County Council. Without this commitment the Trust would not have been able to acquire this property, and members are only entitled to free admission to the mansion and gardens. Members must pay car park charges, and full admission to all other attractions – including the Old Hall, Farm and many special events (including the carriage-driving trials on 28/29 June)

[symbol] 24 March to 26 Oct: **Park:** 10–6 daily. **Gardens:** Tues to Sun 10.30–5. **Mansion:** Tues to Sun 12–4 (open Sat & Sun only 1 to 26 Oct). 27 Oct to 31 March 1998: **Park:** Tues to Sun 11–5. **Gardens:** Tues to Sun 11–4. Opening times for Farm and Old Hall on request (tel. 01565 654822). **Events:** All NT members will be expected to pay the special charges which apply to events, including those at Christmas. Please send s.a.e. for full events programme

[symbol] Park: (incl NT members) cars, motorcycles, mopeds £2.80 (disability badges £1); horse/horse-drawn vehicles £2: cyclists, pedestrians, coaches free. Mansion: adult £2.80, child £1.80; family ticket £8 (NT members free). Gardens: as Mansion. Old Hall: adult £2.50, child £1.50, family ticket £8. Farm: as Old Hall; charges apply to NT members. Explorer ticket (Park plus all 4 attractions): adult £8.50, child £5.50; family ticket £25. Mini Explorer (2 attractions): adult £4, child £2.50; family ticket £12. Discounts on all prices for groups of 12 adults or more; contact the property for details

[symbol] Mansion: 1 April to 26 Sept; weekdays only except school holidays and busy periods. Old Hall: 1 April to 31 Oct: Tues to Fri at 3 & 4. *Note:* on weekdays access to Mansion is by guided tour only except during July & Aug

[symbol] 5 March to 30 Sept; Tues to Sun 11.30–5; Oct: Tues to Sun 11.30–4; 3 Nov to 22 Dec: Sat & Sun 11.30–4. Special opening 21 to 24 Oct & 29 Nov to 21 Dec for Christmas events. Jan to 23 March 1998: Sun only 11.30–4. Shop, housekeeper's

store sells estate and local produce; garden sales area

Comprehensive leaflet available. Parking in stable yard, at Old Hall and farm. Ramped access to ground floor of Mansion; contact cashier for access. Garden, park, farm, restaurant & shop easily accessible. Walking and fishing facilities. WC. Sungift electric vehicles available at garden and farm

Braille guide available at garden entrance

1 April to 31 Oct: daily 10.30–5; 1 Nov to 31 March 1998: Tues to Sun 11.30–3

Adventure playground. Nursing mothers invited to use rest-room (ask for directions)

Living History and Education Programme available for schools. Please tel. 01565 750790 for details. Tatton Outdoor Sailing Centre for group instruction. Please tel. 01565 653141 for details

On leads at farm and in park under close control. No dogs in garden

3½ml N of Knutsford, 4ml S of Altrincham, 5ml from M6, exit 19; 3ml from M56, exit 7, well signposted on A556; entrance on Ashley Road, 1½ml NE of jn. A5034 with A50 [109/118: SJ745815] *Bus:* EMS Travel X2 Altrincham Interchange– Chester, Sun only, otherwise from surrounding areas to Knutsford, thence 2ml (tel. 01244 602666) *Station:* Knutsford 2ml

---

TOWNEND

Troutbeck, Windermere LA23 1LB Tel: 015394 32628

An exceptional relic of Lake District life of past centuries. Originally a 'statesman' (wealthy yeoman) farmer's house, built c.1626, Townend contains carved woodwork, books, papers, furniture and fascinating domestic implements of the past, accumulated by the Browne family who lived here from that date until 1943

2 April to 1 Nov: Tues to Fri, Sun & BH Mon, 1–5 or dusk if earlier. Last admission 4.30

£ £2.70, children £1.30; family ticket £7. No reduction for parties which must be pre-booked. Townend and the village are unsuitable for coaches; 12–15-seater minibuses are acceptable; permission to take coaches to Townend must be obtained from the Transportation and Highways Dept, Cumbria CC, Carlisle, Cumbria (tel. 01228 23456). Car park (no coaches)

♿ Unsuitable for wheelchairs

👁 Access for accompanied visually impaired visitors; Braille guide

🍴 Refreshments available in the village

👶 Unsuitable for baby back-packs or pushchairs. Children's quiz sheet

➜ 3ml SE of Ambleside at S end of Troutbeck village [90: NY407020] *Bus:* From surrounding areas (many passing ⟺ Windermere) to within 1ml (tel. 01946 63222) *Station:* Windermere 3ml

---

WORDSWORTH HOUSE 🏠 ❀ E

Main Street, Cockermouth CA13 9RX Tel: 01900 824805

The house where William Wordsworth was born in 1770. This north-country Georgian town house was built in 1745. Seven rooms are furnished in 18th-century style, with some personal effects of the poet; his childhood garden, with terraced walk, leads down to the Derwent. 25min video display in the old stables, last showing of video at 4

O 26 Mar to 1 Nov: weekdays 11–5. Also Sat 29 Mar, 3 & 24 May, all Sats 28 June to 6 Sept and Sat 25 Oct. Closed remaining Sats and all Suns. Last admission 4.30. **Events**: concerts and other events during the season; tel for details

£ £2.60, children £1.30; family ticket £7. Pre-booked parties £1.90 per person. Parking in the town. Reciprocal discount ticket, available from Wordsworth House, allows visitors to enjoy Dove Cottage, the Wordsworth Museum and Rydal Mount (nr Grasmere, not NT) at reduced prices

🛍 Shop same months as house: Mon to Sat 10–5 (10–1 on Sats when house is closed). Also 3 Nov to 24 Dec: Mon to Wed, Fri and Sat 10–4

♿ Unsuitable for severely disabled people; steps at access points. Shop accessible from Main Street. Garden possible over gravel paths by prior arrangement

👁 Suitable for accompanied visually impaired visitors; Braille guide

🍴 Morning coffee, light lunches & refreshments (licensed for beer and wine); teas in the old kitchen

👶 We regret the house is not suitable for baby back-packs, pushchairs or wheelchairs. Baby sling available (up to 2 yrs), children's menu, children's quiz sheet, toys and books, highchair, mother and baby facilities.

🐕 No dogs

➜ [89: NY118307] *Bus:* Stagecoach Cumberland X5, 34 ⟺ Penrith–Workington (passing close ⟺ Workington); 58 from Maryport (passing close ⟺ Maryport) (tel. 01946 63222) *Station:* Maryport 6½ml

Northern Ireland

Tory Island

Ballyliffin
Carndonagh
Carrickart
R257 Falcarragh
Creeslough
Millford
Buncrana
R228
Bunbeg
N56
R245
Gweedore
Bridge End
Londonderry
R258
N58
A6
Letterkenny
N13
R250
Mass
R250
R252
Glenties
N55
N14
Strabane
Gray's Printing Pre
Glencolumbkille
Ardara
N15
Ballybofey
A5
Carrick
R263
N56
Castlederg
B47
Newtownstewart
Donegal
B72
R232
Omagh
Bundoran
Ballyshannon
A47
Kesh
A32
Dromore
B46
A5
Fintona
A46
Irvinestown
B80
Clogher
A.
N15
N16
Manorhamilton
A32
Enniskillen
A4
Dromore West
Sligo
A4
A4
Castle Coole
N59
Florence
Court
Maguiresbridge
Ballysadare
N4
Lisnaskea
Mona
A509
Crom Estate
N54
R294
N17
A34
Newbli
Tobercurry
N87
R183
Belturbet
N57
Charlestown
R294
Boyle
R202
Cavan
Swinford
Ballinamore
R297
Ballaghaderreen
N5
Carrick-on-Shannon
Fenagh
Knock
R327
N83
Frenchpark
Drumsna
N4
Bellanagh
N3
N20
N17
Mohill
N55
Ballyjamesduff
Ballyhaunis
Castlerea
Dromod
Virgi
R031
N60
N5
R194
Granard
Ballymoe
Longford
R394
Castlepollard
R332
R328
N83
R360
N60
Edgeworthstown
R362
N63
N4
R392
R394
Delvin
Athleague
Ballymahon
R392
Mullingar
N17
Mount
Bellew
N61
N55
N52
N4
R339
Athlone
N6
N6
Kinnegad
N6
Rochfortbridge

COAST

Most of the Trust's coastal holdings in Northern Ireland are in Co. Down and Co. Antrim. The southernmost property in Co. Down is at the mouth of **Carlingford Lough** – **Blockhouse** and **Green Islands** [J254097]. These tiny islands total only 0.8ha, but are important nesting sites for terns, and are leased to the Royal Society for the Protection of Birds. To the north of Carlingford Lough are the Mourne Mountains, and here the Trust owns **Slieve Donard**, the highest mountain in the range, and two sections of the **Mourne Coastal Path** [J389269]. One runs south from Bloody Bridge at the foot of Slieve Donard, along the coast and past the site of St Mary's, Ballaghanary, an early Celtic church; the other leads up the valley of the Bloody River, giving access to the mountains. There is an adapted WC for wheelchair users at the car park, but the path is not recommended for wheelchairs.

On this same stretch of coast lies **Dundrum**, with the Widow's Row cottages and footpath along the old railway; also **Murlough National Nature Reserve**, near Newcastle, Ireland's first such reserve. The oldest dunes here are at least 5,000 years old and the soil ranges from lime-rich to acid, supporting a wide variety of plants including pyramidal orchid, bell heather, primrose and dune burnet rose. In spring many birds nest in the sea buckthorn, including reed bunting, stonechat and whitethroat; in winter its orange berries attract thrushes and finches. Visitor facilities open July and August: daily 10–5, and 1st weekend of Sept, weather permitting; parking £2. There is a special slatted walkway across the dunes, suitable for wheelchair users. Holiday cottages now available on shores of Dundrum Inner Bay. Dogs on leads only.

Strangford Lough: the Trust's **Wildlife Scheme** here embraces the entire foreshore of Strangford Lough [J60615] and some 50 islands, totalling 2,200ha. Vast flocks of wildfowl gather here, as well as nesting birds, seals and other marine animals. The wild flowers merit special attention. Bird hides and refuges are provided for study purposes. Birdwatching facilities, including those for disabled visitors, at Castle Espie and Mount Stewart (tel. 01238 510721 or 01396 881411). The Quoile Estuary and two riverside areas, forming part of the freshwater Quoile Pondage, also come under the Wildlife Scheme. Information at Strangford Lough Wildlife Centre, Castle Ward.

On the extreme easterly point of the Co. Down coastline is the former fishing village of **Kearney** [J650517], where the Trust owns 13 houses. **Ballymacormick Point** [J525837] is 3ml north-east of Bangor on the south side of the entrance to Belfast Lough; there are 18ha of rocky shore and coastal heath of biological interest. **Orlock Point** [J559837] has wildfowl, wading birds and gulls. **Lighthouse Island** [J596858] is a 18ha island with a bird observatory. Visits by arrangement with Mr Neville McKee, 67 Temple Rise, Templepatrick, Co. Down (tel. 01849 433068).

The north coasts of counties Londonderry and Antrim are more dramatic than that of Co. Down. The Trust has a continuous series of coastal properties, beginning in the west with **Downhill** [C758363] (see p.168).

Portstewart Strand consists of 2ml of duneland west of Portstewart [C720360]. Parking £2.50. Visitor facilities May to end Aug: daily 10–6, weather permitting. Beach accessible by car, but only suitable for wheelchair users at low tide when sand is hard. Dogs on leads only during summer months. The **Bar Mouth** and **Grangemore Dunes**, 5ml north-west of Coleraine at the mouth of the River Bann [C792355], is a wildlife sanctuary with wheelchair access to observation hide – key available from Warden (tel. 01265 848728).

Between **Giant's Causeway** (see p.170) and the ruins of **Dunseverick Castle** [C987445] the Trust now owns 42ha of the **North Antrim Cliffpath**. East of Dunseverick is the beautiful curve of **Whitepark Bay**, 72ha of sand and white chalk cliff [D023440] with an information panel. Beyond this bay is the tiny stack of basalt connected in summer by a swinging rope bridge to the mainland: **Carrick-a-Rede**, the 'rock on the road'. This is the road the salmon take on their way to rivers in the north and there is a salmon fishery on the island [D062450]. Access to Carrick-a-Rede via cliffpath from Larrybane where there is a car park, £2; coaches £6. Information centre and tea-room open April, May and Sept: weekends 11–6; June to Aug: daily 11–6, weather permitting; adapted WC for wheelchair users. Adjoining are 23ha of coastline with a disused basalt quarry and lime-workings [D051449].

The distinctive headland of **Fairhead** [D185430] rises 190m and affords dramatic views over the Antrim Plateau, Western Isles of Scotland, and the adjacent property to the east, **Murlough Bay** [D199418]. The Trust has leased parts of these properties from local landowners, whose animals continue to graze the land; dogs are therefore to be kept on leads at all times. This is one of the most outstanding sections of the Antrim Coast, with much to interest both botanist and ornithologist. There are several trails to be discovered around the bay. To the south-east is **Cushleake Mountain** [D2273641]; acquired in 1995, this 1213ha site is the best example of raised blanket bog in the ownership of the Trust. At present, access is limited. Turning south, the lovely village of **Cushendun** at the foot of Glendun [D248327] contains cottages designed and built by the architect of Portmeirion in North Wales, the late Clough Williams-Ellis. The harbour is also owned by the Trust.

ARDRESS HOUSE 🏠 📷 🚶 🍴 E

64 Ardress Road, Portadown BT62 1SQ Tel: 01762 851236

Originally a 17th-century farmhouse, the main front and garden façades were added in the 18th century by the owner-architect George Ensor. The house contains some particularly fine neo-classical plasterwork as well as good furniture and pictures. There is a display of farm implements and livestock in the farmyard, an attractive garden and woodland and riverside walks

House & farmyard: April: weekends & Easter (28 March to 1 April) 2–6; May & Sept: Sat, Sun & BH 2–6; June to end Aug: daily (except Tues) 2–6. Farmyard also open weekdays (except Tues) May & Sept 12–4. **Events**: range of events and demonstrations during season; tel. 01762 851236 for details

£ £2.20, children £1.10; family ticket £5.50. Parties £1.80. Parties outside normal opening hours £3 per person

Shop open as house

Access to 3 rooms on ground floor via 3 steps or side door from farmyard, picnic area and part of farmyard; ground floor farm exhibits in information room accessible. WC in car park by farm. Gravel paths in garden. Sympathetic Hearing Scheme

No on-site facilities but picnics welcome. Picnic area opens at 12

Play area

Pre-booked school groups welcome, especially those involved in the Cross-Community Contact Scheme. Farmyard tours and trails available

In garden only

7m from Portadown on Moy road (B28), 5m from Moy, 3m from Loughgall intersection 13 on M1, 9m from Armagh [H914559] *Bus:* Ulsterbus 67 Portadown–Kesquin Bridge (passing close NIR Portadown Stn) to within ¼ml (tel. 01762 342511) *Station:* Portadown 7ml

THE ARGORY

Moy, Dungannon BT71 6NA Tel: 01868 784753 Fax: 01868 789598

Set in over 130ha of woodland overlooking the Blackwater river, the house dates from 1820 and remains substantially unchanged since the turn of the century. Fascinating furniture and contents, including an 1824 Bishop's barrel organ. There is an imposing stable yard with a coach house and carriages, harness room, laundry and acetylene gas plant. Also, an interesting sundial garden and extensive walks

Note: The house has no electric light. Visitors wishing to make a close study of the interior and paintings should avoid dull days early and late in the season

Easter (28 March to 1 April): daily 2–6. April, May & Sept: Sat, Sun & BH 2–6; June to end Aug: daily (except Tues) 2–6. Open 1–6 on all BH. Last tour 5.15. **Events:** range of events during season. Tel. for details

£2.40, children £1.20; family ticket £6. Parties £2. Parties outside normal opening hours £3 per person. Car park £1.50. Parking 100m. Coaches must book with Administrator

K Please note that numbers on any one tour are restricted. All visitors, including NT members, please report to reception on arrival

Shop Shop open as house, but weekends only in June 2–6; BHols 1–6; weekdays July & Aug 3–5

Access Access to ground floor of house, all driveways, garden and pleasure grounds, walks, tea-room and reception area; some deep gravel round house; wheelchair available. Car-parking near east door of house (ramp) by arrangement at reception; WC by reception area. Sympathetic Hearing Scheme. Special tours for partially-sighted visitors by prior arrangement

Refreshments Light refreshments in tea-room, open as shop. Picnics welcome

Playground Adventure playground

School Pre-booked school groups welcome, especially those in the Cross-Community Contact Scheme. Study centre; teachers' pack and pupil worksheets; Key Stages 1 & 2 tours available

Dogs In grounds and garden only, on leads

Directions 4ml from Moy, 3ml from M1, exit 13 or 14 (signposted) NB coaches must use exit 13; weight restrictions at Bonds Bridge [H872580] *Bus:* Ulsterbus 67, 75 Portadown–Dungannon (both pass close NIR Portadown Stn), alight Charlemont on 67, Verner's Inn on 75, 2½ml from both (tel. 01762 342511)

CASTLE COOLE 🏠 ♣ K E

Enniskillen BT74 6JY Tel: 01365 322690 Fax: 01365 325665

This very fine neo-Classical late 18th-century house with colonnaded wings was designed by James Wyatt. It contains original decoration and furniture dating from before 1830 and is set in a landscaped parkland with mature oak woodland. State Bedroom prepared for George IV in 1821. Exterior attractions include servants' tunnel, laundry house, dairy, ice house, woodland walks, stables and estate display room in Grand Yard

O Easter (28 March to 1 April): daily 1–6; April & Sept: Sat, Sun & BH only, 1–6; May to end Aug: daily except Thur 1–6. Last tour begins 5.15. Grounds open to pedestrians during daylight hours. **Events:** concerts and displays in the house, cricket on the south lawn; tel. for details

£ £2.80, children £1.40; family ticket £7. Parties £2.50 per person. Parties outside normal opening hours £3.50 per person. Estate £2 per car

Shop Shop in Tallow House, open same days as house 1–5 (weekends and BHs only in May)

Access Ramped access to ground floor of house and reception area in car park; disabled visitors may be driven to the house. Wheelchair available. WC in reception centre. Sympathetic Hearing Scheme

Refreshments Tea-room in Tallow House, open as shop (shop and tea-room opening times may vary according to demand). Picnics welcome

Baby Baby-changing facilities in disabled WC

165

■ Pre-booked school groups welcome, especially those involved in the Cross-Community Contact Scheme

🐾 In grounds, on leads only

➜ 1½ml SE of Enniskillen on main Belfast–Enniskillen road (A4) [H260430]
Bus: Ulsterbus 95, Enniskillen–Clones (tel. 01365 322633)

CASTLE WARD 🏠 🏰 ❖ ♠ 🏊 ⊿ ⊥T 🕴 E

Strangford, Downpatrick BT30 7LS
Tel: 01396 881204 Fax: 01396 881729

Castle Ward is set in a 285ha country estate on the shores of Strangford Lough. This unique 18th-century mansion has opposing façades in different styles: the west front is Classical, and the east front Gothick. In the stableyard there is a Victorian laundry and theatre for visiting companies. Also, formal and landscape gardens with specimen shrubs and trees, fortified towers, a sawmill and working cornmill. Strangford Lough Wildlife Centre, located on the water's edge, has audiovisual shows. Caravan park, holiday cottages, and basecamp for young people

O **House:** Easter (28 March to 6 April): daily 1–6; April, Sept & Oct: Sat & Sun 1–6; May to end Aug: daily except Thur 1–6. Last tour 5.10. **Estate & grounds:** open all year dawn to dusk (charge for car park only). **Strangford Lough Wildlife Centre:** open as house 2–6, except May & June when open Sat, Sun & BH only 2–6. **Events:** craft fairs, guided walks, concerts, opera season and other events; tel. for details.

£ £2.60, children £1.30; family ticket £6.50. Parties £2 per person. Parties outside normal opening hours £3 per person. Three car parks; parking £3.50 (£1.75 when house and other facilities are closed). Coaches: booked parties to house free; others £15. Horses (using bridlepath) £5 per single horsebox

🛍 Shop open same days as house (but weekends & BH only in May): weekdays 1–5; Sat, Sun & BH 1–6

♿ Access to formal garden, restaurant and interpretation centre; wheelchairs available. Disabled visitors may be set down at house; car park for disabled drivers behind stables; limited spaces. House accessible via six steps. WC in stableyard and in farmyard and caravan park. Sympathetic Hearing Scheme. Wheelchair access to shore of Strangford Lough

👁 Braille guide available. Scented plants

🍴 Light refreshments, lunches and teas, open as shop. Party organisers should book visits and arrange teas in advance with receptionist. Picnics welcome

👶 Changing facilities in WC. Adventure playground. Victorian Pastimes Centre; toys & dressing up

■ Pre-booked school groups welcome especially those involved in the Cross Community Contact Scheme. Teachers' pack available and pupil worksheet. Nature trails. Key Stage 2 tour available based on 'life in the big house'

🐾 In grounds only, on leads

→ 7ml NE of Downpatrick, 1½ml W of Strangford village on A25, on S shore of Strangford Lough, entrance by Ballyculter Lodge [J752494] *Bus:* Ulsterbus 16E Downpatrick–Strangford, with connections from Belfast (passing close NIR Belfast Central Stn); alight Ballyculter crossroads, 1ml (tel. 01396 612384)

CROM ESTATE 🏠🌳🎣👤🚶🧍 Ⓔ

Newtownbutler BT92 8AP
Tel: 01365 738174 Visitor Centre Tel: 01365 738118

770ha of woodland, parkland and wetland on the shores of Upper Lough Erne. This is one of Northern Ireland's most important nature conservation areas and is of international significance. Nature trails around lakeshore and ruins of Crom Old Castle. Visitor facilities include 7 holiday cottages, boat hire, overnight woodland hide, coarse angling, jetty and slipway

Note: The 19th-century castle is private and not open to the public

🅾 1 April to end Sept: daily 10–6 (Sun 12–6). **Events:** programme available: please contact the visitor centre

£ Admission £3 per car or boat

🚶 Guided walks programme available or by special arrangement

🛍 Shop in visitor centre open April, May, June & Sept: Sat, Sun & BH 2.30–5.30; July & Aug: daily 2.30–5.30

♿ Designated spaces in car park. Wheelchair available for visitor centre. Full access to exhibition, shop and tea-room in visitor centre. Gravel paths on Estate; strong companions necessary. WCs in visitor centre in stableyard. Sympathetic Hearing Scheme

🍴 Tea-room open as shop; also by arrangement

🧒 Children's area in information centre; also baby-changing facilities

🏫 Pre-booked school groups welcome, especially those involved in the Cross-Community Contact Scheme

🐕 On lead only

→ 3ml W of Newtownbutler, on Newtownbutler–Crom road [J363245], or follow signs from Lisnaskea *Bus:* Ulsterbus 95 Enniskillen–Clones (with connections from Belfast), alight Newtownbutler, 3ml (tel. 01365 322633)

CROWN LIQUOR SALOON 🏠

46 Great Victoria Street, Belfast BT2 7BA Tel: 01232 249476

A magnificent high-Victorian public house with rich ornamentation and fine woodwork, glass and tiles, built at the end of the 19th century; managed by Tennents Taverns

🅾 Daily, during licensed hours 11.30am–11pm; Sun 12.30–2.30 & 7–10

Full bar facilities, snack lunches

→ [J738332] *Bus:* From surrounding areas (tel. 01232 246485 (Citybus) or 320011 (Ulsterbus)) *Station:* Belfast Central ¼ml

DERRYMORE HOUSE

Bessbrook, Newry BT35 7EF Tel: 01693 830353

An elegant late 18th-century thatched cottage. Built by Isaac Corry, who represented Newry in the Irish House of Commons for 30 years from 1776. Set amidst a picturesque estate, it is typical of the informal thatched retreats which many estates boasted in the 18th century

O 28 March to 1 April: daily 2–5.30; May to end Sept: Thurs, Fri & Sat 2–5.30

£ £1.60, children 80p, family ticket £4. Parties £1.10 per person

& Access to grounds and one room on ground floor. No WC

🐾 In grounds on lead please

→ Off the Newry–Camlough road at Bessbrook, 1½ml from Newry [J056279]
Bus: Ulsterbus 41/2/4 from Newry (passing close NIR Newry) (tel. 01693 63531)
Station: NIR: Newry 2ml

DOWNHILL CASTLE, MUSSENDEN TEMPLE, BISHOP'S GATE & BLACK GLEN

Bishop's Gate, 42 Mussenden Road, Castlerock, Coleraine BT51 4RP
Tel: 01265 848728

A landscaped estate, laid out in the late 18th century by the energetic Earl-Bishop, Frederick Hervey, Earl of Bristol and Bishop of Derry. The estate includes Mussenden Temple perched on the cliff, ruins of his palatial house, family memorials, garden, fish pond, woodland and cliff walks, as well as panoramic views of Ireland's north coast. Modest camping facilities in Walled Garden

Note: Mussenden Temple may be closed for several weeks during 1997 for essential repairs

O **Temple:** Easter (28 March to 1 April): daily 12–6; April, May, June & Sept: Sat, Sun & BH 12–6; July & Aug: daily 12–6. **Grounds:** open all year, dawn to dusk. Open for groups at other times by arrangement (tel. 01265 848728)

£ Free. Limited access for coaches. WC in Walled Garden (Lion's Gate)

& Paths through garden; cars may be taken to Bishop's Gate. Glen Walk partly accessible

Picnics welcome

Must be kept on leads

→ 1ml W of Castlerock and 5M W of Coleraine on the Coleraine–Downhill coast road (A2) [J757357] *Bus:* Ulsterbus 134 Coleraine–Limavady (tel. 01265 43334) *Station:* Castlerock ½ml

FLORENCE COURT 🏛 🏚 ❊ ♠ ⚎ 🍴 E

Enniskillen BT92 1DB Tel: 01365 348249 Fax: 01365 348873

One of the most important houses in Ulster, built in the mid 18th-century by John Cole, father of the 1st Earl of Enniskillen. Contents include fine rococo plasterwork and good examples of 18th-century furniture. There are pleasure grounds with an ice house and water-powered sawmill, plus a walled garden and fine views over surrounding mountains. Holiday cottage in walled garden

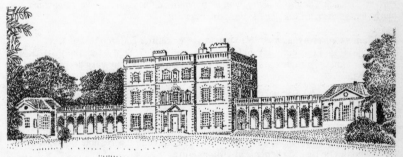

O Easter (28 March to 1 April): daily 1–6; April & Sept: Sat, Sun & BH only 1–6; May to end Aug: daily except Tues 1–6. Last admission 5.15. Grounds open all year 10–7 (Oct to March 10–4). Closed Christmas Day. **Events**: country fairs, craft fairs and other events; tel. for details

£ House: £2.80, children £1.40; family ticket £7. Parties £2.50 per person. Parties outside normal opening hours £3.50 per person. Estate: £2. Parking 50m. Information room

🛍 Shop open as house 1–6 (weekends and BHols only in May). Open from 12 noon July and Aug (tel. 01365 348788)

♿ Access to garden & ground floor only. North Pavilion restaurant accessible. WCs and parking. Self-drive powered vehicle available. Sympathetic Hearing Scheme

Teas & lunches downstairs in North Pavilion; open as shop. Picnic area

Parent and baby room, baby slings and highchair available. Play area

Pre-booked school groups welcome, especially those involved in the Cross-Community Contact Scheme. Teachers' pack and pupil worksheets available. Key Stages 1 & 2 tours available

In grounds and garden, on leads

8ml SW of Enniskillen via A4 Sligo road and A32 Swanlinbar road [H175344], 4ml from Marble Arch Caves *Bus:* Ulsterbus 192 Enniskillen–Swanlinbar to within 1ml (tel. 01365 322633)

GIANT'S CAUSEWAY

44a Causeway Road, Bushmills BT57 8SU
Tel: 012657 31159/31582 Fax: 012657 32963

The unusual basalt rock formations harbour a wealth of local and natural history, which can be enjoyed from the cliff paths. The wreck-site of Armada treasure ship Girona *(1588) is at Port-na-Spaniagh. The visitor centre, with interpretative displays, audiovisual theatre and tourist information, is owned by Moyle District Council*

Giant's Causeway: all year. **NT shop in visitor centre**: 7 March to end May: daily 10–5; June: daily 10–6; July & Aug: daily 10–7; Sept & Oct: daily 10–5. **Tea-room**: open same days as shop 11–5 (closing times may vary according to demand)

Free. Parking £2.50, incl. NT members (Moyle District Council car park)

Open as visitor centre

Parking access close to buildings; minibus with hoist for transport to Causeway during season; ramps to shop, tea-room & visitor centre; accessible walks; WC. Sympathetic Hearing Scheme at visitor centre

Braille guide

Lunch, tea, snacks in tea-room at visitor centre (closes 6.15 in July & Aug)

■ Pre-booked school visits welcome, especially those involved in the Cross-Community Contact Scheme. Activity trail available. Coastal Guardians Scheme

🦮 On leads only, outdoors

➔ On B146 Causeway–Dunseverick road [C945438] *Bus:* Ulsterbus 138 from Coleraine (passing NIR Coleraine Stn & connecting with trains from Belfast Central Stn); 172 Ballycastle–Portrush (tel. 01265 43334) *Station:* Portrush 8ml

---

GRAY'S PRINTING PRESS 🏠 🚻 E

49 Main Street, Strabane BT82 8AU Tel: 01504 884094

An 18th-century printing press. It may have been here that John Dunlap, the printer of the American Declaration of Independence, and James Wilson, grandfather of President Woodrow Wilson, learned their trade. There is a collection of 19th-century hand-printing machines, NT information and an audiovisual display

O April to end Sept: daily except Thur, Sun & BH 2–5.30. At other times by prior arrangement. **Events:** compositor demonstrations once per fortnight; tel. for details

£ £1.60, children 80p; family ticket £4. Parties £1.10 per person. Public car park 100m

🤸 Guided tours by arrangement

♿ Access to audio-visual display only

🛒 In town (not NT)

■ Pre-booked school visits welcome, especially those involved in the Cross-Community Contact Scheme

➔ [H345977] *Bus:* Ulsterbus Express 273 Belfast–Londonderry (passing close NIR Londonderry Stn), alight Strabane centre; few min walk (tel. 01504 382393)

HEZLETT HOUSE 🏠

107 Sea Road, Castlerock, Coleraine BT51 4TW
Tel: 01265 848567

A 17th-century thatched house, with an interesting cruck-truss roof construction. Furnished in late Victorian style. Small museum of farm implements

O Easter (28 March to 1 April): daily 12–5; April, May & Sept: Sat, Sun & BH only 12–5; June to Aug: daily, except Tues 12–5. Guided tours. Parties must book in advance (max. number in house 15 at any one time)

£ £1.60, children 80p; family ticket £4. Parties £1.10 per person. Parties outside normal opening hours £2 per person. Cycles can be parked at side of house

♿ Access to ground floor only

■ Pre-booked school groups welcome

 In garden only, on leads

→ 5ml W of Coleraine on Coleraine–Downhill coast road, A2 [C772349]
Bus: Ulsterbus 134 Coleraine–Limavady, alight crossroads, few min walk
(tel. 01265 43334) *Station:* Castlerock ¾ml

MOUNT STEWART HOUSE, GARDEN & TEMPLE OF THE WINDS 🏠 🔭 ❋ ⚒ E

Newtownards BT22 2AD
Tel: 01247 788387/788487 Fax: 01247 788569

A fascinating 18th-century house with 19th-century additions, where Lord Castlereagh grew up. The garden was largely created by Edith, wife of the 7th Marquess of Londonderry, with an unrivalled collection of plants, colourful parterres and magnificent vistas. The Temple of the Winds, James 'Athenian' Stuart's banqueting hall of 1785, overlooks Strangford Lough

🅞 **House:** Easter (28 March to 6 April): daily 1–6; April & Oct: Sat & Sun 1–6; May to end Sept: daily except Tues 1–6. Last tour 5. **Garden:** March: Sun only 2–5; April to end Sept: daily 11-6; Oct: Sat & Sun only 11–6. **Temple of the Winds:** open same days as house 2–5. **Events:** seasonal guided walks, craft fairs & band concerts; tel. for details

£ House & garden £3.50, children £1.75; family ticket £8.75. Parties £3 per person. Parties outside normal opening hours £4.50 per person. Garden £3, children £1.50, family ticket £7.50, parties £2.50, parties outside normal opening hours £4.30. Parking 300m. Temple of the Winds only £1, children 50p, parties 80p per person

📷 Open same days as house 12.30–5.30, Sun until 6. BH open 12.30–6. Also open Sun in March 2–5; Tues May to Sept, 12.30–5.30

♿ Ramped access to ground floor of house and large parts of garden; restaurant and shop accessible from house; wheelchairs available. Disabled visitors may be set down at house. WCs. Powered buggy available; free route-map of garden; mostly level path round lake. Sympathetic Hearing Scheme

◉ Scented plants

◖ Light refreshments and teas same times as shop

♿ Baby-changing facilities

▮ Pre-booked school groups welcome, especially those involved in the Cross-Community Contact Scheme

🐕 On leads only

→ 15ml SE of Belfast on Newtownards–Portaferry road, A20, 5ml SE of Newtownards [J553695] *Bus:* Ulsterbus 9, 10 Belfast–Portaferry (passing close NIR Belfast Central Stn) to within ¾ml (tel. 01247 812391/2) *Station:* Bangor 10ml

---

PATTERSON'S SPADE MILL 🏠 ❌ 🛗 🍴 E

Antrim Road, Templepatrick BT39 0AP Tel: 01849 433619

The last surviving water-driven spade mill in Ireland. Spades were made here until 1990 and all the original equipment has been fully restored. There are demonstrations of spade making

◯ Easter (28 March to 1 April): daily 2–6; April, May & Sept: Sat, Sun & BH only 2–6; June to end of August: daily except Tues 2–6. **Events:** vintage-vehicle displays; tel. for details

£ £2.50, children £1.25; family ticket £6.25. Parties £1.75. Parties outside normal opening hours £3

🛍 Shop open as mill

♿ Accessible throughout. Ramp gives access to viewing platform. WC in reception area. Wheelchair

▮ Pre-booked school groups welcome, especially those involved in the Cross-Community Contact Scheme

→ 2ml SE of Templepatrick on Antrim–Belfast road, A6; exit 4 or 5 of M2 [J263/856] *Bus:* Ulsterbus 120 Belfast to Ballymena (passing close to NIR Belfast Central & Antrim stations): alight Templepatrick (tel. 01232 320011) *Station:* Antrim 8ml

---

ROWALLANE GARDEN ❃ E

Saintfield, Ballynahinch BT24 7LH
Tel: 01238 510131 Fax: 01238 511242

A 21ha garden, with daffodils and rhododendrons in spring, summer-flowering trees and shrubs, and herbaceous plants, fuchsias and shrub roses in the wall garden. The garden also includes the national collection of penstemon, and the rock garden with primulas, meconopsis, heathers and dwarf shrubs is interesting throughout the year. There are several areas of natural wild flowers to attract butterflies

◯ 1 April to end Oct: daily (weekdays 10.30–6; weekends 2–6); Nov to end March 1998: daily except Sat & Sun 10.30–5. Closed 25, 26 Dec & 1 Jan. **Events:** concerts, teddy bears' picnics, Yuletide market; tel. for details

£ Easter to Oct £2.50, children £1.25; family ticket £6.25. Parties £1.75. Parties outside opening hours £3 per person. Nov to end March 1998 £1.40, children 70p, parties 80p

& Close parking by arrangement. Majority of garden accessible; wheelchair available. WC. Tea-room accessible. Sympathetic Hearing Scheme

Scented plants. Tours arranged by Head Gardener

Light refreshments. Open 28 March to 1 April: daily 2–6; April & Sept: Sat & Sun only 2–6; May to end Aug: daily 12.30–5 (2–6 at weekends)

Must be kept on leads

→ 11ml SE of Belfast, 1ml S of Saintfield, W of the Downpatrick road (A7) [J412581] *Bus:* Ulsterbus 15 Belfast–Downpatrick (passing close NIR Belfast Central Stn) (tel. 01396 612384)

SPRINGHILL 🏠 🏠 ❖ 🧒 🏃 E

20 Springhill Road, Moneymore, Magherafelt BT45 7NQ
Tel: 01648 748210

17th-century 'Planter' house with 18th- and 19th-century additions. Springhill was the home of ten generations of a family which arrived from Ayrshire in the 17th century and the house contains family furniture, a refurbished nursery, paintings, ornaments, curios and 18th-century hand-blocked wallpaper. Outbuildings house an extensive costume collection and there are walled gardens and woodland walks

O Easter (28 March to 1 April): daily 2–6; April, May & Sept: Sat, Sun & BH only 2–6; June to Aug: daily except Thur 2–6. **Events:** children's & family events during the season; tel. for details

£ £2.40, children £1.20; family ticket £6. Parties £2. Parties outside normal opening hours £3 per person. Parking 40m

🛍 Shop open as house

& Access to all ground-floor rooms; close car parking at rear of house and by costume museum; access to small sales point by arrangement with guiding staff; picnic area accessible; gravel paths in garden. WC. Sympathetic Hearing Scheme

Herb garden

Light refreshments in servants' hall, open as house. Picnic areas in garden and woodland

🧒 Baby-changing facilities. Toy collection; children's costumes and activities. Play area

Pre-booked school groups welcome. Study centre. Teachers' pack and pupil worksheets. Key Stages 1–4 tours available

In grounds, on lead

→ 1ml from Moneymore on Moneymore–Coagh road, B18 [H866828] *Bus:* Ulsterbus 110/20 Belfast–Cookstown (passing close NIR Antrim Stn), alight Moneymore village, ¼ml (tel. 01648 32218)

WELLBROOK BEETLING MILL 🍴 💺 🚻 🚶 🔧

20 Wellbrook Road, Corkhill, Cookstown BT80 9RY
Tel: 01648 751715/751735

A hammer mill powered by water for beetling, the final process in linen manufacture. Original machinery is in working order. The mill is situated in an attractive glen, with wooded walks along the Ballinderry river and by the mill race

🅾 Easter (28 March to 1 April): daily 2–6; April, May, June & Sept: Sat, Sun & BH only 2–6; July & Aug: daily, except Tues 2–6

💷 £1.60, children 80p; family ticket £4. Parties £1.10 per person. Pre-booked parties outside normal opening hours £2 per person. Parking. For information contact the Custodian

🛍 Shop open as Mill

👁 'Touch and Sound' tour can be provided for visually impaired visitors

🎒 Pre-booked school visits welcome, especially those involved in the Cross-Community Contact Scheme. Key Stage 2 tour available, based on technology & change in Victorian times

🐕 In grounds only, on leads

➔ 4ml W of Cookstown, ½ml off Cookstown–Omagh road (A505): from Cookstown turn right at Kildress Parish Church [H750792], or follow Orritor Road (A53) to avoid town centre *Bus:* Ulsterbus 90 from Cookstown, with connections from Belfast (passing close NIR Antrim Stn) (tel. 01648 766440)

South East

COAST

In **KENT** the Trust owns 227ha of land on either side of Dover, stretching to over 5½ml of the famous White Cliffs; 27ha of cliff and farmland with fine walks to the south-west at **Great Farthingloe** [179: TR2902393], 65ha of clifftop grassland behind the port of Dover at Langdon Cliffs and Langdon Hole, and the remainder at St Margaret's Bay to the north-east, including **Bockhill Farm** and Kingsdown Leas. Paths across Bockhill Farm are suitable for wheelchair users (a strong pusher is needed) [179: TR372448].

Further north at **Sandwich Bay** [179: TR347620] and **Pegwell Bay** [179: TR343627] are 223ha of coastal saltmarsh, sand dunes, mudflats and foreshore, managed for the Trust as a nature reserve by the Kent Trust for Nature Conservation and forming part of a Site of Special Scientific Interest. Guided walks can be arranged from the Sandwich Bay Bird Observatory. Formed by the serpentine River Stour which finally reaches the sea at Pegwell Bay, the saltings, mudflats and freshwater marshes attract migrant waders as well as British sea- and shore-birds, including some rare species. One of the footpaths is suitable for wheelchairs and leads to an accessible birdhide. Access to this is from the Pegwell Bay side. Send an s.a.e. for a leaflet to the KTNC, Tyland Barn, Sandling, Maidstone, Kent ME14 3BD (tel. 01622 662012).

The South Downs meet the sea at the Seven Sisters, just west of Eastbourne in **EAST SUSSEX**, forming one of the best-known and -loved lengths of coast in England. At **Crowlink**, **Birling Gap** and **Chyngton Farm** [199: TV5497] the Trust owns some 404ha of chalk downland, cliff and river estuary. Here, and on the neighbouring downland, are some of the most delightful walks and unspoilt views. The downs at Crowlink have gradual slopes and short turf over which wheelchairs may be pushed; there are no designated wheelchair routes and visitors may wander where they wish. The beach at Birling Gap remains relatively uncrowded. There is access to the sea and fine views of the Seven Sisters from Chyngton Farm. The coastal strip is a Site of Special Scientific Interest [199: TV5497]. Car-parking at both Crowlink and Birling Gap. To the east of Hastings, public footpaths give access to more Trust-owned cliffland at **Fairlight** with local countryside walks [199: TQ884127].

At West Wittering in **WEST SUSSEX** is the 45ha sand and shingle spit of **East Head**, east of the entrance to Chichester Harbour [181: SU766990]. Vulnerable to the constant battering it receives from the sea and, indeed, from the feet of visitors, East Head is important because it demonstrates how the sea has shaped this part of the coastline, and because it supports a variety of wildlife. The Trust has fenced off part of the spit, while marram grass is encouraged to 'bind' the dunes; naturalists come to see the waders, the plant and marine life, and the insect population.

The Trust owns 16ml of spectacular coastline on the **ISLE OF WIGHT**. The best-known landmark on West Wight is the Needles, the pointed stacks of rock stretching into the sea at the extreme west of the island. Overlooking the famous rocks the Trust owns the **Needles Headland** [196: SZ300848], as well as the **Needles Old Battery** (see p.209) and three coastguard cottages, let as holiday homes. From here Trust land extends to Freshwater Bay, along the chalk cliffs of **Tennyson Down** [196: SZ330855], where the Poet Laureate walked every day when he lived at nearby Farringford.

South-east from Freshwater Bay the Trust also owns much land along the back of the Wight. On the coast **Compton Bay** [196: SZ3785], one of the island's most popular bathing beaches, is protected by the Trust, as is **Brook Chine** [196: SZ378840] (dogs not allowed on Compton beach from June to mid Sept). At the southernmost tip of the island is **St Catherine's Point** [196: SZ495755], where there is another NT holiday cottage.

On the east of the island the Trust owns **Bembridge & Culver Downs** [196: SZ 624869], which look to the north towards the village of Bembridge and its windmill (see p.189). Stretching almost across Bembridge harbour-mouth is **St Helen's Duver** [196: SZ637891], a wide sand and shingle spit which used to be a golf course. The Club House has been converted to a holiday cottage and adapted for disabled visitors.

The Trust owns a spacious Edwardian house facing the sea at Cowes on the north of the island, now converted into two holiday cottages. On the north-west coast the ancient borough of **Newtown** [196: SZ424906] is now reduced to a small village, although the outlines of the 13th-century town are still clearly visible. The Trust owns the Old Town Hall (see p.211) and protects much of the old borough and the entire river estuary, which is now a National Nature reserve.

COUNTRYSIDE

In the far west of the region, in **OXFORDSHIRE**, the **Buscot** and **Coleshill** estates extend to about 3036ha of farmland and woodland [163: SU2694]. This beautiful, rural area includes **Badbury Hill**, where there is a car park. An Iron Age hillfort gives fine views over the upper Thames Valley and south to the Berkshire Downs on which is **White Horse Hill**. Buscot is an attractive stone village close to the Thames, with a popular picnic area at Buscot Weir. You may park in the village a short walk away. There is also a picnic site and small car park by the Thames to the west of Buscot on the road to Lechlade. Coleshill village is a typical estate village of Cotswold stone-and-tile houses and cottages. Box hedges are an attractive feature of the village.

1ml south-east of Watlington, on an escarpment of the Chilterns, **Watlington Hill** [175: SU702935] rises to 210m and gives splendid views over much of Oxfordshire. The scenery alone is rewarding, and for the naturalist the area offers much fascination. This chalk hill is overlaid with clay and flints, so the vegetation includes both clay- and chalk-loving plants. There is a fine yew forest, and whitebeam, dogwood, hawthorn and the wayfaring tree grow in profusion. The hill is skirted by the Upper Icknield Way. It is an ideal spot for picnics or simply enjoying the view.

An interesting feature to look out for on the side of the hill is the White Mark, a triangle cut out of the chalk and kept free of vegetation. Just south of the hill lie **Watlington Woods**, which are especially attractive at bluebell time. There is a small car park for both the hill and woods off the Watlington to Northend road.

Aston Wood [165: SU740973], to the west of Stokenchurch, is a pleasant pocket Chiltern woodland. An area rich in wildlife, it adjoins the Nature Conservancy Council's National Nature Reserve at Aston Rowant. There is parking in a layby beside the A40.

There are some excellent archaeological monuments in the open countryside south of Uffington, south-west Oxfordshire. The famous landmark of **White Horse Hill** has a 80m long figure of a horse cut in the chalk. At the foot of the hill is a sheltered grassy area known as 'The Manger', where traditionally the horse comes to feed. The origin of the White Horse is unknown, but it is probably late Bronze Age and is certainly the oldest chalk figure in Britain. Above it is an ancient barrow. The hill is crowned by the Bronze Age hillfort of **Uffington Castle**, which dates from 1,000 BC and is surrounded by a strong defensive bank and ditch. The smaller, flat-topped **Dragon Hill** is nearby. It is traditionally the site where St George slew the dragon, and legend has it that the distinctive bare patch is where the dragon's blood was spilled on the earth.

All three monuments [174: SU301869] belong to, and are cared for, by the Trust, but are protected under the guardianship of English Heritage. This fascinating area may be approached on foot from the Ridgeway path or by car from the B4507. Large car park 450m from monuments.

South of White Horse Hill, there are beautiful walks at **Ashdown Woods** [174: SU283824], adjoining the 17th-century **Ashdown House** (see p.186), **Weathercock Hill** on the opposite side of the B4000 and **Alfred's Castle**, an Iron Age hillfort where rumour has it that King Alfred defeated the Danes. There is a car park 250m from the house. Please note that the estate and car park are closed to the public for estate management purposes on Fridays throughout the year.

Glimpses of Berkshire, Hampshire and Surrey may be seen from the steep, heather-clad ridge of **Finchampstead Ridges** [175: SU808634], 4ml south of Wokingham in **BERKSHIRE**, south of the B3348. The ridge overlooks the valley of the River Blackwater. North of the Ridges is **Simons Wood** [175: SU814637], a heathland and woodland area with a rich variety of tree species, including clumps of Scots pine over a century old. A popular walk is to **Heath Pool**; its northern bank is bounded by the Devil's Highway, which is part of the old Roman road from London to Silchester. The area has many attractions for naturalists and birdwatchers, with siskins and spotted flycatchers among the species which may be seen. You may park beside the B3348 at the Ridges, and further east along the same road there is a signposted car park in Simons Wood. Nearby is the impressive **Wellingtonia Avenue**, which forms part of the B3348. As its name suggests, it is lined by mature examples of *Wellingtonia*, one of the world's tallest species of tree.

Commonland on the south bank of the Thames at Maidenhead and Cookham provides a range of pleasant country walks. One of the features of **Maidenhead Thicket** [175: SU855810] is a prehistoric Belgic farm enclosure known for some reason as 'Robin Hood's Arbour'. The Thicket is perhaps at its most attractive in springtime, when a mass of primroses bloom here. Visitors may be fortunate enough to hear a nightingale.

Parts of **Cock Marsh** [175: SU890869], on the south bank of the Thames facing Bourne End, provide a fine example of a lowland marsh, a habitat which is increasingly at risk in Britain today. A group of burial barrows remains as evidence of Cock Marsh's ancient history. Adjoining Maidenhead Thicket to the north is **Pinkney's Green**, and in the same area the Trust also owns Cookham Dean village green. **Cookham Moor**, **Widbrook** (or Whitebrook) **Common**, **Bigfrith** and **Tugwood Commons**, and **North Town Moor**, ½ml north of Maidenhead and Winter Hill. Residents of the area bought and gave all these pleasant open spaces to the Trust in 1934. The former **Brick & Tile Works** site at Malders Lane, Pinkney's Green, was acquired in 1989 and comprises scrub, woodland and ponds, with paths for access. Today the 364ha continue to be enjoyed by local people and visitors alike. There are several small car parks in the area, some of which are signposted.

The Holies [174: SU594797], **Lardon Chase** [174: SU588809] and **Lough Down** [174: SU588813] all lie on the west side of the Goring Gap where the Thames divides the Chilterns from the North Wessex Downs. The car park at the top of Streatley Hill [174: SU583806] gives access to all these properties, from which there are magnificent views. The chalk grassland is managed for its nature conservation interest. The Holies comprises grassland, scrub and woodland. A short distance away, just below Pangbourne Bridge, east of the B471, is Pangbourne Meadow [175: SU640768], a 3ha area with some interesting flora, on the south bank of the Thames.

The charming village of **Bradenham** [165: SU823970], to the north-west of High Wycombe in **BUCKINGHAMSHIRE**, belongs almost entirely to the Trust. There are over 400ha of Chiltern beech woodland, hills and farmland to be explored. A network of paths provides easy access for the rambler. The church and 17th-century manor house provide an impressive backdrop to the sloping village green. The manor house, which is let and not open to the public, was once the home of Isaac D'Israeli, whose Prime Minister son Benjamin Disraeli lived at Hughenden Manor nearby (see p.202). Car-parking is available at the village green.

3ml north-east of Princes Risborough, is **Coombe Hill**, the highest viewpoint in the Chilterns, rising to 258m. There are extensive views over the Vale of Aylesbury, towards the Berkshire Downs, to the Cotswolds north of Oxford and the woodland in which is set Chequers, the official country house of the Prime Minister. (The monument on Coombe Hill is not NT property.) During winter, sheep graze the chalk downland turf. In 1906, the then owner of Coombe Hill put fences on his property to keep the public out. However, the outraged people of nearby Wendover tore down the barriers and eventually public rights of way were legally established.

Adjoining Coombe Hill is **Low Scrubs**, bought by the National Trust in 1985. It includes an area of ancient beech coppice which was used for centuries by local people to provide fuel. There is a car park for both properties off the Dunsmore road [165: SP852063].

Pulpit Wood [165: SP832048], south of Coombe Hill, is a typical Chiltern beechwood, on which a hillfort may be seen. This recent acquisition gives fine views over the Vale of Aylesbury. There is a small car park by the roadside [165: SP834045].

West Wycombe Hill [175: SU829947] is situated 2ml west of High Wycombe with fine views over West Wycombe Park (see p.230) and the surrounding countryside. The hill has an Iron Age defended settlement and was given to the National Trust in 1935, just after the acquisition of most of the village a year earlier.

In **BEDFORDSHIRE** at **Whipsnade Downs**, near Dunstable [166/165: TL000190], the Trust owns a 101ha farm on the plateau and 20ha of the chalk grassland on the scarp slope. There are views north towards Dunstable and west towards Ivinghoe Beacon (see Pitstone Windmill, p.214). On this stretch of unimproved downland, the Trust has reintroduced sheep grazing, the traditional form of management of these slopes. The effect has been to conserve the open grassland habitat which supports a rich variety of plants and insects. There is unrestricted access on foot to the chalk downland. Access across the farmland is by footpath and bridleway only. A car park is signposted off the B4540.

Whipsnade Tree Cathedral [166: TL008182] is one of the Trust's most unusual countryside properties. Many species of trees have been planted out in the traditional pattern of a cathedral, with grassy avenues for nave and transepts. This quiet, peaceful area may be reached from Whipsnade village green, beside which there is a car park, signposted from the B4540. (An annual service is held at the end of June; for details tel. the Regional Office.)

At the eastern end of the Chilterns, south-west of Barton-le-Clay, are the steep slopes of **Sharpenhoe Clappers** [166: TL067300]. The hilltop was the site of an Iron Age hillfort. This stretch of the Chiltern scarp contains a wide variety of habitats, ranging from unimproved chalk grassland with its richly varied flora and fauna, through incipient and mature hawthorn scrub, to the beech and ash woodland of the Clappers, crowning the ridge. Access to the viewpoint is from the car park beside the Streatley road, ½ml to the south.

South of London in **SURREY**, the Trust owns a great deal of commonland and some famous viewpoints, such as **Box Hill** (see p.191) and **Leith Hill**, **Coldharbour Common**, **Duke's Warren** and the **Rhododendron Wood** (see p.205). There are many lesser-known properties, which are just as beautiful. **Bookham** and **Banks Commons**, west of Leatherhead [187: TQ1256], are of particular interest for their rich birdlife. The manor of Bocheham is known to have been owned by Chertsey Abbey as early as 666 AD, and in the Domesday Survey the commons are listed as providing pannage (the right to graze pigs on acorns) for the Abbey. Access is by footpaths and bridleways and there are parking facilities. Not far away, **Ranmore Common** [187: TQ1451] and **Denbies Hillside** [187: TQ145503] bound the southern edges of the Polesden Lacey estate (see p.214) and offer good walks on the south slopes of the North Downs. A car-parking fee is charged to non-members at Box Hill, Headley Heath, Leith Hill Rhododendron Wood, Denbies Hillside, Ranmore Common and Abinger Roughs.

North of Abinger Hammer, and 4ml west of Dorking, there is a car park from which you can explore on foot the wooded ridge of **Abinger Roughs** and **Netley Park** [187: TQ111480]. Many of these areas were damaged in the great storms of October 1987 and January 1990, although trees are now growing back at a fast rate. **Holmwood Common** [187: TQ1746], 1ml south of Dorking, offers many attractive walks through oak and birch woodland and many newly-restored ponds.

Nearer London, between Reigate and Banstead Heath [187: TQ250520] are 146ha of open down, copse and beechwood on the North Downs with views towards the South Downs. This includes **Colley Hill**, **Reigate Fort**, **Reigate Hill**, a short strip of the **Pilgrim's Way**, **Margery Wood**, **Juniper Hill**, and wood and parkland at **Gatton**. On the eastern border of the county, almost in Kent, are **Oxted Down**, on the chalk scarp with the North Downs Way running through it, and **Limpsfield**, a charming series of woodlands and small heaths on the greensand. Just to the south, the Harewoods Estate, including **Outwood Common**, offers a good rights-of-way network between farmland and small woodlands, which are rich with flowers in spring.

4ml south of Epsom, near Box Hill, some 215ha of **Headley Heath** (including the Lordship of Headley Manor [197: TQ2053]) were originally grazed by sheep and other stock; continuing management by the Trust enables the various habitats to be maintained for the benefit of a great variety of plants, trees, birds and insects.

Much further south at **Hindhead** are more than 566ha of heathland and woodland, covering valleys and sandstone ridges which radiate from Hindhead Village [186: SU890357]. There are walks through the **Devil's Punch Bowl**, one of the largest spring-eroded valleys in Europe, and **Gibbet Hill**; from the latter are panoramic views to the Chilterns, and over the Weald to the South Downs.

Astride the A287 Hindhead to Farnham road is **Frensham Common** [169: SU8540], nearly 400ha, including Frensham Great and Little Ponds. Part-managed by Waverley Borough Council, there is a wide variety of lowland heathland wildlife and wildfowl.

In **KENT** the Trust owns a row of 16th- and 17th-century houses in the lovely village of **Chiddingstone** near Edenbridge, including the Castle Inn, the post office and stores. There is public-footpath access to the **Chiding Stone**, which stands on 0.2ha of land given to the Trust by Lord Astor of Hever.

East of Trottiscliffe (now popularly spelt Troseley) is **Coldrum Long Barrow** [188: TQ654607], a megalithic burial chamber surrounded by standing stones. The tomb was opened in 1910 and 22 skeletons were found, dating from 3,000 BC – the New Stone Age. Not far away south-west of Wrotham at **Oldbury Hill** [188: TQ582561] is the southern half of an Iron Age hillfort, where flint implements have been found, thought to date back to Neanderthal times. At **Wrotham Water** [188: TQ629597] are 162ha of farmland with footpath access including part of the North Downs Way. Between Chislehurst and Orpington are **Hawkwood** and **Petts Wood**, 135ha of farmland, woodland and heath with extensive footpaths [177: TQ441690] (see London).

South of Brasted, at **Toys Hill** [188: TQ465517] and neighbouring **Ide Hill**, the

Trust owns some 160ha of heath and woodland. Paths and a wheelchair route on Toys Hill provide spectacular views of the countryside to the south. The Trust's founder, Octavia Hill, knew this area well, and 41ha of woodland given by Sevenoaks District Council here bear her name. Part of the area is a Site of Special Scientific Interest.

North of Brighton in **EAST SUSSEX** are the remains of **Ditchling Beacon** hillfort [198: TQ332131], which lie across the South Downs Way; from the NT car park there is a splendid view across the Weald. On a clear day the North Downs can be seen, and nearer at hand Ashdown Forest and Crowborough Beacon.

Between Alfriston and Seaford lies **Frog Firle Farm** [TQ517012], 187ha of unspoilt downland and river valley, with an extensive footpath network and car park (not NT) at High and Over.

Near Tunbridge Wells, the Sussex Wildlife Trust leases 43ha of woodland from the Trust. **Nap Wood** [188: TQ585330], on the A267, is mostly oak woodland maintained as a nature reserve, with a footpath and limited parking.

The Trust has recently acquired **Black Cap**, 252ha of chalk downland and woodland on the South Downs, west of Lewes [198: TQ375120]. Bridleways cross the property. There is no car-parking.

On the borders of Surrey and West Sussex a large acreage of sandstone heathland at **Black Down** and **Marley Common** gives fine views south to the South Downs and the English Channel. The highest point in Sussex, it provides commanding views across the Weald over the South Downs. Part of an Area of Outstanding Natural Beauty, the plateau was once an extensive heath created by common grazing, now woodland with small areas remaining. Magnificent views from the circular panoramic walk from the main car park. At the foot of Marley Lane are two hammer ponds: **Shottermill Ponds** [186: SU883324]. **Lavington Common** [197: SU950190] and **Sullington Warren** [198: TQ096144] are heather-clad heathland properties, well-supplied with footpaths and car-parking areas. A famous landmark, **Cissbury Ring** [198: TQ140082] near Findon, gives views to Beachy Head and the Isle of Wight. There was a flint mining industry on the Ring in Neolithic times and its remains can still be seen at the western end of the hill. **Wolstonbury Hill** [198: TQ285139], **Newtimber Hill** [198: TQ275125], the **Fulking Escarpment** [198: TQ240110] and the **Devil's Dyke** [198: TQ260110] are downland properties which form the **Devil's Dyke Estate**. Providing spectacular views over the Weald and to the sea, they are rich in downland flora and fauna. This estate, well-provided with car parks, rewards those who leave the beaten track. **Harting Down**, near Petersfield [197: SU798184], is a 211ha stretch of chalk downland and woodland, traversed by the South Downs Way, with magnificent views, good walks, and rich in flora and fauna.

Another archaeologically important site is **Highdown Hill** near **Ferring** [197/198: TQ092043]. This has a late Bronze Age settlement, and an early Iron Age hillfort with a pagan Saxon cemetery within its ramparts. Excavations were carried out in the summer of 1988.

The **Slindon Estate** north of Bognor Regis [197: SU9608] includes much of Slindon village, with its 17th-century brick and flint cottages and links with Hilaire Belloc, who lived here. Within the beechwood, devastated by the Great Storm in 1987 and now re-planted with new beech trees, can be found a shingle beach, 39m above sea level, which proves that the sea once reached here – it is now 5ml away! Other archaeological sites on the estate include the Neolithic causewayed enclosure of Barkhale and the largest surviving section (3½ml) of Stane Street, which took the Roman legions to Chichester, past Bignor Hill. The park and Bignor Hill, with spectacular views, and the South Downs Way car park are open daily, and access to the remainder of the 1425ha estate is by public footpaths and bridleways.

SOUTH EAST

The Trust owns some 1500ha of the **ISLE OF WIGHT**, including beautiful flower-rich chalk downland with interesting archaeology and including the Downs from **Afton** to Brook Down [196: SZ376850/SZ395891]. The Trust's **Mottistone Estate** [196: SZ405837] is further east and includes the Manor, the garden (see p.208), two holiday cottages, farmland, woodland, Mottistone Down and most of Mottistone village. In Brighstone, the Trust has the attractive terrace of 18th-century thatched cottages built of chalk blocks, situated in North Street, including the gift shop, local history museum and post office. **St Catherine's Hill** and **St Catherine's Down** [196: SZ494772/495785] give magnificent views over both the eastern and western ends of the island. Also in the south, the Trust protects much of the Ventnor Downs, including the highest point on the island. **St Boniface Down** [196: SZ565782] rises steeply to 224m and is renowned for its beautiful views and New Forest ponies grazing in the summer.

The Trust publishes a visitors' guide to all the coast and countryside it protects on the Isle of Wight. Copies are available from 35a St James' Street, Newport PO30 1LB (tel. 01983 526445), or from the NT shop in Brighstone.

Within the New Forest in **HAMPSHIRE**, to the north the Trust owns 567ha of **Bramshaw Commons** and **Manorial Wastes** [184/185: SU2717], consisting of Cadnam and Stocks Cross Greens and Cadnam, Furzley, Half Moon, Penn and Plaitford Commons; 207ha to the north-west at **Hale Purlieu** near **Fordingbridge** [184: SU200180] and 12ha to the west at **Hightown Common**, near **Ringwood**. All these areas in the New Forest are grazed by commoners' stock.

Further north, 3ml south-west of Newbury, is the woodland area **The Chase** at Woolton Hill, approximately 57ha of woodland, threaded by a chalk stream with a meadow.

On the Hampshire/Surrey border [186: SU855350] **Ludshott** and adjoining commons offer fine examples of lowland heath. At **Waggoners' Wells** a chain of lakes carries one of the sources of the River Wey. There are many footpaths and rides and a number of nature walks. Wheelchair access. **Selborne Common** is a rolling wooded hill of 97ha in an area of outstanding natural beauty [186: SU35333].

Some 10ml due north of **Mottisfont Abbey Garden** (see p.207) is **Stockbridge Down**, 1ml east of Stockbridge [185: SU379349]. The chalk downland is rich in plant and insect life. Pleasant walks here are accessible from two car parks on the A272. Also at Stockbridge is the **Common Marsh** [185: SU354340] with attractive walks beside the River Test. Car park W of A3057, S of Stockbridge. Limited access.

At **Curbridge**, 1ml south of Botley on the A3051 [196: SU523118], the Trust owns 30ha of woods and arable farmland on the River Hamble, part of which is a nature reserve. A further 7ha of downland have been acquired at **Speltham Down**, Hambledon [196: SU645148], to the north-west of Waterlooville.

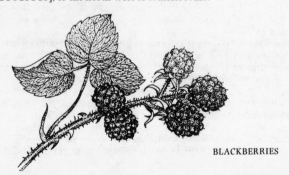

BLACKBERRIES

ALFRISTON CLERGY HOUSE 🏠 ❊ E

The Tye, Alfriston, Polegate BN26 5TL Tel: 01323 870001

This 14th-century Wealden hall house was the first building to be acquired by the Trust, in 1896. The building is half-timbered and thatched, and contains a medieval hall, exhibition room and two other rooms open to the public. The charming garden is filled with traditional cottage favourites, some grown since Roman times and now almost lost to cultivation

🅾 29 March to 2 Nov: daily except Tues & Fri 10–5 or sunset if earlier. Last admission 30min before closing. **Events**: for details tel. 01892 891001

£ £2.20, children £1.10; family ticket £5.50. Pre-booked parties £1.60, children 80p. WCs and parking in car park at other end of village (not NT)

🛍 Shop open as house. Also Christmas shop 11–4; tel. Custodian for details

♿ House unsuitable for wheelchair users

👁 Braille guide

☕ In village (not NT)

🐕 No dogs in garden or house

➔ 4ml NE of Seaford, just E of B2108, in Alfriston village, adjoining The Tye and St Andrews Church [189: TQ521029] *Bus*: Stagecoach South Coast 713 Eastbourne–Lewes (passing close ⭇ Polegate & Seaford); Autopoint 125 from Lewes (tel. 01273 474747) *Station*: Berwick (U) 2½ml

ASCOTT 🏠 ❊

Wing, nr Leighton Buzzard LU7 0PS Tel: 01296 688242 Fax: 01296 681904

The garden contains unusual trees, flower borders, naturalised bulbs, water lilies and a topiary sundial. House closed for refurbishment during 1997

🅾 **Garden**: 28 March to 4 May & 2 to 30 Sept: Tues to Sun 2–6; 7 May to 31 Aug: every Wed & last Sun in each month 2–6. Open Good Fri but closed BH Mon

185

£ Garden £4. Children half-price. No reduction for parties which must book. Parking 220m

& 3 wheelchairs available; limited access to garden; close parking by prior arrangement. WC in car park

✠ In car park only

→ ½ml E of Wing, 2ml SW of Leighton Buzzard, on S side of A418 [165:SP891230] *Bus:* Aylesbury & The Vale/Wycombe Bus X15, 65, 325, Aylesbury–Milton Keynes (passing close ≋ Aylesbury & Leighton Buzzard) (tel. 0345 382000) *Station:* Leighton Buzzard 2ml

ASHDOWN HOUSE 🏛 ❀ 🖼 🕴

Lambourn, Newbury RG16 7RE Tel: 01488 72584

A 17th-century house built by 1st Lord Craven and 'consecrated' to Elizabeth, Queen of Bohemia, 'The Winter Queen'. The great staircase, rising from hall to attic, is impressive, and the house contains important portraits of the Winter Queen's family. There are fine views from the roof; also, a box parterre, lawns, avenues and woodland walks

○ **Hall**, **stairway**, **roof and grounds only:** April to end Oct: Wed & Sat 2–5. Guided tours only; at 2.15, 3.15 & 4.15 from front door. Closed Easter weekend & every BH. Last admission to house 4.15. **Woodland:** all year: Sat to Thur dawn to dusk

£ Grounds, hall, stairway & roof £2. No reduction for parties, which should book in writing. Woodland free. Car park 250m. No WC or refreshments available. No picnicking

& Access to grounds only; house not accessible to wheelchair users

✠ In woodland only (not in house or grounds)

→ 2½ml S of Ashbury, 3½ml N of Lambourn, on W side of B4000 [174: SU282820] *Bus:* Thamesdown 47 Swindon–Lambourn, with connections from Newbury (passing close ≋ Swindon & Newbury) (tel. 0345 090899)

ASHRIDGE ESTATE 🏛 🖼 🕴 🇪

Ringshall, Berkhamsted HP4 1LT Tel: 01442 851227 Fax: 01442 842062

The Ashridge Estate covers some 6sq ml in Hertfordshire and Buckinghamshire, running along the main ridge of the Chiltern Hills from Berkhamsted to Ivinghoe Beacon. It comprises over 1619ha of woodlands, commons and downland. At the northerly end of the Estate the Ivinghoe Hills are an outstanding area of chalk downland which supports a rich variety of plants and insects. The Ivinghoe Beacon itself offers splendid views. This area may be reached from a car park at Steps Hill. The rest of Ashridge is an almost level plateau with many fine walks through woods and open commons. Wildlife is well represented; a wide variety of birds is always in evidence, including the goldcrest and the lesser-spotted woodpecker. Some 400 fallow deer roam freely; muntjac deer, badgers and foxes also abound and almost unique to the area is the edible dormouse. The main focal point of the Estate is the granite Monument erected in 1832 to the 3rd Duke of Bridgewater, the canal Duke

O Estate: open all year, incl. 16ml boundary trail & six self-guided walks. Guide leaflets available from visitor centre shop. **Monument, visitor centre & shop**: 28 March to 2 Nov: Mon to Thur & Good Fri 2–5, Sat, Sun & BH Mon 2–5.30. Last admission to monument 30min before closing. **Events**: for details of events please send s.a.e. to Box Office, PO Box 180, High Wycombe, Bucks HP14 4XT

£ Monument £1, children 50p. *Note*: For further information, shop and party bookings, tel. 01442 851227; Estate office tel. 01442 842488. Riding permits available from riding warden (tel. 01442 842716)

⌂ Shop open 28 March to 2 Nov: Mon to Thur & Good Fri 2–5, Sat, Sun & BH Mon 2–5.30. 8 Nov to 14 Dec: Sat & Sun 12–4 (or dusk if earlier)

♿ Monument area, monument drive and visitor centre accessible. WC (RADAR lock). Parking near visitor centre. Self-drive powered vehicles and one manual wheelchair free of charge from visitor centre; advance booking advisable. Extensive routes with fine views. Some routes may be difficult in poor weather

◉ Volunteer Base Camp used by groups of visually impaired people with sighted companions; details available

▣ Tea kiosk next to visitor centre, summer weekends

▦ Full education programme and study base. Details from the Education Warden (tel. 01442 842448)

🐕 Admitted if kept under control

➔ Between Northchurch & Ringshall just off B4506 [165: SP970131]
Bus: Monument; Seamarks 27; Lucketts 30/1 from ≋ Tring, alight Aldbury, ½ml. Beacon; Aylesbury & The Vale 61 Aylesbury–Luton (passing close ≋ Aylesbury & Luton); Seamarks 327 from Tring to Monument Drive and Beacon, Sun, June to Sept only (tel. 0345 244344) *Station:* Monument: Tring 1¼ml. Beacon: Cheddington 3½ml

BASILDON PARK 🏠 ❀ ♣ **E**

Lower Basildon, Reading RG8 9NR Tel: 0118 984 3040 Fax: 0118 984 1267

A classical 18th-century house by John Carr of York, in a beautiful setting overlooking the Thames Valley. The focal point of the interior is the unusual Octagon Room. The house also contains fine plasterwork, important pictures and furniture, a decorative Shell Room and some of Graham Sutherland's studies for the tapestry in Coventry Cathedral. The restoration of the early 19th-century pleasure grounds is underway and includes the construction of a new ornamental umbrello seat. Waymarked woodland walks

O House: 29 March to 2 Nov: Wed to Fri 2–5.30; Sat, Sun & BH Mon 1–5 (closed Good Fri & Wed following BH). **Park, garden & woodland walks**: 1 March to 23 March: Sat & Sun 12–5; 29 March to 2 Nov as house, but open 12–6 on Sat, Sun & BH Mon. *Note*: House and grounds will close at 5 on 16 August 1997 for jazz concert. **Events**: for details please send s.a.e. marked 'Events' to Property Manager

£ House, park & garden £3.80, children £1.90; family ticket £9.50. Park & garden only £1.50, children 75p; family ticket £3.75. Parties of 15 and over £3 per person, only on application to Property Manager. Parking in grounds, 400m from house

🛍 Shop open 1–23 March: Sat & Sun 12–5; 29 March to 2 Nov: Wed to Fri 2–5.30, Sat, Sun & BH Mon 12.30–5.30; 3 Nov to 21 Dec: Fri 12–4, Sat & Sun 11–5; (tel. 01491 671738)

♿ Access to garden via firm gravel paths; tea-room accessible via ramps. Volunteer-driven buggy between car park and house. Access to first floor of house by stair-climber, strictly by prior arrangement. Shop in stable yard; level access. Parking facilities for disabled drivers near house; please contact ticket office near car park; disabled passengers may be set down at house. Adapted WC in stable yard near car park

👁 Braille guide

☕ Tea-room same months as house: teas Wed to Sun, also light lunches Sat, Sun & BH Mon and by prior arrangement for groups: Wed to Fri 2–5.30; Sat, Sun & BH Mon 12–5.30. Also Nov to 21 Dec: Sat & Sun 12–4 (tel. 0118 9844080). Picnics in grounds except on main lawns near house

🚼 Highchair available in tea-room

🐕 In park, woodland and grounds only, not on main lawns near house; dogs must be on leads at all times

➡ Between Pangbourne and Streatley, 7ml NW of Reading, on W side of A329; leave M4 at exit 12 [175: SU611782] *Bus:* Reading Buses 105 Oxford–Reading (passing ≋ Pangbourne) (tel. 0118 959 4000) *Station:* Pangbourne 2½ml; Goring & Streatley 3ml

---

BATEMAN'S 🏠 🐾 ✖ ❖ 🍽 E

Burwash, Etchingham TN19 7DS Tel: 01435 882302 Fax: 01435 882811

Home of Rudyard Kipling from 1902–36, the house was built by a local ironmaster in 1634. Kipling's rooms and study are as they were during his lifetime. At the bottom of the garden, the watermill grinds corn for flour (Sat pm only). Alongside is one of the oldest working water-driven turbines in the world, installed by Kipling to generate electricity for the house. Kipling's 1928 Rolls-Royce. Gardens including rose, wild and herb gardens, are maintained much as they were in Kipling's time

O **House, mill and garden**: 28 March to 2 Nov: Sat to Wed 11–5.30 (open Good Fri). Last admission 4.30. The mill grinds corn every Sat at 2 in the open season. **Events**: for details tel. 01892 891001

£ £4.50, children £2.25; family ticket £11.25. Pre-booked parties £3.80 except on Sun, BH Mon & Good Fri when £4.50

⌂ Shop open same days as house 11.30–5.30. Also Christmas shop 11–4, tel. Administrator for details

♿ The mill and shop are not suitable for wheelchair users. Access to ground floor of house, tea-room and garden; there are routes which avoid the steps. WC in car park. Map available

👁 Braille introduction to house. Scented plants & flowers; watermill sounds (Sat only)

☕ Morning coffee, light lunches and teas in tea-room (licensed) open 11–5. Picnicking in copse adjacent to car park; no picnicking in garden

👶 Baby-changing facilities. Children's guide

▦ Teachers' resource book

🐕 On leads in car park only. Dog crèche

➔ ½ml S of Burwash (A265); approached by road leading S from W end of village or N from Woods Corner (B2096) [199: TQ671238] *Bus*: RDH 318 Hurst Green–Heathfield (passing ≋ Etchingham) (tel. 01273 474747) *Station*: Etchingham 3ml

---

BEMBRIDGE WINDMILL ✠

Enquiries to the Custodian, Mill Reach, Kings Road, Bembridge PO35 5NT
Tel: 01983 873945 during opening hours

Dating from around 1700. The only windmill to survive on the island. Much of the wooden machinery can still be seen

O 26 March to 31 Oct: daily except Sat (but open Easter Sat & daily in July & Aug) 10–5. Last admission 4.45

£ £1.20. No reduction for groups. All school groups are conducted by an NT guide; special charge applies. Parking 100m. No WC. Picnic field

👤 Conducted school groups and special visits March to end Oct (but not July or Aug), by written appointment

⌂ Small shop

♿ Mill not accessible to severely disabled people; grab ropes are provided for those able to climb the steep stairs. Area around mill is accessible

👁 Braille and large-print guides

▦ Educational quiz sheets

➔ ½ml S of Bembridge on B3395 [196: SZ639874] *Bus*: Southern Vectis 1 Cowes–Sandown (passing ≋ Ryde Esplanade) (tel. 01983 827005) *Station*: Brading (U) 2ml by footpath. *Ferry*: Ryde (Wightlink Ltd) 6ml (tel. 01705 827744). E Cowes (Red Funnel) 13ml (tel. 01703 334010)

BOARSTALL DUCK DECOY ⬛🚶

Boarstall, nr Aylesbury HP18 9UX Tel: 01844 237488

18th-century duck decoy in working order, in 5.26ha of natural woodland; nature trail. Exhibition hall

O 29 March to 31 Aug: Wed 4–7; Sat, Sun & BH Mon 10–5. School parties by arrangement. Talk/demonstration when Warden is available, Sat, Sun & BH Mon at 11 & 3

£ £2; family ticket £5. Parties of six or more, which must book, £1 per person

♿ Nature trail, exhibition hall, bird hide and decoy accessible in dry weather; ramps; wheelchair available

🐕 In car park only

➜ Midway between Bicester and Thame, 2ml W of Brill [164 or 165: SP624151] *Station:* Bicester Town (U), 6½ml; Bicester North, 7½ml

---

BOARSTALL TOWER 🏰

Boarstall, nr Aylesbury HP18 9OX

The stone gatehouse of a fortified house long since demolished. It dates from the 14th century, and was altered in the 16th and 17th centuries, but retains its crossloops for bows. The tower is almost surrounded by a moat

O By written appointment with tenant. May to end Sept: Wed 2–6

£ £1. No reduction for parties. No WC

♿ Access to garden and ground floor of house (1 step); car park near house

🐕 In car park only

➜ Midway between Bicester and Thame, 2ml W of Brill [164 or 165: SP624141] *Station:* as for Boarstall Duck Decoy above

---

BODIAM CASTLE 🏰⬛ E

Bodiam, nr Robertsbridge TN32 5UA Tel: 01580 830436 Fax: 01580 830398

Bodiam Castle was built in 1385 for the defence of the surrounding countryside and as a comfortable dwelling for a rich nobleman. It has been voted one of the top six most popular castles for children. The virtual completeness of the exterior, the best example of its type in the country, makes it an exciting place for children to explore, with spiral staircases and battlements. Although a ruin, the floors have been replaced in some of the towers, and impressive views can be enjoyed from the battlements. There is an audiovisual presentation on life in a medieval castle, and a small museum

Note: Please note that Bodiam Castle is widely used by education groups during term-time mornings

O 8 Feb to 2 Nov: daily 10–6 or dusk if earlier; 4 Nov to 4 Jan: Tues to Sun 10–4 or dusk if earlier (closed 24/25/26 Dec, open New Year's Day). Last admission 1hr before closing. **Events:** for details tel. 01892 891001

£ £3, children £1.50; family ticket £7.50. Parties £2.50. Car park ¼ml, £1 (NT members free); coaches £5

▣ Shop open 8 Feb to end Oct: same days as castle 11–5 (or dusk if earlier). Nov to Dec: Wed to Sun 11–4; tel. Administrator for details

& Access to car park, shop and restaurant function room; WC in car park. Castle (but not its towers) is accessible to wheelchair users, but it is ¼ml from car park over uneven ground; for alternative access details please tel. Administrator before visiting

◉ Braille guide available from ticket office

▣ Lunches, teas and snacks in car park tea-room, open 8 Feb to end Oct: daily 11–5 (or dusk if earlier); Nov to Dec: Wed to Sun 11–4

🚼 Parent and baby room. Children's guide. Highchairs & children's menu in restaurant

▣ Teachers' resource books. Education rooms with hands-on resources; tel. Administrator for details

🐾 On leads in grounds only, not in castle

→ 3ml S of Hawkhurst, 2ml E of A21 Hurst Green [199: TQ782256]
Bus: Fuggles/Stagecoach South Coast 349 from ≋ Hastings; Hastings & District RE Group ≋ Rye–≋ Battle, Sun, July to Aug only (tel. 01273 474747)
Station: Robertsbridge 5ml

BOX HILL ▣ ▣ 🚼 **E**

The Old Fort, Box Hill Road, Tadworth, nr Dorking KT20 7LB
Tel: 01306 885502 Fax: 01306 875030

On the edge of the North Downs, rising some 130m above the River Mole, this Country Park consists of more than 400ha of woods and chalk downland, with magnificent views to the South Downs. Summit buildings include information centre, shop with plant sales and servery, and 1890s fort (partly open to public)

O All year. **Events:** 29 June, Country Day (extra charge for cars, incl. NT members); 5 Dec, special late-night opening in shop (up to 8pm), especially for visitors with disabilities, free glass of sherry and mince pie

£ Countryside free. Coaches must not use the zig-zag road from Burford Bridge on W side of the hill as a weight restriction applies, but must approach from E side of the hill B2032 or B2033; car/coach parks at top of hill; pay-and-display £1.50 (free to NT members displaying membership cards). Annual car park pass available

🚶 Guided walks at intervals throughout the year. Groups by prior arrangement with the Warden (tel. 01306 885502)

▣ Shop & information centre: open all year, daily 11–4 later in summer (weather permitting); closed 25 & 26 Dec (tel. 01306 888793). Plant sales at back of shop, available March to Sept; Christmas trees on sale from 1 Dec

 ♿ Access to summit area, including shop & servery. Parking behind servery. Wheelchair path to viewpoint and beyond. WCs opposite main car park at summit

 👁 Braille guides for short walk and nature walk

 🍽 Servery. Hot & cold snacks & drinks: open all year, daily 11–4 (closed 25 & 26 Dec); longer hours (weather permitting) (tel. 01306 888793)

 🏛 Education Room. Education groups for day visits and residential groups by prior arrangement with North Downs Education Officer (tel. 01306 742809)

 🐕 Must be kept under control (sheep grazing)

 ➡ 1ml N of Dorking, 2½ml S of Leatherhead on A24 [187: TQ171519] *Bus:* London & Country 516, ⇌ Leatherhead–Dorking (tel. 01737 223000) *Station:* Boxhill & Westhumble ½ml

---

BRIGHSTONE SHOP AND MUSEUM

**Enquiries to the Manager, National Trust Shop,
North Street, Brighstone PO30 4AX Tel: 01983 740689**

Attractive terrace of thatched Isle of Wight vernacular cottages. NT shop and Village Museum (Brighstone Museum Trust)

 🅾 6 Jan to 27 March: Mon to Sat 10–1. Good Fri to 1 June: daily 10–4. 2 June to 31 Oct: daily 10–5. 1 Nov to 31 Dec: Mon to Fri 10–4, Sat 10–1. Closed 25 & 26 Dec & 1 Jan

 💷 Free entry, donations welcome

 ➡ *Bus:* Southern Vectis 12 Newport–Alum Bay (tel. 01983 827005) *Ferry:* Yarmouth (Wightlink Ltd) 8ml (tel. 01705 827744); E Cowes (Red Funnel) 12ml (tel. 01703 334010)

BUCKINGHAM CHANTRY CHAPEL ✚

Market Hill, Buckingham

Rebuilt in 1475 and retaining a fine Norman doorway. The chapel was restored by Gilbert Scott in 1875, at which time it was used as a Latin or Grammar School

 🅾 April to end Oct: by written appointment with the Buckingham Heritage Trust, c/o The Book Barn, Church Way, Whittlebury, Northants NN12 8SX

 💷 Free. No WC

 ♿ Wheelchair access

 ➡ On Market Hill [152 or 165: SP693340] *Bus:* Paynes 32, Milton Keynes Citybus 51/A from Milton Keynes (passing close ⇌ Milton Keynes Central); Aylesbury & The Vale 66 from Aylesbury (passing close ⇌ Aylesbury) (tel. 0345 382000) *Station:* Wolverton 10ml

BUSCOT OLD PARSONAGE 🏠 ✻

Buscot, Faringdon SN7 8DQ Tel: (Coleshill Estate Office) 01793 762209

An early 18th-century house of Cotswold stone on the bank of the River Thames; small garden

O April to end Oct: Wed only 2–6 by appointment in writing with tenant

£ £1. Not suitable for parties. No WC

→ 2ml from Lechlade, 4ml from Faringdon on A417 [163: SU231973] *Bus:* Carterton 64 Swindon–Carterton, or Thamesdown 77 Swindon–Cirencester (both passing close ⇌ Swindon). On both, alight Lechlade, 1½ml (tel. 0345 090899)

BUSCOT PARK 🏠 ✻ ♣

Faringdon SN7 8BU Tel: 01367 240786 Fax: 01367 241794

A late 18th-century house with pleasure gardens, set within a park. The property is administered by Lord Faringdon on behalf of the National Trust, and the contents of the house are owned by the Trustees of The Faringdon Collection

O **House & grounds**: 28 March to end Sept (including Good Fri, Easter Sat & Sun): Wed to Fri 2–6. Also open every second & fourth Sat & and immediately following Sun 2–6 (i.e. April 12 & 13, 26 & 27; May 10 & 11, 24 & 25; June 14 & 15, 28 & 29; July 12 & 13, 26 & 27; Aug 9 & 10, 23 & 24; Sept 13 & 14, 27 & 28). Timed entry to house may be imposed if crowding occurs. Last admission 5.30. **Grounds only**: 28 March to end Sept: open as house but also Mon (but not BH Mon) & Tues 2–6

£ House & grounds £4. Grounds only £3. No reduction for parties which must book in writing or by fax (01367 241794) to the Estate office stating numbers and time of arrival

♿ Unsuitable for wheelchair-users due to gradients; gravel paths throughout grounds and steep flight of steps to house

▣ Tea-room open same days as house, 2.30–5.30. Self-pick soft fruit available when advertised or tel. 01367 244243 for details of availability

→ Between Lechlade and Faringdon, on A417 [163:SU239973] *Bus:* Thamesdown 67 Swindon–Faringdon (Fri only); otherwise as for Buscot Old Parsonage (see above) but 2¾ml walk from Lechlade

CHARTWELL 🏠 ✻ 👤 E

Westerham TN16 1PS Information Tel: 01732 866368 Shop Tel: 01732 867837
Restaurant Tel: 01732 863087 Fax: 01732 868193

Home of Sir Winston Churchill from 1924 until the end of his life. The rooms, left as they were in his lifetime, evoke his career and interests, with pictures, maps, documents and personal mementoes. Two rooms are given over to a museum of his many gifts and uniforms.

Exhibition giving visitors an insight into the life of Churchill. Terraced gardens descend towards the lakes, the garden studio contains many of Sir Winston's paintings

Note: Entry to the house is by timed ticket for all visitors (incl. NT members). Occasionally there may be a delay in gaining admission to the house. The waiting time may be spent in the garden, shop or restaurant. Opening days have changed for 1997: please see details below.

House & garden: March & Nov: Sat, Sun & Wed 11–4.30. Last admission 4. **House, garden & studio:** 29 March to 2 Nov: daily (except Mon & Tues) 11–5.30. Last admission 4.30. Open BH Mon 11–5.30, last admission 4.30. (Closed Tues & Wed following BH Mon). **Events:** for details tel. 01892 891001

House, garden & studio £5, children £2.50, family ticket £12.50. Garden & studio only £2.50. March & Nov, house only £3. Coaches and groups by appointment only; no reductions

Guided tours by arrangement; please contact property

Shop open same days as house: 29 March to 2 Nov: 11–5.30; March & Nov: 11–4. Also Christmas shop 11–4

Garden is hilly with steps but magnificent views. Contact Property Manager in advance or enquire at visitor reception on arrival for close parking to house. Ground floor accessible, two steps to small lift to first floor; wheelchairs available. Lower ground floor and exhibition not accessible. Access to shop and restaurant with close parking. 2 WCs in car park

Rose garden; scented plants; Braille guide

Coffee, lunches and teas; licensed self-service restaurant. Open same days as house: 29 March to 2 Nov 10.30–5. March & Nov 11–4. Also Christmas opening 11–4. Function room available

Children's guide; children's meals available. No pushchairs in house. Baby-changing facility

Special tours for schools; for details contact property

In grounds only, on leads

2ml S of Westerham, fork left off B2026 after 1½ml [188: TQ455515] *Bus:* Metrobus 746 ≋ Tunbridge Wells–≋ Bromley South; (Sun, June to Sept only) to house; otherwise London & Country 320, ≋ Bromley N–Westerham (passing ≋ Bromley S); 410 Reigate–Sevenoaks (passing ≋ Oxted and ≋ Sevenoaks), on all alight Westerham, 2ml (tel. 0800 696996) *Station:* Edenbridge (U) 4ml; Edenbridge Town 4½ml; Oxted 5½ml; Sevenoaks 6½ml

---

CHASTLETON HOUSE 🏚 ❀

Chastleton, Moreton-in-Marsh GL56 0SU Tel: 01608 674355

Chastleton House is one of England's finest and most complete Jacobean houses. It is filled not only with a mixture of rare and everyday objects, furniture and textiles collected since its completion in 1612, but also with the atmosphere of four hundred years of continuous occupation by one family. The gardens have a typical Elizabethan and Jacobean layout with a ring of fascinating topiary at their heart and it was in these gardens in 1865 that modern croquet was invented. Since acquiring the property, the Trust has concentrated on conserving rather than restoring it to a pristine state

Note: Chastleton House is opening in 1997 after six years of conservation. The overriding concern is the protection of the house and its contents and so the number of visitors will be restricted. All entry will be by pre-booked timed ticket. Due to narrow access roads, the largest vehicles that can be accommodated are minibuses (25-seater). There will be no shop or tea-room

O 10 Sept to end Oct: Wed to Sat 1–5. Last admission 4.30 or dusk if earlier. Admission for all visitors (incl. NT members) by pre-booked timed ticket only; bookings can be made by letter to the Custodian or tel. 01608 674284, Tue to Sat 9.30–12.30 from 5 Aug to 31 Oct 1997 and from Feb 1998

£ £4.50, children £2.25, family ticket £11.25. Groups (min. 11, max. 25) by prior arrangement only. No access for coaches. Car park on hill 250m from house

⚥ Out-of-hours guided 'Private View' Wed to Fri mornings £7 (incl. NT members); must be booked in advance on tel. 01608 674284

♿ House unsuitable for wheelchairs; please tel. for further information on access for disabled visitors

◉ Braille guide available

◨ No shop or tea-room. Picnic area in car park

🐕 Guide dogs only

➜ 6ml from Stow-on-the-Wold. Approach only from A436 between the A44 (west of Chipping Norton) and Stow [163: SP248291] *Station:* Moreton-in-Marsh 4½ml; Kingham 5ml (for information about transport from Moreton station tel. 01608 650881)

CLANDON PARK 🏠 🔭 ❀ ♣ **E**

West Clandon, Guildford GU4 7RQ
Tel: 01483 222482; Infoline/fax: 01483 223479

Clandon was built in the early 1730s for the 2nd Lord Onslow by the Venetian architect, Giacomo Leoni. This Palladian house, with a magnificent two-storeyed Marble Hall, contains Onslow family pictures and furniture, the Gubbay collection of porcelain, furniture and needlework, also Mortlake tapestries and the Ivo Forde collection of Meissen Italian comedy figures. Also of interest are the old kitchen, the gardens with parterre, grotto, sunken Dutch garden and Maori house, and the Queen's Royal Surrey Regiment Museum (tel. 01483 223419)

O House (**new times**): 30 March to 30 Oct: Tues, Wed, Thur & Sun, plus BH Mon 11.30–4.30; last admission 4. **Garden:** daily 9–7.30 (or dusk if earlier). **Museum:** 30 March to 30 Oct: Tues, Wed, Thur, Sun & BH Mon 12–5. **Events:** concerts are held in the Marble Hall and in the grounds; contact Regional box office (tel. 01372 451596). *Note:* The house is available for civil wedding ceremonies and receptions, as well as private and corporate functions; the Property Manager welcomes enquiries (tel. 01483 222482)

£ House & garden £4; family ticket £10. Special group rate £3.50 Tues, Wed & Thur only. Combined ticket with Hatchlands Park £6. Parking 300m

✠ Groups and morning guided tours by prior arrangement with Property Manager. Connoisseurs' tours; please ring for information

▢ Shop open: March (weekends only 1–5); 1 April to 30 Oct: Tues, Wed, Thur, Sat, Sun and BH Mon 12–5; November (Tues, Wed, Thur, Sat & Sun 1–5); December, daily till 23rd 1–5; tel. 01483 211412

♿ Parking near front of house for disabled drivers only; disabled visitors may be set down at house. Access limited to ground floor and basement only. WCs on lower-ground floor. Ramp to garden. Electric stairclimber available to lift chairs up entrance steps to ground floor only, which is then completely level; upper floor (porcelain collections) only accessible via stairs. Restaurant and shop accessible. 3 wheelchairs and 1 walker available.

◉ Braille guide

▣ Licensed restaurant in vaulted basement of house for lunches and teas, same days as house 11–5. March (Sun), Nov (Tues, Wed, Thur & Sun) and Dec (daily until 23rd) 12–5. Advance bookings for lunch and functions advisable (tel. 01483 222502). Picnicking in grounds and gardens. Tables in car park area

☗ Changing table available. Children's quizzes for house and garden, children's menus and highchairs. Pushchairs allowed in house Tues, Wed & Thur

🐕 On leads in car park area only

➔ At West Clandon on A247, 3ml E of Guildford; if using A3 follow signposts to Ripley to join A247 via B2215 [186: TQ042512] *Bus:* London & Country 563 Guildford–Addlestone (passing ≋ Clandon); otherwise London & Country 408 Guildford–Croydon, 479 Guildford–Kingston, Surrey Hills Leisure Bus 433 Guildford–Dorking (all pass close ≋ Guildford), alight W Clandon Cross Roads, ¼ml (tel. 01737 223000) *Station:* Clandon 1ml. Turn left on main road

CLAREMONT LANDSCAPE GARDEN ✽ E

Portsmouth Road, Esher KT10 9JG Tel: 01372 469421

One of the earliest surviving English landscape gardens, restored by the Trust to its former glory. Begun by Sir John Vanbrugh and Charles Bridgeman before 1720, the gardens were extended and naturalised by William Kent. 'Capability' Brown also made improvements. Features include a lake, island with pavilion, grotto, turf amphitheatre, viewpoints and avenues. The house is not NT

◯ All year: Jan to end March: daily (except Mon) 10–5 or sunset if earlier; April to end Oct: Mon to Fri 10–6; Sat, Sun & BH Mon 10–7. *Note*: Garden closed all day 8 July and closed at 2 on 9 to 13 July. Nov to end March 1998: daily (except Mon) 10–5 or sunset if earlier. Last admission 30min before closing. Closed 25 Dec but special opening New Years Day 1–4 for National Gardens Scheme (£3 incl. NT members). **House (not NT)**: open first weekend each month from Feb to Nov 2–4.30. **Events**: 9 to 13 July, Fête Champêtre and open-air concert; send s.a.e. for booking form to Claremont Box Office, c/o Southern Regional Office, or tel. 01372 459950 for information. Telephone bookings taken from 15 April

£ £3. Family ticket (2 adults & 2 children) £8. Groups of 15+ £2.50. All coach parties must book; no coaches on Sun. Parking at entrance

🚶 Guided tours (min. 15 persons) £1.50 extra per person by prior booking (tel. 01372 469421)

🛍 Shop open 12 Jan to end March: Sat & Sun 11–4.30; April to end Oct: daily (except Mon) 11–5.30; Nov to 14 Dec: daily (except Mon) 11–4; 18 Jan to end March 1998: Sat & Sun 11–4.30. Open BH Mon

♿ Level firm gravel pathway around lake, and level grassland. Wheelchairs available. Access to tea-room and shop. WC in car park. Parking by entrance. Accessible events; for details see above

👁 Braille guide

☕ Tea-room serving morning coffee, home-made lunches (12–2) and teas. Open as shop. Last orders 30min before shop closes

🚼 Baby-changing facilities available in WC. Highchairs in tea-room

🐕 On leads Nov to end March but not admitted April to end Oct

➔ On S edge of Esher, on E side of A307 (no access from Esher bypass) [187: TQ128634] *Bus:* London & Country 415 Victoria–Guildford (passing close ≋ Esher) (tel. 01737 223000) *Station:* Esher 2ml; Hersham 2ml; Claygate 2ml

---

CLAYDON HOUSE 🏠✚Ｅ

Middle Claydon, nr Buckingham MK18 2EY
Tel: 01296 730349 Fax: 01296 738511

The most perfect expression of rococo decoration in England, in a series of great rooms with wood carving in the Chinese and Gothick styles. Relics of the Civil War and a museum with mementoes of Florence Nightingale and the Verney family. All Saints' Church (not NT) in the grounds is also open to the public. Evensong: 25 May, 22 June, 27 July, all at 5

O 22 March to 2 Nov: Sat to Wed & BH Mon 1–5. Last admission 4.30. Closed Good Fri. Leaflets available in French, German and Spanish. **Events**: August, lantern-light concert; for details please send s.a.e. to Custodian

£ £3.80; family ticket £9.50. Parties must book; rates on application to Custodian. No parties on Sun

♿ Wheelchairs available. Car-parking close to front door; 3 steps to front door; ramps; then all ground-floor rooms accessible. Access to garden via 2 steps; ramps. Half-price admission to ground floor only; WC, tea-room accessible

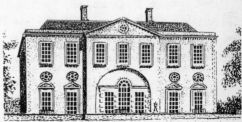

👁 Braille guide. Guided tours by arrangement

☕ Teas open 2–5

👶 Baby changing facilities

🐕 In park on leads only

➔ In Middle Claydon 13ml NW of Aylesbury, 3½ml SW of Winslow; signposted from A413, A421 & A41; entrance by N drive only [165: SP720253] *Bus:* Red Rose 17 and Classic Coaches 78 from Aylesbury (passing close ⚊ Aylesbury) (tel. 0345 382000)

CLIVEDEN 🏠 ❖ ♠ E

Taplow, Maidenhead, SL6 0JA Tel: 01628 605069 Fax: 01628 669461

Set on cliffs above the Thames. The present house, the third on the site, built in 1851 by Sir Charles Barry, and once the home of Nancy, Lady Astor, is now let as an hotel. The 152ha of garden and woodland include a magnificent parterre, a water garden and miles of woodland walks with spectacular views of the Thames

🅾 **Woodlands only**: 1 March to 2 Nov. **Entire estate**: 22 March to 2 Nov: daily 11–6; Nov & Dec: daily 11–4. **House** (three rooms open): April to Oct: Thur & Sun 3–6. Last admission 5.30. Entry by timed ticket from information kiosk. Octagon Temple open same days as house. **Events**: for details please send s.a.e. to Property Manager

£ Grounds £4.50; family ticket £11. House £1 extra. Party rates on application to the Property Manager; parties must book (no parties on Sun or BH Mon). Car-parking 400m from house. *Note*: Mooring charge on Cliveden Reach £6 per 24hrs (up to 4hrs £2) (incl. NT members) but excl. admission fee to Cliveden. Tickets available from River Warden. Mooring at suitable locations for more than ½ml downstream from Cliveden boathouse

🛍 Shop in walled garden open 26 March to end Oct: Wed to Sun & BH Mon (incl. Good Fri) 1–5.30; Nov to 21 Dec: Wed to Sun 12–4 (tel. 01628 665946)

♿ Garden & grounds largely accessible; route-maps, 2 self-drive powered vehicles, plus one two-seater and 4 wheelchairs available. Wheelchair access to house, but some steps; ramped access to terrace. Restaurant and shop accessible. WC. Car park 200m from house but other arrangements available

🌹 Scented rose garden

🍴 Morning coffee, light lunches, teas and vegetarian dishes, open same days as shop 11–5 in Conservatory restaurant (licensed), but Nov to 21 Dec: Sat & Sun only 12–2. Parties of more than 20 must book (tel. 01628 661406). Refreshment kiosk open in walled garden Mon & Tues only 11–5. No picnics in formal gardens

👶 Highchairs available. Baby-changing facilities in WCs near main car park

🐕 In specified woodlands only; not in garden

➔ 3ml upstream from Maidenhead, 2ml N of Taplow; leave M4 at exit 7 onto A4, or M40 at exit 4 onto A404 to Marlow and follow signs. Entrance by main gates opposite Feathers Inn [175: SU915851] *Station:* Taplow (not Sun) 2½ml; Burnham 3ml

DAPDUNE WHARF See River Wey & Godalming Navigations p.216

DORNEYWOOD GARDEN �

Dorneywood, Burnham SL1 8PY

The house was given to the Trust as an official residence for either a Secretary of State or Minister of the Crown; only the 2.5ha garden is open, and consists of herbaceous borders, a rose garden, cottage and kitchen gardens, maintained in the style of the 1930s

O Garden open by written appointment only on Wed 9 & 16 July, and Sat 9 & 16 Aug: 2–5.30. Application to the Secretary, Dorneywood Trust, at above address

£ £2.50. No reduction for parties

& Access to part of garden only

→ Located on Dorneywood Road, SW of Burnham Beeches, 1½ml N of Burnham village, 2ml E of Cliveden [175: SU938848] *Bus:* Chiltern Rover/Bee Line 3, 44, 74, 444 High Wycombe–Heathrow Airport (passing close ⇌ Slough & Beaconsfield), alight Farnham Common, 1½ml walk through Burnham Beeches (tel. 0345 382000) *Station:* Burnham 2½ml

EMMETTS GARDEN ✤ 👤 E

Ide Hill, Sevenoaks TN14 6AY Tel: 01732 750367 Fax: 01732 868193

This charming hillside garden boasts the highest treetop in Kent and is noted for its rare trees and shrubs, bluebells, rose and rock gardens. Wonderful views across the Weald and Bough Beech Reservoir. 7ha of grounds open to public

Note: New opening days and times for 1997

O 29 Mar to 2 Nov: Sat, Sun & Wed, plus BH Mon 11–5.30. Last admission 4.30. **Events:** for details tel. 01892 891001

£ £3, children £1.50; family ticket £7.50. Pre-booked parties £2

👤 Guided pre-booked parties by arrangement; please tel. 01732 868381

📷 Small shop in tea-room, open same days as garden 11.30–4.30

& Parts of garden accessible; volunteer-driven golf buggy (seats 3) available from car park to ticket hut only; three wheelchairs available for garden. WC. Access to shop and tea-room

❀ Fountain and waterfall; scented azaleas in spring and roses in summer. Beware sheer drop at end of shrub garden

☕ Tea-room open same days as garden 11.30–4.30

🚼 Baby-changing facilities

🎋 Tree trail

🦮 On leads only

➔ 1½ml S of A25 on Sundridge to Ide Hill road, 1½ml N of Ide Hill off B2042, leave M25 at exit 5, then 4ml [188: TQ477524] *Bus:* East Surrey 404 from ➤ Sevenoaks, alight Ide Hill, 1½ml (tel. 0800 696996); two buses daily, none at weekends *Station:* Sevenoaks 4½ml; Penshurst (U) 5½ml

---

GREAT COXWELL BARN 🏠

Great Coxwell, Faringdon Tel: (Coleshill Estate Office) 01793 762209

A 13th-century monastic barn, stone-built with stone-tiled roof; interesting timber structure

⭕ All year: daily at reasonable hours. For details please contact Estate Office

💷 50p. No WC

🦮 On leads only

➔ 2ml SW of Faringdon between A420 and B4019 [163: SU269940] *Bus:* Stagecoach Swindon & District 66 Swindon–Oxford (passing close ➤ Swindon & passing ➤ Oxford), alight Great Coxwell Turn, ¾ml (tel. 0345 090899) *Station:* Swindon 10ml

---

GREYS COURT 🏠 🏠 ❄ E

Rotherfield Greys, Henley-on-Thames RG9 4PG Tel: 01491 628529

Rebuilt in the 16th century and added to subsequently, the house is set amid the remains of a 14th-century fortified house. A Tudor donkey-wheel well-house and an ice house are still intact, and the garden contains a maze inspired by Archbishop Runcie's enthronement speech in 1980

⭕ **House (part of ground floor only):** 29 March to end Sept: Mon, Wed & Fri 2–6. (closed Good Fri). **Garden:** daily except Thur & Sun 2–6 (closed Good Fri). Last admission 5.30. **Events:** for details please send s.a.e. to the Box Office, PO Box 180, High Wycombe, Bucks HP14 4XT

💷 House & garden £4.20; family ticket £10.50. Garden only £3; family ticket £7.50. Parking 220m. No picnicking in grounds. No reduction for coach parties, which must book in advance with the Custodian

♿ Garden only, in part accessible; WC

🍴 Teas in Cromwellian stables: 29 March to end Sept: Mon, Wed, Fri & Sat 2.30–5.15

🦮 In car park only

➔ 3ml W of Henley-on-Thames, east of B481 [175: SU725834] *Bus:* Yellow Bus M1 from ➤ Reading, alight Greys Green, ½ml (tel. 01296 613831); otherwise Reading Buses 136–8 from Reading (passing close ➤ Reading), alight Peppard Common, 2ml (tel. 0118 959 4000) *Station:* Henley-on-Thames 3ml

HATCHLANDS PARK 🏠 ❀ ♠ E

East Clandon, Guildford GU4 7RT
Tel: 01483 222482 Infoline/fax: 01483 223479

A handsome brick house built in the 1750s by Stiff Leadbetter for Admiral Boscawen, hero of the Battle of Louisburg. Set in a Repton park, the house has splendid interiors by Robert Adam and in 1988 the Cobbe collection of fine keyboard instruments, paintings and furniture was installed and the house was extensively redecorated. There is a small garden by Gertrude Jekyll (flowering late May to early July) and grounds which have been restored with new walks in the park

O **House:** 30 March to 2 Nov: Tues, Wed, Thur, Sun & BH Mon (and Fri in Aug) 2–5.30. Last admission 5. **Garden:** open same as house. Park walks April to Oct: daily 11.30–6. No dogs on walks. **Events:** concerts are held in the house and garden; please contact Regional Box Office (tel. 01372 451596). Occasional afternoon instrumental performances; please telephone house for details

£ House and grounds £4; family ticket £10. Special group rate £3.50 (Tues to Thur only). Combined ticket with Clandon Park £6. Park walks and garden only £1.50. Parking 300m

🛈 Guided tours are not available. New audio tour available for 1997

🛍 Shop open same days as house 1.30–5.30 (tel. 01483 211412)

♿ Electric buggy service available from car park to house. Access to ground floor, terrace and part of garden. WC. Wheelchair and wheeled walker/seat available. Access to restaurant in courtyard for wheelchair users

👁 Braille and audio guides

🍴 Licensed restaurant for lunches and home-made teas 12.30–5.30 same days as house (tel. 01483 211120). Limited advance booking for lunch available. Picnicking in grounds

👶 Facilities in ladies' WC for nursing mothers; changing table. Children's menu; highchairs

🐕 On lead in car park only

➡ E of East Clandon, N of A246 Guildford–Leatherhead road [187: TQ063516] *Bus:* London & Country 408 Guildford–Croydon, 479 Guildford–Kingston, Surrey Hills Leisure Bus 433 Guildford–Dorking (all pass close ≋ Guildford) (tel. 01737 223000) *Station:* Clandon 2½ml, Horsley 3ml

HINTON AMPNER GARDEN 🏠 ❀

Bramdean, nr Alresford SO24 0LA Tel/fax: 01962 771305

The garden, set in superb Hampshire countryside, combines formal design with informal planting, producing delightful walks with many unexpected vistas. After 5 years of restoration work the garden is now flourishing and highlights include the dell and a sunken garden

Note: The house will be closed throughout 1997 whilst major rewiring work takes place

O **Garden**: 16 & 23 March, then 29 March to end Sept: Tues, Wed, Sat, Sun & BH Mon 1.30–5.30 (last admission 5). Car park opens 1.15

£ Garden £2.80. Special entrance for coaches; please book in advance. No group bookings in Aug

& Most of garden and tea-room accessible; map of wheelchair route available. Four wheelchairs available. Parking in front of house on request at kiosk. WCs by house

◉ Braille guides to house and garden. Scented plants

◗ Tea-room open same days as garden 1.30–5. Picnics in grass car park only

✖ No dogs

→ On A272, 1ml W of Bramdean village, 8ml E of Winchester, leave M3 at exit 9 and follow signs to Petersfield [185: SU597275] *Bus:* Stagecoach Hampshire Bus 67 Winchester–Petersfield (passing close ≊ Winchester & ≊ Petersfield) (tel. 01256 464501) *Station:* Alresford (Mid Hants Rly) 4ml; Winchester 9ml

---

HUGHENDEN MANOR 🏠 ❖ ♠ E

High Wycombe HP14 4LA Tel: 01494 532580

Victorian home of Prime Minister and statesman Benjamin Disraeli from 1847 until his death in 1881. He gave the manor its 'Gothic' appearance and much of his furniture, pictures and books remain. The park and woodland have lovely walks and the garden is a recreation of the original colourful design of his wife, Mary Ann

Note: Certain rooms have little electric light. Visitors wishing to make close study of interior of the house should avoid dull days, particularly early and late in the season

O **House**: 1 to 30 March: Sat & Sun only; 31 March to end Oct: Wed to Sun & BH Mon 1–5. Last admission 4.30. Closed Good Fri. On BH weekends and other busy days entry is by timed ticket only. **Garden**: same days as house 12–5. **Park & woodland**: open all year. **Events**: for details please send s.a.e. to The Box Office, PO Box 180, High Wycombe, Bucks HP14 4XT

£ House & garden: £3.80; family ticket £9.50. Garden only £1, children 50p. Park & woodland free. Parties must book in advance – rates on application to the Estate Office; no parties Sat, Sun or BH Mon. Coach-parking: space for one coach only; car park 200m from house. Please show membership cards and purchase tickets from the stableyard ticket office

🚶 Guided tours available for pre-booked parties on request

🛍 Shop open as house. Also Nov to 21 Dec: Wed to Sun 11–3 (tel. 01494 440718)

& Access to all ground-floor rooms; close car-parking arrangements; garden has some steep paths, best seen from terrace; park and woodland very hilly. WC. Wheelchairs available. Good access to shop and tea-room

◉ Braille and taped guides

◗ Tea-room open same days as house: Wed to Fri 1–5, Sat, Sun & BH Mon 12–5. Also Nov to 21 Dec, Wed to Sun 11–3

⊞ Children's worksheet. Baby-changing facilities. Children's menu and highchairs

▦ Study base available for pre-booked groups, rates on application to the Estate Office. Guided tours linked to Victorian history and environmental education can also be arranged

🏠 Dogs welcome except in house and formal gardens, where only guide dogs are permitted. Dog rings in stableyard and shady parking in car park

→ 1½ml N of High Wycombe; on W side of the Great Missenden road (A4128) [165: SU866955] *Bus:* Chiltern Rover 323/4 High Wycombe–Aylesbury (passing close ⇌ High Wycombe) (tel. 0345 382000) *Station:* High Wycombe 2ml

---

IGHTHAM MOTE 🏠 ✝ ❀ ❁ 🏃 E

Ivy Hatch, Sevenoaks TN15 0NT Tel: 01732 810378 Fax: 01732 811029

Beautiful medieval moated manor house, dating from 1340 with important later additions. Features include the Great Hall, crypt and courtyard. During 1997, as part of the ongoing conservation and repair programme, work will continue on the house, restricting access to the ground floor only. It will not be possible to view the Tudor chapel ceiling, drawing room or billiard room, which will re-open in 1998. However, the Robinson library and south-east courtyard, not normally open, will be shown. A 'Conservation in Action' exhibition explains the work in detail. The house is surrounded by an extensive 6ha garden

🅾 28 March to 2 Nov: daily except Tues & Sat, weekdays 12–5.30; Sun & BH Mon 11–5.30. Last admission 5. Car park open dawn to dusk throughout the year. Estate walks leaflet available. **Events:** for details tel. 01892 891001

£ £4, children £2, family ticket £10. Pre-booked parties of 20 or more weekday afternoons £3 (no reduction Sun & BH)

🏃 Free introductory talks. Pre-booked special guided conservation tour for groups of 20 or more on open weekday mornings only; tel. 01732 810378 for details (group reductions only apply after noon). Guided walks to Old Soar Manor

🛍 Shop open same days as house, 12.30–5.30 except Sun, when 11.30–5.30

♿ Access to most of ground floor, garden (some gravel paths), cobbled courtyard, conservation exhibition, tea pavilion and part of shop only; two wheelchairs available. Woodland estate walk accessible. Contact Property Manager in advance or enquire at ticket office on arrival for closer parking to house. WC

👁 Braille guide. Some contents may be touched on request

🍽 Tea pavilion open same days as house, 11.30–5. Oct hours vary – weather dependent. Picnic area in car park. No picnics in gardens

⊞ Baby-feeding/changing facilities available; children's quiz

▦ Teachers' resource book. Special tours for schools, contact Property Manager for details. Woodland shelter in grounds for use by groups

🏠 No dogs in gardens or house, but welcome on leads on estate walks

→ 6ml E of Sevenoaks, off A25, and 2½ml S of Ightham, off A227 [188: TQ584535] *Bus:* Kentish Bus 710 Sevenoaks–Maidstone (summer Sun only); otherwise

Wealden Beeline 222 ⇥ Borough Green–⇥ Tunbridge Wells, alight Fairlawne,
thence ½ml (footpath); East Surrey 404 Sevenoaks-Plaxtol (passing ⇥ Sevenoaks),
alight Ivy Hatch, ¾ml; otherwise Kentish Bus 306 ⇥ Sevenoaks–⇥ Gravesend
(passing ⇥ Borough Green), alight Ightham Common, 1½ml (tel. 0800 696996).
710 Sniddy Service Westerham–Maidstone (alight Ivy Hatch) *Station:* Borough
Green & Wrotham 3½ml; Hildenborough 4ml

KING'S HEAD 🏠

The Market Square, Aylesbury HP20 1TA
Tel: (Regional Office) 01494 528051 Fax: 01494 463310

*Coaching inn dating from 1450. The large contemporary window in the parlour contains
fragments of 15th-century glass with figures of angels holding shields, some of which bear
the arms of Henry VI and his wife, Margaret of Anjou*

O This property is to be re-let, and at time of going to press opening times are not
yet finalised. Please contact above number for information about opening
arrangements

→ At NW corner of Market Square *Bus:* from surrounding areas (tel. 0345 382000)
Station: Aylesbury 400m

KNOLE 🏛 ❈ ♠ 🛠 **E**

Sevenoaks TN15 0RP
Infoline: 01732 450608 Tel: 01732 462100 Fax: 01732 465528

*Knole is the largest private house in England and sits within a magnificent deer park owned by
Lord Sackville. Dating from 1456, the house was enlarged and embellished in 1603 by Thomas
Sackville, 1st Earl of Dorset, to whom it had been granted by Elizabeth I. The 13 state rooms
open to the public contain a collection of historical portraits, including works by Van Dyck,
Gainsborough, Lely, Kneller and Hoppner and a room devoted to the works of Sir Joshua
Reynolds. Silver, tapestries and a world-renowned collection of 17th-century Royal Stuart
furniture, including three state beds, silver table and the prototype of the Knole Settee*

O **House:** 28 March to 2 Nov: Wed, Fri, Sat, Sun & BH Mon 11–5; Thur 2-5. Last
admission 4. Pre-booked groups accepted on Wed, Fri & Sat 11–4, Thur 2–4.
Park: open daily to pedestrians by courtesy of Lord Sackville. **Garden:** May to Sept:
first Wed in each month only, by courtesy of Lord Sackville, 11–4; last admission
3. **Events:** programme of concerts and lectures; for details tel. 01892 891001

£ **House:** £5; children £2.50; family ticket £12.50. Pre-booked parties £4. Parking
(NT members free) £2.50. Park free to pedestrians. Only vehicles carrying visitors
to the house are allowed in the park. **Garden (note limited opening times):** £1,
children 50p

🛠 Guided tours for pre-booked parties on Thur 10–1 throughout season; normal
admission price plus £2 guiding fee

🛍 Shop open as house. Christmas shop 11–4. (tel. 01732 743748)

♿ Access to Great Hall, Stone Court, Green Court, shop, restaurant, garden (only open on first Wed in month; May to end Sept) and park; WC near restaurant; wheelchair available

👁 Braille guide; several items to touch. Herb and wilderness gardens, subject to limited opening (see above)

🍵 Tea-room open as house, serving morning coffee, lunch and tea (Thur, open from 12)

👶 Children's guide, worksheets and objects of the month. Highchairs in tea-room, children's portions. Baby-changing facilities

📖 Education facilities. Links to Tudor and Stuart aspects of curriculum, living history. Excellent collection of historical portraits. Contact Education Coordinator for details (tel. 01732 462100)

🐕 In park only, on lead. Please do not feed the deer; they can be dangerous

➡ Off M25 London Orbital at S end of Sevenoaks town; just E of A225 [188: TQ532543] *Bus:* Kentish Bus 426, 433, East Surrey 321 from Sevenoaks to House, Wed–Sun, June–Oct only; otherwise from surrounding areas to Sevenoaks, thence ¾ml (tel. 0800 696996) *Station:* Sevenoaks 1½ml

LAMB HOUSE 🏠 ✿

West Street, Rye TN31 7ES
Tel: (Regional Office) 01892 890651 Fax: 01892 890110

The home of the writer Henry James from 1898 to 1916 where he wrote the best novels of his later period. The walled garden, staircase, hall and three rooms on the ground floor containing some of James's personal possessions are on view. Also once home to the author E. F. Benson. The house and gardens are administered and largely maintained on the Trust's behalf by the tenant

🅾 April to end Oct: Wed & Sat only 2–6. Last admission 5.30

💷 £2.20; children £1.10. No reduction for parties. WCs and car park available in Rye

🐕 No dogs in house or garden

➡ In West Street, facing W end of church [198: TQ920202] *Bus:* From surrounding areas to Rye (tel. 01273 474747) *Station:* Rye ½ml

LEITH HILL 🏠 ⛴ 👤

Nr Coldharbour Tel/fax: 01306 711777

A large countryside property with an 18th-century tower at the highest point in south-east England. The top of the tower is 340m above sea level and provides magnificent views to the North and South Downs. The beautiful rhododendron wood is ¾ml to the south-west and at its best in May/June

◎ **Tower**: 1 April to end Sept: Wed 12–5; Sat, Sun & BH 11–5. Last admission 4.30. Also open weekends Oct to end March 11–3.30. Last admission 3 (tel. 01306 712434)

£ Tower: 80p. No reduction for groups. Rhododendron wood: £1.50 per car. Parking in designated areas along road at foot of the hill, ½ml walk from tower, some steep gradients. No direct vehicular access to summit. No coaches. Information room and telescope in tower. Circular trail guide available from dispenser £1

🚶 Guided walks at intervals throughout the year. Groups by prior arrangement with the Warden (tel. 01306 711777)

♿ Access path to upper part of rhododendron wood; car park

🍽 Light refreshments open same times as tower. Picnic area alongside tower and within rhododendron wood

🏫 Education groups for day visits and residential groups catered for by prior arrangement with North Downs Education Officer (tel. 01306 742809)

🐕 Dogs not allowed in rhododendron wood picnic area; elsewhere in rhododendron wood on leads. No dogs in tower

→ On summit of Leith Hill, 1ml SW of Coldharbour A29/B2126 [187: TQ139432]. Rhododendron wood: [187: TQ131427] *Bus:* Surrey Hills Leisure Bus 433 from ≢ Guildford & ≢ Dorking, Sun, May to Sept only; otherwise Tillingbourne 21, 31 Guildford–Dorking (passing close ≢ Guildford and passing ≢ Chilworth and Dorking), alight Holmbury St Mary 2½ml (tel. 01737 223000) *Station:* Holmwood (U), not Sun, 2½ml; Dorking 5½ml

---

LONG CRENDON COURTHOUSE 🏠

Long Crendon, Aylesbury HP18 9AN

A 14th-century building of two storeys, partly half-timbered, probably first used as a wool store. The manorial courts were held here from the reign of Henry V until recent times. The ground floor, rearranged as a flat, is let

◯ Upper floor only April to end Sept: Wed 2–6; Sat, Sun & BH Mon 11–6

£ £1. No reduction for parties. No WC

→ 2ml N of Thame, via B4011, close to the church [165: SP698091] *Bus:* Aylesbury
& The Vale 260/1, Aylesbury–Thame (not Sun) (passing ⇥ Haddenham &
Thame Parkway) (tel. 0345 382000) *Station:* Haddenham & Thame Parkway
2ml by footpath, 4ml by road

MONK'S HOUSE 🏠 ✿

Rodmell, Lewes BN7 3HF Tel: (Regional Office) 01892 890651 Fax: 01892 890110

---

*A small village house and garden, and the home of Leonard and Virginia Woolf from 1919
until Leonard's death in 1969. The house and garden are administered and largely maintained
by the tenant on the Trust's behalf*

◯ April to end Oct: Wed & Sat 2–5.30. Last admission 5

£ £2.20; children £1.10. No reduction for parties; max. 15 people in house at a
time. Parties only by prior arrangement with the tenant. Car park 50m; village
street too narrow for coaches; drivers please set passengers down at main road
junction, and park elsewhere

🐕 No dogs in house or garden

→ 4ml SE of Lewes, off former A275 in Rodmell village, near church (no access from
A26) [198: TQ421064] *Bus:* Stagecoach South Coast 123 Lewes–Newhaven
(passing ⇥ Lewes) (tel. 01273 474747) *Station:* Southease (U) 1¼ml

---

MOTTISFONT ABBEY GARDEN, HOUSE & ESTATE ✿ 🏃 E

Mottisfont, nr Romsey SO51 0LP Tel: 01794 340757 Fax: 01794 341492

---

*The abbey and garden form the central point of an 809ha estate which includes most of the
village of Mottisfont, farmland and woods. A tributary of the River Test flows through the
garden, forming a superb and tranquil setting for a 12th-century Augustinian priory, which,
after the Dissolution, became a house. It contains the spring or 'font' from which the place-
name is derived. The magnificent trees, walled gardens and the national collection of old-
fashioned roses combine to provide interest throughout the seasons. The abbey contains a
drawing room decorated by Rex Whistler and the cellarium of the old priory. In 1996 the
Trust acquired Derek Hill's 20th-century picture collection*

◯ **Garden & grounds** : 23 & 30 March, 1 April to 2 Nov: Sat to Wed 12–6 (or dusk
if earlier). During rose season (9 June to 6 July; check recorded message for state
of roses, 01794 34075) open daily 12–8.30. Last admission to grounds 1hr
before closing. **House: Whistler Room & cellarium:** same days as garden 1–5.
Derek Hill picture collection: Sun, Mon & Tues 1–5. **Events:** open-air events in
summer; for details contact Regional Box Office (tel. 01372 451596). Rooms in
the house are available for private and commercial functions, seminars and civil
wedding ceremonies; please contact Visitor Services Manager (tel. 01794
340757). Free parking

£ Garden, grounds & Whistler Room: £4, family ticket £10; during rose season £5, family ticket £12. No reduction for parties; coaches please book in advance. *Note*: As the roses are renowned for their scent, please refrain from smoking in the walled garden during the rose season. To appreciate the roses evening viewing is recommended

🛍 Shop open same days as garden,12.30–5.30. Closes 8 during rose season and 4 in Oct & Nov. Plant sales available (tel. 01794 341901)

♿ Extensive garden, lawns and gravel drive can be arduous. Easy access to rose garden. Wheelchairs and volunteer-driver buggy available. *Note:* paths not suitable for small/narrow wheelchairs. WC

◐ Braille guide. Many scents in rose garden

◑ Licensed restaurant (capacity 70; parties by arrangement). Lunches and home-made teas 12–5.30 same days as garden; 12–7.30 Fri, Sat & Sun during rose season (approx 9 June to 6 July). Dining rooms available for booked lunches, suppers and dinner parties; contact Visitor Services Manager (tel. 01794 340757)

👶 Baby-changing facilities; children's menus

🐕 Dogs in car park only (no shade). Delightful woodland walks may be enjoyed in Spearywell Woods and Great Copse; details from property

➔ 4½ml NW of Romsey, ¾ml W of A3057 [185: SU327270] *Station:* Dunbridge (U) ¾ml

MOTTISTONE MANOR GARDEN ❀ **E**

Bookings and postal enquiries to the Gardener, Manor Cottage, Hoxall Lane, Mottistone PO30 4ED

The colourful herbaceous borders, flowering fruit trees and delightful sea views combine to make a perfect setting for the 16th- and 17th-century manor house. The manor and village lie at the centre of the Mottistone Estate, which offers footpath walks between downs and the coast

O **Garden**: 26 March to 1 Oct: Wed & BH Mon 2–5.30. Last admission 5. Groups by written appointment. **House:** open Aug BH Mon only. **Events:** July, open air concerts; please tel. 01983 526445 for information

£ Garden £1.80. No reduction for groups. Parking 50m. No WC

& Not recommended for wheelchair users; steep slopes

🐕 On leads

➔ At Mottistone, 2ml W of Brighstone on B3399 [196: SZ406838] *Bus:* Southern Vectis 12 Newport–Alum Bay (tel. 01983 827005) *Ferry:* Yarmouth (Wightlink Ltd) 6ml (tel. 01705 827744) E Cowes (Red Funnel) 12ml (tel. 01703 334010)

THE NEEDLES OLD BATTERY 🐕 🏛 **E**

West Highdown PO39 0JH Tel: 01983 754772 during opening hours

A Victorian coastal fort built in 1862, over 80m above sea level. A 65m tunnel leads to spectacular views of Needles Rocks, lighthouse and Hampshire and Dorset coastline. Two original Rifled Muzzle-Loader gun-barrels are mounted on carriages in the parade ground, and the Laboratory, Searchlight Position and Position-Finding Cells have been restored

O 23 March to 30 Oct: Sun to Thur (but open Easter weekend and daily in July & Aug) 10.30–5. Last admission 4.30. *Note:* Property will be closed during adverse weather conditions; tel. property on day of visit to check. **Events:** send s.a.e. or tel. for information

£ £2.40; family ticket £6. No reduction for groups; school groups can be conducted by an NT guide by prior arrangement; a special charge applies. No vehicular access to Battery. Parking 1ml away at Alum Bay (not NT; charge £2), or park in Freshwater Bay (IOW Council) or Highdown car park (NT) and walk over downs. Children and dogs must be kept under strict control because of the cliffs

👤 School groups/special visits 23 March to 30 Oct (but not Aug) by appointment

🛍 Shop open same days as Battery 10.30–4.30

& Some access; car-parking some distance from Battery, but accompanied wheelchair users may park nearer by prior arrangement with the Administrator

♿ Braille guides for adults and children; large print guide

☕ Tea-room (spectacular views) open same days as Battery 10.30–4.30

📖 Children's guide and quiz sheets; the children's exhibition tells the story of 'The Needles at War' and cartoon information boards throughout explain how the Battery functioned

🐕 Dogs welcome on leads

➔ At Needles Headland, W of Freshwater Bay and Alum Bay (B3322) [196: SZ300848] *Bus:* Southern Vectis 42 Yarmouth–Needles, April to Oct only; otherwise any service to Alum Bay, thence ¾ml (tel. 01983 523831) *Ferry:* Yarmouth (Wightlink Ltd) 5ml (tel. 01705 827744); E Cowes (Red Funnel) 16ml (tel. 01703 334010)

NYMANS GARDEN

**Handcross, nr Haywards Heath RH17 6EB Tel: 01444 400321/400777
Fax: 01444 400253**

One of the great gardens of the Sussex Weald and one which retains much of its distinctive family style and character in the historic collection of plants, shrubs and trees. These are reflected in the house and surrounding estate, including the woodland walks and wild garden. Lady Rosse's library, drawing room and walled garden, showing the Messel family's creative character, will be open for the first time (see below)

Garden: 1 March to 2 Nov: daily except Mon & Tues (but open BH Mon) 11–6 or sunset if earlier; last admission 5.30. Winter 1997/8: Sat & Sun, including restaurant & shop, 12–4, but restricted according to ground conditions; tel. 01444 400321 for information. **House:** Lady Rosse's library, drawing room and walled garden will be open free of charge (as part of garden visit) 12 March to 2 Nov: same days as garden 12–4. Space is very limited and access cannot be guaranteed for every visitor; queuing likely and timed tickets may be in operation. **Events:** Special evening opening: garden & restaurant 13, 20 & 27 June, 4, 11, & 18 July 7–9.30; charge for all, incl. NT members, and booking essential (tel. 01444 400321); 15 & 16 Aug, musical events. Other summer events are held in the garden, for details contact Regional Box Office (tel. 01372 451596)

£ £4.50; family ticket £11. Groups £3.50. Joint party ticket which includes same day entry to Standen £6.50, available Wed to Fri. Car park at entrance; coaches must book

Shop and plant sales open same days and times as garden. Also Nov daily, (except Mon & Tues):10–4; Christmas shop 1 to 24 Dec: 10–4 (tel. 01444 400157)

Garden, licensed tea-room and shop accessible; wheelchair route indicated (map available); wheelchairs on request and self-drive powered vehicle (booking essential). Wheelchair access to house not available at present. WC

Braille guide. Old roses and other scented plants

Light lunches and teas in licensed tea-room 11–5, same days as shop. Restricted menu Nov to end Feb 1998. Available for functions throughout the year and open for Christmas lunches. Kiosk open (weather permitting) May to Sept 11–6.

Changing table in WCs at car park and tea-room. Highchair available in tea-room

In car park only

On B2114 at Handcross, 4.5m S of Crawley, just off London–Brighton M23/A23 [187: TQ265294] *Bus:* Brighton & Hove/London & Country 773 Brighton–Crawley (tel. 01273 886200); Lewes Coaches 33 Haywards Heath–Crawley (tel. 01273 674881). Alight Handcross, ¼ml–¾ml according to direction; all pass ⇌ Crawley *Station:* Balcombe 4½ml; Crawley 5½ml

OAKHURST COTTAGE 🏠 👤

Hambledon, nr Godalming GU8 4HF Tel/fax: 01428 683207

A very small 16th-century timber-framed cottage, restored and furnished as a simple cottager's dwelling in the 1800s. Delightful cottage garden with contemporary plant species

🅾 30 March to end Oct: Wed, Thur, Sat, Sun & BH Mon 2–5. Strictly by appointment in advance only (48hrs' notice required) with Witley Common Information Centre (tel. 01428 683207)

£ £2.20, incl. guided tour. No reduction for groups. Schools & groups by special arrangement any day or evening. Parking 200m. No WC

➡ *Bus:* Guildford & West Surrey 503 from Godalming (Wed only) (passes close ⮕ Godalming); otherwise Stagecoach Hants & Surrey 271, 571 Guildford–Hindhead (passes close ⮕ Godalming), alight Lane End 1ml (tel. 01737 223000) *Station:* Witley 1½ml

OLD SOAR MANOR 🏠

Plaxtol, Borough Green TN15 0QX Tel: 01732 810378

The solar block of a late 13th-century knight's dwelling

🅾 April to end Sept: daily 10–6

£ Free. Exhibition on Manor and surrounding areas. No WCs

👤 Guided walks from Ightham Mote; please tel. for details

🐕 No dogs please

➡ 2ml S of Borough Green (A25); approached via A227 and Plaxtol; narrow lane, unsuitable for coaches [188: TQ619541] *Bus:* Wealden Beeline 222 ⮕ Borough Green–⮕ Tunbridge Wells; East Surrey 404 Sevenoaks–Plaxtol (passing ⮕ Sevenoaks); on both alight E end of Plaxtol, thence ¾ml by footpath (tel. 0800 696996) *Station:* Borough Green & Wrotham 2½ml

OLD TOWN HALL, NEWTOWN 🏠 👤

Enquiries to the Custodian, Ken Cottage, Upper Lane, Brighstone PO30 4AT Tel: 01983 741052

The small, now tranquil village of Newtown once sent two members to Parliament, and the Town Hall was the setting for often turbulent elections. An exhibition depicts the exploits of the anonymous group of benefactors known as 'Ferguson's Gang'

🅾 26 March to 29 Oct: Mon, Wed & Sun (but open Good Fri, Easter Sat and Tues & Thur in July & Aug) 2–5. Last admission 4.45

£ £1.10. No reduction for groups

👤 Guided tours by written appointment

SOUTH EAST

♿ Not recommended for wheelchair users; flights of steps. WC

♿ Braille and large-print guides

■ School groups welcome by appointment

■ No dogs

→ Between Newport and Yarmouth, 1ml N of A3054 [196: SZ424905] *Bus:* Southern Vectis 7 ≟ Ryde Esplanade–Freshwater (passing Yarmouth Ferry Terminal), alight Barton's Corner, 1ml (tel. 01983 827005) *Station: Ferry*: Yarmouth (Wightlink Ltd) 5ml (tel. 01705 827744); E Cowes (Red Funnel) 11ml (tel. 01703 334010)

OWLETTS ■ ⚘

The Street, Cobham, Gravesend DA12 3AP
Tel: (Regional Office) 01892 890651 Fax: 01892 890110

A modest red-brick Charles II house with contemporary staircase and plasterwork ceiling, and small pleasure and kitchen gardens. Former home of the architect, Sir Herbert Baker. The property is now administered and largely maintained on the Trust's behalf by the tenant

◉ April to end Sept: Wed & Thur only, 2–5. Last admission 4.30

£ £2; children £1. Parties by arrangement; please write to tenant. No WC

■ No dogs in house or garden

→ 1ml S of A2 at W end of village, at junction of roads from Dartford and Sole Street [177: TQ665687] *Station:* Sole Street 1ml

---

PETWORTH HOUSE ■ ⚘ E

Petworth GU28 0AE
Tel: 01798 342207 Infoline: 01798 343929 Fax: 01798 342963

Magnificent late 17th-century mansion, set within a beautiful deer park (see following entry) and landscaped pleasure grounds. The house contains the Trust's finest collection of pictures with works by Turner, Van Dyck, Reynolds and Blake. Also ancient and neo-classical sculpture, fine furniture and carvings by Grinling Gibbons. Old kitchens and other servants' rooms recently opened in servants' block. Additional private family rooms open on weekdays. Chapel closed in 1997 for essential repairs

◉ **House:** 28 March to 2 Nov: daily except Thur & Fri (but open Good Fri) 1–5.30. Last admission to house 4.30; old kitchens 5. Additional rooms shown weekdays (not BH Mon). **Pleasure grounds and car park** 12–6 (opens 11 on BH Mon and all of July & Aug) for walks, picnics and access to tea-room, shop and Petworth town. **Events:** 24 to 26 May, Craft Festival; 27 to 29 June, open-air concerts (NT members charged for these events). For details of exhibitions and other events please send s.a.e. or contact Regional Box Office (tel. 01372 451596)

£ £4.50; family ticket £12. Pre-booked groups of 15+ £4. Coach parties alight at Church Lodge entrance, coaches then park in NT car park. Coach parties must book in advance due to limited parking; please contact Administration Office

⫪ Guided tours by arrangement on weekday mornings (additional charge); contact Administration Office

⌂ Shop open same days as house 12–5. BH Mon, July & Aug only open 11–5. Christmas shopping

♿ Car park is 800m from house. Vehicle available to take mobility-impaired visitors to house. Alternatively they may be set down at the Church Lodge entrance; drivers should make arrangements with the Administration Office. All ground-floor public rooms accessible; wheelchairs available. WC in servants' block. Shop and tea-room accessible. Pleasure ground accessible; parts of park possible, but mostly rough grass

⊙ Braille guide. Touch tours by arrangement

♨ Coffee, light lunches and teas in licensed tea-room 12–5 same days as house; BH Mon, July & Aug only 11–5. Private functions catered for; also pre-booked Christmas lunches (tel. 01798 344080)

⫪ Baby-feeding and changing facilities; highchair. No prams in house but pushchairs admitted. Children's guide

▥ Details of educational programme from Education Officer (tel. 01798 343748)

⌖ No dogs

→ In centre of Petworth (A272/A283) [197: SU976218]; car park well signposted *Bus:* Stagecoach Coastline 1/A Worthing–Midhurst, 1B Worthing–⇌ Petersfield (both pass ⇌ Pulborough) (tel. 01903 237661) *Station:* Pulborough 5¼ml

PETWORTH PARK ♣ E

As Petworth House, above

Beautiful 283ha deer park, with lakes, landscaped by Capability Brown and immortalised in Turner's paintings which can be seen in the house

O All year: daily 8 to sunset. Closed 27 to 29 June from 12. **Events:** 24 to 26 May, Craft Festival; 27 to 29 June, open-air concerts (NT members charged for these events). Send s.a.e. for booking form or contact Regional Box Office (tel. 01372 451596)

£ Free. Car park for park only on A283, 1½ml N of Petworth. No vehicles in park. No WC

& Car park and part of park accessible with care; some uneven paths

🐕 Dogs must be kept under close control

➔ Pedestrian access from Petworth town and on A272 & A283 *Bus:* as for Petworth House

---

PITSTONE WINDMILL ⌧

Ivinghoe

One of the oldest post mills in Britain; in view from Ivinghoe Beacon

🅞 June to end Aug (Sun only) and May BH: 2.30–6. Last admission 5.30

£ £1, children 30p. For details of arrangements for parties, contact David Goseltine, Holland Cottage, Whipsnade, Dunstable, Beds LU6 2LG (tel. 01582 872303). Parking 200m (by B488). No WC

& Area around mill accessible but strong pusher needed to negotiate track from car park. Mill machinery not accessible; long flight of wooden steps

➔ ½ml S of Ivinghoe, 3ml NE of Tring, just W of B488 [165: SP946158]
Bus: Aylesbury & The Vale 61 Aylesbury–Luton (passing close ⭰ Aylesbury & Luton) (tel. 0345 382000) *Station:* Tring 2½ml; Cheddington 2½ml

---

POLESDEN LACEY 🏠 ⌧ ♠ 🚶 Ⓔ

Great Bookham, nr Dorking RH5 6BD
Tel: 01372 458203/452048 Fax: 01372 452023

Originally an 1820s Regency villa, situated in a magnificent landscape setting on the Surrey Downs. The house was remodelled after 1906 by the Hon. Mrs Ronald Greville, a well-known Edwardian hostess. Her collection of fine paintings, furniture, porcelain and silver are still displayed in the reception rooms and corridors, which surround an inner courtyard. Extensive grounds, walled rose garden, lawns and landscape walks. King George VI and Queen Elizabeth The Queen Mother spent part of their honeymoon here. Shop, plant sales and restaurant in old stableyard

🅞 **House:** March: Sat & Sun only, plus Good Fri 1.30–4.30; 2 April to 2 Nov: Wed to Sun 1.30–5.30; also open BH Mon (starting with Easter) 11–5.30; last admission to house 30min before closing. **Grounds:** daily all year: 11–6 (or dusk if earlier). **Events:** 15 June to 6 July, open-air theatre: send s.a.e. for booking form to Theatre Box Office, P.O. Box 10, Dorking, Surrey RH5 6FH; tel. 01372 457223. 6 July, Polesden Fair; additional charge for all visitors, incl. NT members. Estate includes a YHA hostel (tel. 01372 452528)

£ Garden, grounds & landscape walks open all year round: £3, family ticket £7.50. House: £3 extra, family ticket £7.50 extra. Pre-booked groups £5 (house, garden & walks) weekdays only. No prams, back-packs or pushchairs in house. Parking 150m. The croquet lawn is available for use; equipment for hire from the house

📷 Shop open from 18 Jan to 23 Feb: Sat & Sun only 11–4.30; 1 to 28 March: Wed to Sun 11–4.30; 29 March to 2 Nov: Wed to Sun & BH Mon 11–5.30 (open daily July & Aug); 5 to 30 Nov: Wed to Sun 11–4.30; 1 to 21 Dec: daily 11–4.30. Plant sales area open same days as shop (tel. 01372 457230)

♿ Access to all showrooms, restaurant, shop and parts of garden; some fairly firm gravel paths. Disabled badge holders car park nearby. Wheelchairs available. Self-drive battery car available by prior appointment. WC near restaurant.
A landscape walk through open farm and woodland has been built for wheelchair users (strong pushers recommended)

👁 Braille guide to house; rose and lavender gardens (rose garden has some crazy paving). The house steward will describe objects and indicate those that may be touched (prior appointment recommended)

🍴 Coffee, lunches and home-made teas in restaurant with table licence. 18 Jan to 23 Feb (light refreshments): Sat & Sun only 11–4; 1 to 28 March (light refreshments) Wed to Sun 11–4; 29 March to 2 Nov: Wed to Sun & BH Mon 11–5; 5 Nov to 21 Dec (limited menu): Wed to Sun 11–4. The Old Stables will serve light refreshments July & Aug, Mon & Tues 11–4 (tel. 01372 456190)

🚼 Changing tables in gents' and ladies' WCs. Highchair available in restaurant

🐕 No dogs in formal gardens, on paths or on lawns. Welcome in rest of grounds on leads and good walks on estate (under close control at all times)

➔ 5ml NW of Dorking, 2ml S of Great Bookham, off A246 Leatherhead–Guildford road [187: TQ136522] *Bus:* Surrey Hills Leisure Buses 410 from Westerham, 433 from ⮑ Guildford, (both passing ⮑ Dorking), Sun, May to Sept only; otherwise 408 Guildford–Croydon (passing close ⮑ Guildford & Leatherhead), alight Great Bookham, 1½ml (tel. 01737 223000) *Station:* Boxhill & Westhumble 2ml

---

PRINCES RISBOROUGH MANOR HOUSE 🏠

Princes Risborough HP17 9AW

A 17th-century red-brick house with Jacobean oak staircase

🕐 House & front garden by written arrangement only with tenant, Wed 2.30–4.30. Last admission 4. Hall, drawing room and staircase shown

💷 £1. No reduction for parties. Public car park 50m

🐕 Admitted by arrangement with tenant

➔ Opposite church, off market square [165: SP806035] *Bus:* Aylesbury & The Vale 323/4 High Wycombe–Aylesbury (passing close ⮑ Aylesbury) (tel. 0345 382000) *Station:* Princes Risborough 1ml

PRIORY COTTAGES 🏠

1 Mill Street, Steventon, Abingdon OX13 6SP
Tel: (Coleshill Estate Office) 01793 762209

Former monastic buildings, converted into two houses. South Cottage contains the Great Hall of the original priory

O **The Great Hall in South Cottage only**: April to end Sept: Wed 2–6; by written appointment with tenant

£ £1. No reduction for parties. No WC. Unsuitable for coach parties

→ 4ml S of Abingdon, on B4017 off A34 at Abingdon West or Milton interchange on corner of The Causeway and Mill Street, entrance in Mill Street [164: SU466914] *Bus:* Thames Transit 32/A, Cityline 35A Oxford–≋ Didcot Parkway (passing close ≋ Oxford) (tel. 01865 772250) *Station:* Didcot Parkway 5ml

QUEBEC HOUSE 🏠

Westerham TN16 1TD Tel: (Regional Office) 01892 890651 Fax: 01892 890110

General Wolfe spent his early years in this gabled, red-brick 17th-century house. Four rooms containing portraits, prints and memorabilia relating to Wolfe's family and career are on view. In the Tudor stable block is an exhibition about the Battle of Quebec (1759) and the parts played by Wolfe and his adversary, the Marquis de Montcalm. The property is administered and maintained on the Trust's behalf by the tenant

O 1 April to 28 Oct: Tues & Sun only 2–6. Last admission 5.30. Parties by arrangement; please write to tenant

£ £2.20, children £1.10. Pre-booked parties £1.60 (prices include exhibition) Public car park 150m E of house

♿ Difficult for wheelchair users; steps, stairs

▣ Refreshments in village (not NT). No picnicking

→ At E end of village, on N side of A25, facing junction with B2026 Edenbridge road [187: TQ449541] *Bus:* All services quoted for Chartwell pass close to the house *Station:* Sevenoaks 4ml; Oxted 4ml

RIVER WEY & GODALMING NAVIGATIONS AND DAPDUNE WHARF 🚤 🛥 🚶

Navigation Office and Dapdune Wharf, Wharf Road, Guildford GU1 4RR
Tel: 01483 561389/455056 Fax: 01483 31667

The Wey, one of the first rivers in Britain to be made navigable, opened for barge traffic in 1653. This 15½ml waterway linked Guildford to Weybridge on the Thames, and thus with London. The Godalming Navigation, opened in 1764, enabled barges to work a further 4ml upriver. At Dapdune Wharf, Guildford, there is Reliance, *a restored Wey barge, as well as models and interactive displays which tell the story of the waterway, the people who lived and worked on it and the barges built there*

🅾 **Dapdune Wharf**: 29 March to 2 Nov: Wed, Sat, Sun & BHols 11–5. Pre-booked groups and school parties welcome throughout the year

£ **Dapdune Wharf**: £2, family ticket £5; pre-booked groups £1.50. **Navigations**: the entire 19½ml towpath is open to walkers and moorings for visiting boats: no charge. Navigation licences (including all lock tolls) are payable on all powered and non-powered craft issued for the year or for 7 or 21 day visits. There is a 10% reduction for visiting NT members on production of current membership card for 7 or 21 days only. There are insurance requirements and restrictions on engine size to protect the property. Please check with Navigation Office in advance of journey. Horse-drawn boat trips on narrow boat *Iona* (tel. 01483 414938); rowboats, punts, canoes and narrow boats at Farncombe Boat House (tel. 01483 421306); restaurant boats, excursion boats, rowboats and canoes at Guildford Boat House (tel. 01483 504494)

🕆 Pre-booked guided tours of Dapdune Wharf available for groups. Please telephone for details

♿ Wheelchair access to main exhibition at Dapdune Wharf. Accessible fishing sites; wheelchair access to some parts of towpath; contact Navigation Office for details

📖 Braille guide

☕ Tea-room at Farncombe Boat House, nr Godalming (not NT) (tel. 01483 418769)

🚼 Baby-changing facilities for 1997

📓 Study centre and facilities available; please tel. for details

🐕 Must be kept under control. All dogs to be kept on leads within lock areas

➔ Dapdune Wharf is on Wharf Road, off Woodbridge Rd, Guildford. Limited parking, so access from town centre on foot or by River Bus; tel. Navigation Office for details. Access to rest of Navigations from A3 & M25. Visiting craft can enter from the Thames at Shepperton or slipways at Guildford or Pyrford *Station:* 🚋 Addlestone, Byfleet & New Haw, Guildford, Farncombe & Godalming all lie close to the Navigation

RUNNYMEDE ♿ 🕆 Ⓔ

Egham Tel: 01784 432891 Fax: 01784 470194

76ha of riverside wildflower meadows where King John sealed the Magna Carta in 1215. Alongside are the 45ha of grassland slopes and broadleaf woods of Coopers Hill. Features include the American Bar Association's Memorial to Magna Carta, the John F. Kennedy memorial and the Fairhaven Lodges and kiosks designed by Edwin Lutyens. 5ha of Langham ponds have been designated as SSSI, rich in diversity of wetland flora and fauna. 1½ml of River Thames towpath

🅾 All year. Riverside grass car park open April to end Sept, daily when ground conditions allow, 10–7. Tea-room car park (hard-standing) open all year, April to Sept 9–7; Oct to March 10–5. **Events**: mid July, Craft Fair; contact Four Seasons Events for information (tel. 01344 874787)

£ Fees payable for parking, fishing and mooring. Fishing: day permits only; all year except during closed season (mid March to mid June); tickets available from riverbank. Mooring available for up to 24hrs only. Please note that mooring fees are also payable by members. *Note:* Seasonal boat trips to Windsor and Hampton Court. Contact boat operators French (not NT) (tel. 01753 851900)

𝄕 Extensive programme of guided walks throughout the year. Please telephone Head Warden for details

🛍 Small shop within tea-room

♿ Limited access to tea-room and meadows by prior arrangement. WC by tea-rooms. Good vehicle access to riverbank during summer months; no charge for orange badge holders. Access to memorials difficult. Riverboats admit people with disabilities. Contact Warden for information

◄ Braille guide; contact Head Warden for information

◖ Apr to end Sept: daily 8.30–5.30; Oct to end March 1998: daily 9.30–4.30; closed 25 Dec. Coach parties welcome by prior arrangement (tel. 01784 477110)

➔ On the Thames, 2ml W of Runnymede Bridge, on S side of A308 (M25, exit 13). 6ml E of Windsor *Bus:* From surrounding areas (tel. 01737 223000) *Station:* Egham 2ml

---

ST JOHN'S JERUSALEM 🏠 ✚ ✿

Sutton-at-Hone, Dartford DA4 9HQ
Tel: (Regional Office) 01892 890651 Fax: 01892 890110

A large garden, moated by the River Darent. The house is the former chapel of a Knights Hospitaller Commandery, since converted into a private residence. The east end of the chapel which is open to view, was retained for family worship, but later was converted into a billiard room. No access to house. The property is occupied as a private residence and is administered and managed by a tenant on the Trust's behalf

◯ **Former chapel and garden only**: April to Oct: Wed only 2–6. Last admission 5.30

£ £1; children 50p

♿ Garden only accessible

➔ 3ml S of Dartford at Sutton-at-Hone, on E side of A225 [177: TQSS8703] *Bus:* Kentish Bus 14/5 from ⇌ Dartford (tel. 0800 696996) *Station:* Farningham Road ¾ml

---

SANDHAM MEMORIAL CHAPEL ✚

Burghclere, nr Newbury RG15 9JT Tel/fax: 01635 278394

The interior walls of this First World War chapel, built in the 1920s, are entirely covered with murals by Stanley Spencer. This extraordinary project illustrates the artist's experiences during the Great War and is considered to be his greatest achievement. Hidden in the depths of rural Hampshire, the chapel sits amid tranquil lawns and orchards with beautiful views across to Watership Down

Note: As there is no lighting in the chapel, it is best to view the paintings on a bright day

◯ March & Nov: Sat & Sun only 11.30–4; Apr to end Oct: Wed to Sun & BH Mon 11.30–6; (closed Wed following BH Mon); Dec to Feb by appointment only

£ £2. No reduction for pre-booked groups. Road verge parking. Picnics on front lawn

♿ Accessible via steps; portable ramp available. Wheelchair users advised to enter through side gate

◉ Braille guide

🐕 On leads only

➔ 4ml S of Newbury, ½ml E of A34 [174: SU463608] *Bus:* Burghfield mini coaches 123/4 from Newbury (passing close ⇌ Newbury) (tel. 01734 590719) *Station:* Newbury 4ml

---

SCOTNEY CASTLE GARDEN 🖼 ✳ ♣ E

Lamberhurst, Tunbridge Wells TN3 8JN Tel: 01892 891081 Fax: 01892 890110

One of England's most romantic gardens, surrounding the ruins of a 14th-century moated castle. Rhododendrons, azaleas, water lilies and wisteria flower in profusion. Woodland and estate walks

◯ **Garden:** 29 March to 2 Nov: (**Old Castle:** May to 14 Sept) Wed to Fri 11–6; Sat & Sun 2–6, or sunset if earlier; BH Sun & Mon 12–6 (closed Good Fri). Last admission 1hr before closing. **Events:** for details tel. 01892 891001

£ £3.60; children £1.80; family ticket £9. Pre-booked parties £2.40 (no party reduction on Sat, Sun or BH Mon)

🛍 Shop open as garden

♿ Garden partly accessible to wheelchair users, but strong companion necessary; approach to garden and paths very steep in places. Wheelchairs available

◉ Herb garden

📇 In Goudhurst & Lamberhurst villages (not NT). Picnicking in car park area only

🐕 On leads on estate walks only

➡ 1ml S of Lamberhurst on A21 [188: TQ688353] *Bus:* Autopoint 256 Tunbridge Wells–Wadhurst (passing ≋ Tunbridge Wells), alight Lamberhurst Green, 1ml (tel. 0800 696996) *Station:* Wadhurst 5½ml

---

SHALFORD MILL

Shalford, nr Guildford Tel: 01483 61617

18th-century watermill on the Tillingbourne, given in 1932 by an anonymous group of benefactors known as 'Ferguson's Gang'. Part-tenanted, part-open

🅾 Daily 10–5

💷 Free but donations in the box (emptied daily) most welcome. No parking at property. Children must be accompanied by an adult

➡ 1½ml S of Guildford on A281 opposite Sea Horse Inn *Bus:* Tillingbourne 21–5, 31/2 Guildford & West Surrey 273, 283 from Guildford (pass close ≋ Guildford) (tel. 01737 223000) *Station:* Shalford (U), ½ml; Guildford 1½ml

---

SHAW'S CORNER 🏠 E

Ayot St Lawrence, nr Welwyn AL6 9BX Tel: 01438 820307

An early 20th-century house, and the home of George Bernard Shaw from 1906 until his death in 1950. Many literary and personal relics are shown in the downstairs rooms, which remain as in his lifetime. Shaw's bedroom and bathroom are also on view, and there is a display room upstairs

🅾 29 March to 2 Nov: Wed to Sun & BH Mon 2–6 (closed Good Fri). Parties by written appointment only, March to end Nov. Last admission 5.30. On busy days admission will be by timed ticket. On events days house and grounds will close at 4. *Note:* No large hand luggage inside property. **Events:** for details of Shaw's birthday play and other events, please send s.a.e. to Custodian

💷 £3.10; family ticket £7.70. No reduction for parties. Car park

♿ Access to garden and house, but some steps. Please enquire about best times for visits; unsuitable for severely disabled visitors

📇 Teas available in village (not NT)

🚼 No back-packs or baby carriers in house, but front sling baby carrier available

🐕 In car park only

➡ At SW end of village, 2ml NE of Wheathampstead; approx. 2ml from B653 [166: TL194167] *Bus:* Sovereign 304 ≋ St Albans City–Hitchin, alight Gustardwood, 1¼ml (tel. 0345 244344) *Station:* Welwyn North 4ml; Harpenden 5ml

SHEFFIELD PARK GARDEN ❀ 𝄢 E

Uckfield TN22 3QX Tel: 01825 790231 Fax: 01825 791264

A magnificent 40ha landscape garden, with 4 lakes linked by cascades and waterfalls, laid out in the 18th century by Capability Brown. Carpeted with daffodils and bluebells in spring, its rhododendrons, azaleas and stream garden are spectacular in early summer. In autumn the garden is ablaze with colour. Its collection of rare trees and shrubs makes the garden wonderful to visit at any time of year

🅾 March: Sat & Sun only 11–6; 28 March to 16 Nov: Tues to Sun & BH Mon 11–6 or sunset if earlier; 19 Nov to 21 Dec: Wed to Sun 11–4. Last admission 1hr before closing. **Events**: for details tel. 01892 891001

£ £4, children £2; family ticket £10. Parties £3. No reduction for parties on Sat, Sun & BH Mon

𝄢 Pre-booked guided tours in groups of 10 or more Tues to Fri mornings; tel. 01825 790231 for rates

🛍 Shop as garden. Also Christmas shop; tel. 01825 790655 for details

♿ Most parts of garden accessible with the exception of woodland path beyond lower lakes; paths mostly firm and level; two powered self-drive cars and wheelchairs available. WCs. Car parking near entrance

👁 Water sounds; scented trees and shrubs

🍴 Restaurant (not NT) and picnic area adjoining car park; no picnics in garden

🚼 Baby-changing facilities

🐕 Dogs on leads in car park only

➔ Midway between East Grinstead and Lewes, 5ml NW of Uckfield, on E side of A275 (between A272 & A22), ½ml from Sheffield Park station (Bluebell Rly [198: TQ415240] *Bus:* Lewes Coaches 21 from Lewes (Sat only); RDH 246 from Uckfield (Mon, Fri only); otherwise Stagecoach South Coast 781 Eastbourne–Haywards Heath (passing ≋ Haywards Heath and Uckfield), alight Chailey Crossroads,1¾ml (tel. 01273 474747) *Station:* Sheffield Park (Bluebell Rly) ½ml; Uckfield 6ml; Haywards Heath 7ml

SISSINGHURST CASTLE GARDEN 🏠 🏠 ❀ ⚘

Sissinghurst, nr Cranbrook TN17 2AB Tel: 01580 715330

The 2ha famous connoisseurs' garden created by Vita Sackville-West and her husband, Sir Harold Nicolson, between the surviving parts of an Elizabethan mansion. A series of small, enclosed gardens, intimate in scale and romantic in atmosphere with much to see in all seasons. Also, the study where Vita Sackville-West worked, and the Long Library

Note: Due to the limited capacity of the garden, timed tickets are in operation and visitors may have to wait before admission. Daily visitor numbers are restricted; visitors may still visit the Oast House exhibition,woodland and lakes walks, restaurant and shop. No tripods or easels in the garden

[O] 28 Mar to 15 Oct: Tues to Fri 1–6.30; Sat, Sun & Good Fri 10–5.30. Closed Mon, incl. BH. Last admission 30min before closing. Ticket office & exhibition open at 12 on weekdays. (The garden is quieter in April, Sept & Oct, and Wed to Fri after 4)

[£] £6. Coaches and parties by appointment only; no reduction. Contact Bookings Secretary for details (tel. 01580 715330 or fax 01580 713911)

[◻] Shop open same days as garden. Tues to Fri 12–5.30; Sat, Sun & Good Fri 10–5.30. Christmas shop, for details tel. 01580 713090

[♿] Admission restricted to two wheelchairs at any one time because of narrow and uneven paths. Limited access to visitors with powered wheelchairs – if transfer to a manual wheelchair is not possible please tel. 01580 715330 in advance. Wheelchairs available on loan. Disabled visitors may be set down at ticket office. Disabled drivers may park near ticket office. Plan of recommended wheelchair route available. Restaurant and shop accessible. WC

[👁] Braille garden plan; scented plants & flowers; herb garden

[🍽] Coffee, lunches, teas in Granary Restaurant (licensed – no spirits) Tues to Fri 12–5.30, Sat, Sun & Good Fri 10–5. Christmas opening, contact restaurant for details tel. 01580 713097. Picnics in car park and field in front of castle

[👶] Not ideal for children. No pushchairs admitted, as paths are narrow and uneven but baby carriers available. No children's games in garden

[🐕] No dogs in garden or picnic areas, but welcome on leads in surrounding areas

[→] 2ml NE of Cranbrook, 1ml E of Sissinghurst village (A262) [188: TQ8138]
Bus: Maidstone & District/Renoun 4/5 Maidstone–Hastings (passing ⇌ Staplehurst), alight Sissinghurst, 1¼ml (tel. 0800 696996)
Station: Staplehurst 5½ml

SMALLHYTHE PLACE [⌂] [❀] [E]

Smallhythe, Tenterden TN30 7NG Tel: 01580 762334

An early 16th-century half-timbered house, home of the Victorian actress Ellen Terry from 1899 to 1928. The house contains many personal and theatrical mementoes. Charming cottage garden including Ellen Terry's rose garden. The Barn Theatre also open most days by courtesy of the Barn Theatre Society

[O] 28 March to 29 Oct: Sat to Wed & Good Fri 2–6, or dusk if earlier. Last admission 30min before closing. (The Barn Theatre may be closed some days at short notice). National Gardens Scheme: house & garden open 13 June, 2–5.30. **Events:** for details tel. 01892 891001

[£] £2.80, children £1.40; family ticket £7. Pre-booked parties Tues am only; no reduction. Max. 25 people in the house at any one time; garden has shelter for a further 25. No picnicking

[👶] Children must be accompanied by an adult

[🐕] No dogs except guide dogs in garden or house

→ 2ml S of Tenterden, on E side of the Rye road (B2082) [189: TQ893300] *Bus:* Autopoint 312 ➤ Rye–Tenterden (tel. 0800 696996) *Station:* Rye 8ml; Appledore 8ml; Headcorn 10ml

SOUTH FORELAND LIGHTHOUSE 🏠 🖼 🔧 👤

St Margaret's-at-Cliffe, Dover
Tel: (Regional Office) 01892 890651 Fax: 01892 890110

A distinctive landmark on the White Cliffs of Dover with views to France. The lighthouse was built in 1843 and used by Marconi for first radio communications as an aid to navigation in 1898. Tower, information room and spiral stairs to balcony around the light are open

🅾 29 March to 27 Oct: Sat, Sun & BH Mon 2–5.30. Last admission 5 (or dusk if earlier). Access on foot from NT car park at Langdon Cliffs (2ml) or from St Margaret's village only

£ £1, children 50p. No reduction for parties, must pre-book with Regional Office. No parking facilities or access for vehicles

♿ Parking for disabled visitors at lighthouse

👤 Model and exhibition on display

🐕 No dogs in lighthouse

→ At St Margaret's-at-Cliffe [179: TR359433] *Bus:* Stagecoach East Kent 90 Folkestone–Deal (passing ➤ Dover Priory & Walmer) (tel. 0800 696996) *Station:* Martin Mill 2½ml

SPRIVERS GARDEN ✿

Horsmonden TN12 8DR Tel: (Regional Office) 01892 890651 Fax: 01892 890110

This garden includes flowering and foliage shrubs, herbaceous borders and old walls. It is administered and maintained on the Trust's behalf by the tenant

🅾 31 May, 14 June & 28 June: 2–5.30. Last admission 5

£ £1; children 50p. No parties. Parking limited; space for one coach only. No WC

→ 2ml N of Lamberhurst on B2162 [188: TQ6940] *Bus:* Maidstone & District/ Fuggles 297 ➤ Tunbridge Wells–Tenterden (tel. 0800 696996) *Station:* Paddock Wood 4ml

STANDEN 🏠 ✿ 🍴 👤 E

East Grinstead RH19 4NE Tel: 01342 323029 Fax: 01342 316424

A family house of the 1890s, designed by Philip Webb, friend of William Morris. A showpiece of the 19th-century Arts & Crafts Movement, it is decorated throughout with William Morris carpets, fabric and wallpaper, Pre-Raphaelite paintings and tapestries. Beautiful hillside garden and woodland walks

🅾 26 March to 2 Nov: Wed to Sun & BH Mon. **Garden:** 12.30–6. **House:** 12.30–4.
Property may close at peak times for limited periods to avoid overcrowding.
7 Nov to 21 Dec: garden only, Fri, Sat & Sun 1–4. **Events:** please send s.a.e.
or tel. for information

£ House & garden £5; family ticket £12.50. Garden only £3, (£2 in Nov/Dec).
Joint party ticket which includes same day entry to Nymans Garden £6.50,
available Wed to Fri. Groups £4 weekdays only, if booked in advance; other
times by prior booking with Property Manager. Parking 180m

🚶 By special arrangement; Wed, Thur, Fri am. Extra charge for out of hours opening

🛍 Shop open as house, plus 7 Nov to 21 Dec: Fri, Sat & Sun 1–4 (admission charge
refunded for purchases over £5)

♿ Ground floor of house, restaurant, shop and part of garden accessible; some steps
in house; wheelchairs available. Disabled drivers only may park adjacent to ticket
office and forecourt of house as directed, but thick gravel. Steps and gravel paths
in garden. WC

👁 Braille guide to house and garden; scented plants & flowers. Stewards will
describe contents and indicate those that may be touched

🍽 Light lunches & afternoon teas. Open 12.30–5. Picnics in lower car park and
picnic area. *Note*: The Barn (Restaurant) is available for non-residential private
and commercial functions with limited associated use of the house. The Property
Manager welcomes enquiries

👶 2 reins, 2 baby carriers available; suitable for children aged up to 16 months;
no back-packs; pushchairs not allowed in house

📖 Education groups welcome; tel. Property Manager for details

🐕 In lower car park and woodland walks only (via lower car park)

➜ 2ml S of East Grinstead, signposted from B2110 (Turners Hill road) [187:
TQ389356] *Bus:* London & Country 474 ⇌ East Grinstead–Crawley (passing
⇌ Three Bridges), alight at approach road just north of Saint Hill, ½ml, or at
Saint Hill, thence ½ml by footpath (tel. 0181 668 7261) *Station:* E Grinstead 2ml

---

STONEACRE 🏠 ✤

Otham, Maidstone ME15 8RS Tel: 01622 862871 Fax: 01622 862157

---

*A half-timbered mainly late 15th-century yeoman's house, with great hall and crownpost,
surrounded by a lovely and newly restored cottage-style garden. The property is administered
and largely maintained on the Trust's behalf by the tenant*

Note: Children's trail proposed for 1997 in conjunction with Kent Gardens Trust

🅾 April to end Oct: Wed & Sat 2–6. Last admission 5

£ £2.20; children £1.10. No reduction for parties. Car park 100m; drive narrow,
coach drivers please set passengers down at road junction in village

👁 Garden recommended to accompanied visually impaired visitors; herb gardens
and other scented plants

No dogs please

→ At N end of Otham village, 3ml SE of Maidstone, 1m S of A20 [188: TQ800535]
Bus: Maidstone & District 13 Maidstone–Hollingbourne (passing close
≢ Maidstone E & W), alight Otham, ½ml (tel. 0800 696996) *Station:* Bearsted 2ml

---

STOWE LANDSCAPE GARDENS 🏠 ✳ ♣ E

Buckingham MK18 5EH Tel: 01280 822850 Fax: 01280 822437

One of the supreme creations of the Georgian era. The first, formal layout was adorned with many buildings by Vanbrugh, Kent and Gibbs: in the 1730s Kent designed the Elysian Fields in a more naturalistic style, one of the earliest examples of the reaction against formality leading to the evolution of the landscape garden. Miraculously, this beautiful garden survives; its sheer scale must make it Britain's largest work of art. The House (not NT) has been owned and occupied by Stowe School since 1923. The State Rooms and Marble Hall may be visited and the view of the gardens from the South Portico should not be missed

O **Gardens:** 24 March to 14 April: daily; 15 April to 5 July: Mon, Wed, Fri, Sun;
6 July to 8 Sept: daily; 10 Sept to 2 Nov: Mon, Wed, Fri, Sun; 27 Dec to 5 Jan
1998: daily 10–5 or dusk if earlier. Last admission 1hr before closing.
House: (not NT) 24 March to 14 April; 6 July to 9 Sept: daily 2–5 (closed Sat).
House occasionally closed for private functions; please check before visiting
(tel. 01280 813650). During school term time, groups on Sun by prior
arrangement. *Note:* visitors should allow plenty of time as gardens are extensive.
Events: for details please send s.a.e. to 'Box Office', Stowe Landscape Gardens
(tel. 01280 823334/822850)

£ Gardens £4.20; family ticket £10.50. House (incl. NT members) £2. Party visits
by prior arrangement with Property Manager (tel. 01280 822850)

🎋 Guided tours available by prior arrangement with Property Manager

🛍 NT gift shop in Menagerie, open as gardens: Mon to Fri 10–5; Sat & Sun
11.30–5.30. For other times of opening (tel. 01280 813164/822850)

♿ Unsuitable for manual wheelchairs; powered self-drive cars (some 2-seaters)
available free (please
pre-book if possible);
details from Estate
Secretary. Access to tea-
room. WC

👁 Braille and audio-
cassette guides available

☕ Morning coffee, light
lunches and teas. Same
days as gardens 11–5
(Dec & Jan 11–4).
Picnics permitted in
gardens

🍼 Highchairs available

■ School visits welcomed

🐕 On leads only

➜ 3ml NW of Buckingham via Stowe Avenue, off A422 Buckingham–Banbury road
[152: SP665366] *Bus:* Classic Coaches 66 from ⇌ Aylesbury to Gardens, Sun
only (May to Sept), otherwise Paynes 32, Milton Keynes Citybus 51/A from
Milton Keynes (passing ⇌ Milton Keynes Central); Aylesbury & The Vale 66 from
Aylesbury (passing close ⇌ Aylesbury) (tel. 0345 382000). On all (except
summer Sun), alight Buckingham, thence 3ml

TUDOR YEOMAN'S HOUSE 🏠

Sole Street, Cobham DA12 3AX
Tel: (Regional Office) 01892 890651 Fax: 01892 890110

---

*A 15th-century yeoman's house of timber construction. The property is administered and
maintained on the Trust's behalf by the tenant*

◉ Main hall only, by written application to the tenant

£ 50p. No reduction for children or parties. No WC

➜ 1ml SW of Cobham, on W side of B2009, just N of Sole Street Station
[177: TQ657677] *Station:* Sole Street, adjacent

UPPARK 🏠 ❀ 🍽 🚹 🅴

South Harting, Petersfield GU31 5QR
Tel: 01730 825415 Infoline (24hrs): Tel: 01730 825857 Fax: 01730 825873

---

*Fine late 17th-century house situated high on the South Downs with magnificent views
towards the Solent. Important collection of paintings and decorative art formed by members of
the Fetherstonhaugh family; interesting below stairs servants' rooms, links with H. G. Wells
whose early years were spent here. Extensive multi-media exhibition in Sun Alliance visitor
centre, fully detailing restoration of house and contents*

Note: The property reopened in 1995 after restoration, following a major fire in 1989
and is likely to continue to be very popular. The house has been fully restored to its
state 'the day before the fire' and the garden replanned and replanted

◉ 30 March to 30 Oct: daily except Fri & Sat; **House:** 1–5; **Car park, woodland
walk, ticket office, exhibition, garden, shop & restaurant:** 11.30–5.30; last
admission to house 4.15. Print room open only on first Mon of each month.
Admission to house is by timed ticket (incl. NT members) so visitors may have to
wait before being admitted. Tickets will be marked with an entry slot (eg. 1–1.15),
visitors enter the house during that slot, but may stay as long as the house is
open. On Sun, BH and other busy days tickets may sell out. Some Sun & BH
tickets are bookable in advance (small charge); tel. 01730 825415 during office
hours Mon to Fri. **Events:** 'Putting to Bed' days; contact Property Manager

£ House, garden and exhibition: £5; family ticket £12.50. Groups (no reduction)
weekdays only and must be pre-booked

⚷ By arrangement some mornings

📷 Open same days as house 11.30–5.30

♿ Exhibition, (stairlift to upper floor) shop, garden and house accessible; lift to basement showrooms. Wheelchairs available. WC. Disabled visitors are advised to tel. before visiting

👁 Braille guide to house; material samples available to handle from stewards

🍴 Light lunches and afternoon teas. Open same days as house 11.30–5.30. Picnic area near car park and in woodland. Kiosk near car park serving sandwiches, hot and cold drinks, open from 11.30

👶 Front carriers available for loan at house (no back carriers please) pushchairs not allowed in the house; changing facilities, highchairs. Children's guide, hands-on exhibits in exhibition

🐕 Woodland walk and car park only, on leads please (no shade in car park)

➡ 5ml SE of Petersfield on B2146, 1½ml S of South Harting [197: SU775177]
Bus: Sussex Bus 54 ⇌ Petersfield–⇌ Chichester (tel. 0345 023067)
Station: Petersfield 5½ml

THE VYNE 🏠 ❖ ⚷ **E**

Sherborne St John, Basingstoke RG24 9HL
Tel: 01256 881337 Fax: 01256 881720

A house of diaper brickwork, dating back to the time of Henry VIII. It was built by William, 1st Lord Sandys, in the early 16th century, and extensively altered in the mid 17th century, when John Webb added the earliest classical portico to a country house in England. Grounds with herbaceous and wild gardens, lawns and lake. Woodland walks

Note: **The house will be closed throughout 1997 while essential internal repair work is undertaken**

O **Grounds:** weekends in March, then 2 April to end Oct: daily except Mon & Fri 12.30–5.30. Also open Good Fri & BH Mon 11–5.30, but closed Tues following. **Events:** please send s.a.e. or telephone Regional Box Office for details (tel. 01372 451596)

£ Grounds only £2. Parking 100m

📷 Shop open weekends March to end Oct: 12.30–5.30, Good Fri & BH Mon 11–5.30; also open 5 July to 13 Sept: daily except Mon & Fri 2–5.30. For Christmas shopping tel. 01256 880039

♿ Access to grounds. Wheelchairs available. Shop accessible via ramp. Old Brewhouse tea-room accessible. WC

🍴 Tea-room times as shop, serving afternoon teas in Old Brewhouse. Light lunches served at weekends, Good Fri & BH Mon only; last orders 30min before closing

👶 Baby-changing facilities

🐕 In car park only

227

➡ 4ml N of Basingstoke between Bramley and Sherborne St John [175 & 186: SU637566]. From Basingstoke Ring Road, follow Basingstoke District Hospital signs until property signs are picked up. Follow A340 Aldermaston Rd towards Tadley. Right turn into Morgaston Rd. Right turn into Vyne Road *Bus:* Hampshire Bus 45 from Basingstoke (passing ⇌ Basingstoke) (tel. 01256 464501) *Station:* Bramley 2½ml

---

WADDESDON MANOR 🏠 ❄ ♣ E

Waddesdon, nr Aylesbury HP18 0JH
Recorded Information Tel: 01296 651211 Booking Office Tel: 01296 651226
Administration Tel: 01296 651282 Fax: 01296 651293

Waddesdon Manor, designed in the style of a French Renaissance château, was built in the 1870s by Baron Ferdinand de Rothschild from the Austrian branch of the famous Rothschild banking family. The interior evokes 18th-century France and is furnished with panelling, furniture, carpets and porcelain, much of which has a royal French provenance. There is an important collection of English 18th-century portraits by Gainsborough and Reynolds and of Dutch 17th-century Old Masters. In addition to the State Reception rooms and the bedrooms there are display areas devoted to Sèvres porcelain, an exhibition on the Rothschild family and important rooms on the first floor recently restored with more of Baron Ferdinand's 18th-century panelling. The family's long association with wine is represented in the Wine Cellars. Set in the garden is a rococo-style aviary housing exotic birds. In the recently restored formal parterre, the elaborate raised ribbon Victorian display is planted twice a year with spring and summer bedding. The shrubberies have been revived around the garden in the style of the 19th century. Daffodil Valley boasts a display of daffodils in March followed by a mass of wild flowers. Many magnificent trees can be seen throughout the garden

Note: The Batchelors' Wing is closed for refurbishment

🅾 **Grounds (incl. gardens, aviary, restaurant & shops):** 1 March to 21 Dec: Wed to Sun & BH Mon 10–5. **House (incl. Wine Cellars):** 27 March to 26 Oct: Thur to Sun & BH Mon, plus Wed in July & Aug only 11–4. Due to the capacity of the house, entry is by timed ticket. Tickets are available from 10 on a first-come, first-served basis and can also be booked in advance (tel. 01296 651226; booking charge £2.50 per transaction). The number of tickets is limited, but a proportion will be retained for on-the-day allocation. Children under 6 are not admitted to the house. Babies must be in front slings (some available). **Events:** an active programme is planned for 1997; please tel. 01296 651226 for details

💷 Grounds (incl. gardens, aviary, restaurant & shops): 1 March to 26 Oct £3, children £1.50, family ticket (2 adults & 2 children) £7.50; 29 Oct to 21 Dec free. House £6 (no reduction for children). In order to visit the house a grounds ticket must be purchased

🚶 A variety of guided tours, workshops and courses are available to individuals and groups; for details tel. 01296 651226

🛍 Gift and wine shops open 1 March to 21 Dec, Wed to Sun & BH Mon 10–5

♿ Tel. 01296 651226 to book timed ticket in advance. Designated parking with drop-off at house if required. Garden, ground floor, first floor (lift), restaurant and shops accessible. No wheelchair access to wine cellars. Most of garden easy, some deep gravel. Free garden map shows suitable route for disabled visitors. Some wheelchairs available, but only two allowed on each floor at any one time for safety reasons

🦮 Braille guide to house. Guide dogs in gardens only

🍽 Licensed restaurant open as shop (last orders 30min before closing). Additional tea-room in stables, open on busy days. Private dining facilities available for groups by arrangement. Picnics welcome except on north lawns, terrace, parterre and aviary garden. No barbecues

👶 Baby-changing facilities. Small play area

🐕 No dogs allowed on the property, except guide dogs in the grounds only

➡ Access via Waddesdon village [165: SP740169], 6ml NW of Aylesbury on A41; M40 (westbound) exit 6 or 7 via Thame & Long Crendon or M40 (eastbound) exit 9 via Bicester *Bus:* Aylesbury & The Vale 16/17, Classic Coaches 77/8, from Aylesbury (passing close ≅ Aylesbury) (tel. 0345 382000) *Station:* Aylesbury 6ml; Haddenham & Thame Parkway 9ml

---

WAKEHURST PLACE ❀ E

Ardingly, nr Haywards Heath RH17 6TN Tel: 01444 894066 Fax: 01444 894069

Managed as part of the Royal Botanic Gardens Kew, Wakehurst Place has been described as one of the most beautiful gardens in England. A series of ornamental features containing a great diversity of exotic plants provides year-round colour and interest. Extensive woodlands, with an informal arboretum, offer delightful walks. Rooms in the Elizabethan mansion, the focal point of the estate, provide visitors with information about Wakehurst Place and its many interesting features. The Loder Valley Reserve may also be visited on the issue of a permit (24hrs notice required)

Note: Wakehurst Place is administered and maintained by the Royal Botanic Gardens Kew; tel. 01444 894066 for up-to-date information

🅾 All year: daily (except 25 Dec & 1 Jan). Nov to end Jan: 10–4; Feb & Oct: 10–5; March: 10–6; April to end Sept: 10–7. Last admission 30min before closing. Mansion closes 1 hr before gardens. **Events**: Aug BH weekend, Craft Fair; tel. 01444 894066 for information on this and other events throughout the year

💷 Prices under review; tel. 01444 894066 for details. Discounts for pre-booked groups of 10+. Parking 400m from mansion. Exhibition in mansion.

🚶 Guided tours available most Sat & Sun: tel. 01444 894004 from Tues onwards for times & availability. Pre-booked tours available on request; please write to Administrator

🛍 Books & gifts are sold in the shop located in the mansion (not NT)

♿ Most of upper garden accessible, but steep paths elsewhere (strong companions essential). A self-service restaurant is accessible via ramps. Wheelchairs available. WC. It may be possible for visitors with disabilities to be set down by the mansion by prior arrangement with Administrator

🌳 Year-round interest

[symbol] Fully-licensed self-service restaurant (not NT), serving a large selection of homemade cakes, hot & cold snacks, salads and full meals. Open all year. Picnics welcome in gardens

[symbol] Baby-changing room in restaurant WCs

[symbol] Contact the Education Officer (tel. 01444 894094)

[symbol] No dogs, except guide dogs

[symbol] 1½ml NW of Ardingly, on B2028 [187: TQ339314] *Bus:* London & Country 472 Haywards Heath–Crawley (tel. 0181 668 7261). Lewes Coaches 772 Brighton–Crawley (tel. 01273 480122). Both pass [symbol] Haywards Heath & Three Bridges *Station:* Balcombe 5ml; Haywards Heath 6ml; E Grinstead 6½ml

WEST GREEN HOUSE GARDEN [symbol]

West Green, Hartley Wintney RG27 8JB Tel: 01252 844611

Delightful gardens surrounding an early 18th-century house of great charm. The gardens have been under restoration since 1992 and access will be restricted to the walled gardens. The lake field and nymphaeum will open when restoration is completed. Open by kind permission of the lessee

Note: The house is privately tenanted and not open to visitors

[symbol] 20 May to end July: Wed only 10–4; last admission 3.30. The garden will open regularly at other times during this period courtesy of the lessee, but at a charge to all visitors (incl. NT members); tel. property for details

[symbol] £3. No reduction for groups

[symbol] Gravel paths and steps in garden

[symbol] No refreshments available; no picnics

[symbol] No dogs allowed

[symbol] 1ml W of Hartley Wintney, 10ml NE of Basingstoke, 1ml N of A30 [175: SU745564] *Bus:* Stagecoach Hampshire Bus 200 Basingstoke–Camberley (passing [symbol] Winchfield), 30/A Basingstoke–Guildford (passing [symbol] Fleet). On both alight Phoenix Green 1ml (tel. 01256 464501) *Station:* Winchfield 2ml

WEST WYCOMBE PARK [symbol] [symbol] [symbol] [symbol]

West Wycombe HP14 3AJ Tel: 01628 488675

A perfectly preserved rococo landscape garden created in the mid 18th century by Sir Francis Dashwood, 2nd baronet, founder of the Dilettanti Society and the Hellfire Club. The house is among the most theatrical and Italianate in England, its façades formed as classical temples. Palmyrene ceilings and decoration, pictures, furniture and sculptures date from the 2nd baronet's time.

Note: The West Wycombe Caves and adjacent café are privately owned, and National Trust members are liable to admission fees

O **Grounds only**: 30 March to end May: Sun & Wed 2–6; Easter, May & spring BH Sun & Mon 2–6. **House & grounds**: June, July & Aug: Sun to Thur 2–6. Weekday entry by timed ticket. Last admission 5.15

£ House & grounds £4.20; family ticket £10.50. Grounds only £2.50. Parties must book: no reductions. Parking 250m

K Guided tours of house on weekdays. Guided tours of the grounds by written arrangement

& Some access to ground floor; designated parking approx. 150m from house; one wheelchair available – please pre-book by tel. Grounds partly accessible

• Braille guide

K In car park only (guide dogs included)

→ At W end of West Wycombe, S of the Oxford road (A40) [175: SU828947]
Bus: Cambridge Coaches 75 Oxford–Cambridge; Classic Coaches 79 ⮂ High Wycombe–Aylesbury; Chiltern Rover 290/2; Wycombe Bus 331/2, 340/1 High Wycombe–Thame (all pass close ⮂ High Wycombe); (tel. 0345 382000)
Station: High Wycombe 2½ml

WEST WYCOMBE VILLAGE AND HILL 🏠 ✝

This Chilterns village is made up of buildings representing six centuries, including fine examples from 16th to 18th centuries. The hill is part of the 18th-century landscape of West Wycombe Park; it is surmounted by an Iron Age hill-fort, now the site of the church and Dashwood mausoleum, and commands fine views

Note: The church, mausoleum and caves do not belong to the National Trust

O All year. Parking available at top of hill and in village. Village architectural trail leaflet available in village store (50/51 High St) and newsagent (36/37 High St)

♦ George and Dragon, Plough, and Swan public houses. Also Bread Oven tea-room in village store (50/51 High St)

→ 2ml W of High Wycombe, on both sides of A40. Public transport: as for West Wycombe Park above

---

WILLINGTON DOVECOTE & STABLES 🏠

Willington, nr Bedford

16th-century stables and stone dovecote, lined internally with nesting boxes for 1,500 pigeons

O April to end Sept: by appointment with Mrs J. Endersby, 21 Chapel Lane, Willington MK44 3QG (tel. 01234 838278)

£ £1. No reduction for parties. Car park 30m. No WC

& Accessible, but floors uneven

• Guide dogs admitted by arrangement

➔ 4ml E of Bedford, just N of the Sandy road (A603) [153: TL107499]
Bus: Stagecoach United Counties 176–8 Bedford–Biggleswade (passing
⇌ Bedford St John's & Biggleswade and close ⇌ Sandy), alight Willington
crossroads, ½ml (tel. 01604 20077) *Station:* Bedford St John's (U), not Sun, 4ml;
Sandy 4½ml; Bedford 5ml

WINCHESTER CITY MILL 🍴 ❀

Bridge Street, Winchester SO23 8EJ Tel/fax: 01962 870057

Built over the river in 1744, the mill has a delightful small island garden and an impressive millrace. Waterwheel restored 1995. Part of the property is used by the Youth Hostels Association

🅾 March: Sat & Sun 11–4.45; 1 April to 31 Oct: Wed to Sun & BH Mon 11–4.45.
Last admission 4.30

💷 £1. No reduction for groups. Parking in public car park, 200m. No WC

👤 Groups by arrangement

🛍 Shop open Sat & Sun in March; 1 April to 30 Nov: Wed to Sun & BH Mon;
1 to 24 Dec, daily 11–5

♿ Unsuitable for severely disabled visitors; many steps

🕭 Braille guide; sound of rushing water; some tactile contents. Informal talks can
be arranged

📰 Children's quiz sheets. School groups welcome by appointment

➔ At foot of High Street, beside City Bridge [185: SU487294] *Bus:* From surrounding
areas (tel. 01256 464501) *Station:* Winchester 1ml

WINKWORTH ARBORETUM ❀ 🌳

Hascombe Road, Godalming GU8 4AD Tel: 01483 208477

Hillside woodland with two lakes, many rare trees and shrubs and fine views. The most impressive displays are in spring for bluebells and azaleas, autumn for colour. Wildlife abounds

Note: The car park is reserved for visitors to the arboretum. Those who wish to use the
car park but are not visiting the arboretum are asked to contact Head of Arboretum
in advance

🅾 All year: daily during daylight hours, but may be closed during bad weather

💷 £2.50, family ticket £6.25 (2 adults, 2 children, additional family member
£1.25). No reduction for groups. Coach parties must book in writing with Head
of Arboretum to ensure parking space

👤 All groups must book in writing to Head of Arboretum. Guided tours £2 extra per
person. NT members free, but donations welcome

⌂ Shop open 1 April to 14 Nov: daily 11–5.30 or dusk if earlier; 15 Nov to 21 Dec & 11 Jan to 1 April 1998: weekends 11–5.30 (or dusk if earlier). Open BH Mon. May be closed during bad weather

♿ Limited access along level paths from upper and lower car parks; viewpoint and lake from lower entrance are accessible. Adapted WC (RADAR key); tea-room and shop accessible via ramp

👀 Water sounds, scented trees and shrubs, songbirds

☕ Tea-room for light refreshments near upper car park; open daily same hours as shop (tel. 01483 208265 when tea-room open). Also open weekends from 11 Jan until end March (weather permitting; may be closed during bad weather, tel. 01483 20477 to check). Picnickers welcome

👶 Baby-changing facilities

🐕 Dogs on leads please

➔ Near Hascombe, 2ml SE of Godalming on E side of B2130 [169/170/186: SU990412] *Bus:* Tillingbourne 42/4 Godalming–Cranleigh (passing close ⏝ Godalming), 448 from ⏝ Guildford, Sun, June to Sept only (tel. 01737 223000) *Station:* Godalming 2ml

---

WITLEY COMMON INFORMATION CENTRE 🚌 👶 ⚿ E

Witley Centre, Witley, Godalming GU8 5QA Tel/fax: 01428 683207

A purpose-built nature information centre set in pinewoods on the edge of the common. An exhibition explains the importance of lowland heath and how it is managed. Walks with interesting and varied flora and fauna

🕑 **Information centre:** 1 April to end Oct: Mon to Thur & BH Mon 11–1 & 2–4; also Sat & Sun 2–5, car park 9–6. **Common:** open at all times. **Events:** August Fun Days; tel. for details

£ Free to centre. Guided groups £1.60 (min. charge £10). Parking 100m from centre; all groups must pre-book

⚿ Guided walks at intervals throughout the year; tel. for details

⌂ Small shop offering limited souvenirs in the centre

♿ Ground floor of centre and 2 trails accessible but strong companions advisable. RADAR lock WC

👀 Braille guides to Witley and Milford Commons

☕ Soft drinks. Picnic tables

▣ Education parties by prior arrangement with West Weald Education Officer (tel. 01428 683207). Residential group accommodation available on application

🐕 Must be kept under close control on trails; no dogs in information centre

➔ 7ml SW of Guildford between London–Portsmouth A3 and A286 roads, 1ml SW of Milford [186: SU9341] *Bus:* Stagecoach Hants & Surrey/Coastline 60 Guildford–Bognor Regis (passing close ⏝ Godalming & passing ⏝ Haslemere) (tel. 01737 223000) *Station:* Milford 2ml

South West

Caerllan
Penparc
Lochtyn
Mwnt
Gernos
Penbryn
Dolaucothi
Gold Mines

Pwllcaerog
St David's Head
St David's Commons
Upper & Lower Treginnis
Nine Wells
Solva
Dinefwr Pa
Paxton's Tower

Colby Woodland Garden
Little Milford
Deer Park
Lawrenny
Williamstone Park
Kete
Llanrhidian Marsh
Rhossili

Tudor Merchant's House
Lydstep Headland
Worms Head
Pennard
Bishopston Valley
Port Eynon Point
Stackpole Estate

Foreland Point & Countisbury Hill
Highveer Point
Holdstone Down
Great Hangman
Little Hangman
Damage Cliffs
Lundy Island
Morte Point
Heddon Valley
Baggy Point
Arlington Court

The Brownshams
Clovelly
Peppercombe Valley
Morwenstow
Duckpool
Sandy Mouth

Crackington Haven
High Cliff
Boscastle Harbour & Valency Valley
Tintagel Old Post Office
Lydford Gorge
Trebarwith Strand
Lawrence House
Pentire Point
New Polzeath
Port Gaverne
Rough Tor
The Church Hous
Doyden & Port Quin
Holne
Park Head
Goodameavy
Hembur
Cotehele
Buckland Abbey
Lanhydrock
Porth Joke
Crantock Beach
Elizabethan House
Holywell Bay
Trerice
Antony
Plymouth
St Agnes Beacon
Saltram
Black Head
The Old Mill
Wembury Cliffs
Chapel Porth
Polperro
Yealm Estuary
Zennor Head
Trencrom
Lansallos Cove
Gurnard's Head
The Gribbin
Lantic Bay
Bolt Tail
Bosigran
Godrevy Point
Nare Head
Overbecks Museum & Garden
Chapel Carn Brea
Cornish Engines
The Dodman
Levant Beam Engine
Trelissick Garden
Bolt Head & Snapes Point
Cape Cornwall
Trengwainton Garden
Rinsey Cliff
St Anthony Head
Mayon Cliff
Glendurgan Garden
Treryn Dinas
St Michael's Mount
Loe Pool
Helford River
Penberth Cove
Mullion Cove
Chynalls Point
Kynance Cove
Poltesco
Lizard Point

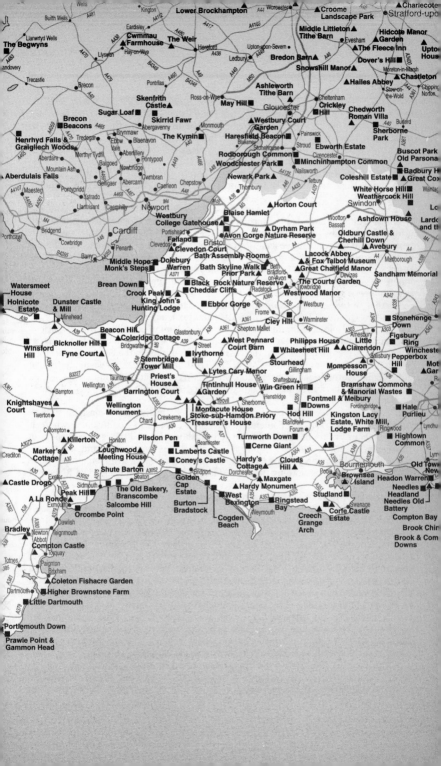

COAST

In the north of the region at Kewstoke, north of Weston-super-Mare [182: ST325660], a coastal path traverses the Trust properties of **Sand Point** and the adjoining 2ml of coastline at **Middle Hope**. The limestone headland of **Sand Point** includes 'Castle Batch', thought to be a Norman motte. New walk from Sand Point car park through to Woodspring Priory (owned by the Landmark Trust). NT car park and WCs. The **Monk's Steps** at Kewstoke give views over the Severn estuary [182: ST336632]. Views from Middle Hope over the Bristol Channel to the Welsh mountains and to the Mendip Hills.

South-west of Weston-super-Mare in **SOMERSET**, **Brean Down** forms the southern arm of Weston Bay, jutting out into the Bristol Channel [182: ST2959]. A steep path with steps cut into the hillside leads to the top of this limestone headland, once the site of a Roman temple. The ruins of a large 19th-century fort, owned by Sedgemoor District Council, remain at the seaward end, built when it was feared that the French might sail up the Bristol Channel to attack the mainland. There is a bird sanctuary here, and good sea fishing from the rocks.

Further to the south-west, on the southern edge of Bridgwater Bay, the beautiful range of the Quantock Hills meets the sea at Quantoxhead.

The Trust's **Holnicote Estate** (see p.242) covers $4\frac{1}{2}$ml of coastline between Porlock Bay and Minehead. The South-West Peninsula Coastal Path, which begins at Minehead, curves inland to avoid the possibility of landslips in the Foreland sandstone which predominates at Hurlstone Point. The Trust has, however, made an alternative but tougher footpath along the clifftop which is recommended for more experienced walkers. There are over 100ml of footpaths through fields, woods, moors and villages.

The Trust owns over 80ml of coastline in **DEVON**. On the **north coast** the Trust's ownership begins near the Somerset border and extends to Countisbury, where it protects about 700ha of **Foreland Point**, **Countisbury Hill** and the wooded valleys of **Watersmeet** [180: SS744487]. There is an information point, shop and self-service restaurant at **Watersmeet House** (see p.291) and miles of signposted footpaths traverse the hanging oakwoods clothing the steep sides of the valleys of the East Lyn River and Hoar Oak Water.

On the West Exmoor Coast the Trust now protects over 6ml of coastline between aptly named Woody Bay [180: SS675487] and Combe Martin. An information point with new exhibition area and shop at Hunters Inn in the deep **Heddon Valley** [180: SS655481] is central to many cliff, woodland and riverside circular walks behind Heddonsmouth. The high coastal heaths of **Trentishoe** and **Holdstone Downs** [180: SS626480] can be enjoyed from many small car parks, whereas the spectacular **Great Hangman** [180: SS601480] is a little more remote. Here the highest cliffs in North Devon fall west to the striking **Little Hangman** [189: SS584481] immediately to the east of Combe Martin, where the Trust also owns the medieval **West Challacombe** farm.

105ha at **Ilfracombe** [180: SS5047] include most of the coastal land from the town's outskirts to the village of Lee, where the Trust owns 5ml of fine coastline as far as Woolacombe, including **Morte Point** [180: SS554445] and **Damage Cliffs** [180: SS470465]. South-west to Croyde more coastal holdings include the viewpoint of **Baggy Point**, where there is a path suitable for wheelchair users [180: SS4241].

Lundy's vessel, *Oldenburg*, sails from Bideford and Ilfracombe to the island in the Bristol Channel (see p.274). At Bideford Bay, the Trust owns 5ml of remote coastline between **Abbotsham** and **Bucks Mills**, acquired in 1988. Although footpaths are being upgraded, access by vehicle is limited, with small car parks only at each end, and very few linking footpaths back to the main coast road. Further west at **Clovelly** more than 243ha of cliff, farm and woodland – with two ancient farmhouses at **The Brownshams** [190: SS285260] – are protected by the Trust. The Trust's most westerly coastal stretch in Devon was acquired in 1995 and includes 1½ml of spectacular coastline at South Hole, near Hartland, through which the coastal footpath runs.

On the south coast, near Plymouth, 5½ml of cliff and woodland are owned, on both sides of the **Yealm Estuary**. **Wembury Cliffs** extend for 1¼ml from **Wembury Head** (see also p.279) [201: SX530480]. A further 101ha of spectacular countryside near Ringmore [202: SX645457] have recently been acquired, including Aymer Cove, the valley inland and 1ml of coastline.

From **Bolt Tail** [202: SX6639] to **Overbecks** near Salcombe (see p.279) are 6ml of rugged cliffland traversed by the coast path, which dips to give access to safe bathing at **Soar Mill Cove** and **Starehole Bay**. At **Bolberry Down** car park a path leads to the west and is suitable for wheelchair users. **Bolt Head** and **Bolt Tail** are the best places from which to observe seabirds. The Trust's first property in the Kingsbridge Estuary, **Snapes Point** [202: SX745394], is the keystone to the conservation of the estuary landscape and has a footpath around the unspoilt headland, and a small car park.

Another extensive holding lies between **Portlemouth Down** [202: SX740375] and Prawle Point [202: SX773350]. 133ha of low cliffs with walks, views and sandy coves. The walker can choose whether to use higher or lower paths, and the cliffs grow higher and more craggy further east towards **Gammon Head** [202: SX765355].

In the beautiful estuary of the river Dart, the Trust protects, on the Dartmouth side, woodland, hilltop and 67ha at **Little Dartmouth** [202: SX880490] – cliff and farmland forming the western approach to Dartmouth Harbour for 1¼ml from the Dancing Beggars rocks off Warren Point to the harbour entrance. Across the estuary at Kingswear, 121ha at **Higher Brownstone Farm** [202: SX901505] gives access to paths to the coast on the **Coleton Fishacre Estate** (see p.254). On 393ha and nearly 5ml of coast, the Trust has created a coastal footpath and several linking paths to small car parks. There are two popular beaches at Man Sands and Scabbacombe along this stretch of coast between Kingswear and Brixham.

In East Devon the Trust owns **Orcombe Point**, Exmouth [192: SY021795], and on either side of Sidmouth, **Peak Hill** [192: SY109871] and **Salcombe Hill** (where there are two pleasant circular walks beginning at the car park [192: SY143882]). Following the acquisition of **Coxes Cliff** at Weston, the Trust now protects the 3½ml of coastline between Salcombe Hill and Branscombe, including farmland and foreshore in places. Some cottages, farms, the forge and the bakery (now a tea-room and baking museum with a small information room housed in the bakery outbuildings) are also owned by the Trust at Branscombe.

The Trust's Devon properties can be enjoyed more fully with the aid of an OS map. A set of leaflets giving information on the Trust's coast and countryside in Devon is in production: please ring the Regional Public Affairs Office (tel. 01392 881691) for details. Three leaflets (West Exmoor Coast, Watersmeet and Countisbury & Arlington) are already available.

The Trust's countryside holdings in **CORNWALL** are mainly of truly spectacular coastline – more than 110ml, including many famous and beautiful holiday stretches.

On the north coast between the Devon border and Bude the Trust owns three blocks of coastline. The most northerly, centred on Morwenstow [190: SS2015], has associations with the celebrated 19th-century cleric and poet, Hawker of Morwenstow. The Trust property, from north of **Duckpool** to south of **Sandy Mouth**, extends up the Coombe Valley; 2½ml inland is the 12th-century motte and bailey

Kilkhampton Castle. There is a café, WCs and a car park at **Sandy Mouth**. A narrow strip at **Maer Cliff** [190: SS2008] runs between Northcott Mouth and Crooklets beach.

Crackington Haven [190: SX1497] is flanked by **Dizzard Point**, where there is a stunted oakwood; **Penkenna Point**; and **High Cliff**, the loftiest height on the Cornish coast at 219m. **Trevigue Farm** has a shop, café and information point (open in high season only).

At **Boscastle** [190: SX1091] the Trust owns both sides of the picturesque harbour, a natural haven still used by fishermen. The NT shop and information centre, in the Old Smithy, is open in summer and has wheelchair access. The Trust owns land up the wooded **Valency Valley** towards St Juliot, rich with Thomas Hardy connections.

Visitors to **Tintagel Old Post Office** (see p.288) can walk out to the cliffs to see **Willapark** [200: SX0689], where there is a cliff castle; **Barras Nose**, the Trust's earliest coastal acquisition in England; or the lengthy stretch of coast extending from Tintagel south to **Trebarwith Strand**. The old cliffside slate quarries are worth seeing, and at **Glebe Cliff** a viewpoint has wheelchair access. The wild cliffs at **Tregardock** and adjoining **Dannonchapel** are best viewed from the coast path. The Trust owns a cluster of old fish 'cellars' and the foreshore at **Port Gaverne**. 8ml inland, the Trust owns 70.5ha of **Rough Tor**, Cornwall's second highest point.

The next highlight is the wonderful 6ml stretch from **Port Quin** to **Polzeath** [200: SW9380]. The main features are **Pentire Point**; the **Rumps** with its cliff castle – probably the finest on the Cornish coast; **Lundy Bay**; **Doyden Castle**, a 19th-century folly; and **Port Quin** itself, where there is a car park and a clutch of NT holiday cottages.

The remote, convoluted coastline at **Park Head** [200: SW8471], with its seabird breeding colonies, provides a tranquil alternative to the activity usually found at **Carnewas** [200: SW8569]. The justly famous beauty spot of Bedruthan Steps (not NT) can be viewed from the Trust's clifftop land or reached by the newly restored **Staircase**. There is an NT shop and information centre, café and WCs in the car park.

Immediately west of Newquay the trio of sandy beaches, **Crantock Beach**, **Porth Joke** and **Holywell Bay**, are backed and separated by an extensive Trust hinterland [200: SW7760]. This is wonderful walking country.

The high ground of **St Agnes Beacon** (189m) is Trust-owned, and the whole area is rich in industrial relics from mining days. **Chapel Porth** [203: SW7050] is another fine beach, at low tide; the ruin of **Towanroath engine house** stands prominently above it.

Between Gwithian and Portreath the Trust owns over 6ml of almost continuous coastline [203: SW6545 to 5842]. The awesome drop at **Hell's Mouth** and the headlands of **Godrevy** and **Navax Point** are the most dramatic features.

Not on the coast, but only 2ml inland from Carbis Bay, is **Trencrom Hill** [203: SW5236], a 26ha granite eminence which sits in its strategic position at the gateway to the Land's End peninsula. Two main rock piles are surrounded by lesser outcrops which are linked by an Iron Age wall, and the remains of stone dwellings can be seen.

Once west of St Ives the character of the landscape changes. This is West Penwith, a coastline of rocky headlands and coves backed by a flattish plateau of small fields where traditionally managed farms are overlooked by a serrated ridge of granite outcrops called carns; **Carn Galver** is the most prominent, although adjoining **Watchcroft** is higher. The Trust owns a number of the headlands, as well as larger areas at **Treveal**, **Rosemergy** and **Bosigran** [203: SW4237]. A walk out to **Zennor** and **Gurnard's Head** will give the visitor a flavour of this very Celtic, unspoilt coast.

From **Cape Cornwall** [203: SW3532], England's only cape, there are good views up and down the coast. It marks the centre point of 4½ml of spectacular Trust-owned coastline of particular archaeological and geological interest: **Kenidjack**, to the north, features extensive and fragile mining remains; south of the Cape, towards Land's End, **Bollowall Common** includes a Bronze Age entrance grave managed by the Trust, **Porth**

Nanven a striking stretch of raised beach, and **Nanjulian** a prehistoric courtyard settlement.

The properties nearest to Land's End are ¼ml of Mayon Cliff [203: SW3526] between Sennen Cove and Land's End; and **Chapel Carn Brea** [203: SW3828], a 22ha hilltop reaching 197m, 2ml inland from Whitesand Bay, which claims the widest sea view from the British mainland.

Once round Land's End the south coast of Cornwall begins, and the first Trust property encountered is the point called **Pedn-men-an-mere** [203: SW3821], which protects the open-air Minack Theatre (not NT) from south-westerly gales. The delightful cove beach of **Porthcurno** (given to the Trust in 1994 by Cable & Wireless plc) is the start of more than 2ml of Trust-owned cliffs culminating at **Penberth**, perhaps Cornwall's most perfect fishing cove [203: SW4023]. Between the two is the thrusting cock's-comb peninsula of **Treryn Dinas**, the famous 67-tonne Logan Rock perched on its rocky crest.

St Michael's Mount (see p.282) is the first Trust property east of Penzance, followed by three detached sites at **Cudden Point**, **Lesceave Cliff** and **Rinsey Cliff**, the last-named having a restored 19th-century mine engine house on the cliff slope.

East of Porthleven the **Penrose Estate** [203: SW6425] spreads to the outskirts of Helston and south to **Gunwalloe Church Cove**. It contains the remarkable **Loe Pool**, Cornwall's largest natural freshwater lake, separated from the sea by the shingle barrier of Loe Bar. A 5ml footpath follows the lake edge, and a bird hide looks onto the reedbed. **Gunwalloe Towans** is a fine sweep of sand dunes used by Mullion Golf Club.

Trust ownership along the west-facing Lizard coast is fragmented into a number of properties. South of Poldhu the **Marconi Memorial** site marks Guglielmo Marconi's first trans-Atlantic wireless message. **Mullion Cove** and **Island** [203: SW6617] are owned by the Trust. About 1ml to the south, at **Predannack Head**, the 273ha Predannack holding spreads inland almost to the A3083. Biologically, this is one of the Trust's most interesting sites. **Kynance Cove** [203: SW6913], which is accessible to wheelchair users, offers good bathing at low tide, and the Trust has just landscaped and improved the clifftop car park. The ½ml of rugged coast to the east of **Lizard Head** includes **Pistil Meadow**, where the bodies of 200 people are buried – drowned in one of the worst wrecks off this most treacherous point. Britain's most southerly outpost, **Lizard Point**, and the surrounding area have recently benefited from a major landscape improvement programme. Parking is available in Lizard village, whence a footpath leads down to the Point, or in the NT car park adjacent to the lighthouse. On the east side of Housel Bay are **Pen Olver** and **Bass Point** and the white castellated structure which was a Lloyds signal station.

On the east-facing Lizard coast, on either side of the stone and thatch village of **Cadgwith** [203: SW7214], where fishermen still winch their brightly-coloured craft up the beach, the Trust owns several miles of cliffland. Of particular interest are the remains of the 19th-century serpentine works – serpentine is the local stone – at **Poltesco**. Three detached properties at **Beagles Point**, **Chynhalls Point and Cliff** and **Lowland Point** flank the next village along the coast, Coverack [204: SW7818].

The shores of the **Helford River** [204: SW7626], probably Cornwall's most beautiful estuary, together with its subsidiary **Gillan Creek**, are protected by the Trust along several miles of its length, and at the northern approach, **Rosemullion Head** [204: SW8028]. One of these safeguarded areas is the enchanting **Frenchman's Creek**, the location of Daphne du Maurier's novel. **Glendurgan Garden** (see p.263) fronts the mouth of the estuary. Between the Helford River and Falmouth is 1ml of open cliff flanking either side of the popular beach of **Maenporth**.

Trelissick Garden (see p.289) and estate, including Pill Farm, straddle the western approach to the King Harry Ferry on the B3289, and **Turnaware Point** [204: SW8338] on the east side marks the end of Carrick Roads and the beginning of the Fal Estuary. The Trust owns 2ml of farmland between **St Just** [204: SW8434] and **St Mawes**, the footpath through which provides wide views over Carrick Roads and the town of Falmouth.

St Anthony Head and **Zone Point** [204: SW8631] form the once-fortified eastern approach to Falmouth harbour. The old defences are largely cleared away, but some of the accommodation is available as holiday lets (see p.19), with wheelchair access and facilities in the cottages. A viewfinder on the highest point, approached by a path suitable for wheelchair users, identifies the features in the wide-ranging panorama.

East of here, Trust ownership extends from the sea on both sides of **Porthmellin Head** [204: SW8732] across the waist of the St Anthony peninsula to the creek and estuary waterfronts facing St Mawes. This is largely farmland, but paths give good access to the main places of interest. Other properties front the **Percuil River** on its eastern bank.

Nare Head [204: SW9137], with its off-lying **Gull Rock**, is the focus for a concentration of Trust properties, with a 4½ml coastline, and extending to about 364ha. A Trust car park at **Penare** is part of a major tidying-up scheme. A wheelchair ramp and picnic area overlook **Kiberick Cove**.

The Dodman [204: SX0039] is the grandest headland on the south Cornish coast. The remains of an Iron Age promontory fort can be seen across its broad back and there are Bronze Age barrows. To the west and east are the detached properties of **Lambsowden Cove** and **Maenease Point** and, further on, **Turbot Point** and **Bodrugan's Leap**, where Sir Henry Trenowth of nearby Bodrugan is said to have jumped into the sea to make his escape by boat to France. Within St Austell Bay is **Black Head**, where yet another Iron Age earthwork can be seen, together with a rifle range from more recent times.

Much of the coastline to the east and west of Fowey is owned by the Trust. **Gribbin Head** [200: SX1050] with its boldly striped navigational daymark begins the sequence of properties. There is a gap at **Polridmouth Cove** (always called Pridm'th) where the Trust owns only the east side of the cove, then a wide strip of mostly Trust land to the outskirts of Fowey. Upstream, overlooking the china clay loading quays, the Trust safeguards the 13ha of woods and meadow at **Station Wood** [200: SW1252]. Across Fowey harbour is the tree-fringed creek of **Pont Pill** [200: SX1451], where the lovely **Hall Walk** passes through the woods. Much of the farmland encircling Polruan was acquired, with the help of a local appeal, in 1991. Thereafter, Trust ownership follows the coast for several miles to beyond the village of **Lansallos** [201: SX1751], and extends some distance inland. There are attractive beaches at **Lantic Bay** and **Lansallos Cove**.

On each side of **Polperro** [201: SX2151] the Trust has 1ml of coastline. The eastern strip was willed to the Trust by Miss Angela Brazil, the author of school stories for girls, and another mile of Trust land projects into the Channel at **Hore Point** [201: SX2451].

Trust ownership east of Looe consists of smallish properties at **Bodigga**, **Trethill Cliff**, **Higher Tregantle Cliffs** and **Sharrow Point**, where there is a cliffside folly called Sharrow Grot [201: SX3952].

A series of detailed leaflets, with maps, has been produced about the Trust's Cornish coastal properties. They are available from NT shops in Cornwall or from the Regional Trading Manager (see address on p.21). Please include a donation to cover postage.

In the east of the region in **DORSET**, the coast is rich in variety; hills, coombes, cliffs, bays and islands. One such island in Poole Harbour is **Brownsea** (see p.249), and immediately south is the Trust's **Studland** peninsula, part of the 2833ha **Corfe Castle** estate (see p.256). This includes Corfe Castle Common, a 162ha common, much of which has never been ploughed and is thus rich in wildlife, and of particular archaeological interest. The peninsula encompasses the whole of Studland Bay, with Old Harry Rocks and Shell Bay (see p.287). The heathland behind Studland beach is designated a National Nature Reserve, of particular interest to naturalists in winter because of its variety of overwintering birds. There are several public paths and two nature trails here. Spyway Farm & Blackers Hole, near Langton Matravers, supports important bird and butterfly habitats and many rare plants. There are several public paths. Access to the sea is at Dancing Ledge. NT car parks at Spyway Farm and Acton village. Extensive information boards are sited at Spyway farmbuildings. Restoration work and conservation-grazing continues in 1997. Hartland Moor National Nature Reserve is a 607ha block of lowland heath, approximately one-third of which is owned by English Nature. 162ha of grassland is currently being restored from farmland to lowland heath and new footpaths have been created. New Purbeck Walks pack available from Corfe Castle, NT shops and tourist information centres.

At **Golden Cap** [193: SY4092] the Trust owns more than 810ha of hill, farmland, cliff, undercliff and beach (7½ml of coastline from the Devon border to Eype). Here is the highest cliff in southern England – so named because of the yellow limestone forming a cap above the blue lias clay cliffs and clumps of golden gorse near its summit. This splendid viewpoint and the remainder of the estate have 25ml of paths for walkers, including a 7½ml coastal footpath. There is a campsite at St Gabriel's on the estate; booking through the Warden (tel. 01297 489628). **Stonebarrow Hill** has an NT shop and information point, public toilets and an adapted WC with RADAR lock for wheelchair users and the paths here are accessible. **Langdon Woods** also has a circular path (RADAR padlocks). Parking prohibited at St Gabriel's.

The shingle and sand beach at **Burton Bradstock** is accessible to wheelchair users, from its grassy car park; no dogs on beach from June to Sept. There are riverside and cliff walks through this 41ha Trust property which includes a stretch of the South-West Coastal Footpath [193/194: SY491889]. **Cogden Beach** [194: SY5088] to the east of Burton Bradstock is accessible on foot. 14ha including part of Chesil Beach. Small free car park off main road. The Trust also owns 89ha of **Cogden Farm**. Circular walks.

Ringstead Bay 5ml E of Weymouth [194: SY7582] 182ha of land including Burning Cliff and Whitenothe Cliff. Car-parking at the top of the down. Access to the sea on foot.

COUNTRYSIDE

At **Rainbow Wood** [172: ST777630] on Claverton Down near **BATH**, and **Smallcombe Wood** and fields [172: ST764640], at Bathwick, 227ha of wood and farmland are part of the **Bath Skyline Walk**. A leaflet describes a 6ml (or shorter) walk, past Iron Age field enclosures, ancient woodland, and remains of the 18th-century expansion of Bath under Ralph Allen, with breathtaking views across the city. Leaflet from NT Shop, Abbey Churchyard, Bath and Prior Park Landscape Garden.

The Avon Gorge Nature Reserve on the west bank of the River Avon is approached from Bristol across the Clifton Suspension Bridge [172: ST560734]. Leigh Woods has flowers and fungi peculiar to the gorge, and an Iron Age hillfort. Leaflet available on site.

Blaise Hamlet, 4ml N of central Bristol, W of Henbury village, just N of B4057 [172: ST559789], is a hamlet of nine different cottages designed in 1809 for John Harford by John Nash, for Blaise Estate pensioners. Free access to the Green, cottages not open. **Dolebury Warren**, 12ml S of Bristol [182: ST450590] at Churchill, is a wild and barren hilltop with one of the finest viewpoints in the Mendips, dominated by an impressive Iron Age fort. The site is managed by the Bristol & Bath Wildlife Trust.

Farms and woodland at **Failand**, 4ml W of central Bristol on S side of A369, with magnificent views overlooking the Severn Estuary.

In **SOMERSET** the Trust owns more than 445ha of the Quantock Hills; some of the more dramatic parts are **Beacon and Bicknoller Hills**, east of Williton – some 255ha of moorland with the Iron Age fort of **Trendle Ring**, which is an Ancient Monument. From these hills are magnificent views over the Bristol Channel, the Vale of Taunton Deane and Exmoor [181: ST125410/124397]. At **Fyne Court** (see p.263) there are three walks over the eastern Quantocks, taking in heathland, forest and farmland.

Inland to the east of the Quantocks the long low ridge of the Polden Hills overlooks Sedgemoor and Athelney, the large wetland area of Somerset once drained and used for agricultural purposes by the monks of Glastonbury Abbey. **Glastonbury Tor** dominates the area. At the summit (158m) an excavation has recovered the plans of two superimposed churches of St Michael, of which only the 15th-century tower remains. Amongst the several small properties owned by the Trust in this area is land around the **Ivythorn**, **Walton** and **Collard Hills**, 52ha of high land and woodland on the A39 which runs along the crest of the Poldens [182: ST474348].

On Exmoor on the Somerset/Devon border the Trust owns the 5042ha **Holnicote Estate** [181: SS8844], including the high tors of Dunkery and Selworthy Beacons with breathtaking views in all directions, 15 farms and part or all of many small villages and hamlets, one of which is the beautiful village of **Selworthy** with its cream cob walls and thatched roofs. There is a shop and information centre at Selworthy (see page 284). There are tea-rooms (not NT) at Selworthy, Bossington and Horner.

On the limestone Mendip Hills above Wells a smaller but no less interesting valley vies with the famous Cheddar Gorge (caves not NT). **Ebbor Gorge**, managed by English Nature, offers two nature walks, one takes 30min and is recommended to wheelchair users (strong pusher needed); the other takes 1½hrs and climbs to 240m giving superb views. In this woodland badgers are plentiful and birds of prey such as buzzard and sparrowhawk may be seen. The caves are home to greater and lesser horseshoe bats [182: ST525485]. The Trust also owns the **Black Rock Nature Reserve**, managed by the Somerset Wildlife Trust, at Cheddar and the northern slopes of Cheddar Gorge; a circular walk from the B3135 road at Black Rock Gate traverses plantations, natural woodland, limestone scree, rough downland and dramatic rock faces [182: ST468543].

3ml west of Cheddar lies the only pointed hill in the Mendips, **Crook Peak**.

In **DEVON** the Trust owns over 2227ha in the **DARTMOOR NATIONAL PARK**, over which there are miles of spectacular walks. Between the ancient **Whiddon Deer Park** [191: SX725888] and Fingle Bridge [191: SX743898] the Trust owns over 243ha of woodland within the dramatic Teign Gorge, whilst downstream at **Steps Bridge** [191: SX802883] are over 154ha of spectacular hanging oak woodlands. In the south are **Holne Woods** [202: SX712708] and **Hembury Woods** [202: SX726685] with its Iron Age hillfort. Further west is the 1349ha estate of **Hentor**, **Willings Walls** and **Trowlesworthy Warren** [202: SX595653], with its extensive archaeological sites, whilst at **Goodameavy** [201: SX536639] is the impressive Dewerstone topped by its Iron Age hillfort. This is one of the best climbing faces in the southwest (permits available from the warden). To the north of Plymouth lies **Plym Bridge Woods**, a 50ha property containing a wealth of industrial archaeological remains, whilst to the south-east of the National Park, the **Parke Estate** at Bovey Tracey forms a beautiful approach to Dartmoor with walks through the woods, beside the river Bovey and along the route of the old railway line. North of Exeter, 2551ha of farmland and woods surround **Killerton** mansion and park. Several specially laid-out walks start from the visitor reception.

The Trust's estate at Fontmell Down in **DORSET**, between Shaftesbury and Blandford [183: ST884184] includes **Melbury Beacon** and **Melbury Down** [184: ST900193], a total of 295ha; with magnificent walks across chalk downland overlooking the Blackmore Vale. Fontmell Down was bought by public appeal to commemorate the Dorset of Thomas Hardy. Car park at the top of Spread Eagle Hill and at Compton Abbas airfield. Limited access for disabled visitors.

Magnificent views from **Creech Grange Arch**, a folly near Corfe Castle (see p.256) [195: SY212818] may be enjoyed.

Dorset is dominated by Iron Age forts and many of these are now in the permanent care of the National Trust, including **Pilsdon Pen**, near Broadwindsor [193: ST414012], **Lambert's Castle**, north of Lyme Regis [193: SY370986] and the adjacent **Coney's Castle**. Hod Hill and Turnworth Down, north-west of Blandford, are equally rewarding as archaeological sites and for superlative views. The familiar ancient figure of the **Cerne Giant** is cut in the chalk of Giant's Hill near Cerne Abbas, 8ml N of Dorchester.

On the **Kingston Lacy Estate** (see p.268) the Trust has opened a number of walks (some of which are accessible to wheelchair users). The 2833ha agricultural estate is crossed by public footpaths, many still following Roman and Saxon tracks past medieval cottages. The estate is dominated by the Iron Age hillfort of **Badbury Rings**. Leaflets on the Kingston Lacy Estate walks and on Badbury Rings are available from the shop at Kingston Lacy, the estate office at Hillbutts and from Badbury Rings at weekends, April to October. The Rings are regularly grazed to manage grassland and, for the protection of livestock, dogs are not permitted. Point-to-point races are held at Badbury on three Saturdays early in the year. On these days a charge is made for car-parking.

The Trust's countryside properties in **WILTSHIRE** are typified by open downland and archaeological features. The major sites of Avebury and Stonehenge Down are described elsewhere in more detail (see pp.246 and 285).

The Iron Age hillfort of **Figsbury Ring** lies to the north-east of Salisbury [184: SU188338] and gives fine views over the city and cathedral, as does **Pepperbox Hill** to the south-east (A36) [184: SU215248], with its curious octagonal tower, a 17th-century folly which gives its name to the site. **Win Green**, in the extreme south of the county, [184: ST925206] is the highest point of the Cranborne Chase at 273m. With the distinctive clump of trees on its summit shielding a bowl barrow, it affords extensive views south-east to the Isle of Wight and north-west to the Quantocks. Another Iron Age hillfort, together with a Neolithic enclosure, lies on **Whitesheet Hill**, close to Stourhead [183: ST7735]. The Iron Age hillfort of **Cley Hill** lies 3ml west of Warminster [183: ST838450].

To the west of Avebury [173: SU050693], the Iron Age earthwork of Oldbury Castle crowns **Cherhill Down** along with the conspicuous Lansdown Monument. Together with the spectacular folds of the newly-acquired Calstone Coombes, the property now provides over 200ha of open downland and walking country.

A LA RONDE

Summer Lane, Exmouth EX8 5BD Tel: 01395 265514

A unique 16-sided house built on the instructions of two spinster cousins, Jane and Mary Parminter, on their return from a grand tour of Europe. Completed c.1796, the house has many 18th-century contents and collections brought back by the Parminters. The fascinating interior decoration includes a feather frieze and shell-encrusted gallery which, due to its fragility, can only be viewed on closed circuit television

◎ 27 March to 2 Nov: Sun to Thur 11–5.30. Last admissions 30min before closing. Closed Fri & Sat

£ £3.20, children £1.60. No party reduction; unsuitable for coaches or large groups except by prior arrangement with the Custodian

⌂ Same days as house: 10.30–5.45

🍴 Same days as house: 10.30–5.30. Morning coffees, lunches and afternoon teas

➔ 2ml N of Exmouth on A376 [192: SY004834] *Bus:* Stagecoach Devon 57 Exeter–Exmouth to within ¼ml (tel. 01392 427711) *Station:* Lympstone Village (U) 1¼ml

ANTONY

Torpoint, Plymouth PL11 2QA Tel: 01752 812191

One of Cornwall's finest early 18th-century houses, faced in the lustrous silvery-grey Pentewan stone, offset by colonnaded wings of red brick and set within grounds landscaped by Repton. These include the formal garden with a national collection of day lilies and fine summer borders, and the superb woodland garden with its outstanding displays of rhododendrons, azaleas, camellias and magnolias. Also of note is an 18th-century dovecote and the 1789 Bath Pond House. Antony has been the home of the Carew family for almost 600 years

◎ 31 March to 30 Oct: Tues, Wed, Thur & BH Mon 1.30–5.30; also Sun in June, July & Aug 1.30–5.30. Bath Pond House can be seen by prior written application to Custodian and only when house is open. Woodland garden (Carew Pole Garden Trust) open 1 March to 31 October, daily 11–5.30

£ £3.80. Pre-arranged parties £3. £2 for access to woodland garden (NT members free on days when house open). Combined gardens-only ticket for Antony garden and adjoining woodland garden £3. Pre-arranged parties £2.40 per person

ℷ Available at less busy times. Last tour 4.45

🛍 Shop open as house

♿ House not suitable for wheelchair users. Garden largely accessible. Shop, tea-room & family history exhibition accessible. WC

👁 Braille guide

🍽 Tea-room, lunches available from 12.30 on open days

➔ 5ml W of Plymouth via Torpoint car ferry, 2ml NW of Torpoint, N of A374, 16ml SE of Liskeard, 15ml E of Looe [201: SX418564] *Bus:* Western National 80/1, from Plymouth (passing close ⇌ Plymouth), alight Great Park Estate, Sm, (tel. 01752 222666) *Station:* Plymouth 6ml via vehicle ferry *Ferry:* Torpoint 2ml

---

ARLINGTON COURT 🏠 ❁ ♣ 🐎 ♿ ℷ E

Arlington, nr Barnstaple EX31 4LP Tel: 01271 850296 Fax: 01271 850711

The house, built for the Chichesters in 1822 and still with much of its original furniture, is full of collections for every taste. Many of these were amassed by Miss Rosalie Chichester, and include model ships, costume, pewter, shells and other fascinating objects. The Trust's large collection of horse-drawn carriages is housed in the stables. Carriage rides through the 11ha of pleasure grounds and past the terraced Victorian garden start from the front of the house. There are miles of walks through woods and parks grazed by Shetland ponies and Jacob sheep.

O **House, Victorian garden & park**: 28 March to 2 Nov: daily except Sat but open Sat of BH weekends 11–5.30. Last admissions 5. **Park**: footpaths across parkland open during daylight hours Nov to March. **Events**: carriage driving tuition and other activities; please ring 01271 850296 for details

£ £4.90; family ticket £12.20. Garden only £2.60. Pre-arranged parties of 15 or more paying visitors £4.10 per person. Parking 300m

🛍 Same days as house 11–5.30 (tel. 01271 850348)

♿ Garden (gravel paths), grounds & shop accessible. Ramps at rear of house, help available; then ground floor accessible. Limited access to carriage collection. Close parking arrangements; disabled visitors may be driven to house by arrangement with Property Manager. WC. Wheelchairs available; ask at visitor reception

👁 Braille guides for house and carriage collection; audio tapes for house; carriages and horses may be touched

🍽 Licensed restaurant and tea-room at house, open as house, but restaurant open 12–5.30, also Sun 12–4 in Nov for pre-booked roast Sunday lunches & open for pre-booked Christmas lunches in Dec (tel. 01271 850629). Restaurant opening during Oct may vary from that printed, although light refreshments will always be available during opening hours. If in doubt, please telephone the property when you are planning a visit

Parent and baby facilities; children's quiz; children's menu; babies in back carriers admitted to all areas

Schools' room available; book with Property Manager. Children's study book

Welcome, on short leads please

7ml NE of Barnstaple on A39 [180: SS611405] *Bus:* Red Bus 13 from Barnstaple, Tues, Fri only; Lynn Valley 07 from Lynmouth, Mon, Tues (May to Sept); otherwise 310 Barnstaple–Lynmouth (passing close Barnstaple), alight Blackmoor Gate, 3ml (tel. 01271 45444). *Note*: Lanes from 310 bus stop to house narrow and difficult *Station:* Barnstaple 8ml

AVEBURY

nr Marlborough SN8 1RF Tel: 01672 539250

One of the most important megalithic monuments in Europe, this 12ha site with stone circles enclosed by a ditch and external bank is approached by an avenue of stones. The site also includes the Alexander Keiller Museum and the Wiltshire Life Society's display of Wiltshire rural life in the Great Barn. The NT also owns 623ha which provide the setting for the stone circle. Museum collection on loan to NT

Stone Circle: open daily. **Alexander Keiller Museum**: 1 April to 31 Oct, daily 10–6 (or dusk if earlier); 3 Nov to late March 1998: daily 10–4 (closed 24 to 26 Dec, 1 Jan). **Great Barn**: for opening times tel. 01672 539555

Alexander Keiller Museum: Adult £1.50; children 80p. English Heritage Members free (tel. 01672 539250). Great Barn: NT members 50p

Open 22 March to 2 Nov: daily 11–5; (minimum opening hours); 3 Nov to 14 Dec: Sat & Sun only 11.30–4 (tel. 01672 539384)

Access to museum, barn and parts of circle (access for disabled drivers to barn area). WC at Great Barn and off village High St

Some objects in Museum may be touched

- Lunches & teas at licensed Stones Restaurant and Red Lion Inn (not NT)
- Study centre available
- On leads in stone circle
- 6ml W of Marlborough, 1ml N of the Bath road (A4) on A4361 and B4003 [173: SU102699] *Bus:* Thamesdown 49A Swindon–Devizes/Marlborough (passing close ⇌ Swindon); Wilts & Dorset 5, 6 Salisbury–Swindon (tel. 0345 090899) *Station:* Pewsey, no practical Sun service, 10ml; Swindon 11ml

---

AVEBURY MANOR AND GARDEN 🏠 ❁

nr Marlborough SN8 1RF Tel: 01672 539250

A much-altered house of monastic origin, the present buildings date from the early 16th century, with notable Queen Anne alterations and Edwardian renovation by Colonel Jenner. The topiary and flower gardens contain medieval walls, ancient box and numerous compartments

Note: Parts of the house are open in 1997

- **Garden**: 22 March to 2 Nov: daily except Mon & Thur (open BH Mon) 11–5.30. Last admission 5 or dusk if earlier. **House**: 23 March to 2 Nov: Tues, Wed, Sun & BH Mon 2–5.30. Last admission as garden
- House and garden: £3.50, children £1.75. Parties £3.15, children £1.60; garden only: £2.20, children £1.40. Parties £2, children £1.20
- See Avebury
- Garden mostly level and accessible
- No dogs
- As Avebury *Bus:* As Avebury

BARRINGTON COURT 🏠 🏠 ❁ E

Barrington, nr Ilminster TA19 0NQ Tel: 01460 241938

A beautiful garden influenced by Gertrude Jekyll and laid out in a series of rooms, including the White Garden, the Rose and Iris Garden and the Lily Garden. The working kitchen garden has apple, pear and plum trees trained along high stone walls. The Tudor manor house was restored in the 1920s by the Lyle family. It is let to Stuart Interiors and is also open to NT visitors

- **Garden & House**: 22 March to 30 Oct: daily except Fri 11–5.30. Last admission 5. Coach parties by appointment only (tel. 01460 241938). **Events**: outdoor theatre and guided walks. 30 March, Easter Egg Hunt; for details tel. 01985 843601
- £4, children £2. Parties £3.50, children £1.80.
- 22 March to 30 Oct: daily except Fri 11–5.30 (tel. 01460 241244)

Garden & restaurant accessible, ideal for wheelchairs. Powered self-drive buggy available. WC

Braille guide and restaurant menu; scented plants and flowers

Licensed restaurant facilities open 22 March to 30 Oct: daily except Fri; fresh produce from kitchen garden; morning coffees, lunches & cream teas. Open as garden. Also available for functions and meetings (tel. 01460 241244)

In Barrington village, 5ml NE of Ilminster, on B3168. Visitors approaching from A303 follow signs for Ilminster town centre *Bus:* Southern National 33 Martock–Ilminster with connections from Taunton on Southern National 31 (passing close ⟨image⟩ Taunton) (tel. 01823 272033) *Station:* Crewkerne 7ml

---

BATH ASSEMBLY ROOMS

Bennett Street, Bath BA1 2QH Tel: 01225 477789 Fax: 01225 444793

Designed by John Wood the Younger in 1769. The Rooms were bombed in 1942, but are restored to their Georgian splendour and let to Bath & North East Somerset Council. The Museum of Costume (not NT) housed in basement

The Rooms are open to the public all year daily (Mon to Sat 10–5, Sun 11–5; closed 25 & 26 Dec), when not in use for pre-booked functions. Access is guaranteed during Aug, but otherwise visitors are advised to check in advance

No admission charge to Rooms; admission charge to Museum of Costume (incl. NT members)

Hourly, when Rooms not in use for pre-booked functions

Open daily

Street parking not always available; disabled visitors may be set down at door. Level access; WC

No refreshments available

Guide dogs only

N of Milsom Street, E of the Circus [156: ST749653] *Bus:* From ⟨image⟩ Bath Spa and surrounding areas (tel. 01225 464446) *Station:* Bath Spa ¼ml

BRADLEY

Newton Abbot TQ12 6BN Tel: 01626 54513

A small medieval manor house set in woodland and meadows. Bradley is occupied and administered by Mrs A. H. Woolner and family

O 2 April to 24 Sept: Wed 2–5; also Thur 2 & 9 April, 18 & 25 Sept. Last admission 4.30

£ £2.60. No party reduction; organised parties by appointment with Secretary. Lodge gates are too narrow for coaches. No refreshments. No WC

→ Drive gate (with small lodge) is on outskirts of town, on Totnes road (A381) [202: SX848709]; ½ml walk to house from lodge *Bus:* Western National 175, 189, Stagecoach Devon 75 Newton Abbot–Totnes (passing close ⇌ Newton Abbot) (tel. 01392 382800) *Station:* Newton Abbot 1½m

BROWNSEA ISLAND

Poole Harbour BH13 1EE Tel: 01202 707744 Fax: 01202 701635

A 202ha island of heath and woodland, with wide views of the Dorset coast. The island includes an 81ha nature reserve leased to the Dorset Wildlife Trust

Note: Boats run from Poole Quay, Swanage & Bournemouth. The service from Sandbanks is under review and visitors should tel. 01202 707744 in advance to check the latest position. Visitors may land from own boat at Pottery Pier at west end of island, accessible at all stages of the tide

O 22 March to 30 Sept: daily 10–5 (6 in July & Aug). **Events:** open-air theatre, and other events in summer; for details tel. 01985 843601

£ Landing fee: £2.30, children £1.10; family ticket £5.70 (2 adults & 2 children). Parties £2, children 90p, by written arrangement with Property Manager

🏃 Guided tours of nature reserve; please contact Dorset Wildlife Trust Warden (tel. 01202 709445)

🛍 Shop open 22 March to 30 Sept: daily 10.30–4.45 (closes 5.45 in June, July & Aug); (tel. 01202 700852)

♿ Island paths hilly and rough, but area around quay accessible; two self-drive powered vehicles, and two manual wheelchairs available; mainland car parking near Poole Quay; all boats will accept and help wheelchair users; WC near island quay. Access to cafeteria and shop from quay; enquire at reception desk

◈ Braille guide

☕ Coffee, snacks and teas in the café near landing quay. Open daily 22 March to 30 Sept from 10.15; closes 30min before last boat departs (tel. 01202 700244). Tuck shop open daily

👶 Nursing room, baby-changing facilities

▮ Portman Study Centre. School groups welcome (tel. 01202 707744)

🐕 No dogs allowed on to the island

➔ In Poole Harbour [195: SZ032878] *Bus:* From surrounding areas to Poole Quay. To Sandbanks: Wilts & Dorset 150 Bournemouth–Swanage (passing ≷ Branksome); 152 from Poole (passing close ≷ Parkstone) (tel. 01202 673555); Yellow Buses 12 from Christchurch, summer only (tel. 01202 557272) *Station:* Poole ½ml to quay; Branksome or Parkstone 3½ml to Sandbanks

---

BUCKLAND ABBEY 🏠 🏛 ✝ ✿ 🧍 E

Yelverton PL20 6EY Tel: 01822 853607 Fax: 01822 855448

Tucked away in its own secluded valley above the River Tavy, Buckland Abbey holds the secret to over 700 years of history, from Cistercian monastery to home of Sir Francis Drake and Sir Richard Grenville. Exhibitions, furnished rooms and ancient buildings lead visitors on a voyage of discovery. Introductory video presentation, craft workshops, estate walks and herb garden

Note: Buckland Abbey is jointly managed by the National Trust and Plymouth City Council

🅾 28 March to 2 Nov: daily except Thur 10.30–5.30; also 8 Nov to end March 1998: Sat & Sun 2-5 (Wed for pre-arranged parties only). Last admissions 45min before closing. Closed 5–23 Jan 1998. *Note*: Some rooms in the Abbey may be

closed during the early part of the year for refurbishment – please ring to check.
Events: please contact Property Manager for details of concerts and other events.
An additional entrance charge (incl. NT members) may be applied on special
event days, including the June Craft Fair

£ £4.30; family ticket £10.70. Grounds only £2.20. Pre-arranged parties of 15
or more £3.50. Winter admission (Nov to March), grounds only no charge.
Workshops only free. NB: There may be an increased charge on certain days
(incl. NT members) when special events are in progress. See Events above. Car
park 150m, £1 refundable on admission

Shop open as house (tel. 01822 853706), but 8 Nov to end March 1998 Sat &
Sun 12.30–5. Additional opening Nov/Dec – please ring to check. Independent
craft workshops throughout year, variable opening (not Thur). Please check with
individual workshops: Basket-maker (tel. 01822 841187), Potter (tel. 01822
841220), Wood-turners (tel. 01364 631485/631585)

Car park area for disabled drivers near reception. Disabled passengers may be set
down at the Abbey after admission at main reception. Access via gravel paths
from car park. Site steep with access to lower levels of house only; restaurant
accessible via path with short steep incline. Motorised volunteer-driven buggy
may be available; please enquire at reception. Wheelchairs available at reception.
WC. Information leaflet on request

Scented herbs and plants. Braille audio guides. Advice leaflet on request

Licensed restaurant/tea-room open as shop. Restricted menu Nov to March 1998.
Last servings 30min before closing. Also open for pre-booked Christmas lunches
and candlelit dinners in Dec (tel. 01822 855024). Picnics in car park only

Children's guide, parent and baby room, baby slings available, special children's
menu, children's activities and events (leaflet available)

Fully equipped school base and handling collection; book with Property Manager.
Resource book available

In car park only, on leads. Dog posts in shade

6ml S of Tavistock, 11ml N of Plymouth: turn off A386 ¼ml S of Yelverton
[201: SX487667] *Bus:* Plymouth Citybus 55 from Yelverton (not Sun) (with
connections from ⇌ Plymouth), not Sun (tel. 01392 382800) *Station:* Bere
Alston (U), not Sun (except June to Sept), 4½ml

CASTLE DROGO 🏛 ✝ ❀ 🌳 ♨ 👶

Drewsteignton, nr Exeter EX6 6PB Tel: 01647 433306 Fax: 01647 433186

*This granite castle, built between 1910 and 1930, is one of the most remarkable works of
Sir Edwin Lutyens. It stands at over 300m above sea level overlooking the wooded gorge of
the River Teign with beautiful views of Dartmoor. The rooms on view include the purpose-
designed kitchen and scullery, as well as the well-appointed rooms of the Drewe family, who
commissioned the building. Delightful rose garden and herbaceous borders; early spring
shrubs and bulbs in woodland areas. Spectacular walks through surrounding 243ha estate*

Castle: 26 March to 2 Nov: daily except Fri 11–5.30 (open Good Fri).
Garden: 26 March to 2 Nov: daily 10.30–5.30. Last admission 5

£ Castle, garden & grounds £4.90; family ticket £12.20. Garden & grounds only £2.30. Pre-arranged parties £4.10 per person. Car park 400m. The croquet lawn is normally open; equipment for hire. Please book through visitor reception

🟊 Occasional guided walks on estate

🏛 Shop and plant centre by car park, open daily 26 March to 2 Nov 10.30–5.30. Also 5 Nov to 21 Dec Wed to Sun 11–4.30 (tel. 01647 433563)

♿ Limited access to part of castle. Lift available (via two steps) to lower floor, dining and kitchen area; too small for most wheelchairs, but seat in lift. Garden accessible. Close parking and access by arrangement at visitor reception. Restaurant and shop accessible. WC near shop. Wheelchairs available

❀ Scented plants. Braille guide; audio guide to castle

🍽 Licensed restaurant at castle, open 26 March to 1 Oct, same days as castle: 12–5.30. Tea-room in grounds, open daily 26 March to 2 Nov: 10.30–5.30; also limited refreshments available in Nov & Dec. Restaurant open for pre-booked Christmas lunches and suppers in Nov & Dec (tel. 01647 432629)

👶 Children's guide, children's menu, baby-changing facilities, babies in back carriers admitted to all areas

🐕 On leads in car park and surrounding public footpaths only

➔ 5ml S of A30 Exeter–Okehampton road via Crockernwell or A382 Moretonhampstead–Whiddon Down road; coaches must use the latter and turn off at Sandy Park [191: SX721900] *Bus:* DevonBus 359 from Exeter (passing ⇌ Exeter Central), Carmel 174 from Okehampton (with connections from ⇌ Exeter St David's) (tel. 01392 382800) *Station:* Yeoford (U) 8ml

THE CHURCH HOUSE 🏠

Widecombe in the Moor, Newton Abbot TQ13 7TA Tel: 01364 621321

Originally a brewhouse dating back to 1537, this former village school is now leased as a village hall and occasionally open to the public. The adjacent Sexton's Cottage is an NT and Dartmoor National Park Information Centre and gift shop

🕐 1 May to 25 Sept: Thur only 10–4

£ Church House free (donation box)

🏛 Information centre and shop in Sexton's Cottage, open daily: mid Feb to 27 March 10–4.30; 28 March to end Sept 10–6; Oct to 24 Dec 10–5; closed Jan 1998

♿ Ground floor only

🍽 In village (not NT)

🐕 Not admitted

➔ In centre of Dartmoor, N of Ashburton, W of Bovey Tracey [191: SX718768] *Bus:* Western National 170/1 & Stagecoach Devon 70, Newton Abbot–Tavistock (tel. 01392 382800)

CLEVEDON COURT 🏠 ❊

Tickenham Road, Clevedon BS21 6QU Tel: 01275 872257

Home of the Elton family, this 14th-century manor house, once partly fortified, has a 12th-century tower and 13th-century hall. Collection of Nailsea glass and Eltonware. Beautiful terraced garden

O 23 March to 28 Sept: Wed, Thur, Sun & BH Mon 2–5. Last admission 4.30

£ £3.60, children £1.80. Parties of 20 or more by prior arrangement; no reduction. Coaches by appointment. Unsuitable for trailer caravans or motor caravans

𝕏 Evening and afternoon tours by prior arrangement

♿ Access to ground floor via 4 steps. No wheelchair available

▶ Tea-room in Old Great Hall 2–4.45 (not NT)

⛑ Children's trail

▦ School parties in the mornings by prior arrangement

➔ 1½ml E of Clevedon, on Bristol road (B3130), signposted from M5 exit 20 [172: ST423716] *Bus:* Badgerline X7, X25/6, 360–3, Swiftlink 662/3 from Bristol; X23/4, 823 from Weston-super-Mare; 360, 660, 823 from Yatton (pass close ⇌ Yatton). On all alight Clevedon Triangle ¾ml (tel. 0117 955 3231). For information on Waverley Paddle Steamer trips tel. 01446 720656 *Station:* Yatton 3ml

CLOUDS HILL 🏠

Wareham, Dorset BH20 7NQ Tel: 01929 405616

T. E. Lawrence (Lawrence of Arabia) bought this cottage in 1925 as a retreat; it contains his furniture

O 23 March to 2 Nov: Wed, Thur, Fri, Sun & BH Mon 12–5 or dusk if earlier; no electric light. Party viewing outside these times by prior arrangement with the Custodian (tel. 01929 405616)

£ £2.20. No reduction for parties or children. Unsuitable for coaches or trailer caravans. No WC

🛍 T. E. Lawrence books on sale

◈ Braille guide

➔ 9ml E of Dorchester, 1½ml E of Waddock crossroads (B3390), 4ml S of A35 Poole–Dorchester road, 1ml N of Bovington Camp [194: SY824909] *Bus:* Southern National 67, Dorchester Coachways from ⇌ Wool, alight Bovington, 1ml (tel. 01305 783645) *Station:* Wool 3½ml; Moreton (U) 3½ml

COLERIDGE COTTAGE

35 Lime Street, Nether Stowey, Bridgwater TA5 1NQ Tel: 01278 732662

Coleridge's home for three years from 1797. It was here that he wrote The Rime of the Ancient Mariner, *part of* Christabel *and* Frost at Midnight

O Parlour and reading room only shown: 23 March to 1 Oct: Tues to Thur & Sun 2–5. In winter by written application to the Custodian. Parties please book

£ £1.70, children 80p. No reduction for parties which must book

◧ In village (not NT)

➔ At W end of Nether Stowey, on S side of A39, 8ml W of Bridgwater [181: ST191399] *Bus:* Southern National 15 Bridgwater–Minehead (passing close ⇌ Bridgwater) (tel. 01823 272033) *Station:* Bridgwater 8ml

---

COLETON FISHACRE GARDEN ✿ ⛰ ⚐ **E**

Coleton, Kingswear, Dartmouth TQ6 0EQ Tel: 01803 752466

8ha garden in a stream-fed valley set within the spectacular scenery of this National Trust coast. The garden was created by Rupert and Lady Dorothy D'Oyly Carte between 1925 and 1948, and is planted with a wide variety of uncommon trees and rare and exotic shrubs

Note: Coleton Fishacre House is lived in by tenants, Brian & Susan Howe, who offer bed & breakfast throughout the year; please tel/fax for details on 01803 752683 or write to Mr & Mrs Howe at the above address. The house can be viewed by written appointment only with Mr & Mrs Howe

O March: Sun only 2–5; also 26 March to 2 Nov: Wed, Thur, Fri, Sun & BH Mon 10.30–5.30 or dusk if earlier. Last admissions 30min before closing. **Events:** for details please send s.a.e or telephone the property

£ £3.30. Pre-booked parties £2.70

🚶 Occasional guided walks by arrangement or as advertised under special events

🛍 Small selection of garden gifts, postcards and unusual plants for sale at reception

♿ Limited access to parts of garden, steep slopes (strong companions essential). Wheelchair available; can be pre-booked. Tea-hut area has wheelchair-accessible tables

👁 Braille guide. Scented herbs and plants

☕ Tea-garden open as garden for morning coffee, light lunches and afternoon teas, weather permitting. Picnics in car park area only

👶 Baby-changing facilities in women's WC; children's trail leaflet

🐕 In car park only

→ 3ml from Kingswear; take Lower Ferry road, turn off at toll house [202: SX910508] *Bus:* Stagecoach Devon 200 Torquay–Kingswear (passing ⇌ Paignton); otherwise Stagecoach Devon 22 Brixham–Kingswear (with connections from ⇌ Paignton). On both, alight ¾ml SW of Hillhead, 1½ml walk to garden (tel. 01803 613226) *Station:* Paignton 8ml; Kingswear (Paignton & Dartmouth Rly) 2¼ml by footpath, 2¾ml by road

---

COMPTON CASTLE 🏠 ✚ ✿

Marldon, Paignton TQ3 1TA Tel: 01803 872112

A fortified manor house with curtain wall, built at three periods: 1340, 1450 and 1520, by the Gilbert family. It was the home of Sir Humphrey Gilbert (1539–1583), coloniser of Newfoundland and half-brother of Sir Walter Raleigh; the family still lives here

Note: Compton Castle is occupied and administered by Mr & Mrs G. E. Gilbert

O 31 March to 30 Oct: Mon, Wed & Thur 10–12.15 and 2–5, when the courtyard, restored Great Hall, solar, chapel, rose garden and old kitchen are shown. Last admission 30min before closing

£ £2.70. Pre-booked parties £2.10; organisers should notify Secretary. Additional parking and refreshments at Castle Barton opposite entrance

🛍 Guidebooks, postcards and slides available

♿ Limited access for wheelchair users

☕ Morning coffee, lunches and teas at Castle Barton (not NT) from 10 (tel. 01803 873314)

👶 Children's guidebook available

🐕 On leads in car park only

→ At Compton, 3ml W of Torquay, 1ml N of Marldon; from the Newton Abbot–Totnes road (A381) turn left at Ipplepen crossroads and W off Torbay ring road via Marldon [202: SX865648] *Bus:* Stagecoach Devon 7 ⇌ Paignton–Marldon, thence 1½ml (tel. 01803 613226) *Station:* Torquay 3ml

CORFE CASTLE

Corfe Castle, Wareham BH20 5EZ Tel/fax: 01929 481294

Corfe Castle's majestic ruins guard the gateway to the Isle of Purbeck. The royal castle was an important stronghold, treasury and prison before being slighted by Parliamentary forces in 1646. The ruins retain many fine Norman and early English features and there are extensive views over the unique Purbeck landscape. There is a new display at Castle View

◙ 1 March to 2 Nov: daily 10–5.30 (4.30 in early March/late Oct); 3 Nov to 1 March 1998: daily 11–3.30 (closed 2 days at end Jan for training). **Events:** medieval and civil war events, archaeology days, evening opening and tours; for details tel. 01985 843601

£ £3.50, children £1.80, family tickets £8.80/£5.30. Parties £3, children £1.50. Car- & coach-parking available at Castle View off A351; also at Norden park & ride and West St (not NT)

✗ Guided tours are often available during normal opening hours. Private groups by arrangement; please contact the castle for details

⌂ Shop open 22 March to 30 Sept: daily 10–6; 1 to 31 Oct: daily 10–5; 1 Nov to 1 March 1998: daily 10–4 (closed 1 week at end Jan for stock-taking); 2 to 31 March 1998: daily 10–5 (tel. 01929 480921)

♿ WC at ticket office (RADAR lock). Wheelchair access to ruins very difficult; not recommended beyond outer bailey. Shop, tea-rooms and Castle View visitor centre accessible (RADAR WC)

◉ Braille guide and menu. Many items and surfaces can be enjoyed by touch

◖ Tea-room (at castle entrance) serves coffee, lunches and cream teas, open 1 March to 1 Nov: daily 10–5.30; 2 Nov to 1 March: daily 10–4.30 (closed end Jan/early Feb for redecoration; tel. for dates)

✦ Children's guidebook; baby-changing facilities at castle and visitor centre; baby carriers, highchairs and children's menu in tea-room. Children should be accompanied by an adult within the castle

■ Education pack, schools' room with hands-on materials and guided tours available; for details tel. 01929 481294

🐕 On leads only

→ On A351 Wareham–Swanage road [195: SY959824] *Bus:* Wilts & Dorset 142/3/4 Poole–Swanage (passing ⮑ Wareham) (tel. 01202 673555) *Station:* Wareham 4½ml; Corfe Castle (Swanage Railway) a few mins walk (park & ride from Norden Station)

___

CORNISH ENGINES 🔛 🛠

Pool, nr Redruth Tel: 01209 216657

___

Two great beam engines (one with a cylinder 2.3m in diameter), used for pumping water from over 566m and for winding men and ore. They impressively evoke the days when the tin and copper mining industry dominated Cornish life. ¼ml to the west is the Geological Museum of the Camborne School of Mines, where the Trust's Norris collection of minerals can be seen. The engines exemplify the use of high pressure steam patented by the Cornish engineer Richard Trevithick in 1802. The winding engine is rotated today by electricity

Note: The property is managed by the Trevithick Trust on behalf of the National Trust. Trevithick's Cottage is nearby at Penponds and is open every Wed 2–5, free of charge (donations welcome)

🅾 28 March to 2 Nov: daily 11–5 (Geological Museum Mon to Fri, 9–5, free entry). For group visits outside these times, please contact Trevithick Trust (tel/fax 01209 612142)

£ £2.50. Pre-arranged parties £2.25; concessions £2; students £1

🛠 Available

🛍 Shop open as above

♿ Unsuitable for disabled visitors, many flights of stairs. No WC

👁 Braille guide

🍴 Refreshments and WCs available nearby

■ Mining diagrams and working models in both properties

→ At Pool, 2ml W of Redruth on either side of A3047 [203: SW672415] *Bus:* From surrounding areas (some passing ⮑ Redruth) (tel. 01209 719988) *Station:* Redruth 2ml; Camborne 2ml

___

COTEHELE 🏠 🏡 🎨 ✝ ❀ 🏺 🔛 🛠 🅴

St Dominick, nr Saltash, PL12 6TA Tel: 01579 351346

___

Built 1485–1627, and home of the Edgcumbe family for centuries, the house contains original furniture, armour and a remarkable set of tapestries and other textiles. There is a series of formal gardens near the house and a richly planted valley garden including a medieval dovecote, stewpond and Victorian summerhouse, as well as an 18th-century tower with fine views. Cotehele Mill has been restored to working condition, with adjoining workshops. Also of interest is Cotehele Quay, on the River Tamar, with 18th- and 19th-century buildings, an outstation of the National Maritime Museum, an art and craft gallery, and the restored Tamar sailing barge Shamrock. *There are woodland walks throughout the estate*

Note: The number of visitors to this small and fragile house has to be limited to no more than 600 per day. Please arrive in good time and be prepared to wait to gain entry. There is no electric light in the rooms, so visitors should avoid dull days early and late in the season

House: 28 March to 2 Nov: daily except Fri (open Good Fri) 11–5 (11–4.30 in Oct). Last admission 30min before closing or dusk if earlier (tel: 01579 350434). **Mill:** 28 March to 2 Nov: daily except Fri (open Good Fri and Fri in July & Aug) 12–5.30 (12–6 in July & Aug, 12–4.30 in Oct). Last admission 30min before closing or dusk if earlier (tel. 01579 350606). **Garden:** open daily 11 to dusk (tel. 01579 350909). **Events:** Please contact the Property Manager for details (tel. 01579 351346)

House, garden & mill £5.60; family ticket £14. Garden & mill only £2.80; family ticket £7. Pre-arranged parties £4.50 by prior written arrangement only with the Property Manager. Coach party organisers must book and obtain a copy of the route from the Property Manager. No parties Sun or BH weekends

Shop open 28 Mar to 2 Nov: daily 11–5.30 (11–5 in Oct). Also limited opening Nov to Christmas (tel. 01579 350072). Cotehele Quay Art & Craft Gallery: open daily 12–5; limited opening Nov to Christmas (tel. 01579 351494)

Hall and kitchen only accessible to wheelchairs. Ramps available at house, restaurant and shop (please enquire); most of garden unsuitable as very steep; loose gravel. Close parking by prior arrangement. WC. Tea-room on quay & some woodland walks accessible

Braille guides for house, garden & mill; scented plants

Coffee, lunches and teas in the Barn (closed Fri) and on Cotehele Quay (open daily) during season, and limited opening Nov to Christmas (tel. 01579 350652)

Parent & baby room

Schools' resource pack available. Environmental education facilities available. National Maritime Museum Outstation on Quay. The Loft education room available on Quay

🐕 Dogs under control allowed on woodland walks

➔ On W bank of the Tamar, 1ml W of Calstock by footpath (6ml by road), 8ml SW of Tavistock, 14ml from Plymouth via Saltash Bridge; 2ml E of St Dominick, 4ml from Gunnislake (turn at St Ann's Chapel); Calstock can be reached from Plymouth by water (contact Plymouth Boat Cruises Ltd, tel. 01752 822797) [201: SX422685] *Bus:* Western National 79, X79 ⇌ Liskeard–Tavistock (passing ⇌ Gunnislake), 190 Tavistock–Callington (tel. 01752 222666) *Station:* Calstock (U), not Sun (except June to Sept), 1½m (signposted from station)

THE COURTS GARDEN ❂

Holt, nr Trowbridge BA14 6RR Tel: 01225 782340

A 3ha garden of mystery flanking an 18th-century house (not open to the public), with an ornamental façade

🅾 **Garden only**: 23 March to 2 Nov: daily except Sat 2–5. Out of season by appointment

💷 £2.80, children £1.40. Parties by arrangement in advance with the Head Gardener. No WC. NT shop in Melksham, 4ml (tel. 01225 706454)

🐕 No dogs

➔ 3ml SW of Melksham, 3ml N of Trowbridge, 2½ml E of Bradford-on-Avon, on S side of B3107 [173: ST861618] *Bus:* Badgerline 237 Chippenham–Trowbridge (passing close ⇌ Chippenham & Trowbridge) (tel. 01225 464446) *Station:* Bradford-on-Avon 2½ml; Trowbridge 3ml

---

DUNSTER CASTLE 🖼 ❂ ♠ E

Dunster, nr Minehead TA24 6SL Tel: 01643 821314

The fortified home of the Luttrell family for 600 years, with a 13th-century castle building below a Norman motte. The 17th-century mansion was remodelled by Salvin in 1870, but retains its fine staircase and plasterwork. There is a terraced woodland garden with rare shrubs, and an 11ha park

🅾 **Castle**: 22 March to 1 Oct: daily except Thur & Fri (closed Good Fri) 11–5; also 4 Oct to 2 Nov: daily except Thur & Fri 11–4. **Garden and park**: Jan to March, Oct to Dec: daily 11–4 (closed 25 Dec); April to Sept 10–5 (open Good Fri). Last admission in all cases 30min before closing. **Events**: 11 & 12 June, Shakespeare's 'Twelfth Night'; for full events programme tel. 01985 843601

💷 Castle, garden & park: £5, children (under 16) £2.60; family ticket £13 (2 adults & up to 3 children). Pre-booked parties £4.50. Garden & park only £2.70, children (under 16) £1.30; family ticket £6.50. A 10min steep climb to castle from car park, but electrically powered vehicle available to give lifts when necessary. Car park in grounds

🏃 Contact Visitor Services for details of out of hours guided tours of house and/or attics & basements

🛍 Shop open daily 22 March to 28 Sept 10–5; 29 Sept to 24 Dec 11–4; 27 Dec to end March 1998 11–4, weather permitting (tel. 01643 821626)

♿ Castle & garden are situated on a steep hill. Volunteer-driven multi-seater and self-drive vehicle available from car park. Castle accessible to manual wheelchairs via stairclimber, but no access for heavy powered chairs; shop accessible. WC. Property plan shows wheel-friendly routes

👁 Braille guide. Guided tours can be booked. Scented plants & flowers in conservatory and garden. Members of staff have British Sign Language, Stage I

☕ In Dunster watermill and village (not NT). Picnic area in park, near car park

🧒 Children's guidebook. Exploration & nature trails available for grounds. Baby-changing facilities. Buggy park; backpacks, slings and reins available at front porch. Activity days; tel. for details

🎒 Study centre. Teachers' resource book (£3.50). For assistance and bookings, contact Education Coordinator

🐕 No dogs in garden, but welcome in park area on leads

➡ In Dunster, 3ml SE of Minehead. NT car park approached direct from A39 [181: ST995435] *Bus:* Southern National 38/9 from Minehead; otherwise 28, 300 Taunton–Minehead (passing ⇌ Taunton), alight Dunster Steep, ½ml (tel. 01823 272033) *Station:* Dunster (W Somerset Steam Rly) 1ml

---

DUNSTER WORKING WATERMILL ✕ E

Mill Lane, Dunster, nr Minehead TA24 6SW Tel: 01643 821759

Built on the site of a mill mentioned in the Domesday Survey of 1086, the present mill dates from the 18th century and was restored to working order in 1979

🕐 28 March to end June: daily except Sat (open Easter Sat) 10.30–5. July & Aug: daily 10.30–5. Sept & Oct: daily except Sat 10.30–5. **Events:** 11 May, National Mills Day; mill in operation. Opportunity to taste samples of products baked with mill flour. Normal admission charges apply

£ £1.60; family tickets available; party rates by prior arrangement. The mill is run and maintained by private funding; NT members must pay normal admission charge. Parking, ¾ml

 🏃 For groups by arrangement

 🛍 Selling mill flour, muesli & mill souvenirs

 ♿ Ground floor only at no charge

 ☕ Tea-room and tea-garden (not NT)

 🏫 School parties welcome, but please book in advance

 → On River Avill, beneath Castle Tor; approach via Mill Lane or Castle Gardens on foot; from car park in Dunster village or in old park [181: ST995435] *Bus:* As Dunster Castle

DYRHAM PARK 🏛 ❀ ♣ E

nr Chippenham SN14 8ER
Property office Tel: 0117 937 2501; Warden's office Tel: 01225 891364; Recorded information (24hrs): Tel: 0891 335215 (45p per min cheap rate, 50p at other times)

Built for William Blathwayt, Secretary at War and Secretary of State to William III, between 1691 and 1710. The rooms have been little changed since they were furnished by Blathwayt and their contents are recorded in his housekeeper's inventory. Surrounding the house, the 106ha ancient parkland, with herd of fallow deer, overlooks the Severn Valley. Featured in the award-winning film Remains of the Day

Note: Due to the fragile nature of the contents, it is necessary to control the light levels in certain rooms

 ⭕ **Park:** all year: daily 12–5.30 or dusk if earlier (opens 11 on days when garden open). Last admission 5. Closed Christmas Day. **Garden:** 22 March to 2 Nov: 11–5.30 except Wed & Thur. **House:** 22 March to 2 Nov: daily except Wed & Thur 12–5.30. Last admission 5 or dusk if earlier. *Note:* Property closed 4/5 July 1997, for jazz concerts. **Events:** 4/5 July, Jazz Festival; for details tel. 01985 843601

 £ House, garden & park £5.20, children £2.60; family ticket £12.90 (2 adults & 3 children). Park only £1.60, children 80p. Park & Garden only £2.60. Party rate available weekdays only. Please contact Property Manager. Coaches by prior arrangement

 🛍 Shop open same days as house, 12–5.30; Nov to 22 Dec (weekends only) (tel. 0117 937 4300)

 ♿ Access to ground floor, orangery and terrace, stable restaurant and small shop; disabled drivers may park near house; disabled passengers may be set down and collected from front door. Photograph album of inaccessible rooms available. WC. Wheelchairs available. Sympathetic Hearing Scheme

 👁 Taped guide to house; Braille guide and menu

 ☕ Coffee, lunches and teas in new licensed stable restaurant. Open 22 March to 2 Nov: daily except Wed & Thur, 11–5.30, last orders 5; 8 Nov to 21 Dec & March 1998: weekends only 12–4; also available for functions and meetings all year round (tel. 0117 937 4293). Special Winter programme in restaurant. Picnics welcome in park, but parties over 20 please advise. No barbecues

⛄ Children's guide

📷 School parties by appointment only; below stairs activities may be arranged

🐕 Dog-walking area: no dogs in deer park. No shaded areas in main car park

➔ 8ml N of Bath, 12ml E of Bristol; approached from Bath–Stroud road (A46), 2ml S of Tormarton interchange with M4, exit 18 [172: ST743757] *Bus:* Ryans Coaches from ≕ Bath Spa, Fri & Sat only (tel. 01225 424157) *Station:* Bath Spa 8ml

---

ELIZABETHAN HOUSE 🏠

32 New Street, The Barbican, Plymouth Pl1 2NA Tel: 01752 253871

A rare, surviving typical Tudor sea captain's timber-framed house, in the heart of Plymouth's historic Barbican. Features period furniture. National Trust shop and information centre. Managed by the National Trust in partnership with Plymouth City Council, which owns it

🅾 28 March to 2 Nov: daily except Mon & Tues 10–5

💷 £1 (including NT members). No WC

🔓 Open as house

📷 In Barbican area (not NT)

➔ Near the Barbican, which overlooks Plymouth Harbour *Bus:* Plymouth Citybus 25 from ≕ Plymouth (tel. 01752 222221) *Station:* Plymouth ¼ml

---

FINCH FOUNDRY 🏠 🔧 ⛄

Sticklepath, Okehampton EX20 2NW Tel/fax: 01837 840046

Fascinating 19th-century water-powered forge which produced agricultural hand tools. Regular demonstrations of working water wheels, forge with huge tilt-hammers and grindstone

🅾 26 March to 2 Nov: daily except Tues 11–5.30. Last admission 30min before closing

💷 £2.50. *Note:* access to car park is narrow and therefore unsuitable for coaches and wide vehicles

🔓 Open as foundry

♿ Disabled drivers may park in front of building. Access to shop; foundry may be viewed through shop windows. Workshop and museum difficult

👁 Braille guide; objects can be touched; volunteers will explain history of foundry

☕ Light refreshments kiosk open same time as foundry

➔ 4ml E of Okehampton off the A30 *Bus:* Jennings 629 Exeter–Bude; Stagecoach Devon 51 Exeter–Okehampton; Western National 187 Exeter–Gunnislake. All pass ≕ Exeter St David's (tel. 01392 382800)

FYNE COURT 🏠🏕️🦌🚶

Broomfield, Bridgwater TA5 2EQ Tel: 01823 451587

Headquarters of the Somerset Wildlife Trust and visitor centre for the Quantocks. The former pleasure grounds of the now demolished home of the pioneer electrician, Andrew Crosse (1784–1855). Now managed as a nature reserve

🅾️ All year: daily 9–6 or sunset if earlier

💷 Free. Car park charge. Coach-parking by prior arrangement only

🏠 Shop (not NT) open Easter to Christmas daily 2–5

♿ Trail for disabled visitors. Access to patio outside tea-room in fine weather. WC

🍽️ Teas on Sun and BH, May to Sept (not NT). Picnic sites

🐕 Strictly no dogs allowed

➡️ 6ml N of Taunton; 6ml SW of Bridgwater [182: ST222321] *Station:* Taunton 6ml

GLENDURGAN GARDEN 🌼

Mawnan Smith, nr Falmouth TR11 5JZ
Tel: 01208 74281 or 01326 250906 (opening hours only)

A valley garden of great beauty with fine trees and rare and exotic plants. The 1833 laurel maze, recently restored, and the Giant's Stride are unusual and popular features, especially with children. The garden runs down to the tiny village of Durgan and its beach. The house is privately occupied

🅾️ 1 March to 1 Nov: Tues to Sat & BH Mon (closed Good Fri) 10.30–5.30. Last admission 4.30

£ £3. Family ticket £7.50. Pre-arranged parties £2.50 per person

⬛ Shop and plant sales open as garden

♿ All access paths are steep, a viewing point is accessible but a strong companion is needed

Braille guide

Snacks and light refreshments

Giant's Stride (a pole with ropes to swing from) and the maze

No dogs allowed in the garden

➔ 4ml SW of Falmouth, ½ml SW of Mawnan Smith, on road to Helford Passage [204: SW772277] *Bus:* Truronian 324 from Falmouth (passing close ≷ Penmere) (tel: 01872 73453) *Station:* Penmere (U) 4ml

GREAT CHALFIELD MANOR 🏠 ✝ ❀

nr Melksham SN12 8NJ Tel: (Regional Office) 01985 843600

Dating from 1480, the manor house is set across a moat between parish church and stables. Restored early this century by Major R. Fuller, whose family still lives here

🅾 1 April to 30 Oct: Tues, Wed, Thur by guided tours only, starting 12.15, 2.15, 3, 3.45 & 4.30. Guided tours of the manor take 45min and numbers are limited to 25. It is suggested that visitors arriving when a tour is in progress visit the church and garden first. Closed on public holidays. *Note:* Members of historical and other societies wishing to visit the Manor in organised parties can usually be shown the church, house and garden on other weekdays, by written appointment with Mrs Robert Floyd

£ £3.50. No reduction for children or parties. No WC

♿ Limited access to garden only

➔ 3ml SW of Melksham via Broughton Gifford Common (sign for Atworth, drive on left) [166: ST860630] *Bus:* Badgerline 237 Chippenham–Trowbridge (passing close ≷ Chippenham & Trowbridge), alight Holt, 1ml by footpath (tel. 01225 464446) *Station:* Bradford-on-Avon, 3ml

HARDY MONUMENT 🏠 ⛽

Black Down, Portesham Tel: (Regional Office) 01985 843600

A monument erected in 1844 in memory of Vice-Admiral Sir Thomas Masterman Hardy, Flag-Captain of HMS Victory at the battle of Trafalgar. Now restored by the Trust

🅾 22 March to 28 Sept: Sat & Sun only 11–5. Staffed by volunteers. Numbers at the top of the monument are limited. Children must be accompanied by an adult. No WC

£ £1; no reduction for children

  No wheelchair access

  From the B3157 Weymouth–Bridport road, turn off at Portesham; the road climbs steeply to a car park signposted 'Hardy Monument' [194: SY613876] *Bus:* Weybus 6 Weymouth–Abbotsbury (passing close ⬛ Weymouth), alight Portesham, thence 2ml (tel. 01305 767023) *Station:* Dorchester South or Dorchester West (U), both 6ml

HARDY'S COTTAGE 🏠 🟦

Higher Bockhampton, nr Dorchester DT2 8QJ Tel: 01305 262366

A small thatched cottage where the novelist and poet Thomas Hardy was born in 1840. It was built by his great-grandfather and little altered; furnished by the Trust. (See Max Gate, p.277)

  23 March to 2 Nov: daily except Fri & Sat (but open Good Fri) 11–5 (or dusk if earlier). Approach only by 10min walk from car park through woods

  Interior £2.50. No reduction for children or parties. School parties and coaches by prior arrangement only. No WC. Hardy's works on sale

  Shop at 65 High West St, Dorchester (tel. 01305 267535)

  Access to garden only; special car-parking arrangement with Custodian

  3ml NE of Dorchester, ½ml S of A35 [194: SY728925] *Bus:* Wilts & Dorset X84, 184/6 Weymouth–Salisbury, 187/9 Poole–Dorchester (all pass ⬛ Dorchester South & close Dorchester West), alight Bockhampton Lane, ½ml (tel. 01202 673555) *Station:* Dorchester South 4ml; Dorchester West (U) 4ml

HEDDON VALLEY SHOP 🟦 🟦 🧍

Heddon Valley, Parracombe, Barnstaple EX30 4PX Tel: 01598 763402

Information centre and gift shop set in spectacular NT wooded valley at centre of West Exmoor Coast property. Focal point for many coastal and woodland walks

  26 March to 30 Sept: daily 10–6; Oct: daily 10–5. Open BHols

  Free, voluntary contributions welcome. Car park

  See local listings for programme of guided walks on the surrounding coastal estate. Walks leaflet available from shop

  Gift shop

  Confectionery, ice cream and cold drinks

  By arrangement with the Warden (tel. 01598 763476)

  Halfway between Combe Martin and Lynton, off the A39 at Hunters Inn *Bus:* Lyn Valley from Lynmouth, Wed only (May to Sept only); otherwise Red Bus 310 Barnstaple–Lynmouth (passing close ⬛ Barnstaple), alight just N of Parracombe, thence 2ml (tel. 01392 382800)

⬛ Licensed restaurant serving coffee & lunches 11–2, teas 2.15–5. Also open as shop in Nov & Dec. Parties to book in advance with Restaurant Manager (tel. 01386 438703). Light refreshments available in plant centre, open same days as garden to end Sept:10.30–5.45

➔ 4ml NE of Chipping Campden, 1ml E of B4632 (originally A46), off B4081 [151: SP176429] *Bus:* Stagecoach Midland Red 216 from Stratford-upon-Avon (tel. 01242 425543) *Station:* Honeybourne (U) 4½ml

HORTON COURT 🏠 🏚

Horton, nr Chipping Sodbury, Bristol BS17 6QR
Tel: (Regional Office) 01985 843600

The 12th-century Norman hall and exceptionally fine detached late Perpendicular ambulatory of a limestone manor house, with early Renaissance features

🅾 2 April to 29 October: Wed & Sat 2–6 or dusk if earlier. Other times by written appointment with tenant

💷 £1.60, children 80p. Unsuitable for coaches. No WC

♿ Ambulatory only accessible; allocated parking on application to tenant

➔ 3ml NE of Chipping Sodbury, ¾ml N of Horton, 1ml W of the Bath–Stroud road (A46) [172: ST766851] *Station:* Yate 5ml

KILLERTON 🏠 🏚 ✝ ✿ ♣ 🐚 🏚 🚶 🅴

Broadclyst, Exeter EX5 3LE Tel: 01392 881345

The house, home of the Aclands, was rebuilt in 1778 to the design of John Johnson. It is furnished as a comfortable family home and includes the Paulise de Bush costume collection, dating from the 18th century to the present day, set in period rooms, and a Victorian laundry. The 8ha hillside garden is beautiful throughout the year, with rhododendrons, magnolias, herbaceous borders and rare trees; also an ice house and early 19th-century rustic style summer-house known as The Bear's Hut. The surrounding parkland and woods offer lovely walks; a number of specially designed circular walks have been created and leaflets are available at reception. Also of interest are the 19th-century chapel, an introductory exhibition in the stable courtyard, and the site of an Iron Age hillfort. Discovery centre with historical and environmental activities

🅾 **House:** 15 March to 2 Nov: daily 11–5.30 (but house closed Tues). Last admission 5. **Park & garden:** open all year from 10.30 to dusk. **Events:** 1997 costume exhibition 'Flowers in Dress', an exhibition of dress and textiles reflecting the use of flowers in design; from mid-June, 'Mansions in Miniature', an exhibition of dolls' houses; 19 & 20 July, Exeter Festival open-air concerts. Full events programme from Property Manager, s.a.e. please. *Note:* on 19 & 20 July, only ticket holders to the Exeter Festival Concerts will be admitted to the garden after 4.30; house will close at 4.30

💷 £4.80; family ticket £12. Garden and park only £3.20. Garden and park reduced winter rate (Nov to Feb). Pre-booked parties £3.90

 Introductory talks by arrangement with Property Manager

 Shop and plant centre in stable courtyard. 5 March to end Sept: open daily 11–6; Oct: open daily 11–5; 1 Nov to 21 Dec: Wed to Sun 11–5, plus special opening 22 & 23 Dec 11–5; Jan to mid March 1998: Wed to Sun 11–4. The shop may not open during adverse weather conditions in winter – please ring to check (tel. 01392 881912)

 Three steps to house (ramp available on request), wheelchairs available. Wheelchair stair climber for access to costume displays, but please check availability in advance. Lower levels of garden accessible, but gravel paths and grass. Volunteer-driven buggies available for tour of garden on days **when house open**; by arrangement at other times. WCs. Designated parking for disabled drivers and transfer by buggy to house and garden. Wheelchair lift to upper level of shop

 Braille guides for house and costume collection; scented plants. Grand piano and organ may be played by visually impaired musicians

 Licensed restaurant open same days as house 12–5 and for pre-booked Christmas lunches (tel. 01392 882081). Tea-room in stable courtyard open 15 March to end Sept: daily 10.30–5.45; Oct: 10.30–4.30; 1 Nov to 21 Dec: Wed to Sun 11–4.30, plus 22 & 23 Dec 11–4.30; Jan to end March 1998: Sat & Sun only 11–4. The tea-room may not open in adverse weather conditions in winter – please ring to check (tel. 01392 881345)

 Table & chair in women's WCs near stable courtyard, and at house; children's guide; quiz sheet for house; children's menu and highchairs available; babies in back carriers and single pushchairs admitted to all areas. Discovery centre open most weekends when house open

 Discovery centre for pre-booked parties; teachers' resource guide (£2.50). Orienteering course

🛌 In park only; parking in shade available in overflow car park

➡️ Off Exeter–Cullompton road (B3181, formerly A38); from M5 northbound, exit 29 and follow A30 Exeter/Honiton road for 3ml, then take left turn signed 'Broadclyst & Killerton'; from M5 southbound, exit 28 (192: SX9700)
Bus: Stagecoach Devon 54A, DevonBus 327, 375 from Exeter (all passing close ⇌ Exeter Central), some pass the house, but on most alight Killerton Turn ¾ml (tel. 01392 382800) *Station:* Pinhoe (U), not Sun, 4½ml; Whimple (U), not Sun, 6ml; Exeter Central & St David's, both 7ml

KING JOHN'S HUNTING LODGE 🏠

The Square, Axbridge BS26 2AP Tel: 01934 732012

An early Tudor merchant's house, extensively restored in 1971. The house is run as a local history museum by Sedgemoor District Council in cooperation with the Somerset County Museums Service and Axbridge Archaeological and Local History Society

🅞 Easter to end Sept: daily 2–5

💷 Free. School parties by arrangement. Council car park, 2min walk

♿ Access limited to ground floor

🐾 In Axbridge (not NT)

➡️ In the Square, on corner of High Street [182: ST431545] *Bus:* Badgerline 126, 826 Weston-super-Mare–Wells (passing close ⇌ Weston-super-Mare) (tel. 01934 621201) *Station:* Worle (U) 8ml

KINGSTON LACY 🏠 ❀ ♣ 🕅 E

Wimborne Minster BH21 4EA Tel: 01202 883402

A 17th-century house, designed by Sir Roger Pratt for the traveller Sir Ralph Bankes, and altered by Sir Charles Barry in the 19th century. As well as an outstanding collection of paintings, the house contains an exhibition of Egyptian artefacts. The house and garden are set in a wooded park with waymarked walks now open to visitors. The park also boasts a fine herd of red Devon cattle

🅞 Feb/Mar & Nov/Dec: Fri, Sat & Sun only. **Park, garden, shop & restaurant (house closed)** 11–4 (or dusk if earlier); 22 March to 2 Nov: daily except Thur & Fri: **House** 12–5.30 (last admission 4.30), **park, garden, shop & restaurant** 11.30–6. **Events:** July, Bournemouth Sinfonietta with firework display; to book tel. 01985 843601; for other events and talks, tel. 01202 883402

💷 Park & garden: Feb, March, Nov & Dec £1 car-parking only; House, park & garden: March to Nov £5.50, children £2.70. Park & garden only March to Nov £2.20, children £1.10. Pre-booked parties (15 or more) £4.80.

🕅 Parties of 15 or more; for details tel. 01202 883402

🛍 22 March to 2 Nov: daily except Thur & Fri 11.30–5.30. Also open Fri, Sat & Sun in Feb, March, Nov & Dec: 11–4 (tel. 01202 841424)

♿ Park (centenary walk), garden, restaurant and shop all accessible; some thick gravel. Wheelchairs and self-drive buggy available. WC. House not suitable for wheelchairs, except for two days (May & Sept) which are reserved for special access to main state rooms only; for details tel. 01202 883402

♿ Braille guide

♿ Coffee, lunches & teas in licensed stable restaurant, open as shop. Party bookings, special occasions and Christmas lunches (tel. 01202 889242). Picnics in park only

♿ Baby-changing facilities in ladies' and disabled WC. Highchairs in restaurant

♿ Frizzell Study Centre & active education programme. Children's guide

♿ In park and woods only, under strict control when near livestock and picnickers

→ On B3082 Blandford–Wimborne road, 1½ml W of Wimborne [19: SY980019]
Bus: Wilts & Dorset X13, 132/3/9 from Bournemouth, Poole, Shaftesbury (passing ⊜ Bournemouth & close ⊜ Poole). On all alight Wimborne Square 2½ml. An occasional service from Bournemouth to the house operates in the summer (tel. 01202 673555) *Station:* Poole 8½ml

KINGSTON LACY ESTATE: LODGE FARM ⚑

Kingston Lacy Estate Office Tel: 01202 882493

Lodge Farm is a stone first-floor hall house of the early 15th century built for Henry V or VI. Documentary sources suggest that it was the residence of the head park keeper, warrener and forester of Kingston Lacy manor

◎ By appointment; write to the Estate Office, Hillbutts, Wimborne, Dorset BH21 4DS

£ £1.50 (free to NT members)

→ *Bus:* Wilts & Dorset X13, 132/3/9 from Bournemouth, Poole, Shaftesbury (passing ⊜ Bournemouth & close ⊜ Poole). On all alight Wimborne Square, 3ml. An occasional service from Bournemouth to Kingston Lacy, 1ml walk, operates in the summer (tel. 01202 673555) *Station:* Poole 9ml

KNIGHTSHAYES COURT 🏠 ❀ ♠ 🧍 E

Bolham, Tiverton EX16 7RQ Tel: 01884 254665 Fax: 01884 243050

Begun in 1869, the rich interiors combine medieval romanticism with lavish decoration. Designed by William Burges, the house is a rare survival of his work and gives an interesting insight into grand Victorian life with its smoking and billiard rooms and elegant boudoir and drawing room. Of equal beauty and interest is the 12ha garden, one of the finest in Devon, with specimen trees, rare shrubs, spring bulbs and summer borders. Woodland walks

🅾️ 28 March to 2 Nov: **House** open daily except Fri (but open Good Fri) 11–5.30; **Garden** open daily 11–5.30. Last admission 5. Nov & Dec: Sun 2–4 for pre-booked parties only; please note that some items normally on view may not be displayed due to conservation work. **Events**: for details please tel. 01884 254665

💷 £5. Garden & grounds only £3.30. Pre-booked parties £4.20. Parking 450m. Visitor reception: (tel. 01884 257381)

🧍 By appointment with the Property Manager (tel. 01844 254665)

🅲 Shop and plant centre open 8 & 9 March, then Wed to Sun 11–4.30 until 27 Mar; 28 March to 2 Nov: open daily 10.30–5.30. 5 Nov to 21 Dec: open Wed to Sun 11–4.30; from mid March 1998: open Wed to Sun 11–4.30 (tel. 01884 259010)

♿ Ground floor of house, shop and restaurant accessible. Small lift to first floor of house unsuitable for wheelchairs, unless user can stand while chair is folded for carriage in lift. Some gravel paths in garden, but recommended signed routes. Access to picnic area in car park. Disabled drivers may park near house, or passengers may be set down by house entrance. Note: please show membership cards or purchase tickets at stables first. WC

👁️ Scented plants; audio and braille house guides; audio guide indicates tactile objects

🍽️ Licensed restaurant open for coffee, lunches and teas: 8 & 9 March, then Wed to Sun 11–4 until 27 March; 28 March to 2 Nov: daily 10.30–5; 5 Nov to 21 Dec: Wed to Sun 11–4; from mid March 1998: Wed to Sun 11–4. Also open for pre-booked Christmas lunches and candlelit dinners (tel. 01884 259416). Picnic area in car park. Restaurant opening hours during Oct may vary from those printed, although light refreshments will always be available during opening hours. If in doubt, please telephone when you are planning a visit

[icon] Changing facilities in women's WC; children's menu; highchair available; children's guide and quizzes for house and garden; baby back carriers admitted to all areas

[icon] In park only, on leads

[icon] 2ml N of Tiverton; turn right off Tiverton–Bampton road (A396) at Bolham [181: SS960151] *Bus:* East Devon 216/7, 717 Tiverton–Dulverton, alight Bolham, thence ¼ml; otherwise Tiverton & District 373/4 from ⇌ Tiverton Parkway; Devon General 55/A/B Exeter–Tiverton (passing close ⇌ Exeter Central), alighting Tiverton, 1¼ml (tel. 01392 382800) *Station:* Tiverton Parkway 8ml

---

LACOCK ABBEY, FOX TALBOT MUSEUM & VILLAGE
[icons]

Lacock, nr Chippenham SN15 2LG
Abbey Tel: 01249 730227 Museum Tel: 01249 730459 Fax: 01249 730501

The abbey was founded in 1232 and converted into a country house c.1540. The fine medieval cloisters, sacristy, chapter house and monastic rooms are largely intact. There is a 16th-century stable courtyard with half-timbered gables, clockhouse brewery and bakehouse. The wooded garden has a fine display of spring flowers, magnificent trees, an 18th-century summer house, Victorian rose garden and ha-ha. The museum of photography commemorates the achievements of William Fox Talbot (1800–77), inventor of the modern photographic negative, who lived in the Abbey. His descendants gave the abbey and village to the Trust in 1944. The village dates from the 13th century and has many limewashed half-timbered and stone houses, a 14th-century tithe barn, 18th-century lock-up and attractive 18th-century packhorse bridge and ford

[icon] **Museum, cloisters & grounds**: 1 March to 2 Nov: daily (closed Good Fri) 11–5.30. **Abbey**: 22 March to 2 Nov: daily, except Tues, 1–5.30; last admission 5. Museum also open 3 Nov to Feb 1998: weekends only 11–4. **Events**: for details of concerts and outdoor theatre events tel. 01985 843601; for special exhibitions, check with museum

[icon] Abbey, grounds, cloisters and museum £5.20, children £3; parties £4.70, children £2.50. Grounds, cloisters and museum only £3.50, children £2. Winter opening of museum £2, children £1

[icon] Guided tours by arrangement

[icon] Shop in village: 22 March to 2 Nov: daily 10–5.30; 3 Nov to 22 Dec: daily 11–4; 4 Jan to end March 1998: daily 11–4 (tel. 01249 730302). Museum shop selling photographic books, films, postcards; open as museum

[icon] All areas of grounds, cloisters and museum are accessible (stairlift in museum). Abbey is difficult with 4 sets of steps; limited parking at abbey by arrangement; wheelchairs and batricar available at museum; WC at abbey and at Red Lion car park (RADAR lock). Sympathetic Hearing Scheme

[icon] Braille and taped guides; pre-booked guided tours

[icon] In village (not NT)

[icon] Children's guide to abbey

🏫 Pre-booked school parties welcome

🐕 No dogs in abbey or grounds

➔ 3ml S of Chippenham, just E of A350 [173: ST919684]; signposted to car park
Bus: Badgerline 234/7 Chippenham–Trowbridge (passing close ≽ Chippenham
& Trowbridge) (tel. 01225 464446) *Station:* Chippenham 3½ml

LANHYDROCK 🏫 ❋ ♣ ♨ 𝒊 E

Bodmin PL30 5AD Tel: 01208 73320 Fax: 01208 74084

Superbly positioned above the River Fowey in 182ha of woods and parkland, this 17th-century house is a blend of Victorian splendour with some elements from the original house, before the disastrous fire which almost destroyed it in 1881. The gatehouse (1651) and the north wing, including a 32m gallery with fine plaster ceiling, are unaltered. A total of 49 rooms are open, including the newly furnished nursery wing (allow at least 1½ hours for tour of house). Formal and shrub gardens are of interest and beauty in all seasons

Note: A cloakroom with lockers is provided in the house for large bags and backpacks

⭕ **House:** 26 March to 2 Nov: daily except Mon, but open BH Mon, 11–5.30 (closes 5 in Oct). Last admission to house 30min before closing. **Garden:** 1 March to 2 Nov: daily 11–5.30 (closes 5 in Oct); Nov to end Feb: daily during daylight hours. **Events:** programme details available from the Property Manager

£ House, garden & grounds £6; family ticket £15. Garden & grounds only £3. Pre-arranged parties £5. Car park at end of long drive, 600m

🛍 Shop open: March, weekends only 11–4; 26 March to 2 Nov, daily 11–5.30 (5 in Oct); Nov & Dec, daily 11–4. Plant sales (in the cark park), open daily March to 2 Nov (tel. 01208 74099)

♿ Disabled visitors may be driven to house; close parking, for assistance please contact reception. Wheelchair access to house via ramp to restaurant; most ground-floor rooms easily accessible; small lift to first floor; WC. No powered wheelchairs allowed in house. Shop has some steps. Garden has a few steps and sloping gravel paths, steep in places – access via steps; ramp available. Powered self-drive buggy available if booked. Indoor and outdoor wheelchairs available

👁 Aromatic plants; water sounds. Braille guides for house & garden. Tactile route through house

🍴 Refreshments available daily 1 March to 2 Nov. Licensed restaurant open daily except Mon (but open BH Mon) 26 March to 2 Nov. Limited opening in Nov & Dec (tel. 01208 74331)

👶 Parent and baby room; baby slings and harnesses available; pushchair storage area in house

🏫 Schools' resource book. Schools' base; children's guide; handling collection; education stewards

🐕 In park and woods only, on leads

➔ 2½ml SE of Bodmin, overlooking valley of River Fowey; follow signposts from either A30, A38 Bodmin–Liskeard or B3268 Bodmin–Lostwithiel roads [200: SX085636] *Bus:* Western National 55, 151 from ⬫ Bodmin Parkway (tel. 01209 719988) *Station:* Bodmin Parkway 1¼ml by original carriage-drive to house, signposted in station car park; 3ml by road

LAWRENCE HOUSE 🏛

9 Castle Street, Launceston PL15 8BA Tel: 01566 773277/774518

Georgian house given to the Trust to help preserve the character of the street, and now leased to Launceston Town Council as a museum and civic centre

🅾 April to early Oct: Mon to Fri 10.30–4.30. Open BH Mon. Other times by appointment

💷 Free, but visitors are invited to contribute towards museum expenses

🛍 Small shop, open as museum

◀ Braille guide

➔ [201: SX330848] *Bus:* Western National 76 from Plymouth (passing ⬫ Plymouth); Tilleys from Exeter (tel. 01392 382800)

THE LEVANT STEAM ENGINE 🔧 🚶

Trewellard, Pendeen, nr St Just
Tel: 01209 216657 or 01736 786156 (opening hours only)

After sixty idle years, the famous Levant beam engine is steaming again. In its tiny engine house perched on the cliff edge, the sight, sounds and smells of this 155-year-old engine make a visit to Levant an unforgettable experience. ½ml along the cliff is Geevor mine (not NT) and a mining museum

🅾 Open Easter, May & Spring BH Sun & Mon; June: Wed, Thur, Fri & Sun; July to 5 Oct: daily except Sat 11–5

💷 £3. Familt ticket £7.50. Stewarded by volunteer members of the Trevithick Society. Members are invited to contribute to the cost of the project

🚶 Available

🦽 Limited access – assistance if required

◀ Recommended to accompanied visually impaired visitors; machinery sounds, smells, and atmosphere

🍴 At Geevor mine or Pendeen village

🚩 Suitable for small groups only (max. 40) by prior arrangement

➔ 1ml W of Pendeen, on B3306 St Just–Zennor road [203: SW368346] *Bus:* Western National 10A from ⬫ Penzance (tel. 01209 719988) *Station:* Penzance 7ml

LITTLE CLARENDON 🏠

Dinton, Salisbury SP3 50Z Tel: (Regional Office) 01985 843600

A Tudor house, but greatly altered in the 17th century

O By appointment only; please tel. 01985 843600

£ £1.50. No reduction for children or parties. House not suitable for pushchairs or prams. No coaches

→ ¼ml E of Dinton Church [184: SU015316] *Bus:* As for Philipps House, p.279

LOUGHWOOD MEETING HOUSE ✝

Dalwood, Axminster EX13 7DU Tel: 01392 881691

Built c.1653 by the Baptist congregation of Kilmington. The interior was fitted in the early 18th century

O All year

£ Free (donation box provided)

→ 4ml W of Axminster; turn right on Axminster–Honiton road (A35), 1ml S of Dalwood, 1ml NW of Kilmington [192/193: SY253993] *Bus:* Red Bus 380 Axminster–Ottery St Mary (passing close ⭢ Axminster) (tel. 01392 382800) *Station:* Axminster 2½ml

LUNDY 🏛 🏠 ✝ ♨ 🚜 🔛 📷 🐾 🚶

Bristol Channel EX39 2LY Tel: 01237 431831 Fax: 01237 431832

An unspoilt island, with rocky headlands and fascinating animal and birdlife. It is the ideal place to explore for a day trip, with no cars to disrupt the peace. The small island community includes a church, tavern and castle. There is a steep climb to the village from the landing beach. Lundy is financed, administered and maintained by the Landmark Trust

O Always. Sea passages from Bideford all year round, also from Ilfracombe in summer season, by the island vessel MS *Oldenburg* (300 tons, 267 passengers, refreshments on board). For sailing details tel. 01237 470422. Groups and passenger ships by prior arrangement

£ Entrance fee included in fare price for passengers on MS *Oldenburg*, but £3.50 per person for those arriving by other means. Discount for NT members who book in advance and arrive on *Oldenburg*

🛍 Shop selling the famous Lundy stamps, souvenirs and postcards, along with general supplies and groceries

♿ Disabled visitors are very welcome but should telephone in advance so that disembarking arrangements may be made

◗ Food and drink at the Marisco Tavern. Accommodation: 23 holiday cottages;

camping site for up to 40 people. For bookings, apply to: The Landmark Trust, Shottesbrooke, Maidenhead, Berkshire SL6 3SW (tel. 01628 825925)

[†] Baby-changing facilities in women's WC. Children in particular find Lundy a fascinating place

[→] 11ml N of Hartland Point, 25ml from Ilfracombe, 30ml S of Tenby [180: SS1345] *Bus:* Bus services available from ⇌ Barnstaple to Bideford or Ilfracombe (tel. 01392 382800) *Station:* Barnstaple: 8½ml to Bideford, 12ml to Ilfracombe

LYDFORD GORGE ⊞ [†]

The Stables, Lydford Gorge, Lydford, nr Okehampton EX20 4BH
Tel: 01822 820441/820320

This famous gorge is 1½ml long. The walk starts high above the river, passing through the oak woodland before the path drops down to the spectacular 30m White Lady waterfall. The path then proceeds along the enchanting riverside walk through the steeply-sided ravine scooped out by the River Lyd as it plunges into a series of whirlpools, including the thrilling Devil's Cauldron

[○] 24 March to 2 Nov: daily 10–5.30; also Nov to March 1998: daily 10.30–3, but from waterfall entrance as far as waterfall only; 3 Nov to 21 Dec: Sat & Sun only 11–4, top path open from main entrance shop. There are delays at the Devil's Cauldron during busy periods. The walk is arduous in places; visitors should wear stout footwear. *Note:* Not suitable for visitors with heart complaints or walking disabilities. Car parks at both entrances

[£] £3.10. Pre-arranged parties £2.50

[🛍] Shop at main entrance open as gorge. Small shop at far end of gorge 1 April to end Oct as gorge, but 2 Nov to 22 Dec: Sat & Sun 11–4

[♿] Gorge unsuitable for disabled visitors. Accessible picnic area; WC

[☕] Main entrance; tea-room serving morning coffee, hot meals, homemade cakes and ice cream, open 24 March to 2 Nov: daily 10.30–5.30; 3 Nov to 21 Dec: Sat & Sun 11–4

[†] Children's guide; baby-changing facilities; babies in back carriers welcome; difficult for pushchairs in places due to terrain and width of some paths

[▦] Teachers' geology pack and guide

🐕 Must be kept on leads at all times

➡️ At W end of Lydford village; halfway between Okehampton and Tavistock, 1ml W off A386 opposite Dartmoor Inn; main entrance at W end of Lydford; second entrance near Mucky Duck Inn [191 & 201: SX509846] *Bus:* Western National 86, Plymouth–Barnstaple (most passing 🚃 Plymouth); 187 🚃 Gunnislake–Exeter (passing 🚃 Exeter St David's), Sun, May to Sept only (tel. 01392 382800)

LYTES CARY MANOR 🏠 ✝️ ❀

Charlton Mackrell, Somerton TA11 7HU Tel: (Regional Office) 01985 843600

A manor house with a 14th-century chapel, 15th-century hall and 16th-century Great Chamber. The home of Henry Lyte, translator of the Niewe Herball (1578). Hedged garden with long herbaceous border

🅾️ 24 March to 29 Oct: Mon, Wed & Sat 2–6 or dusk if earlier; last admission 5.30

💷 £3.80, children £1.90. No reduction for parties. Large coaches cannot pass the gate piers so must stop in narrow road, ¼ml walk. Coaches strictly by appointment only

♿ Access to garden only. Scented plants in herbaceous borders. WC

👁️ Braille guide

🧒 Children's trail

🐕 In car park only

➡️ Signposted from Podimore roundabout at junction of A303, A37 take A372 [183: ST529269] *Bus:* Badgerline 376 Bristol–Yeovil (passing 🚃 Bristol Temple Meads) (tel. 0117 9553231); Southern National 54 Yeovil–Taunton (passing close 🚃 Taunton) (tel. 01823 272033). Both pass within ½ml 🚃 Yeovil Pen Mill. On both, alight Kingsdon, 1ml *Station:* Yeovil Pen Mill 8½ml; Castle Cary 9ml; Yeovil Junction 10ml

---

MARKER'S COTTAGE 🏠

Broadclyst, Exeter EX5 3HR Tel: 01392 461546

Fascinating medieval cob house which contains a cross-passage screen decorated with a painting of St Andrew and his attributes

🅾️ 30 March to 2 Nov: Sun, Mon, Tues 2–5

💷 £1. House unsuitable for coach parties. WC. Please park in village car park

♿ Access difficult; four steps into house

➡️ Off Exeter–Cullompton road (B3181) in village of Broadclyst. Turn right opposite church (coming from Exeter direction) and then second right [192:SX985973] *Bus:* Stagecoach Devon 54 Exeter–Cullompton (passes close 🚃 Exeter Central) (tel. 01392 427711) *Station:* Pinhoe (U), not Sun, 2½ml; Polesloe Bridge (U) 4ml; Whimple (U) 4½ml; Exeter Central 5½ml; Exeter St David's 6ml

MAX GATE 🏠 ❀

Alington Avenue, Dorchester DT1 2AA Tel: 01305 262538 Fax: 01305 250978

Poet and novelist Thomas Hardy designed and lived in the house from 1885 until his death in 1928. The house is leased to tenants and contains several pieces of Hardy's furniture

O **Dining & drawing rooms:** 23 March to 1 Oct: Mon, Wed & Sun 2–5. Open at other times for private visits, tours and seminars by schools, colleges and literary societies, by appointment with the tenants, Mr & Mrs Andrew Leah

£ Dining & drawing rooms and garden £2, children £1. No WC

🛍 Shop at 65 High West St, Dorchester (tel. 01305 267535)

♿ Some level access to ground floor

◐ Braille guide

➡ 1ml E of Dorchester on the A352 Wareham road. From Dorchester follow A352 until you reach the roundabout named Max Gate (at the junction of the A35 Dorchester bypass). Turn left and left again into the cul-de-sac outside the house *Bus:* Southern National D from town centre (tel. 01305 783645) *Station:* Dorchester South 1ml; Dorchester West (U) 1ml

MOMPESSON HOUSE 🏠 ❀

The Close, Salisbury SP1 2EL Tel: 01722 335659

One of the finest 18th-century houses in the Cathedral Close, containing notable plasterwork, an elegant oak staircase, fine period furniture, the important Turnbull collection of 18th-century English drinking glasses and a china collection. The attractive walled garden is enclosed on one side by the great wall of the Cathedral Close

O 22 March to 2 Nov: daily except Thur & Fri 12–5.30. Last admission 5

£ £3.20, children £1.60. Parties £2.80. Garden only 80p. Visitor sitting room. Parking in Cathedral Close (a charge is made by the Dean & Chapter). Coach-parking in Central Car Park

🏃 Out of hours tours of house and/or garden, by prior arrangement

🛍 Shop at 41 High Street, Salisbury (tel. 01722 331884)

♿ Access to ground floor, garden and tea-room

◐ Braille guide; scented plants

☕ Teas in Garden Room 12–5

🐕 No dogs permitted

➡ On N side of Choristers' Green in the Cathedral Close, near High Street Gate [184: SU142295] *Bus:* From surrounding areas (tel. 01722 336855); Rickshaw service from ≋ Salisbury to house (tel. 01722 334956) *Station:* Salisbury ½ml

MONTACUTE HOUSE 🏠 ❈ ♣ E

Montacute TA15 6XP Tel: 01935 823289

A magnificent Elizabethan house, with an H-shaped ground plan and many Renaissance features, including contemporary plasterwork, chimneypieces and heraldic glass. The house contains fine 17th- and 18th-century furniture, an exhibition of samplers dating from the 17th century, and Elizabethan and Jacobean portraits from the National Portrait Gallery. The formal garden includes mixed borders and old roses; also, a landscaped park

Note: For conservation reasons some rooms in the house do not have electric light. Visitors wishing to make close study of tapestries, textiles or paintings should avoid visiting on dull days

🅾 **House:** 22 March to 2 Nov: daily except Tues 12–5.30. Last admission 5. **Garden and park:** 22 March to 2 Nov: daily except Tues 11–5.30 or dusk if earlier; 5 Nov to March 1998: Wed to Sun 11.30–4. **Events:** 12/13 July, horse trials; for further details of all events tel. 01985 843601

💷 House, garden & park: £5, children £2.50; family ticket (2 adults & 2 children) £12.50. Pre-booked parties (15 or more) £4.60, children £2.20. Limited parking for coaches which must be booked in advance. Garden and park only, 22 March to 2 Nov: £2.80, children £1.20. No reduction for parties; from 5 Nov to March 1998 £1.50; party organisers please book in writing with s.a.e. to the Property Manager

🛍 Open same days as house 11–5.30; also for Christmas shopping, 5 Nov to 21 Dec: Wed to Sun 11–4; March 1998: Wed to Sun 11–4 (tel. 01935 824575)

♿ Designated parking for disabled drivers. Disabled visitors are very welcome, but access to garden, restaurant & shop only; we regret there is no access to house for wheelchair users (many steps and stairs). WC. 2 wheelchairs available

👁 Braille guides for house, garden and park; Braille restaurant menu. Fragrant plants & shrubs

🍽 Licensed restaurant open as shop; light refreshments only 11–12, lunches & teas (tel. 01935 826294). Christmas menu and pre-booked parties catered for: 5 Nov to 21 Dec: Wed to Sun 11–4; March 1998: Wed to Sun 11–4 (light refreshments only). Limited seating available so party organisers please book lunches & teas in writing to the Property Manager. Picnic area adjacent to car park

👶 Children's guidebook and quiz sheets. Parent & baby room. Children's portions and highchairs available

📖 Teachers' resource book

🐕 In park only, on leads, not allowed in garden. Shaded parking limited

➡ In Montacute village, 4ml W of Yeovil, on S side of A3088, 3ml E of A303 [183 & 193: ST499172] *Bus:* Safeway 681 Yeovil–South Petherton (passing within ¼ml ≠ Yeovil Pen Mill) (tel. 01460 240309) *Station:* Yeovil Pen Mill 5½ml; Yeovil Junction 7ml; Crewkerne 7ml

THE OLD BAKERY, BRANSCOMBE 🏠 ♿ 🚻

Branscombe, Seaton EX12 3DB Tel: 01297 680333

A traditional stone-built and partially rendered building beneath a thatched roof which was, until 1987, the last traditional bakery in use in Devon. The baking room has been preserved and houses traditional baking equipment. The remainder of the building is used as tea-rooms. An information room is in an adjacent outbuilding

O Baking room and licensed tea-rooms: daily Easter to Oct and weekends in winter 11–5

£ Free. Car park adjacent to village hall on opposite side of road, donations in well

♿ WC

🍴 Morning coffee, light lunches and teas

🐕 Admitted to garden and information room only

➔ In the village of Branscombe off A3052 [192: SY198887] *Bus:* Axe Valley 899 Sidmouth–Lyme Regis (connections from 🚆 Axminster or Honiton) (tel. 01392 382800) *Station:* Honiton 8ml

THE OLD MILL 🏠 🚻

Wembury Beach, Wembury PL9 0HP Tel: 01752 862314

Café housed in a former mill house, standing on a small beach near the Yealm estuary

🚶 Regular guided rock pool rambles and other marine-related events are led by the Devon Wildlife Trust wardens from Wembury Marine Centre (open Easter to end Sept), tel. 01752 862538 for details

📷 28 March to end Oct: Beach goods and souvenirs (not NT), peak periods only. Car park beside beach, parking charge to non-members

♿ Access difficult, several stone steps

🍴 28 March to end Sept: daily 10.30–5. Limited opening Mar, Oct, Nov & Dec. Drinks, refreshments, ice cream (not NT)

🐕 Admitted, except to café

➔ At Wembury, nr Plymouth [201: SX517484] *Bus:* Western National 48 from 🚆 Plymouth, thence ½ml (tel. 01752 222666) *Station:* Plymouth 10ml

OVERBECKS MUSEUM AND GARDEN 🏠 ❀ 🚻 🚶 E

Sharpitor, Salcombe TQ8 8LW Tel: 01548 842893

Spectacular views over Salcombe estuary can be enjoyed from the beautiful 2.4ha garden, with its many rare plants, shrubs and trees. The elegant Edwardian house contains collections of local photographs taken at the end of the last century, local ship building tools, model boats, toys, shells, birds, animals and other collections; also a secret room for children with a ghost hunt. Also of interest is an exhibition showing the natural history of Sharpitor and new collection of Otto Overbeck's pencil and wash drawings

O **Museum:** 24 March to 30 June: Sun to Fri 11–5.30; July & Aug: daily 11–5.30, last admission 5; Sept & Oct: Sun to Thur 11–5, last admission 4.30.
Garden: daily throughout year 10–8 or sunset if earlier. WC open same days as museum 11–4.45 due to joint use with YHA. No WC facilities during winter months. **Events:** please tel. for details

£ Museum & garden £3.60; garden only £2.40. No party reduction. Small car park; charge refundable on admission. Roads leading to Overbecks are narrow (single track) and therefore unsuitable for coaches or large vehicles

✗ By arrangement, outside normal opening hours

🛍 Shop open same days as museum 10.45–5.30

♿ Garden is steep with some gravel paths, but largely accessible with a strong companion; details of parking and other facilities available from Administrator. Ground floor, shop and tea-room accessible via ramp into museum. Wheelchair available

👁 Braille guides to museum for adults and children; also Braille ghost hunt certificate!

🍽 Tea-room for snacks and light refreshments same days as museum 12–4.15. Picnics allowed in parts of garden

👶 Secret room with dolls, toys and other collections; quiz guide; ghost hunt for children; baby-changing facilities, single pushchairs admitted to house and garden

📖 Teachers' pack

🐕 No dogs in garden. Estate walks from car park

➜ 1½ml SW of Salcombe, signposted from Malborough and Salcombe [202: SX728374] *Bus:* Tally Ho! 606 from Kingsbridge (with connections from Plymouth, Dartmouth & ≈ Totnes), Western National 164 from Totnes (Sun only); on both alight Salcombe, 1½ml (tel. 01392 382800)

PHILIPPS HOUSE AND DINTON PARK 🏠 🌳 ✗

Dinton, Salisbury SP3 5HJ Tel: 01985 843600

A neo-Grecian house by Jeffry Wyattville, completed in 1816

Note: The house is undergoing a major repair programme during 1997. However, the 48ha park is open at all times of the year; car park off St Mary's Road, next to the church

O **House:** no access due to repairs. When the repairs are complete access will be possible to the principal rooms on the ground floor; tel. 01985 843600 for details

£ Access to the park is free

✗ A series of recommended walks around the park starts from the car park; leaflets are available from the village shop/post office and the NT shop in Salisbury

⬧ Access to the park is limited, but good views of the lake can be obtained from the main access point from the car park

⬧ Braille guide available

⬧ Penruddocke Arms and Swordsman Inn, Dinton (not NT)

→ 9ml W of Salisbury, on N side of B3089 [184: SU004319] *Bus:* Wilts & Dorset 25, 26, 27 from Salisbury (passing ⮂ Salisbury & Tisbury) (tel. 01722 336855) *Station:* Tisbury 5ml

---

PRIEST'S HOUSE 🏠

Muchelney, Langport TA10 0DQ Tel: 01458 252621

A late medieval hall house with large Gothic windows, originally the residence of priests serving the parish church across the road. The house is occupied by tenants and has recently been extensively repaired

🅞 23 March to 29 Sept: Sun & Mon 2.30–5.30; last admission 5.15

£ £1.50. No reductions for parties or children. No WC. Unsuitable for coaches and trailer caravans

→ 1ml S of Langport [193: ST429250] *Bus:* Southern National 54 Yeovil–Taunton (passing close ⮂ Taunton & within ¾ml Yeovil Pen Mill), alight Huish Episcopi, ½ml (tel. 01823 272033)

PRIOR PARK LANDSCAPE GARDEN ✥

Ralph Allen Drive, Bath BA2 5AH Tel: 01225 833422; Recorded information (24hrs): 0891 335242 (45p per min cheap rate, 50p at other times)

Beautiful and intimate 18th-century landscape garden created by Bath entrepreneur Ralph Allen (1693–1764) with advice from the poet Alexander Pope and Lancelot 'Capability' Brown. Sweeping valley with magnificent views of the City of Bath. Palladian Bridge and lakes. Major restoration of the garden continues. Prior Park College, a co-educational school, operates from the mansion (not NT)

Note: Planning permission to open the property was granted until Sept 1998 only; renewal is likely to be conditional on the success of the 'green transport' scheme, as no car park can be provided. See details below

🅞 Daily, except Tues 12–5.30 (or dusk if earlier). Closed 25 & 26 Dec & 1 Jan 1998

£ £3.80, children £1.90. To thank visitors for using public transport, all those who produce a valid bus or train ticket will receive £1 off admission; NT members will receive a £1 voucher (to be used towards the cost of a guidebook, cream tea or a purchase of £1 or more at the NT shops in either Bath centre or Dyrham Park). There is a bus and coach drop-off point outside the gates to the garden. Coach parties should book in advance on tel. 01225 833422; every passenger qualifies for a discount

🗍 In Abbey Churchyard, Bath (tel. 01225 460249)

⬧ There are three parking bays for disabled drivers. It is essential to reserve these in advance on tel. 01225 833422. The garden is extremely steep in places, but offers good views from the top, which is easily accessible

⬧ Braille guide

⬧ No dogs allowed due to grazing cattle

→ All visitors must use public transport as there is no parking at Prior Park or nearby. To obtain a leaflet explaining how to reach the garden, tel. 01225 833422 *Bus:* Badgerline 2, 4, 733 ⬧ Bath–Combe Down (tel. 01225 464446). As Bath is very congested, use Park & Ride to centre *Station:* Bath Spa 1ml

---

ST MICHAEL'S MOUNT ⬧ ⬧ ✝ ⬧ ⬧

Marazion, nr Penzance TR17 0EF Tel: 01736 710507 Fax: 01736 711544

Originally the site of a Benedictine chapel, the spectacular castle on top of this famous rocky island dates from the 12th century. Approached by a causeway at low tide, the castle has magnificent views towards Land's End and The Lizard, fascinating early rooms, an armoury, a rococo Gothic drawing room and, at the highest point, a 14th-century church

Note: Owing to narrow passages within the castle, visitors are warned that some delays may occur at the height of the season. On Sun from June to Sept a short non-denominational service is held in the Castle Chapel at 11; seating is limited

⬧ 28 March to 31 Oct: Mon to Fri 10.30–5.30. Last admission 4.45. Nov to end March: It is essential to telephone the property before setting out, in order to ascertain the opening arrangements for that day. The times stated above apply from the visitors' entrance on the island; therefore ample time should be allowed for travel from the mainland. *Note*: The Mount is also open most weekends during the season; these are special charity open days, when NT members are asked to pay for admission

£ £3.90; family ticket £10. Pre-arranged parties £3.50 per person

⬧ Audio tour available. Introductory video in cinema

⬧ Shop open 28 March to 31 Oct daily (tel. 01736 711067)

⬧ The causeway and paths are cobbled, and therefore unsuitable for wheelchairs, prams and pushchairs

⬧ Braille and taped guides

⬧ Island café (not NT), open daily 28 March to end Oct. Coffee, lunches and teas in The Sail Loft restaurant, 28 March to 31 Oct: daily; limited out of season service (tel. 01736 710748)

🔳 Special educational visits for schools and organisations on Tues from March to end May, weather permitting, by prior arrangement with The Manor Office, Marazion (tel. 01736 710507). Schools' resource pack available

🐕 No dogs allowed

➡️ ½ml S of A394 at Marazion, whence there is access on foot over the causeway at low tide or, during summer months only, by ferry at high tide (return ferry tickets should not be taken) [203: SW515298]. Tide and ferry information only: tel. 01736 710265 *Bus:* Western National 2, 2X Penzance–Falmouth; 17/A Penzance–St Ives. All pass ⇌ Penzance. (tel. 01209 719988) *Station:* Penzance 3ml

---

SALTRAM 🏠 🏠 ✝ ✤ ♠ 🧍 E

Plympton, Plymouth PL7 3UH Tel: 01752 336546

Said to be the most impressive house in Devon, this is a remarkable survival of a George II mansion complete with its original contents, set in an attractive landscape park. Robert Adam worked here on two occasions to create magnificent state rooms. There is exquisite plasterwork throughout and several rooms are decorated with original Chinese wallpaper. The house contains fine period furniture, china and pictures, including many portraits by Reynolds and Angelica Kauffmann. There is an interesting orangery and the superb 18th-century gardens contain a chapel and several follies as well as beautiful shrubberies and imposing specimen trees. The 202ha park was laid out by Richmond, a follower of 'Capability' Brown

🅾️ **House:** 28 March to 2 Nov: Sun to Thur 12.30–5.30, closed Fri & Sat (but open Good Fri). **Garden:** 2–23 March: Sat & Sun only 11–4; from 28 March as house but from 10.30. **Art gallery & Great Kitchen:** open as house but from 10.30. Last admission 5. Timed tickets may be issued at busy times. **Events:** full programme, including traditional candlelight concerts in Adam Saloon, Nov & Dec (tel. 01752 336546 to join mailing list)

£ £5.30; garden only £2.50. Parking 500m, £1

🏃 Walks with the Warden throughout the year. Tel. 01752 336546 for programme

🛍️ Shop in stable block. Open same days as house 10.30–5.30; 3 Nov to 21 Dec: daily except Fri 11–5; Jan 1998: daily except Fri 11–4; Feb & March 1998: Sat & Sun 11–4 (tel. 01752 330034). Work by West Country artists on sale in chapel gallery; open same days as house

♿ House, ground floor of art gallery, and garden accessible; disabled visitors may be set down at front door by prior arrangement; lift (66cm wide by 86.5cm deep) to first floor. Information from ticket office in stable block. Wheelchairs at house and also at ticket office for use in garden. WC on ground floor

👁️ Scented plants; Braille and audio guides

🍽️ Licensed restaurant open same days as house 12–5.30, last admission 5 (entrance from garden at garden admission price); also for pre-booked Christmas lunches (tel. 01752 340635). Coach house tea-room in stable block near car park, open same days as house 10.30–5. Nov to end March 1998: Sat & Sun 11–4

👶 Pushchairs, children's guide, baby-changing facilities available on request from entrance hall. Highchairs, children's menu and baby foods available in restaurant

⬛ Education room available; advance bookings essential. For details contact Property Manager (tel. 01752 336546)

🐕 In park only. Dogs must be on leads in areas being grazed by cattle. Shaded 'dog park' near stable block entrance

➡ 3½ml E of Plymouth city centre, between Plymouth–Exeter road (A38) and Plymouth–Kingsbridge road (A379); take Plympton turn at Marsh Mills roundabout [201: SX520557] *Bus:* Plymouth Citybus 19/A, 20/A, 21, 22, 51 from Plymouth, alight Plymouth Road–Plympton Bypass Jn, ¾ml footpath (tel. 01752 222221) *Station:* Plymouth 3½ml

---

SELWORTHY VILLAGE ⬛ ✝ 🧍

Tel: (Holnicote Estate Office) 01643 862452

Situated below Selworthy Woods in the heart of the Trust's beautiful Holnicote Estate (5042ha), seven thatched cottages with cream cob walls are grouped around a traditional village green and overlooked by its white-painted church

Note: The church is not NT

🅾 At any reasonable time throughout the year. Parking available 100m past the village

🛍 Shop & information centre located on the green, open 1 to 30 March daily 10.30–3.30; 31 March to 2 Nov: daily 10–5; Nov: weekends only 10.30–3.30. Closed for lunch 1–1.30. Spring and autumn opening reduced in bad weather

☕ Tea-room (not NT) on the green. Closed Mon

➡ Off A39 Minehead–Porlock, 3ml W of Minehead *Bus:* Southern National 38, 300 Minehead–Porlock, alight Holnicote, thence ½ml (tel. 01823 272033) *Station:* Minehead (West Somerset Rly) 5ml

---

SHUTE BARTON 🏰 ⬛ 🏃

Shute, nr Axminster EX13 7PT Tel: 01297 34692

One of the most important surviving non-fortified manor houses of the Middle Ages. Commenced in 1380 and completed in the late 16th century, then partly demolished in the late 18th century, the house has battlemented turrets, late Gothic windows and a Tudor gatehouse

🅾 The house is tenanted; there is access to most parts of the interior for conducted tours only: 2 April to 29 Oct: Wed & Sat 2–5.30. Last admission 5

💷 £1.60. No party reduction; unsuitable for coaches or large groups. No WC

➡ 3ml SW of Axminster, 2ml N of Colyton on Honiton–Colyton road (B3161) [177/193: SY253974] *Bus:* Red Bus 380 Axminster–Honiton (passes close ≈ Axminster and Honiton), alight Shute Cross, ¾ml; Axe Valley 885/Red Bus 378 ≈ Axminster–Seaton, alight Whitford, thence 1½ml (tel. 01392 382800) *Station:* Axminster, 3ml

STEMBRIDGE TOWER MILL ✖

High Ham TA10 9DJ Tel: 01458 250818

The last thatched windmill in England, dating from 1822 and in use until 1910

🅾 30 March to 29 Sept: Sun, Mon & Wed 2–5; special arrangements may be made for coach and school parties

£ £1.60, children 80p. Parties by prior appointment with the tenant; no reduction. Parking for coaches ¼ml. No WC

🐕 No dogs allowed

➔ 2ml N of Langport, ½ml E of High Ham [182: ST432305]; take the Somerton road from Langport and follow High Ham signs. Take road opposite cemetery in High Ham. Mill is ¼ml along on right *Bus:* Southern National 54 Yeovil–Taunton (passing close ≋ Taunton & within ¾ml Yeovil Pen Mill), alight Langport, 2½ml (tel. 01823 272033) *Station:* Bridgwater 10ml

STOKE-SUB-HAMDON PRIORY 🏛

North Street, Stoke-sub-Hamdon TA4 6QP Tel: (Regional Office) 01985 843600

A complex of buildings, begun in the 14th century for the priests of the chantry chapel of St Nicholas, which is now destroyed

🅾 31 March to 2 Nov: daily 10–6 or dusk if earlier. Great Hall only open

£ Free

🐕 No dogs allowed

➔ Between A303 and A3088. 2ml W of Montacute between Yeovil and Ilminster *Bus:* Safeway 681 Yeovil–South Petherton (passing within ¾ml ≋ Yeovil Pen Mill) (tel. 01460 240309) *Station:* Crewkerne or Yeovil Pen Mill, both 7ml

STONEHENGE DOWN ⛴ 🏛 🚶

Amesbury, nr Salisbury SP4 7DE Tel: (English Heritage) 01980 623108

The Trust owns 587ha of land surrounding the monument, including some fine Bronze Age barrow groups and the Cursus. There are recommended walks and an archaeological leaflet, available at Stonehenge shop, from the leaflet dispenser in the car park, and at the NT shop in Salisbury

Note: The monument itself is owned and administered by English Heritage

🅾 Monument opening details are obtainable from English Heritage at the address and tel. no. above. NT members free. NT land open at all times, but may be subject to closure at the Summer Solstice (21 June) for up to 2 days

🛍 Shop run by EH adjacent to the monument

♿ Wheelchair access to the monument but not to land. WC

🔈 Taped guide available for monument only; also refers to the landscape

🔦 Refreshments available adjacent to the monument (not NT)

🐿 No dogs on archaeological walks

→ Monument 2ml W of Amesbury, at junction of A303 & A344/A360 [184: SU1242] *Bus:* Wilts & Dorset 3 ⚭ Salisbury–Stonehenge (tel. 01722 336855) *Station:* Salisbury 9½ml

---

STOURHEAD 🏠 ❈ ♠ E

The Estate Office, Stourton, Warminster BA12 6QD Tel: 01747 841152
Recorded information: 0891 335205 (45p per min cheap rate, 50p at other times)

The landscape garden, an outstanding example of the English landscape style, was laid out between 1741 and 1780. Classical temples, set amongst rare and mature trees and shrubs, surround the lake. The house, begun in 1721 by Colen Campbell, contains furniture by the younger Chippendale, and fine paintings. King Alfred's Tower, an intriguing red-brick folly built in 1772 by Flitcroft on the edge of the 1052ha estate, is almost 50m high, giving magnificent views across the three counties of Somerset, Dorset and Wiltshire

◎ **Garden**: all year daily 9–7 or sunset if earlier (except 24–26 July when garden will close at 5; last admission 4). **House**: 22 March to 2 Nov: Sat to Wed 12–5.30 or dusk if earlier; last admission 30min before closing (tel. 01747 840348). **King Alfred's Tower**: 22 March to 2 Nov: Tues, Wed & Thur 2–5.30; Sat & Sun 11.30–5.30 or dusk if earlier. Closed Fri & Mon, except Good Fri and BH Mon (tel. 01985 844785). **Events**: 24 to 26 July Fête Champêtre; midsummer event, open-air Shakespeare and other events, tel. 0891 335203. Regional Box Office 01985 843601/2 or Stourhead Box Office 01747 841142

£ Garden: March to Oct: £4.30, children £2.30; family ticket £10, pre-booked parties (15 or more) by written appointment £3.70; Nov to end Feb: £3.30, children £1.50; family ticket £8, no reduction for parties. House £4.30, children £2.30; family ticket £10, pre-booked parties £3.70. Combined Garden & House ticket: £7.70, children £3.60; family ticket, £20, parties £7.40. King Alfred's Tower: £1.50, children 70p

🔑 Exhibition about Stourhead Estate in reception building in the main car park

🛒 Open daily 1 April to 2 Nov 11–6; 3 Nov to end March 1998 11–4 (tel. 01747 840591). Plant centre open daily 1 to 22 March 12–4; 23 March to 28 Sept 12–6 (tel. 01747 840894)

[♿] Wheelchairs and parking at house and garden for disabled drivers. WC available at main car park and in Spread Eagle courtyard. Garden: 1½ml path around lake accessible to wheelchair users, but steep in places and more than one strong companion essential. Wheelchairs & battery-powered self-drive buggy. House: 13 steps up to house accessible by stairclimber, all showrooms on one level accessible by wheelchair. Sympathetic Hearing Scheme. House congested at weekends and in May & June. Shop and refreshments in Spread Eagle courtyard accessible; plant centre off main car park accessible. King Alfred's Tower: level walk across grass and along 1½ml terrace walk to house

[👁] Braille short house guide; items to touch. Braille garden guide; scented azaleas in early summer

[🍴] Spread Eagle Inn (NT) situated close to garden entrance, the only village inn owned and managed by NT, providing en-suite accommodation and home-cooked food to guests and visitors. Open all year with log fires in winter. Weekend and mid-week breaks available 1 Nov to end Feb. Breakfast 8–9.30, lunch 12–2, dinner 7–9. Special party bookings and seminar group bookings welcome (tel. 01747 840587). Village Hall self-service tea-toom serving coffee, light lunches, teas and ice creams, open daily 22 March to 2 Nov 10.30–5.30 (tel. 01747 840161). Picnicking near car parks and in garden

[👶] Parent & baby room next to reception building in main car park

[📷] Special events and projects can be organised by contacting the Estate Office. History of Tower by arrangement

[🐕] Dogs are allowed in the garden on lead, Nov to end Feb; in woods throughout year. Please keep your dog on a lead whenever near to farming stock; King Alfred's Tower: dogs may be tied up outside but are not allowed in the Tower

[→] At Stourton, off B3092, 3m NW of Mere (A303) [183:ST7834]. Parking 300m from house, garden and catering facilities. King Alfred's Tower: 3½ml by road from Stourhead House; parking 350m *Bus:* Wilts & Dorset 26, Wakes 125 Salisbury–Stourhead (Wed & Fri only); otherwise Southern National 59 from [🚉] Gillingham–Yeovil, some to garden, but on others alight Zeals, 1¼ml (tel. 0345 090899) *Station:* Gillingham 6½ml; Bruton (U) 7ml

---

STUDLAND BEACH & NATURE RESERVE [🏖][🏞][🐕][🚻]

Countryside Office, Studland, Swanage BH19 3AX Tel: 01929 450259

Three miles of fine sandy beaches backed by the Studland Heath National Nature Reserve, extending from South Haven Point to the chalk cliffs of Handfast Point and Old Harry Rocks

[🕐] All year. **Car parks:** Shell Bay: all year; The Knoll & Middle Beach: 9–8 summer months only (reduced parking area in winter); South Beach: 9–11pm

[£] Car parks (Shell Bay, The Knoll, Middle Beach and South Beach): April & Sept £2, £1 after 2; May & June £2.60, £2.10 after 2; July & Aug £3.50, £2.50 after 2. Rest of year donations only. NT members free. Coaches £9. Motorcycles £1. Boat launching: powered craft £14 per day, catamarans £9. Others, incl. sail boards, £4.50 per day (incl. NT members). WCs at Knoll & Middle Beach. Bicycle racks are sited at all car parks

🚹 Guided tours of nature reserve given by NT wardens and English Nature wardens. Information from the countryside office (tel. 01929 450259)

🛍 Knoll visitor centre: shop open daily 1 March to 30 June 11–4; 1 July to 7 Sept 10–5; 8 Sept to Feb 1998 11–4, weather permitting. Longer opening in fine weather (tel. 01929 450500)

♿ Knoll car park has good access. In summer, boardwalks for wheelchairs along part of Knoll beach and to visitor facilities. RADAR WC at Knoll Beach; RADAR WC at Middle Beach car park

☕ NT beach café at Knoll Beach open same days and times as Knoll visitor centre shop (tel. 01929 420305). Concessionary cafés at Middle Beach and Shell Bay

🚼 Baby-changing facilities in WC at Knoll visitor centre

ℹ Information in Knoll visitor centre and old coastguard hut at Middle Beach

🐕 Must be kept on leads May to end Sept and not allowed to foul the beach. 'Poop Scoops' are available for sale at the visitor centre and most car park kiosks

➡ [195: SZ036835] *Bus:* Wilts & Dorset 150 Bournemouth–Swanage (passing ⇌ Branksome) to Shell Bay and Studland; 152 Poole–Sandbanks (passing close ⇌ Parkstone) (tel. 01202 673555); Yellow Buses 12 Christchurch–Sandbanks, summer only (tel. 01202 557272). Vehicle ferry from Sandbanks to Shell Bay *Station:* Branksome or Parkstone, both 3½ml to Shell Bay or 6ml to Studland via vehicle ferry

TINTAGEL OLD POST OFFICE 🏠

Tintagel PL34 0DB Tel: 01840 770024 (opening hours only)

Small and fascinating 14th-century stone house built to the plan of a medieval manor house, with a large hall. It was used in the 19th century for nearly fifty years as the letter-receiving office for the district and is now restored to that period and function

🅾 28 March to 2 Nov: daily 11–5.30 (closes 5 in Oct)

💷 £2. Pre-arranged party rate £1.50

🛍 Shop open as property

♿ Unsuitable for disabled visitors

📖 Braille guide

➡ In centre of village [200: SX056884] *Bus:* Western National 122/4/5, X4 Wadebridge–Bude (with some from ⇌ Bodmin Parkway) (tel. 01209 719988); Fry's service from Plymouth (tel. 01840 770256)

TINTINHULL HOUSE GARDEN ❀

Farm St, Tintinhull, Yeovil BA22 9PZ Tel: 01935 822545

A 20th-century formal garden surrounding a 17th-century house. The garden layout, divided into areas by walls and hedges, has border colour and plant themes, including shrub roses and clematis; there is also a kitchen garden

📅 22 March to 28 Sept: Wed, Thur, Fri, Sat, Sun & BH Mon 12–6

💷 £3.50; children £1.70. No reduction for parties. Coach parties by arrangement in advance with the Gardener

🚶 In advance with the Gardener

♿ Parking in courtyard by arrangement; some access for wheelchair users but cobbles, uneven paths and steps make progress difficult

🌹 Roses, honeysuckles and other scented plants

🍵 Tea-room in stable block; open same times as property. Light refreshments and teas 12–5.30

🐕 No dogs in courtyard or garden

➔ 5ml NW of Yeovil, ½ml S of A303, on E outskirts of Tintinhull [183: ST503198] *Bus:* Southern National 52 Yeovil–Martock (passing within ¾ml ≋ Yeovil Pen Mill) (tel. 01935 76233) *Station:* Yeovil Pen Mill 5½ml; Yeovil Junction 7ml

---

TREASURER'S HOUSE 🏠

Martock TA12 6JL Tel: (Regional Office) 01985 843600

A small house dating from the 13th and 14th centuries and recently refurbished by the Trust. Medieval hall, wallpainting and kitchen

📅 30 March to 30 Sept: Sun, Mon & Tues 2.30–5.30. Parking is limited and unsuitable for coaches and trailer caravans

💷 Medieval hall, wallpainting and kitchen £1.50. No reduction for children or parties. No WC

🏪 In Martock (not NT)

➔ Opposite church in middle of village; 1ml NW of A303 between Ilminster and Ilchester [193: ST462191] *Bus:* Southern National 52 Yeovil–Martock (passing within ¾ml ≋ Yeovil Pen Mill) (tel. 01935 76233) *Station:* Crewkerne 7½ml; Yeovil Pen Mill 8ml

---

TRELISSICK GARDEN 🌼 🍴 🐕 🖼 🚶 E

Feock, nr Truro TR3 6QL Tel: 01872 862090 Fax: 01872 865808

A superb collection of tender and exotic plants bring colour to this tranquil garden at all times. There are extensive park and woodland walks beside the river, with panoramic views across the estuary to Falmouth. The house is not open, but there is an art and craft gallery, shop, two restaurants and fine Georgian stable block.

📅 Garden open 1 March to 2 Nov: Mon to Sat 10.30–5.30, Sun 12.30–5.30 (5 in March & Oct). The woodland walks are open throughout the year. **Events:** programme of theatrical and musical events; details from the Property Manager (tel. 01872 862090)

£ £4; family ticket £10. Pre-arranged parties £3.20 per person. £1 car park fee refundable on admission

🛍 Shop and plant sales, open daily 1 March to 2 Nov (tel. 01872 865515). Art and craft gallery open as shop (tel. 01872 864084). Shop and gallery also open daily 3 Nov to Christmas

♿ Upper parts of garden reasonably flat with loose gravel paths; parking near shop & restaurant, both accessible; powered self-drive buggy. Access to ground floor of gallery. WC near shop & car park

👁 Small walled garden with aromatic plants, near entrance. Braille guide.

🍽 Coffee, lunches and teas in Trelissick Barn. Light refreshments in the Courtyard Room, 1 March to 2 Nov: Mon to Sat 10.30–5.30, Sun 12–5.30 (closes at 5 in Mar & Oct); additional limited daily opening in Nov & Dec (tel. 01872 863486)

🎒 Schools' resource pack

🐕 In woodland walks and park only

➔ 4ml S of Truro, on both sides of B3289 above King Harry Ferry [204: SW837396] *Bus:* Truronian 311 from Truro (tel. 01872 73453); Western National 51B Truro–St Mawes via King Harry Ferry, Sun only (tel. 01209 719988). Both pass close ☒ Truro *Station:* Truro 5ml; Perranwell (U), not Sun, except July & Aug, 4ml

---

TRENGWAINTON GARDEN 🏵

nr Penzance TR20 8RZ
Tel: 01736 63021/68410 (during opening hours) Fax: 01736 68142

Perhaps the garden on mainland Britain most favoured for the cultivation of exotic trees and shrubs, this is a beautiful place throughout the year and a plantsman's delight. The walled garden has many tender plants which cannot be grown in the open anywhere else in the country

🕐 1 March to 1 Nov: Wed to Sat, BH Mon & Good Fri 10.30–5.30 (closes 5 in March & Oct). Last admission 30min before closing

£ £3. No reduction for parties

🛍 Shop and plant sales in new reception lodge

♿ Close parking on request. Jubilee Garden and Lower Stream area best for wheelchair users. Flat firm gravelled viewpoint around house. One wheelchair and one powered self-drive buggy available; please pre-book. Some access to walled garden. Shop and plant sales accessible. Accessible refreshments in farmhouse garden (not NT). WC

👁 Fragrant plants, stream, pools, water sounds; Braille guide

🍽 Light refreshments available in the farmhouse garden (not NT), weather permitting

🐕 Dogs allowed on leads

➡️ 2ml NW of Penzance, ½ml W of Heamoor on Penzance–Morvah road (B3312), ½ml off St Just road (A3071) [203: SW445315] *Bus:* Western National 10/A Penzance–St Just (tel. 01209 719988) *Station:* Penzance 2ml

TRERICE 🏠 ✤ Ⓔ

nr Newquay TR8 4PG Tel: 01637 875404 Fax: 01673 879300

A delightful, small, secluded Elizabethan manor house, built in 1571 with an early gabled façade, containing fine fireplaces, good plaster ceilings, oak and walnut furniture and clocks. A small museum in the barn traces the development of the lawn mower. The summer garden has some unusual plants and there is also an orchard of old varieties of fruit trees

🅾️ 28 March to 2 Nov: daily except Tues & Sat (but open daily 28 July to 7 Sept), 11–5.30 (closes 5 in Oct). Last admission 30min before closing. **Events:** programme available from the Property Manager (s.a.e. please)

💷 £3.80. Family ticket £9.50. Pre-arranged parties £3.20

🛍️ Shop and plant sales open as house

♿ Ground & upper (via grass slope) floors of house, tea-room & shop accessible; some loose gravel and cobbles. Garden more difficult. Close parking by prior arrangement with Property Manager. WC. *Note:* Winner of British Gas ADAPT award for Historic Houses, 1992

👁️ Braille guide and taped tour available. Access leaflet for disabled visitors

☕ Coffee, lunches and teas in the Barn. Organisers of parties should arrange for meals beforehand (tel. 01637 875404)

🚼 Parent & baby room

🏫 Schools may visit the house from 10 by prior arrangement with the Property Manager. School hut available. Schools are welcome to picnic in the orchard

🐕 Dogs in car park only

➡️ 3ml SE of Newquay via A392 and A3058 (turn right at Kestle Mill) [200: SW841585] *Bus:* Western National 50 from Newquay (June to Sept); otherwise 90 Newquay–Truro, alight Kestle Mill, ¾ml (tel. 01209 719988) *Station:* Quintrell Downs (U), not Sun, except July to Sept, 1½ml

WATERSMEET HOUSE 🏠 ♿ 🎣 🚶

Watersmeet Road, Lynmouth EX35 6NT Tel: 01598 753348

A fishing lodge c.1832 in a picturesque valley at the confluence of the East Lyn and Hoar Oak Water, used for information, recruiting, refreshments and an NT shop. The site has been a tea-garden since 1901 and is the focal point for several beautiful walks (steep in places)

🅾️ 27 March to 30 Sept: daily 10.30–5.30; Oct: daily 10.30–4.30

💷 Free. Pay-and-display car park, or free car parks at Combepark Wood, Hillsford Bridge and Countisbury

🚶 See local listings for programme of guided walks on Watersmeet Estate. Walks leaflet available from shop

📷 27 March to 30 Sept: daily 10.30–5.30; Oct: daily 10.30–4.30

♿ Limited access arrangements for disabled visitors strictly by appointment with Catering Manager (tel. 01598 753348)

🍴 Morning coffee, lunches and cream teas in tea-garden beside the river; 27 March to end Sept: daily 10.30–5.30; Oct: 10.30–4.30. Party catering by arrangement

🚼 Baby-changing facilities in both men's and women's WCs

📷 By arrangement with the Warden (tel. 01598 753580)

🐕 Admitted, but not to restaurant or shop

➡️ 1½ml E of Lynmouth, in valley on E side of Lynmouth–Barnstaple road (A39) [180: SS744487] *Bus:* Red Bus 310 Barnstaple–Lynmouth (passing close ⇌ Barnstaple), 300 Minehead–Ilfracombe. On both, alight Lynmouth, thence walk through NT Gorge (tel. 01392 382800)

WEST PENNARD COURT BARN 🏛️

West Pennard, nr Glastonbury BA6 8NL Tel: (Regional Office) 01985 843600

A 15th-century barn of five bays with a roof of interesting construction. Repaired and given by the Society for the Protection of Ancient Buildings in 1938

🔑 Visitors to collect key from Mr P. H. Green, Court Barn Farm, West Bradley, Somerset; prior telephone arrangement is welcomed (tel. 01458 850212)

💷 Free

➡️ 3ml E of Glastonbury, 7ml S of Wells, 1½ml S of West Pennard (A361) [182/183: ST547370] *Bus:* Badgerline 160 Wells–Street, to within 1ml (tel. 01934 621201) *Station:* Castle Cary 8ml

WESTBURY COLLEGE GATEHOUSE 🏛️

College Road, Westbury-on-Trym, Bristol Tel: (Regional Office) 01985 843600

The 15th-century gatehouse of the College of Priests (founded in the 13th century) of which John Wyclif was a prebend

🔑 Access by key only, to be collected by prior written or tel. 0117 962 1536 arrangement with the Rev. G. M. Collins, The Vicarage, 44 Eastfield Road, Westbury-on-Trym, Bristol BS9 4AG

💷 £1, children 50p

➡️ 3ml N of the centre of Bristol [172: ST572775] *Bus:* Frequent from surrounding areas except Sun (U) (tel. 0117 955 3231) *Station:* Clifton Down 2ml

WESTWOOD MANOR 🏠 ✤

Bradford-on-Avon BA15 2AF Tel: 01225 863374

A 15th-century stone manor house, altered in the late 16th century, with late Gothic and Jacobean windows and Jacobean plasterwork. There is a modern topiary garden

Note: Westwood Manor is administered for the National Trust by the tenant

O 1 April to 1 Oct: Sun, Tues & Wed 2–5. At other times parties of up to 20 by written application with s.a.e. to the tenant

£ £3.30. No reduction for parties or children. No WC

♿ No wheelchair access

➡ 1½ml SW of Bradford-on-Avon, in Westwood village, beside the church; village signposted off Bradford-on-Avon to Rode road (B3109) [173: ST812590]
Bus: Trowbridge Taxibus 97 from Trowbridge (passes close ≥ Trowbridge); otherwise from surrounding areas to Bradford-on-Avon, thence 1½ml (tel. 0345 090899) *Station:* Avoncliff (U), 1ml; Bradford-on-Avon 1½ml

WHITE MILL ✕ 𝕏

Sturminster Marshall, nr Wimborne BH21 4BX Tel: 01258 858051

Rebuilt in 1776 on Domesday site this corn mill was extensively repaired in 1994 and contains much of the rare original 18th-century timber machinery (now too fragile to be operative). Peaceful setting by River Stour. Riverside picnic area nearby

O 22 March to 2 Nov: weekends & BHols 12–5. Pre-booked parties welcome at other times (subject to additional charge) (tel. 01202 882493)

£ £1.50, children £1. Parties by arrangement

𝕏 The mill is shown by guided tour and numbers within the building must be restricted for safety reasons. No WC

♿ Limited parking in front of mill. Access around the mill is via narrow steps, but wheelchair access is available to most of the ground floor via ramps. A viewing platform and internal mirrors enable visitors to view much of the remainder of the mill

👁 Handling collection, audio guide. Braille and large-print guide available

🐕 No dogs in mill, but access to Stour Valley Way from White Mill (south) to Wimborne

➡ On the River Stour north of Sturminster Marshall. From B3082 Blandford to Wimborne road take right-hand turn signposted Sturminster Marshall. Mill is 1ml on right. Car park nearby *Bus:* Wilts & Dorset 129, X13 Poole–Blandford (passes close ≥ Poole); 139, X13 Bournemouth–Shaftesbury (passes ≥ Bournemouth), alight Sturminster Marshall, 1½ml (tel. 01202 673555) *Station:* Hamworthy 7ml; Poole 8½ml

Wales

WALES

Mae'r wybodaeth sydd yn y llawlyfr hwn am feddiannau'r Ymddiriedolaeth Genedlaethol yng Nghymru ar gael yn Gymraeg o Swyddfa Rhanbarth Gogledd Cymru, Sgwâr y Drindod, Llandudno, LL30 2DE. Ffôn 01492 860123 neu Swyddfa Rhanbarth De Cymru, Pen y Brenin, Heol y Bont, Llandeilo, SA19 6BN. Ffôn 01558 822800.

COASTLINE

The Trust owns 132ml of Wales's spectacular coastline, and it is fascinating to remember that the first property ever given to the Trust in 1895 was Dinas Oleu [124: SH615158], 2ha on the headland above Barmouth in North Wales. Since then the Trust has added many miles to its coastal properties in Wales, from the rugged cliffs in Llŷn and Pembroke to the tranquil bays of Gower.

The lovely and varied scenery of the Gower Peninsula, the first area to be designated an Area of Outstanding Natural Beauty, lies just west of the coastal city of Swansea. It is renowned for its wildlife, sandy beaches and magnificent coast – yet much of it is remote, wild and unpopulated save for vast colonies of seabirds and waders. The Trust owns about 2227ha in Gower, ranging from saltmarsh at **Llanrhidian** on the north coast [159: SS490932] to the limestone cliffs between **Port Eynon** [159: SS468845] and **Rhossili** (see p.313), with prehistoric caves and a medieval dovecote known as the Culver Hole; the lovely wooded valley at Bishopston; and the elongated rocky headland of **Worms Head** [159: SS383878] at the extreme westernmost point of the peninsula, which is a national nature reserve leased to the Countryside Council for Wales.

The 186ml long Pembrokeshire Coast Path begins at Amroth on Carmarthen Bay and ends at St Dogmaels, a village on the outskirts of Cardigan. It traverses Trust property for much of its length, beginning with the 397ha **Colby Estate** at Amroth, giving views of Somerset, Caldy and Gower. The Trust owns the fine section of coastal slope and undercliff between Amroth and Wisemans Bridge. Once part of a coal mining area, it is rich in bird and insect life. This forms part of the Colby Estate, offering miles of footpaths through deciduous woodland. The Woodland Garden (see p.303) lies at the heart of the estate. 1½ml east of Manorbier is **Lydstep Headland** [158: SS090976], accessible by footpath from Lydstep village NT shop in Pembroke.

The 810ha **Stackpole Estate**, 6ml south of Pembroke [158: SR977693], includes freshwater lakes at Bosherston, thick with waterlilies in summer; woods, 8ml of cliffs, two beaches, farmland and sand dunes. From the tiny and beautiful Stackpole Quay, where the Trust has several holiday cottages and a tea-room, you can walk over the headland to Barafundle Bay, where there is a wide sweep of pale golden sand and good bathing. The tea-room, serving light refreshments, is situated by the Quay and has accessible indoor and outdoor seating; for opening times tel. 01646 672058. A recreation area near the Quay has been developed for able-bodied and disabled people (tel. 01646 661359, or the Warden on 01646 672169). A small exhibition in the former Game Larder tells the story of Stackpole Court, the mansion overlooking the lake which was demolished in 1963. There are car parks at Stackpole Quay and Broadhaven – the second of the bathing beaches. About 1ml from Broadhaven is St Govan's Chapel (not NT), a tiny 13th-century building clinging to a crevice halfway down three steep cliffs, and reached by a long flight of extremely uneven stone steps. The Ministry of Defence controls access and closes the road at certain times when the nearby firing ranges are in use. At Freshwater West, the Trust owns a farm and a large part of **Kilpaison Burrows**, one of the finest sand dune systems in Pembrokeshire; and **Castlemartin Corse**, an important wetland.

On the northern side of Milford Haven at **Kete**, west of Dale, the Trust owns 68ha, giving views of Skomer and Skokholm Islands [157: SM800045]. From here is a good walk to the cliffs of St Anne's Head. Free car park.

The Trust owns about about 15½ml of the coastline of **St Bride's Bay**, including the **Deer Park** at Marloes, which is separated from the adjacent headland by a high stone wall built at the beginning of the 19th century, although deer were never introduced. It provides a suitable feeding habitat for chough. There are marvellous views of Skomer and Skokholm to the south [157: SM78091]. Car park, information panel and WC at Martin's Haven.

Nearby at **Marloes Sands** [157: SM7707], a 2½ml walk can be followed along the Pembrokeshire Coast Path. It takes in the sandstone cliffs, an Iron Age fort and Marloes Mere; ravens, choughs and grey seals may be seen; the mere is an exciting place to watch birds. Leaflet from DWT, 7 Market Street, Haverfordwest, Dyfed SA61 1NF (45p by post). Access to the mere is by permit only from DWT.

In the **St David's** area [145: SM740278] the Trust owns land extending from west of Newgale Beach to St David's Head [145: SM721278], incorporating 530ha of unspoilt coastline with four farms, and 870ha of commons, all within the Pembrokshire Coast National Park. The landscape is one of rocky outcrops, coastal plateau and spectacular coastline, important for geology and natural history. The views are extensive and beautiful along the coast to Marloes, west to Ramsey Island and north towards Strumble Head. NT shop at **Solva** (seasonal); visitor centre with shop at St David's (also seasonal).

Further acquisitions have added to the Trust's ownership on the North Pembrokeshire coastline. 81ha of coastal farmland at **Ynys Barri**, Llanrhian [151/157: SM805328] includes 2ml of coastland between Porthgain Harbour and Abereiddy. Near Abercastle, **Long House Farm** [157: SM853337] comprises 61ha of farmland with 2½ml of scenic rugged coastline. Two small islands are included with the land: Ynys-y-Castell and Ynys Deullyn. There is an Iron Age promontory fort on the property. **Dinas Island Farm** [157: SM0140] lies 5ml east of Fishguard and 18ml west of Cardigan; 168ha of farmland with 2½ml of coastline lying within the Pembrokeshire Coast National Park. Just to the east of Strumble Head, 3ml north-west of Fishguard on the Pembrokeshire coast, is 39ha of rugged coastal outcrop and largely unimproved pasture, known as **Good Hope** [157: SM912407]. 2.5ha are owned at **Ceibwr Bay**, Moylegrove [139(168): 109485]. **Abermawr** [157: SN891347] is 10ml from St Davids and a little to the south of Strumble Head; 109ha, comprising a shingle beach backed by a freshwater marsh lying in a wooded valley and forming about ½ml of coast. At **Gernos**, St Dogmaels, Cardigan [145: SM1340], the Trust protects a further 2ml of the North Pembrokeshire coast; 43ha to the west of Cemmaes Head, near St Dogmaels, including the promontory of Pen-yr-Afr.

Between Cardigan and Newquay the Trust owns **Mwnt** [145: SN1952], a family beach with parking, lavatories and a refreshment kiosk; **Penbryn** [145: SN295519], just north-east of Tresaith with extensive beaches, car-parking, lavatories and café/refreshment facilities (no dogs at Mwnt and Penbryn beaches between 1 May and 30 Sept); **Caerllan** at Cwmtudu [145: SN355577], with 3½ml of cliff walks to Newquay; and **Lochtyn** [145: SN315545], a rocky headland near the village of Llangrannog; from the highest point, **Pen-y-Badell**, splendid views can be Cardigan Bay to the Llŷn Peninsula and Snowdonia. **Penparc Farm** consists of 49ha south-west of Cwmtudu including 1ml of coastline and ¾ml of valley bluff.

Between Aberaeron and Aberystwyth, the Trust has acquired **Mynachdy'r Graig** [135: SN563742], a 62ha coastal farm with stunning views to the extremities of Cardigan Bay.

Recent acquisitions on the Pembrokeshire coast include 4 farms, comprising over 324ha of farmland, and further areas of coastal land, totalling some 10ml of coastline.

WALES

In Anglesey the Trust now owns 7½ml of coastline including the beautiful **Mynachdy Estate** on the north-western coast of the island (Note: there is a covenanted area which is not Trust-owned; access to this area is not permitted between 15 Sept and 1 Feb). Also on the coast is **Plas Newydd**, the home of the Marquess of Anglesey (see p.310). **Glan Faenol** [114: SH530695], more than 122ha of farm and woodland stretching from Faenol Wood to Y Felinheli, was acquired to protect the view across the Menai Strait from Plas Newydd.

The most spectacular coastal scenery in North Wales can probably be seen from the beautiful Llŷn Peninsula. The Trust's benefactresses on Llŷn – the **Misses Keatings** – were three sisters who gave **Plas yn Rhiw** (see p.311), their lovely manor house and garden above Porth Neigwl. From 1950–66 they were tireless in their quest to rescue threatened land in the vicinity and present it to the Trust, and as a result the original 168ha estate has been reclaimed, 166ha of which is coastal land. The Trust has kept up the Misses Keatings' good work, and with Enterprise Neptune funds has acquired more of the Llŷn coast – at **Penarfynydd**, **Mynydd Bychestyn**, **Porth Gwylan** and **Carreg**. In 1990 **Porthor**, a delightful sandy cove, was acquired. The beach is also known as 'Whistling Sands', owing to the whistling noise produced when the dry sand is walked on. The most recent acquisition is **Porthdinllaen**, an unspoilt fishing village and harbour set in sweeping bay.

COUNTRYSIDE

The Trust owns over 40,486ha of countryside in Wales much of it in Snowdonia and the Brecon Beacons. Many of its holdings are within the Snowdonia National Park, the two largest properties being the **Ysbyty** and **Carneddau Estates** [115/116: SH8448 and 115: SH6760], of 8097ha and 7287ha respectively, both of which were transferred to the Trust with **Penrhyn Castle** through the National Land Fund in 1951.

Ysbyty has 51 farms, and includes the upper valleys of the Conwy, Eidda and Machno rivers, whilst the **Carneddau Estate** has some of the most exciting scenery in Snowdonia. The Trust owns ten of the main mountain peaks over 900m, including Tryfan, where the first successful Everest climbers trained, together with land through the Ogwen and Nant Ffrancon valleys between Capel Curig and Bethesda.

The **Cwm Idwal** Nature Reserve near Ogwen has a low-level mountain walk around Llyn Idwal. The cwm or corrie has been famous since the 17th century for its rich variety of mountain flora. The reserve is in the care of the Countryside Council for Wales, Penrhos Road, Bangor, who can provide detailed information.

South-west of Betws y Coed is **Tŷ Mawr** in the little valley of Wybrnant. The Wybrnant Trail is a short waymarked walk; a leaflet (s.a.e. please) is available from Tŷ Mawr (see p.315). Parts of trail accessible to wheelchair users from car park.

At **Cregennan** [124: SH6614] are two lakes, hill farms and mountain land giving fine views to Cadair Idris, where two sheepwalks are owned on the north face – **Tan-y-Gadair** and **Llyn-y-Gadair** [124: SH7013/7115] – both with spectacular views.

North-west of Dolgellau, the **Dolmelynllyn** estate of 506ha includes one of Wales's most spectacular waterfalls, Rhaeadr Ddu on the Gamlan, reached by footpath from the village of Ganllwyd; also two sheepwalks on **Y Llethr** [124: SH7222]. To the south of Beddgelert lies the Aberglaslyn Pass, with the famous view north from the stone bridge, Pont Aberglaslyn [115: SH595463].

In the **Brecon Beacons** [160: SO010200], the Trust owns over 3644ha of the main part of the range including **Penyfan**, at 872m the highest peak in the Beacons and **Cwm Oergwm**, 36ha of fields and woods in a sheltered valley on the northern slopes of the Beacons. **Cwm Sere** is a small wood at the base of the Brecon Beacons, of high nature conservation value. **Blaenglyn Farm** and **Carno Wood**, a typical working Welsh hill farm at the head of the Tarrell Valley, is crossed by the Taff trail, the new long-distance path from Cardiff to Brecon.

Berthlwyd Farm [160: SN913133] is a traditionally run family farm in the head of the Neath Valley with extensive archaeological and nature conservation interest. **Henrhyd Falls**, the highest single drop falls in South Wales, are in a beautiful spot near the edge of the South Wales coalfield. Formed by the River Llech, they tumble for 27m into a deep wooded ravine; there is a car park and circular walk. **Graigllech Woods** are also Trust-owned [160: SN850119].

The Trust has more recently acquired 526ha of the **Begwns Commons** [161: SO154444], a heavily used common 4ml west of Hay-on-Wye with outstanding views. The 6680ha of **Abergwesyn Common** [127/128/141: SN8359/9861] comprise a 12ml stretch of high, beautiful and remote commonland between Rhayader and the Irfon Gorge near Llanwrtyd Wells, with an unrestricted right of access; but only recommended to the hardy hill walker! Dogs must be kept on a lead at all times.

1ml east of the border town of Monmouth is **The Kymin**, a 240m high hill giving views over the valleys of the Wye and the Monnow. The 'first gentlemen in Monmouth' built a tower they called The Round House as a dining club on the summit, a bowling green, and a Naval Temple which was visited by Nelson and Emma Hamilton in 1802 [162: SO02718]. Access from A4136.

The **Sugar Loaf**, just west of Abergavenny [161: SO2718], is 600m high and cone-shaped. There is access to the summit across commonland, open mountainside, woodland and valleys. **Parc Lodge Farm**, a 202ha working hill farm crossed by footpaths, lies beneath the Sugar Loaf. Another nearby viewpoint is **Skirrid Fawr** [161: SO330180], 480m, giving views of the Sugar Loaf, the Usk valley and the Black Mountains.

With the Usk Valley, **Coed y Bwnydd**, a well-preserved Iron Age hillfort close to Bettws Newydd, has magnificent displays of bluebells in spring. The Trust also owns the attractive parkland of **Clytha**, on the banks of the River Usk, with distant views of the Black Mountains; there is a riverside picnic site here and walks along waymarked paths. Clytha Castle, the folly overlooking the estate, is leased to the Landmark Trust as holiday accommodation.

The **Dolaucothi Estate** [146: SN656406] includes over 1000ha of unspoilt countryside centred on the Cothi Valley. Facilities include an estate car park with walks through farm and woodland, and a new visitor centre in Pumsaint village.

The Trust owns two areas of woodland near Milford Haven; one at **Little Milford** on the Western Cleddau, south of Haverfordwest [158: SM967118], with public foot-paths; the other a 29ha hanging wood at **Lawrenny** on the east side of Castle Reach.

Two other rivers which enter this estuary are the Creswell and the Carew. **Williamston Park**, a promontory between these rivers south-east of Lawrenny, is one of the two deer parks of Carew Castle – now a dramatic ruin (not NT). The Park is a nature reserve, managed by the Dyfed Wildlife Trust; access is by footpath only [158: SN030057].

The Trust owns 6ha at **Paxton's Tower**, 7ml east of Carmarthen [159: SN541191]. This folly was once known as Nelson's Tower, and was built in the early 19th century on a hill giving fine views over the countryside. A car park is available adjacent to the site. Access for less able visitors is via a key available at the Regional Office in nearby Llandeilo.

The **Dinefwr Estate**, [159: SN625225] was split up and sold in the 1970s, and since 1986 the Trust has been trying to reassemble the core elements. These now include the ancient deer park, Newton House and 197ha of parkland. Dinefwr Castle (Dyfed Wildlife Trust) was established in 877 and was the seat of the Welsh princes.

ABERCONWY HOUSE 🏠

Castle Street, Conwy LL32 8AY Tel: 01492 592246 Fax: 01492 585153

Dating from the 14th century, this is the only medieval merchant's house in Conwy to have survived the turbulent history of this walled town for nearly six centuries. Furnished rooms and an audiovisual presentation show daily life from different periods in its history

Note: The house has limited electric lighting and therefore is dark on dull days

O 26 March to 2 Nov: daily except Tues 10–5. Last admission 4.30

£ £2, children £1; family ticket (max. 2 adults & 2 children) £5. Pre-booked groups £1.80 per person. NT members free

🛍 Shop open all year: daily 9.30–5.30, except 25/26 Dec

♿ No WC. Steps up to entrance

■ Educational visits welcome. Pre-booked groups only

➔ At junction of Castle Street and High Street [115: SH781777] *Bus:* From surrounding areas (tel. 01492 575415) *Station:* Conwy 300m

ABERDULAIS FALLS 🔌 🔧 E

Aberdulais, nr Neath, SA10 8EU Tel: 01639 636674 Fax: 01639 645069

For over 300 years this famous waterfall has provided the energy to drive the wheels of industry, from the first manufacture of copper in 1584 to present-day remains of the tinplate works. It has also been visited by famous artists such as J.M.W.Turner in 1796. The site today houses a unique hydro-electrical scheme which has been developed to harness the waters of the Dulais river. The Turbine House provides access to an interactive computer, fish pass, and display panels. A special lift has been installed to allow disabled visitors access to the roof level, which affords excellent views of the Falls. The new water wheel, the largest currently used in Britain to generate electricity, makes Aberdulais Falls self-sufficient in environmentally-friendly energy

Note: The operation of the fish pass, water wheel and turbine is subject to river levels

O 27 March to 2 Nov: Mon to Fri 10–5, Sat, Sun, BHols 11–6. Last admission 30min before closing. **Events:** held throughout the year; contact Property Warden for full details

£ £2.80, children £1.40. One child (16 or under) free with each paying adult. Parties (min. 15) by prior arrangement with Property Warden: adults £2.20, children £1.10. Children should be accompanied by an adult. NT members free. Car park signposted to Dulais Rock Inn, 2min walk. Also, on-road parking on A4109 outside the property entrance; coaches please check beforehand as parking is limited

𝄪 Guided tours every day during July and Aug, at other times by arrangement for pre-booked parties

🛍 Located near the entrance and open during normal property opening times

♿ Much of the property is accessible to disabled visitors. In the Turbine House a special lift, capable of carrying two wheelchair visitors and their helpers, provides access to the roof level with excellent views of the falls, gorge and water wheel. WC and wheelchair available. *Note*: Won British Gas ADAPT Commendation 1993 for access

🔊 Taped guide with information for sighted companions

🍴 Light refreshments are served in the Old Works Library and Victorian schoolroom by Friends of Aberdulais Falls during summer weekends and public holidays. At other times by arrangement. Lunches and bar meals available at Dulais Rock Inn (not NT)

📖 Education facilities provided for pre-booked groups by arrangement with the Property Warden. In Victorian schoolroom: tours and talks on hydro-electrical scheme, industrial archaeology, history for educational and other organisational groups. Teachers' resource pack available

🐾 Must be kept on leads

➡️ On A4109, 3ml NE of Neath [170: SS772995]. 4ml from M4 exit 43 at Llandarcy, take A465 signposted Vale of Neath *Bus:* Route 158: Swansea–Banwen 161, N10 from Neath, X75 Swansea–Merthyr Tydfil (tel. 01792 580580); Silverline Brecon–Swansea (tel. 01874 623900). All pass close ➡ Neath *Station:* Neath 3ml

---

BODNANT GARDEN 🏠 ❖ E

Tal-y-Cafn, Colwyn Bay LL28 5RE Tel: 01492 650460 Fax: 01492 650448

The 32ha garden at Bodnant is one of the finest in the world, situated above the River Conwy and looking across the valley towards the Snowdon range. The garden is in two parts. The upper part around the house (the private residence of Lord and Lady Aberconway) consists of the Terrace Gardens as well as informal lawns shaded by trees. The lower portion, known as 'The Dell', is formed by the valley of the River Hiraethlyn, a tributary of the Conwy, and contains the pinetum and wild garden. In March and April masses of daffodils and other spring bulbs make a very colourful display. Pride of place amongst the shrubs is held by rhododendrons, magnolias and camellias, which flower from March until the end of June. The famous laburnum arch, embothriums and many of the azaleas are at their best at the end of May/early June. In summer the Terrace Gardens are very colourful with herbaceous borders, roses, water lilies, clematis and unusual wall shrubs and climbers. Eucryphias and hydrangeas are a special feature in late summer, whilst an October visit is very worthwhile to see the splendid autumn colours. Bodnant Garden and refreshment pavilion are managed by Lord Aberconway VMH

🅾 15 March to 31 Oct: daily 10–5. Last admission 4.30. **Events:** 29 June, open-air Shakespeare

💷 £4.20, children £2.10. Parties of 20 or more £3.80 per person. NT members free. Car park 50m from garden entrance

🛍 Plant centre and gift shop (not NT), open as garden

♿ The garden is steep in places, has many steps, and is not easy for wheelchairs. Five wheelchairs available, but cannot be reserved. Restaurant and plant centre accessible. WC

◉ Braille guide. Scented roses and other plants

⬛ Refreshment pavilion serving light lunches and teas, open as garden: daily 11–5. Picnicking in car park area only

🧒 Baby-changing facilities. Baby slings available. Highchairs in tea-room

🐕 No dogs allowed

➡ 8ml S of Llandudno and Colwyn Bay off A470, entrance ½ml along the Eglwysbach road [115/116: SH801723]. Signposted from A55 *Bus:* Crosville Cymru 25, D & G 65 from Llandudno (passing close ⊞ Llandudno Junction) (tel. 01492 575415) *Station:* Tal-y-Cafn (U) 1½ml

---

CHIRK CASTLE 🏰 ✝ ❀ ♠ 🧍 E

Chirk, Wrexham LL14 5AF Tel: 01691 777701 Fax: 01691 774706

A magnificent Marcher fortress, completed in 1310, commanding fine views over the surrounding countryside. Elegant state rooms with elaborate plasterwork, superb Adam-style furniture, tapestries and portraits. In the formal gardens there are clipped yews, roses and a variety of flowering shrubs. Elaborate entrance gates made in 1719 by the Davies brothers. 18th-century parkland

🅾 26 March to 28 Sept: daily except Mon & Tues but open BH Mon; 4 Oct to 2 Nov: Sat & Sun only. **Castle:** 12–5. **Garden:** 11–6. Last admission 4.30. **Events:** please contact Property Manager for details of programme, which includes open-air plays and family fun days

💷 £4.40, children £2.20; family ticket (max. 2 adults & 2 children) £11. Pre-booked parties of 15 or more £3.50 per person. Garden only, adults £2.20, children £1.10. NT members free. Parking 200m

🧍 Connoisseurs' tour by prior arrangement (minimum group of 20)

🛍 Shop open as castle

♿ Access to state rooms by stairclimber. Garden mostly accessible; gravel paths. Tea-room accessible. Courtesy coach from car park. Room for CAPD. WC

Braille guide

Licensed tea-room: morning coffee, light lunches and teas; open 11–5. Picnicking in car park only

Parent & baby room. Baby carriers for loan. Highchairs in tea-room

Educational visits particularly welcome. 'Hands-on' facilities. Education officer and room available. School parties must be pre-booked

Allowed on walks and in car park

→ ½ml W of Chirk village off A5; 8ml S of Wrexham, signposted off A483
Bus: Midland Red 2/A Wrexham–Oswestry (tel. 01978 363760) *Station:* Chirk (U) 1½ml

CILGERRAN CASTLE 🏛 E

nr Cardigan, SA43 2SF Tel: 01239 615007

This 13th-century ruin has inspired many artists, including Turner

Note: Cilgerran Castle is in the guardianship of Cadw (Welsh Historic Monuments)

All year: daily. Summer (late March to late Oct): 9.30–6.30. Winter (late Oct to late March 1998): 11–4. **Events:** Shakespeare plays held each year; contact Custodian for details

£ Adult £1.70, children (under16)/OAP/student £1.20; family ticket (2 adults & 3 children under 16) £4

Shop open daily except Sat, same hours as castle

Access to grounds and inner bailey only

No dogs allowed

→ On rock above left bank of the Teifi, 3ml SE of Cardigan, 1½ml E of A478 [145: SN195431] *Bus:* Midway 430 from Cardigan; otherwise Davies Bros 460/1
� Carmarthen–Cardigan, alight Llechryd. 1¾ml by footpath (tel. 01437 764551)

COLBY WOODLAND GARDENS 🌼 🍀 🏖 🎨 🧍 E

Amroth, Narberth SA67 8PP Tel: 01834 811885

Attractive woodland gardens with a fine collection of rhododendrons and azaleas. The early 19th-century house is not open (Mr & Mrs A. Scourfield Lewis kindly allow access to the walled garden during visiting hours). There are walks through secluded valleys along open and wooded pathways

21 March to 31 Oct: daily 10–5. **Walled garden:** 1 April to 30 Oct: 11–5. **Events:** 28 May, family fun day; 15 June, rare plant sale; 26 June, open-air production of *The Tempest*; 14 Aug, open-air play *Peter Pan*; 27 Aug, family fun day. Tel. 01834 811885 for details

💷 £2.60, children £1.30; family ticket £6.50. Group: adult £2.10, child £1.10. Coaches welcome (narrow approaches). Open evenings by arrangement

🛍 Shop, gallery and plant sales, open as property

♿ Limited facilities, shop and parts of garden accessible; disabled visitors may park closer to the garden on request

👁 Braille guide available

☕ Tea-room (not NT) serving morning coffee, home-made light lunches and afternoon tea; open as property. Large car park with picnic facilities

🚼 Baby-changing facilities. Children's quiz and safari packs

🐕 Not in walled garden

➡ 1½ml inland from Amroth beside Carmarthen Bay [158: SN155080]. Follow brown signs from A477 Tenby–Carmarthen road or off coast road at Amroth Castle *Bus:* Silcox 350/1 from Tenby (passing ≋ Kilgetty) (tel. 01437 764551) *Station:* Kilgetty (U) 2½ml

CONWY SUSPENSION BRIDGE 🔧

Conwy LL32 8LD Tel: 01492 573282

Designed and built by Thomas Telford, the famous engineer, this elegant suspension bridge was completed in 1826: it replaced the ferry, previously the only means of crossing the river. The toll-keeper's house has recently been restored and furnished as it would have been a century ago

🅾 26 March to 30 June and 1 Sept to 2 Nov: daily except Tues 10–5. July & August: daily 10–5. Last admission 4.30

💷 Adults £1, children 50p. NT members free

🎓 Educational visits welcome; pre-booked groups only

➡ 100m from Conwy town centre, adjacent to Conwy Castle [115: SH785775] *Bus:* From surrounding areas (tel. 01492 575415) *Station:* Conwy ¼ml; Llandudno Junction ½ml

DINEFWR PARK 🏠 🌳 E

Llandeilo SA19 6RT Tel: 01558 823902 Fax: 01558 822036

An 18th-century landscape park, situated on the outskirts of the market town of Llandeilo. This was the capital of South Wales and the home of Welsh kings and princes, including Hywel Dda c.920 and the Lord Rhys. Newton House has a Victorian Gothic façade, which envelops the earlier 17th-century building. The ground floor and basement are now open after restoration and an exhibition explains the importance of Dinefwr in Welsh history. The newly restored Victorian garden at the rear of the house overlooks the ancient deer park, an internationally important SSSI, with fallow deer and the famous Dinefwr white park cattle. Paths through the estate give fine views over the Towy Valley and a 750m boardwalk, suitable for families and wheelchair users, meanders through Bog Wood. There is limited access to the privately owned walled garden. Access to Dinefwr Castle

O **House, garden, deer park, parkland & boardwalk**: 27 March to 2 Nov: Thur to Mon 11–5. Last admission 4.30. The library and old drawing room are available for conferences on Tues & Wed. Parkland also open during winter in daylight hours. **Events**: for details of full programme please send s.a.e. marked 'Events' to Property Manager

£ £2.60, children £1.30; family ticket (max. 2 adults & 2 children) £6.50; 1 child (16 and under) free per paying adult from 24 July to 1 Sept. Parties £2.40, children/school groups £1.20. Coaches by prior appointment only due to narrow access. WCs in car park

🚶 Guided tours through the deer park by prior arrangement with Warden

🛍 Christmas shop and tea-room open Nov & Dec: Fri to Sun 10.30–4.30

♿ Ramped access to ground floor of house, exhibition and tea-room. WC. Parts of grounds accessible: boardwalk through Bog Wood to lake

👁 Braille guide

🍽 Tea-room (not NT) open as house

👶 Baby-changing facilities, highchairs & children's menu. Activities available

🐕 In outer park only, on leads. No dogs in deer park

➜ On N outskirts of Llandeilo A40(T); from Swansea take M4 to Pont Abraham, thence A48(T) to Cross Hands and A476 to Llandeilo; entrance by police station [159: SN625225] *Bus*: From surrounding areas to Llandeilo, thence 1ml (tel. 01267 231817) *Station*: Llandeilo 1ml

---

DOLAUCOTHI GOLD MINES 🏊 🛗 🚶

Pumsaint, Llanwrda SA19 8RR Tel: 01558 650359

These unique Roman gold mines are set amid wooded hillsides overlooking the beautiful Cothi Valley on the Dolaucothi Estate. Exploited by the Celts and Romans some 2,000 years ago and last worked in 1938, the Trust's exhibition centre vividly illustrates the ancient and modern mine workings. Gold-panning and displays of 1930s mining machinery in the mine yard, video and bilingual interpretation and guided tour (overground)

🅾 27 March to 30 Sept: daily 10–5. Underground tours, 17 May to 21 Sept: 10.30–5. Underground tours last about 1hr, involving rugged climbing; helmets with lights provided; stout footwear recommended. The underground tour is unsuitable for disabled or infirm visitors; the Trust regrets children under 5 not allowed underground. Limited places are available on underground tours; tours are very busy during late July and Aug; please come early to avoid disappointment

💷 Site admission £3, children £1.50, family ticket (2 adults, 2 children) £7.50. NT members free. Guided underground tour: £3.50, children £1.75, family ticket (2 adults, 2 children) £8.50. NT members £2, members' children £1, members' family ticket £5. All-inclusive family ticket £15

🚶 Stout footwear recommended. Unsuitable for disabled or infirm visitors and under-5s

📷 Shop and tea-room open as property

♿ Wheelchair access to reception and exhibition centre; mines not accessible

🍽 Light lunches and refreshments available

🎪 Room available for school groups

🐕 On leads, but no dogs on tours

➡ Between Lampeter and Llanwrda on A482 [146: SN6640] *Bus:* Thomas Bros 284 from Llandeilo, Tues only (tel. 01267 231817) *Station:* Llanwrda (U), not Sun, except June to Sept, 8ml

---

ERDDIG 🏠 🏠 ✝ 🌸 ♣ 🏊 🚶 Ⓔ

nr Wrexham LL13 0YT Tel: 01978 355314 Infoline/fax: 01978 313333

This late 17th-century house, with 18th-century additions, is the most evocative upstairs-downstairs house in Britain. The range of outbuildings includes kitchen, laundry, bakehouse, stables, sawmill, smithy and joiner's shop, while the state rooms display most of the original 18th- and 19th-century furniture and furnishings. A large walled garden restored to its 18th-century formal design with Victorian parterre and yew walk; also contains the national ivy collection. Surrounding parkland with extensive woods. 10min video programme

Note: Due to the extreme fragility of their contents, the Tapestry and Small Chinese Rooms are open on Wed & Sat only. Most rooms have no electric light; visitors wishing to make close study of pictures and textiles should avoid dull days

🅾 22 March to 2 Nov: daily, except Thur & Fri (open Good Fri); **House:** 12–5;

Garden: 11–6. (July & Aug: 10–6; from 4 Oct house & garden close 1hr earlier). Last admission to house 1hr before closing. **Events:** 20 to 22 June, craft show in garden (additional charge, incl. NT members); 10/11 July, open-air classical music; 26 July, open-air opera gala. Please send s.a.e. to Property Manager for full events programme

£ All-inclusive ticket £5.40, children £2.70; family ticket (max. 2 adults & 2 children) £13.50. Parties (15 or more) £4.40 per person. Belowstairs (incl. outbuildings & garden) £3.60, children £1.80, family ticket (max. 2 adults & 2 children) £9. Parties (15 or more) £2.90 per person. NT members free. Parking 200m

Garden tours available by prior arrangement (15 or more)

Shop and plant sales open as property. Christmas shop: 7 Nov to 21 Dec: Fri, Sat & Sun 11–4 (tel. 01978 311919). Joiner's shop manufacturing quality garden furniture, open same times as property; catalogue available (tel. 01978 363816)

Access over rough gravel and cobbled yard to ground floor, garden (ramps) and outbuildings only; not an easy property for wheelchair users; please discuss visits in advance with the Property Manager. Tea-room difficult but table by shop accessible. WC in main yard; wheelchairs provided. Good access provided in Country Park; RADAR key WCs

Braille guide

Licensed restaurant: morning coffee, lunches and teas, open as property 22 March to 2 Nov. Also open for pre-booked functions, incl. pre-booked Christmas lunches. Catering Manager (tel. 01978 311919). Picnicking in car park area only

Feeding and baby-changing facilities. Highchairs in restaurant. Baby carriers on loan. Children's guide

🔲 School and Youth Groups Mon, Tues & Wed am only by prior arrangement. Please send s.a.e. for details of education programme at the house and on the estate

🐕 In car park and country park only, on leads

➡️ 2ml S of Wrexham, signposted A525 Whitchurch road, or A483/A5152 Oswestry road [117: SJ326482] *Station:* Wrexham Central (U) 1ml, Wrexham General 1½ml via Erddig Rd & footpath

---

LLANERCHAERON 🖊️ E

nr Aberaeron SA48 8DG Tel: 01545 570200 Fax: 01545 571759

A rare survivor of a Welsh gentry estate acquired by the Trust in 1994. The core area includes the principal house, designed and built by John Nash in 1794–6; service wing and courtyard; model home farm; kennels and stables, pleasure grounds and parkland

Note: The property has been accepted unendowed. An ambitious programme of repair and regeneration has commenced with minimal finance and will only continue for as long as funds permit. Access may be restricted in some areas for safety reasons. The house is under restoration

🅾️ **Home farm, gardens and grounds:** 23 March to 6 April, 8 May to 5 Oct: Thur to Sun & BH Mon 11–5. Last admission 4. **Parkland:** all year, dawn to dusk. **Events:** details from Property Manager (s.a.e. please)

💷 £2, children £1. Parties £1.50/75p. Guided tours: 70p, additional to admission (incl. NT members)

🖊️ During opening periods at 2 every Thur; also at 2 on Sun in July & Aug. Groups of 15+ please book in advance

♿ Access to whole site including walled garden. WCs. Wheelchair available

👁️ Braille guide

🐕 On leads in parkland only

➡️ 2ml east of Aberaeron off A482 [146:SN480 602] *Bus:* Davies Bros 202 ⊨ Carmarthen–Aberaeron (with connections from ⊨ Aberystwyth (tel. 01267 231817)

LLYWELYN COTTAGE 🏠 🛍️ 🖊️

Beddgelert LL55 4YA Tel: 01766 890293 Fax: 01766 890545

An information centre, exhibition and shop situated in the picturesque village of Beddgelert, near the Aberglaslyn Pass and within the Snowdonia National Park. Superb walks, including a stroll to the legendary Gelert's grave, and a level path along the track of the former Welsh Highland Railway. An interactive display will help you learn about the area's history, wildlife and walks

🅾️ 27 March to 2 Nov: daily 11–5

£ Free admission

⬛ Open daily 11–5

♿ Accessible to wheelchairs; interactive display accessible

➜ At junction of A498 and A4085. Well-signposted from A5 and A487 [115: SH590481] *Bus:* KMP/Crosville Cymru 95/A from Caernarfon (with connections from ⬛ Bangor), Express 97 from Porthmadog (passes close ⬛ Porthmadog) (tel. 01286 679535) *Station:* Penrhyndeudraeth (U) or Porthmadog (U) both 6ml

---

PENRHYN CASTLE 🏛️ ✝️ ✿ 🔆 🚶 🅴

Bangor LL57 4HN
Tel: 01248 353084 Infoline: 01248 371337 Fax: 01248 371281

A neo-Norman castle placed dramatically between Snowdonia and the Menai Strait. Built by Thomas Hopper between 1820 and 1845, the castle contains interesting 'Norman' furniture, panelling and plasterwork designed by Hopper, and houses the best private collection of paintings in North Wales. There is also an industrial railway museum, a countryside exhibition, a Victorian terraced walled garden and an extensive tree and shrub collection

🔘 26 March to 2 Nov: daily except Tues. **Castle:** 12–5 (July & Aug 11–5). **Grounds and stable block exhibitions:** 11–5 (July & Aug 10–5). Last admission 30min before closing (last audio tour 4). **Events:** a programme including open-air plays, concerts and family fun days runs throughout the season; send s.a.e. for details. Events information line (tel. 01248 371337)

£ £4.60, children £2.30; family ticket £11.50 (max. 2 adults & 2 children). Booked parties of 20 or more £3.70 per person. Garden and stable block exhibitions only £3, children £1.50. NT members free. Audiotour 50p, for adults and children in Welsh and English. School and youth groups by arrangement. Parking 200m

🚶 Garden tours arranged throughout the season. Specialist guided tours by prior arrangement

⬚ Shop open as Castle

♿ Access to all ground floor rooms; access ramps and handrail (but no access to shop in basement). Wheelchair available. Castle is least congested on Sat. Park paths are firm. Parking and volunteer-driven golf buggy seating 3, for garden and park by arrangement. WC. Induction loop audio tour for hard of hearing, Sympathetic Hearing Scheme

◉ Braille guide. Audio tour

◖ Licensed tea-room; morning coffee, light lunches and teas. Picnicking in grounds. Tea-room opens 1hr before Castle

♟ Industrial railway museum. Adventure playground. Young Adventurers' audio tour. Baby-changing facilities; baby carriers on loan. Highchairs in tea-room. Permanent orienteering course in grounds; maps and instructions available from shop. Activity sheets for children

▦ Pre-booked educational visits particularly welcome. Hands-on educational facilities, Education Officer on site. Permanent orienteering course. Send s.a.e. for education programme

🐕 In grounds only, on leads

➔ 1ml E of Bangor, at Llandegai on A5122 [115: SH602720]. Signposted from junction of A55 and A5 *Bus:* Crosville Cymru 5/B Caernarfon–Rhyl; Purple 6/7 Bangor–Bethesda; D & G 65/6 Bangor–Gerlan. All pass close ⊷ Bangor and end of drive to Castle (tel. 01286 679535) *Station:* Bangor 2ml

---

PLAS NEWYDD ▦ ❈ ♠ ⧄ E

Llanfairpwll, Anglesey LL61 6DQ Tel: 01248 714795 Fax: 01248 713673

An impressive 18th-century house by James Wyatt in unspoilt surroundings on the Menai Strait, with magnificent views of Snowdonia. The house contains Rex Whistler's largest wallpainting and an exhibition about his work. In the military museum are campaign relics of the 1st Marquess of Anglesey and the Battle of Waterloo. There is a fine spring garden, summer terrace and, later, massed hydrangeas and autumn colour. Also woodland walk with access to a marine walk

Note: The Rhododendron Garden is open from 27 March to early June only

🅞 **House:** 27 March to 30 Sept: daily except Sat 12–5; 3 Oct to 2 Nov: Fri & Sun 12–5. **Garden:** same days as house 11–5.30. Last admission 30min before closing. **Events:** extensive programme of tours, plays and music (incl. 19 July, open-air concert; 23 Aug, open-air jazz concert); details from Property Manager

£ £4.20, children £2.10; family ticket (max. 2 adults, 2 children) £10.50. Pre-booked parties of 20 or more £3.40 per person. Garden only £2, children £1. NT members free. Parking 400m

♟ Connoisseurs' and garden tours by prior arrangement

⬚ Shop open daily (incl. Sat) 11–5. Also Christmas shop: 7 Nov to 21 Dec: Fri, Sat & Sun 11–4

🦽 Ground floor and Whistler Room accessible via ramps. Stairclimber to first floor. Close parking, enquire at reception desk; wheelchairs available. Easy access to garden (all main paths accessible), tea-room and shop. WC near tea-room

📖 Braille guide

🍽 Licensed tea-room: morning coffee, light lunches & teas; open daily (incl. Sat) 11–5. Picnicking in car park and playground area

👶 Parent & baby facilities. Baby carriers available. Highchairs in tea-room. Children's quiz and adventure playground

🏫 Pre-booked school groups welcome

🐕 No dogs allowed in house or gardens

➜ 1ml SW of Llanfairpwll and A5 on A4080 to Brynsiencyn; turn off A5 at W end of Britannia Bridge [114/115: SH521696] *Bus:* Crosville Cymru 42 from Bangor (passing ≋ Bangor & Llanfairpwll) (tel. 01248 351879) *Station:* Llanfairpwll (U), no practical Sun service, except May to Sept, 1¼ml

---

PLAS YN RHIW 🏛 ❄ 🖼 E

Rhiw, Pwllheli LL53 8AB Tel: 01758 780219

A small manor house, with garden and woodlands, overlooking the west shore of Porth Neigwl (Hell's Mouth Bay) on the Llŷn Peninsula. The house is part-medieval, with Tudor and Georgian additions, and the ornamental gardens have flowering trees and shrubs, divided by box hedges and grass paths, rising behind to the snowdrop wood

Note: In the interests of preservation, numbers of visitors admitted to the house at any one time may be limited, particularly in July and Aug and on BHs

🅾 27 March to 19 May: daily (except Tues & Wed) 12–5. 21 May to 30 Sept: daily (except Tues) 12–5. Last admission 4.30. **Events:** open-air concert and play; tel. for details

💷 £2.60, children £1.30, family ticket (max. 2 adults & 2 children) £6.50. NT members free. Pre-booked parties evenings only (incl. full guided tour) £3.50 per person. Parking 80m. No coaches

🧑 Advance notice is required; no tours during July & Aug

🛍 Shop open as house

🦽 Wheelchair access to ground-floor rooms only; most of garden very difficult for wheelchairs. WC

📖 Braille guides

🏫 School visits are encouraged, but Custodian must be informed 2 weeks in advance

🐕 On the woodland walk, on leads only

➜ 12ml from Pwllheli, signposted from B4413 to Aberdaron (drive gate at the bottom of Rhiw Hill) [123: SH237282] *Bus:* Crosville Cymru 17B Pwllheli–Aberdaron (passing ≋ Pwllheli) (tel. 01248 351879) *Station:* Pwllheli 12ml

POWIS CASTLE & GARDEN 🏰 ❀ ♣ E

Welshpool SY21 8RF Tel: 01938 554338 Infoline/fax: Tel: 01938 554336

The world-famous garden, overhung with enormous clipped yews, shelters rare and tender plants. Laid out under the influence of Italian and French styles, the garden retains its original lead statues, an orangery and an aviary on the terraces. In the 18th century an informal woodland wilderness was created on the opposing ridge. Perched on a rock above the garden terraces, the medieval castle contains one of the finest collections in Wales. It was originally built c.1200 by Welsh princes and was subsequently adapted and embellished by generations of Herberts and Clives, who furnished the castle with a wealth of fine paintings and furniture. A beautiful collection of treasures from India is displayed in the Clive Museum

◯ **Castle & museum:** 26 March to 31 May & 3 Sept to 2 Nov: daily except Mon & Tues 12–4; June, July & Aug: daily except Mon; 12–4.30 (open BH Mon during season). **Garden:** same days as castle & museum, 11–6. Last admission 30min before closing. **Events:** programme of concerts, plays, walks, talks and demonstrations throughout the year: for details tel. 01938 554338

£ Garden £4, children £2; family ticket (max. 2 adults & 2 children) £10. Parties £3.20 per person. All-in ticket (incl. castle, museum & garden) £6, children £3; family ticket (max. 2 adults & 2 children) £15. Parties for castle, museum & garden £5.50, by written appointment only. No group rates Sun & BH Mon

🏃 Out of hours guided tours of the castle and/or garden by prior arrangement

🛍 Open same days as castle & garden. Also Christmas shop open 7 Nov to 21 Dec: Fri, Sat, Sun 11–4

♿ Due to the layout of the garden and design of the castle, access for disabled visitors is very limited and it is not possible to use wheelchairs inside the castle. The garden approach is steep, and not recommended for disabled walkers or wheelchair-users, but access to the tea-room, shop and plant shop is good. Wheelchair available. Elderly and disabled visitors may be driven up to entrance but drivers should return car to car park; disabled drivers should park on the reserved area in the coach park. Adapted WC

📖 Braille guide; scented flowers

🍴 Licensed tea-room; counter service for morning coffee, light lunches and teas. Open same days as castle & garden, 11–5

👶 Baby-feeding and changing facilities. Front baby carriers available on loan. Castle unsuitable for back baby carriers and pushchairs. Highchairs in restaurant. Family quiz trails in garden during school holidays

👦 Children's guides and questionnaires. School groups by appointment

🐕 Guide dogs only, allowed in castle and garden. Dogs cannot be walked in the park as it does not belong to the Trust and there is no public access on this private land

➔ 1ml S of Welshpool; pedestrian access from High Street (A490); cars turn right 1ml along main road to Newtown (A483); enter by first drive-gate on right [126: SJ216064] *Bus:* Midland Red D71 Oswestry–Welshpool; D75 Shrewsbury–Llanidloes, alight High Street, 1ml (tel. 0345 056785) *Station:* Welshpool 1¼ml via footpath in town

---

RHOSSILI VISITOR CENTRE 🏛 👶

Coastguard Cottages, Rhossili, Gower, Swansea SA3 1PR Tel: 01792 390707

Situated adjacent to extensive NT ownership of the Raised Terrace, the Down, the beach, coastal cliffs and Worm's Head. Exhibition and shop

🅾 22 March to 30 March: Sat & Sun 11–4; 31 March to 26 Oct: daily 10.30–5.30; 27 Oct to 2 Nov: daily 11–4; 6 Nov to 21 Dec: Sat & Sun 11–4

💷 Free admission to visitor centre. Car park and WC nearby (not NT): charge for parking

♿ Visitor centre ground floor and shop accessible. Rough surface in car park (not NT); disabled visitors may be set down at visitor centre. No separate parking facilities. Excellent view from outside building

🍴 Available nearby (not NT)

🐕 Guide dogs only in the visitor centre

➔ SW tip of Gower Peninsula, approached from Swansea via A4118 and then B4247 *Bus:* South Wales 18/A/C from Swansea (passing close ≉ Swansea) (tel. 01792 580580)

SEGONTIUM 🏛

Caernarfon LL55 2LN Tel: 01286 675625

The remains of a Roman fort, with a museum containing relics found on-site. Segontium is in the guardianship of Cadw (Welsh Historic Monuments)

🅾 All year. March, April & Oct: Mon to Sat 9.30–5.30, Sun 2-5. May to Sept: Mon to Sat, 9.30–6, Sun 2–6. 2 Nov to end Feb: Mon to Sat 9.30–4, Sun 2–4. Closed 24 to 26 Dec, New Year's Day, Good Fri & May BH

£   Adult £1, children/over-60/student 60p. NT members free. Parking on main road nearby

♿   Wheelchair access to most parts of site. Discounted entry

🐾   No dogs

→   On Llanbeblig road, A4085, on SE outskirts of Caernarfon [115: SH485624]
Bus: From surrounding areas to Caernarfon, KMP 95 from Beddgelert & Arvonia 93 pass museum, on others ½ml walk to castle (tel. 01286 679535)
Station: Bangor 9ml

SKENFRITH CASTLE 🗺

Skenfrith, nr Abergavenny

A Norman castle, built to command one of the main routes between England and Wales. A keep stands on the remains of the motte, and the 13th-century curtain wall with towers has also survived

Note: Skenfrith Castle is in the guardianship of Cadw (Welsh Historic Monuments) (tel. 01222 500200)

●   All year

£   Free

♿   Wheelchair access

→   6ml NW of Monmouth, 12ml NE of Abergavenny, on N side of the Ross road (B4521) [161: SO456203]

TUDOR MERCHANT'S HOUSE 🏠

Quay Hill, Tenby SA70 7BX Tel: 01834 842279

A late 15th-century town house, characteristic of the building tradition of south-west Wales. The ground-floor chimney at the rear of the house is a fine vernacular example, and the original scarfed roof-trusses survive. The remains of early frescos can be seen on three interior walls. Access to small herb garden, weather permitting. Furniture and fittings re-create the atmosphere from the time when a Tudor family was in residence

●   27 March to 30 Sept: Mon to Sat (except Wed) 10–5, Sun 1–5; 1 to 31 Oct: Mon, Tues, Thur & Fri 10–3, Sun 12–3

£   £1.60, children 80p. Groups £1.30 per person, children 60p. NT members free. No WC. Car-parking in town

♿   Not recommended for wheelchair-users; difficult steps and stairs

→   [158: SN135004] *Bus:* From surrounding areas (tel. 01437 764551)
Station: Tenby 700m

TŶ MAWR WYBRNANT 🏠 🖼 🚶

Penmachno, Betws-y-coed LL25 0HJ Tel: 01690 760213

Situated in the beautiful and secluded Wybrnant Valley, Tŷ Mawr was the birthplace of Bishop William Morgan, first translator of the entire Bible into Welsh. The house has been restored to its probable 16th/17th-century appearance, with a display of Welsh Bibles. The surrounding fields are traditionally managed, and the Wybrnant Walkers' Guide covers approximately 1ml from the house and back

Note: No access for coaches

🅾 27 March to 29 Sept: Thur to Sun, BH Mon 12–5. Last admission 4.30; 2 Oct to 2 Nov: Thur, Fri & Sun 12–4

💷 £1.80, children 90p; family ticket (max. 2 adults & 2 children) £4.50. Pre-booked parties (20 or more) £1.50 per person

🏛 Educational visits particularly welcome for house and nature trail tours. Pre-booked school parties only

🐕 In countryside only

➔ At the head of the Wybrnant valley. From A5 3ml S of Betws-y-coed, take B4406 to Penmachno. House is 2½ml NW of Penmachno by forest road [115: SH770524] *Bus:* Selwyns 64 Llanrwst–Cwm (passes ⭙ Betws-y-coed), alight Penmachno, thence 2ml (tel. 01492 575415) *Station:* Pont-y-pant (U) 1½ml

TY'N-Y-COED UCHAF 🏠 🖼 📷 🚶

Penmachno, Betws-y-coed LL24 0PS Tel: 01690 760229

A smallholding with 19th-century farmhouse and outbuildings which provide a record of the traditional Welsh way of life. The house is approached by an interesting walk along the River Machno through fields of nature and conservation interest

🅾 27 March to 29 Sept: Thur, Fri & Sun: 12–5; 2 Oct to 2 Nov: Thur, Fri & Sun 12–4. Last admission 30min before closing. Ty'n-y-Coed Uchaf is occupied by a tenant family, so please observe the property opening times. Car park can be approached through the car park for Penmachno Woollen Mill

💷 £1.80, children 90p; family ticket (max. 2 adults & 2 children) £4.50. Parking at Penmachno Woollen Mill ¾ml

♿ Wheelchair-accessible path through first 3 fields only from Penmachno Woollen Mill car park; thereafter access not possible

🏛 Educational groups are especially welcome. Pre-booked only

🐕 No dogs allowed

➔ 1½ml S of Betws-y-coed on the A5. Turn right at the sign for Penmachno Woollen Mill, then follow B4406 for ½ml [116: SH803521] *Bus:* Selwyns 64 Llanrwst–Cwm (passes ⭙ Betws-y-coed) (tel. 01492 575415) *Station:* Betws-y-coed (U) 3ml

INDEX

INDEX

INDEX